FICTIONS OF WESTERN AMERICAN DOMESTICITY

Fictions of Western American Domesticity

Indian, Mexican, and Anglo Women in Print Culture, 1850–1950

AMANDA J. ZINK

UNIVERSITY OF NEW MEXICO PRESS • ALBUQUERQUE

Printed in the United States of America

Library of Congress Cataloging-in-Publication Data

Names: Zink, Amanda J. (Amanda Jane), 1977– author.

Title: Fictions of western American domesticity: Indian, Mexican, and Anglo women in print culture, 1850–1950 / Amanda J. Zink.

Other titles: Indian, Mexican, and Anglo women in print culture, 1850–1950

Description: First edition. | Albuquerque: University of New Mexico Press, 2018. | Includes bibliographical references and index. |

Identifiers: LCCN 2017027176 (print) | LCCN 2017041994 (e-book) | ISBN 9780826359193 (e-book) | ISBN 9780826359186 (printed case: alk. paper)

Subjects: LCSH: Women and literature—West (U.S.)—History. | Women in literature. | Sex role in literature. | Racism in literature. | Stereotypes (Social psychology) in literature. | Housewives in literature. | Housekeeping in literature. | American literature—Women authors—History and criticism. | American literature—19th century—History and criticism. | American literature—20th century—History and criticism.

Classification: LCC PS152 (e-book) | LCC PS152 .Z56 2018 (print) | DDC 810.9/35640978—dc23

LC record available at https://lccn.loc.gov/2017027176

Cover illustration: The Santa Fe Railway and other railroads increased the incidences of contact between white women and American Indian and Mexican American women. This advertisement for the California Limited, a train that took passengers through the American Southwest, depicts such an encounter between a white woman and, presumably, a Pueblo woman in New Mexico. Author's collection.

Designed by Lisa C. Tremaine
Composed in ITC Baskerville Pro

For Carson and Madilyn

CONTENTS

ILLUSTRATIONS

ACKNOWLEDGMENTS

I often joke, "If this professor gig doesn't work out, I'll open an interior design business." From my youngest years, my primary preoccupations have been reading books and enhancing spaces. It is no surprise, then, that my first book is also preoccupied with these activities, with the many American women—both fictional and historical—who made it their life's work to read, write, and teach about the physical and ideological power of domesticity. Thanks to a vast company of encouraging people, reading, writing, and teaching about American domesticity is now part of my life's work.

First and foremost, this company of encouragers includes professors from the various institutions where I have studied and worked: Becky Belcher-Rankin, Betsy Klimasmith, Susan Tomlinson, Patricia Smith, Jodi Byrd, Stephanie Foote, Ricky Rodriguez, and Robert Dale Parker. I am especially grateful to Bob for his invaluable and tireless guidance on this project, from inception to publication. My gratitude also extends to Nina Baym, who, in her "retirement," happily suggested names of women writers of the American West before her most recent book on the subject went to print. I am grateful for the many librarians and curators who have helped me locate materials for this book, including those at the Newberry Library; the Haskell Indian Nations University; the Kansas Historical Society; the Library of Congress; the Smithsonian Institution; Washington State University; the University of Illinois at Urbana–Champaign; the Illinois State Library in Springfield; the University of Iowa Special Collections & University Archives; the Webb Library in Morehead City, North Carolina; the New York Public Library; and the Kansas City Public Library. Special thanks go to the librarians at the following institutions and my students who, at the eleventh hour, helped me locate higher-resolution files of several images reproduced in this book: Laura Griffith and the Multnomah County Library, Tommy Flynn and the Boise Public Library, and Emily Ward and the Special Collections Division at the University of Utah's J. Willard Marriott Library. And, though I will always treasure the feel and smell of physical books—especially old ones!—I owe a debt to the tireless, invisible force of librarians that has spent hours and hours scanning texts and making them available digitally. Archival research will never be the same, and in that there's much to be grateful for.

In addition to my professor-readers, I am deeply appreciative of the many anonymous reviewers, editors, and graphic artists whose generous and insightful feedback on various stages of this book's production made this finished product possible. I can thank one reviewer by name—Siobhan Senier—whose own scholarship, as well as her encouraging and exacting suggestions, made this book better than it would have been without her. I can also thank Elise McHugh, my editor at the University of New Mexico Press, for seeing potential in the manuscript and for guiding me through the process of making it into this book. Additionally, I thank the reviewers who gave feedback on portions of this book that have been published as articles as well as the publishers who granted me permission to reprint them. A portion of chapter 1 first appeared as "Peyote in the Kitchen: Gendered Identities and Imperial Domesticity in Edna Ferber's *Cimarron*" in *Western American Literature* 47, no. 1 (Spring 2012). Portions of chapter 4 appeared as "Carlisle's Writing Circle: Boarding School Texts and the Decolonization of Domesticity" in *Studies in American Indian Literatures* 27, no. 4 (Winter 2015). I reprint both with the permission of the Regents of the University of Nebraska–Lincoln.

I am so grateful to the artists who entrusted reprints of their work to this project: Cathy Ashworth and her 2015 painting, *La Llorona*, and Maria Cristina Tavera and her 2014 woodblock print, *La Llorona (The Crying Woman)*, make visible the Weeping Woman who haunts Leti in Felicia Luna Lemus's *Trace Elements of Random Tea Parties* (2003). Thanks too, to the Estate of Alberto Vargas, pinup-girl artist extraordinaire, for permission to reprint one of his famous Vargas Girls.

To my department chair and dean at Idaho State University—Jennifer Attebery and Kandi Turley-Ames—and to ISU's Office for Research, I extend gratitude for support in the form of funding for conference travel and course release time. I also thank Jennifer and Kandi for their encouragement and excitement as they watched me see this project to completion in the first few years of my assistant professorship. I am especially grateful for Bethany Skidmore and Price L. Worrell's help with indexing this book and for Jessica Hoffman-Ramirez's feedback on new content I wrote late in the process. I am truly grateful for all of my students—especially those who took my graduate seminar in fall 2014—for helping me articulate more clearly the ideas that make up this book. I am a lucky girl to have landed such a great gig (that I won't be trading in for my own interior design company!).

Finally, my heartfelt gratitude goes out to the countless friends and family members who have offered support and encouragement over the several years of this project. I offer my deepest gratitude, though, to my wonder-twins, Carson and Madilyn, who have grown up while I have grown into my vocation as a scholar. And to Corey, who, after all, joined me in our own journey west to set up housekeeping here in the Rockies of southeast Idaho.

INTRODUCTION

The Literature of Modern American Domesticity

Throughout the mission fields workers are found using their utmost strength in their endeavors to raise the standards of family life. Home has seldom been a sacred place, and family relations have not been held sacred. Missionaries who have been engaged in teaching have been able to improve conditions to a great extent but if the home, the citadel of family life, is to be permanently strengthened there must be more Bible women, more district nurses, and more settlement workers whose primary duty is to go into the homes. It is a most important work that women be taught to make the home attractive to the men and children of the family, for to the average Spanish American home is the place where he occasionally eats and sleeps. A real home would tend to make husbands more faithful and women's lot brighter. There are occasional homes that are worthy of the name—the homes of women who have been trained in mission schools.

—Robert McLean and Grace Petrie Williams, *Old Spain in New America,* 1916

You have your beautiful homes filled with many treasures, ordered households where courtesy reigns; food of the best, served graciously. . . . I say this: Seek the Americano officials who have influence and invite them to your homes and entertainments. Show them that we have much to give them in culture, that we are not the ignorant people they take us to be, that to remain as we are will neither harm nor be a disgrace to their union of states. They are far too well acquainted with the lowest of the Mexicans and not at all with the best.

—Jovita González and Eve Raleigh, *Caballero: A Historical Novel,* 1996

In *Cimarron,* Edna Ferber's best-selling novel (1929) turned blockbuster film (1931), Sabra Cravat finds herself in Oklahoma Territory with an often-absent husband, a newspaper that needs running, and a household that needs keeping. Raised in the American South and accustomed to having servants (i.e., slaves), Sabra eventually realizes that, as her husband is frequently away for increasingly long periods of time and the work of editing and printing the newspaper falls to her, she needs someone to help clean the house and mind her two children, a redistribution of labor that pleases her (210). Her parents' youngest servant, Black Isaiah—who "was as much her slave as though the Emancipation Proclamation had never been" (64)—had been a stowaway member of their westward journey, but he was more useful to Sabra for outside chores. So she hires Arita Red Feather, a fifteen-year-old Osage girl "who had been to the Indian school and had learned some of the rudiments of household duties" (210). In addition to Sabra's annoyance that Arita "had to be told everything over again, daily," this hire has disastrous consequences. Arita and Black Isaiah fall and love and have a baby, and all three are one morning found dead in the desert, having been brutally murdered by, presumably, other Osages.[1] Because "there was no other kind of help available," Sabra soon employs another Osage housekeeper, Ruby Big Elk. To avoid repeating the "hideous experience" of Arita Red Feather and Black Isaiah, she is careful to hire an older girl (288). But an event transpires that, to Sabra, is even more hideous than the terrible deaths of Arita and Isaiah: her own son, Cimarron, falls in love with, marries, and has children with Ruby Big Elk.

Conventional narratives of American modernism tell us that most women writers at the turn into the twentieth century abandoned the themes of domesticity and true womanhood that typified the writings of their nineteenth-century foremothers. On the contrary, as I show in this book, white writers sometimes drew characters that use domesticity to colonize American Indian and Mexican American women, as if to enable and legitimize their own public activities. As can be seen in the example of *Cimarron,* this transfer of domesticity is not without physical and ideological threat, and the exchange of cross-cultural influence goes both ways, in lived history and in literary constructs. Further, this book shows how Indian and Mexican American women writers manipulate domestic colonization and rhetoric to assert a syncretic domesticity that negotiates resistance and assimilation in sophisticated ways. Interpreting memoirs, novels, Indian boarding school narratives, Mexican American cookbooks, and the visual culture that surrounds their publication, I demonstrate that such responses were in no way isolated or exceptional, nor were they merely responses. American Indian and Mexican American women collectively rewrite colonial domesticity and write their own domesticity.

As I use it in this study, *domesticity* indicates an ideology centered on the household and is characterized by a particular devotion to home life. Many literary scholars have discussed and defined the conventions of domestic or sentimental fiction. Donna Campbell provides a useful summary of the genre, citing such features as a heroine's quest to master herself and her desires, her struggle to navigate social pressures and personal passions, and her ability to endure suffering "at the hands of abusers of power before establishing a network of surrogate kin" ("Domestic"). The plots often feature two main stories: the heroine successfully navigates the pitfalls of coming of age, and the heroine marries at the end, either reforming a corrupt man or returning to the stalwart man. But in the literary texts I consider in this book, domesticity becomes an ideology and a set of rituals that white heroines transfer to nonwhite women, ostensibly so the latter might master a particular brand of American femininity. The social pressures these heroines must learn to navigate are far more complex than those the typical sentimental heroine deals with. In addition to pressures regarding sexual purity, for example, Indian and Mexican American sentimental heroines both withstand the nearly crushing pressures of American racism and colonialism and learn to redirect these social forces for their own benefit. Euro- and Anglo-American women writers and thinkers, from the mid-nineteenth to the mid-twentieth century, worked to legitimize, politicize, professionalize, organize, and proselytize the rhetoric, values, and rituals of domesticity. These women—particularly Protestant missionaries, federal agents, and relocated artists—preached a gospel that made sacred the domestic labors of American women and propagated a political platform that made domesticity the very definition of American femininity, what Barbara Welter describes as the "cult of true womanhood" and Linda Kerber discusses as "republican motherhood." As I show, Willa Cather, Edna Ferber, Elinore Cowan Stone, and Evelyn Hunt Raymond fictionalized the ways white women colonized western women of color by creating characters who brought "the right ways of living" to the Other women in their western adventures.

This book builds on the foundational scholarship of Jane Tompkins, Mary Kelley, Gillian Brown, Ann Douglas, Lora Romero, and others who broke new ground by encouraging scholars to see the public and political qualities of a nineteenth-century genre previously thought only private and personal. I use Amy Kaplan's concept of "Manifest Domesticity" to help characterize the white characters in the texts I discuss here, a concept that seems to shape the particular politics that the characters—and perhaps their authors—espouse. Starting with but pushing past the nineteenth century, this book shows how American women writers carry the literary conventions of sentimentalism and domesticity into the twentieth century and, thinking along with Lauren Berlant, probes the persistence of sentimentality as a mode for engaging public life. Taking as a given that the personal and private is also political and public—an individual's spheres of influence are not, as Cathy Davidson (1998) points out, entirely separable—and running with Kaplan's argument that literary domesticity works to naturalize the internal foreigner, this project shows how the politics of modernist sentimentalism are distinctly colonial. To make a profession out of spreading this domestic gospel, late nineteenth- and early twentieth-century white women subjugated their own performance of domestic labor to *writing and speaking* about the performance of domestic labor by Others.

A double standard regarding American domesticity was then born; someone had to perform the actual labors of domesticity, and Euro-American speakers and writers needed pupils who presumably required lessons in domesticity. African American, Mexican American, and American Indian women living within the political borders of the United States served as these students. Woven through the arguments of this book is the zigzag narrative of domesticity. What promises to be a pathway to power (i.e., republican motherhood, true womanhood) for women turns out to be another means of oppression for women who are not white and/or middle class. White women reformers disavowed domesticity for themselves but then displaced it onto women of color. It might be argued that Harriet Beecher Stowe and her incredibly and lastingly popular sentimental novel, *Uncle Tom's Cabin* (1852), is the first example of such duplicitous domesticity. Louise Michele Newman, for example, asserts that Stowe—and other white female abolitionists such as Angelina Grimké—used abolition as a thinly veiled guise for her primary agenda: gaining a public platform for (white) women's rights. Stowe constructs the character of Mrs. Shelby, who is adored as an American domestic goddess and enjoys all the rights and privileges of a true woman but does not perform domestic labor. Rather, like historical plantation owners' wives, Mrs. Shelby passes off this labor to her female black slaves, thereby teaching them how to perform American femininity, even if these black women primarily labor in their mistresses' homes. In *Uncle Tom's Cabin*, Mrs. Shelby helps Eliza escape slavery to raise her child in freedom not only because Eliza's complexion is light enough for her to pass as white, but also because Eliza's sacrificial motherhood signifies that she passes the tests of American femininity. Presumably, Mrs. Shelby trusts Eliza to implement her lessons of domesticity—regarding motherhood, housekeeping, and religious education—with her own son and in her own home.

As Brian Dippie and others discuss, Helen Hunt Jackson fancied herself the Harriet Beecher Stowe for Indians and hoped her books, *A Century of Dishonor* (1881) and *Ramona* (1884), would influence federal Indian reform the same way that *Uncle Tom's Cabin* contributed to the abolition of slavery (156). *Ramona* is perhaps the most-discussed example of white women—historical authors and fictional characters—who take up the cause of uplifting Indian and Mexican women through the civilizing, evangelizing, and Americanizing tenets of domesticity. Indeed, Siobhan Senier argues that Jackson's reform work and writings "reveal how the desire for self-authorization erupted into the political projects of white reformers who claimed to speak for Indians" (*Voices* 30). Jackson, like Stowe, uses the rhetoric of domesticity in ways that domesticate the nonwhite female characters in *Ramona* and show that they are already well versed in the art of housekeeping. Even though she treats Ramona cruelly, Señora Morena runs a meticulous and mannered household, and Jackson carefully crafts the señora's scenes to connect her with the physical spaces of the house. And even though Ramona and Alessandro are on the run during their entire marriage, Jackson describes in great detail how Ramona keeps an amazingly clean and well-appointed home. See, Jackson seems to argue, Indians know what they're doing—they're either domesticated already or quick studies in domesticity.

This book also engages histories of colonial domesticity by Margaret D. Jacobs, Jane E. Simonsen, Peggy Pascoe, Laura Wexler, Anne McClintock, Cathleen D. Cahill, and others who document the lives of white women reformers. The white heroines in Cather's, Ferber's, Stone's, and Raymond's novels can be read as caricatures of the historical female missionaries, teachers, and reformers who lived among Indian and Mexican women of the West in efforts to "civilize" and Americanize them. Fictional reformers both represent and complicate the lived histories of female reformers at the turn into the twentieth century who left the confines of domesticity but brought it with them and enforced it on the Other women they encountered in their travels. The first epigraph to this chapter offers a prime example of the ways Euro-American women moved and lived among indigenous women of the southwestern states. Surely fueled by what they believed to be the best intentions—evangelism and uplift—these white missionaries viewed Indian and Mexican domesticity through their own cultural lenses, which, not surprisingly, led them to erroneous conclusions. The authors of the epigraph, Robert McLean and Grace Petrie Williams, are but two such missionaries and *Old Spain in New America* is but one such tract that "reports" the status of America's nonwhite "internal foreigners." In addition to *Old Spain*, the Council of Women for Home Missions (CWHM) published several other field reports, including *From over the Border: A Study of the Mexicans in the United States*; *In Red Man's Land: A Study of the American Indian*; *From Darkness to Light: The Story of Negro Progress*; *Comrades from Other Lands: What They Are Doing for Us and What We Are Doing for Them*; *Mormonism: The Islam of America*; and *Christian Americanization: A Task for the Churches*. See figures I.1–4 for propagandistic images published in these texts.

As the titles imply, the writers of these missionary reports signal the Protestant Church's agenda for Americanization-through-Christianization. The directors of the CWHM apparently targeted for conversion a wide variety of the groups living in America that were not considered WASPs: Mexicans, Indians, blacks, Slavs, Mormons, and Muslims. Many of the writers are women, and most tracts include sections on conversion efforts that were the particular province of women—namely, training in domesticity and religious education. Female missionaries, however, did not practice the domestic message they preached. They were not spending most of their time keeping house or raising children or teaching school—comfortably acceptable roles for women under the auspices of domesticity—but were writing and speaking about domesticity to women who presumably lacked such feminized knowledge. Indeed, white women writers such as these missionaries might be illustrative of Cathryn Halverson's paradigm of western housekeeping as "play" instead of labor, as "playing house" instead of "keeping house." For Halverson, whose 2013 *Playing House in the American West: Western Women's Life Narratives, 1839–1987* focuses on life narratives instead of fiction, "playing house is at once a symptom of estrangement and a manifestation of agency." If play can be defined as "a form of conquest" and an "active mastery of a situation,"

FIGURE I.1 *Present Day Warriors.* Two "warriors" defend the border of "Red Man's Land." Courtesy Eli M. Oboler Library, Idaho State University, Pocatello.

then narratives of western housekeeping "distance narrators and protagonists from the domestic work they do and the identity it connotes. They appear not as 'housekeepers' but as women playing the role of such" (4). Following this logic, one could ask what this play at housekeeping conquers and what situation are these writers mastering? Halverson's answer is: "glossing over American Indian dispossession and seemingly oblivious to class and racial privilege, these writers do not acknowledge as a 'legacy of conquest' the western experiences that absorb them," seeing in their "emphasis on disruption" authors who "little resemble 'gentle tamers,' women bent on extending civilization's reach" (12). But it seems that

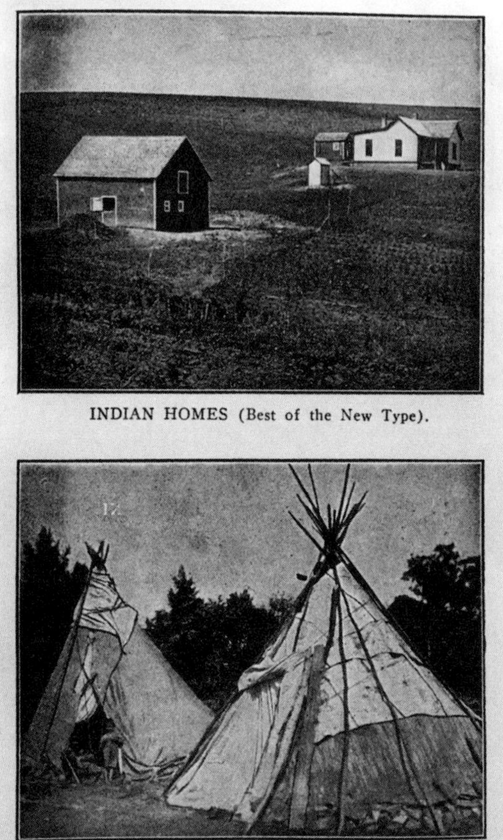

FIGURE I.2 *Indian Homes (Best of the New Type)* and *Ojibway Tepees (Typical of the Passing Old Life).* Encapsulating the Euro-American preoccupation with indigenous homes, these photos tell the master narrative of the "Vanishing Indian." Courtesy Eli M. Oboler Library, Idaho State University, Pocatello.

"glossing over American Indian dispossession" *is* an act of imperial privilege, regardless of how unaware of such privilege these women writers might be, and even if some writers do not seem to align themselves with "the project of oppressing nonwhite others" (13). After all, missionaries and reformers would not have described their own westering as exercises in colonial oppression or conquest but as endeavors in philanthropy.

Historical missionaries were not the only white American women to escape the confines of domesticity only to enforce it on or celebrate it in nonwhite women's cultures. Cather and Mary Austin are often paired as prime examples of early twentieth-century American writers who abandoned practical and literary domesticity. In her autobiography, *Earth Horizon* (1932), Austin compares the "purely objective domesticity" of her childhood home, where her mother was an "efficient housekeeper," to the "moral implications" of how an American household is adorned and organized that, for her, symbolized the "repressive conventions hedging femininity on every side" (108, 124, 115). But even Austin does not altogether abandon literary domesticity; she praises "primitive" Indian domesticity in "The Basket Maker" and ridicules repressive Euro-American domesticity in *Santa Lucia, a Common Story* (1908). Newman writes,

FIGURE I.3 *New Citizens from Over the Border.* Women for Home Missions attempted to override the authority of Mexican mothers by teaching Mexican children to be American. Author's collection.

FIGURE I.4 *Mexicans? No! They Are Americans in the Making!* The original caption on this photo of Mexican children metaphorically abducts Mexican children and renames them "American." Author's collection.

> White woman's rights activists measured the (lack of) "social progress" of non-white races in terms of their (lack of) conformity to Anglo-American Protestant middle-class gender relations. One of the most profound ironies of this history, then, is that at the very moment that the white woman's movement was engaged in a vigorous critique of patriarchal gender relations, it also called for the introduction of patriarchy into those cultures deemed "inferior" precisely because these cultures did not manifest these gender practices. White leaders' critique of the cult of domesticity—as too restrictive and oppressive when applied to themselves—went hand in hand with their defense of domesticity as necessary for the "advancement" of "primitive" women. (7–8)

As reformers lived it and writers fictionalized it, then, modern American domesticity—or as Suzanne Clark dubs it, "sentimental modernism"—is remodeled into a colonial enterprise. Clark traces the ways modernist women writers both deny and recuperate the sentimental (13), but though she touches on questions of race when she briefly discusses "womanist" fiction and Alice Walker, she does not explore the colonial underpinnings of modernist domesticity. As I show in the chapters to follow, white women writers indeed brought the conventions of domestic sentimentalism with them into modernism. Building on the histories of women reformers by Jacobs, Simonsen, and others, as well as the makeover of American modernism by Clark and others, this project explores another layer of texts motivated by "reform" efforts: popular magazines and popular culture events such as fairs and contests, boarding school publications, children's books, and novels. The archive for this project consists of materials that use domesticity as a common platform—a modernist domesticity that is also decidedly colonial.

The central questions driving this project—where and how do white writers fictionalize colonial domesticity? how do indigenous women write about colonial domesticity?—led me to amass an unconventional, materialist archive of primary sources that includes advertisements in magazines, pamphlets and circulars printed by fair organizers, scorecards and award medals produced by fair judges, and illustrations in children's books. In this way, the illustrations this book includes do not serve merely as visual representations of the textual argument. Rather, the book's illustrations offer their own, distinct, material-cultural argument. Devising a method that follows the lead of American print culture scholars and innovative archivists such as Janice A. Radway, Carl F. Kaestle, Trish Loughran, Ronald and Mary Saracino Zboray, Terence Whalen, David M. Henkin, Robert Dale Parker, and others, I examine texts and read extra-textual spaces to uncover ways that texts engage cultural discourses and circulate cultural ideologies. Part of what makes domesticity modernist in the early twentieth century is the myriad of forms this traditional content takes. In addition to the usual suspects one looks for when embarking on a literary project—novels, stories, nonfiction prose, poetry—I show instances when American print culture moves away from depicting white women as "angels in the house" and instead propagates a doctrine that seeks to persuade Other women to be angels in their houses so they can be American and so white women can get out of the house. The sheer volume of stories and images circulating in popular print sources that feature Great White Mothers uplifting poor, ignorant black, brown, and red mothers (even *Uncle Tom's Cabin* was first published in a newspaper) suggests attempts to normalize the ideas that domestic labor is not for white women but for nonwhite women and that white women need to teach nonwhite women how to be American.

American novels—both canonical and noncanonical—and other popular print sources are treasure troves of colonial domesticity. It is no secret among Cather scholars that, in a review in the *Lincoln Courier* on November 9, 1895, she harshly disparaged modern print culture, touting her conviction that "journalism is the vandalism of literature. It has brought to it endless harm and no real good. It has made art a trade. The great American newspaper takes in intellect, promise, talent; it gives out only colloquial gossip. It is written by machines, set by machines, and read by machines" (Cather 272). But whether financial hardship or change of opinion influenced her later publishing decisions, most of Cather's novels were, in fact, serialized in popular periodicals, both highbrow and middlebrow. Exploring the "enmeshed" state of fiction and advertising between the 1890s and 1910, Ellen Gruber Garvey asserts that fiction does not emerge from some "pure sphere of literature" where it can remain "untouched by the commercial nexus within which its writers live and work" but instead "constantly if uneasily reflects on its place within commerce" (5). Aleta Feinsod Cane and Susan Alves argue that, since the 1830s, American women writers have used periodicals to reinforce or subvert prevailing or ideal models of and for

American femininity. If modernist domesticity is distinctly colonial, it is also inextricably linked to the publishing market, making popular novels and magazines another frontier of capitalism as well as colonialism.

This new frontier—this juncture of domesticity, sentimentalism, modernism, capitalism, and colonialism—provides the setting, the rhetoric, and the opportunity for indigenous women of North America to write back to the empire. Cane and Alves argue that while

> many white women writers from the middle class sought to expand the opportunities for American women within the context of the dominant social norms, others—white women of the working classes, Mexican American, Native American, and African American women writers—urged the expansion of American readers' consciousness of countries and cultures beyond and within this nation's borders. (11)

Through their "sentimental educations" in boarding schools and with federal field agents and Christian missionaries—as well as their mundane exposure to mainstream American print culture—American Indian and Mexican American women learned the feminized discourse of domesticity so well that they too could manipulate its principles.

Thus, while I use historical categories of and models for American womanhood (republican motherhood, true womanhood, new womanhood) and theoretical concepts or generic conventions for women's writing (domesticity, sentimentalism) as if they are stable, the work of this book is to *de*stabilize these categories, models, concepts, and conventions.[2] This book deconstructs historical, gendered structures that white women (and men) built on the backs of women (and men) of color—Native Americans, Mexican Americans, and, though I do not discuss in depth their history or literature in this project, African Americans—to expose the fragility and pliability of these seemingly monolithic, approaching divine, ways of organizing and policing American gendered life. The historical and literary white women reformers featured in this book were themselves invested in the stability of these categories, using terms and concepts as tools to police women of color but also to police their own anxieties about their choices to move outside these categories. Even as their reform efforts seemed to bolster the constancy of gendered ideals, they also belie the shakiness of such constructs. As this book shows, the gendered categories some white women clung to were always already empty signifiers defined on other women's bodies. White women spent decades trying to fill these signifiers as true women or new women, but saying that they have passed through them—that they are now free to pursue other more diverse and more public activities—lays bare the vacuity of the signifiers. The irony, then, is that, knowing (at least unconsciously) that the constructs might crumble if they could abandon them, white women still imbued the categories with enough meaning as to pass them on to Other women.

If the goal of republican mothers or true women or even new women was to be a best version of American femininity while influencing people around them to be the best Americans they could be, it follows that the ultimate work of domesticity would be to use its tenets to Americanize women who haunted the periphery of American femininity. In English and Anglo-American literature of "feminist individualism in the age of imperialism," as Gayatri Chakravorty Spivak asserts, what is at stake is "precisely the making of human beings, the constitution and 'interpellation' of the subject." Spivak shows how these stakes play out in two registers: in "domestic-society-through-sexual-reproduction cathected as 'companionate love'" and, most relevant to the argument of this book, in "the imperialist project cathected as civil-society-through-social mission" ("Three Women's Texts" 244). Domesticity and sentimentalism, both literarily and historically, attest to be the sites all women must traverse in order to claim subjectivity and Americanness, even when the sites are but empty markers on the way to fuller participation in American public and political life and even when, as Spivak argues, the "'native female' is excluded any share" in these categories.

This emptiness, though, allows for a refilling of the signifiers of domesticity in ways that best serve whoever is now doing the filling. Anticipating Spivak's rhetorical question, Mexican American and American Indian women writers show that the subaltern do indeed speak. As early as the mid-nineteenth century, Mexican and Native women in the United States had at least some access to the same print outlets as did Euro-American women. Many scholars have documented a literary history of subaltern interventions in the discourses of domesticity and sentimentality, showing how colonized writers negotiate colonial pressures in ways that cannot be categorized simply as "assimilative" or "resistant" and are not evidence of selling out to dominant cultural ideologies. A caveat: to include as subaltern the Mexican American women writers interpreted in this study is to engage a complex scholarly debate. The women who had access to print from the mid-nineteenth through the early twentieth centuries were typically from landed families who identified more with their Spanish ancestors than with their indigenous Mexican heritage.

But it is on this point that this debate becomes complex, since the best way to refer to any group of people is to use the term they call themselves. In this book, I name tribal affiliations as often as possible. When speaking of collectives, I use the inept but inevitable catchall terms European and Anglo settlers invented to categorize indigenous peoples and use them interchangeably: *American Indian, Native American, Indian, Native.* Similarly, when discussing Hispanic (Spanish-speaking) writers, I avoid using the now popular catchall term *Latina/o* because the writers I discuss were mostly Spanish Mexicans. They often use the term *Spanish American* to describe themselves, privileging their Spanish heritage over their indigenous Mexican heritage. I sometimes use that term in chapter 2, but for the most part I use *Mexican American*, or sometimes *Mexican*, to describe people who were born or some of whose ancestors were born in Mexico. I use the term *indigenous* to indicate a historical, social, or cultural collective of peoples who, from precontact to the present, inhabit the territories now designated as North America. In the same way, I use *Euro-American, Anglo-American*, and *white* interchangeably to describe women who had themselves or whose ancestors migrated from Europe and England to North America.

For American Indian women writers who engage sentimental and domestic discourses, the goal is not to claim whiteness in a clash of colonial powers but to survive whiteness in a settler colonial nation. Chapter 4 of this book joins a conversation about the exigency of Indian iterations of sentimentality and domesticity to ongoing struggles among Native peoples for self-determination. For instance, Susan K. Bernardin argues that sentimentality provided a "nominally shared vocabulary and set of affective values with which to broach socially unspeakable issues of race and sexuality . . . and their implications for national self-definition" ("Meeting Grounds" 209–10). As Cari M. Carpenter argues in *Seeing Red: Anger, Sentimentality, and American Indians*, "early Native American women writers use sentimentality as one means of buttressing their own nationhood. Sentimentality as a means of nation-making is not, in other words, the sole prerogative of white women" (17). In *Domestic Subjects*,

Beth H. Piatote (Nez Perce) plays with the double entendre of her title to show how, in a settler colonial society, questions of Indian citizenship and the law are bound up with gender. Native literature of domesticity, she argues, centers "the intimate domestic" as the "primary site of struggle against the foreign force of U.S. national domestication" in order to "illuminate the web of social relations the law seeks to dismantle" (4, 10). Writing novels, poetry, school essays, cookbooks, memoirs, magazine articles, and stories, Indian and Mexican women used print culture to process which elements of American domesticity they would accept, which they would reject, and which they would synthesize with their own preexisting rituals of indigenous domesticity. As the work of Bernardin, Carpenter, and Piatote suggest, colonized women writers—particularly American Indian writers—engage the cultural work of domesticity and sentimentality and all its political import to be present at this site of self-determination and to assert what I am terming a *sovereign domesticity*.

Here the arguments of this book intersect with scholarship on indigenous sovereignty. Evoking this multifaceted and historically contentious term as a nonnative scholar, I suggest that Indian domesticity is, ultimately, a matter of self-determination, of continuance, of futurity. The decades surrounding the turn into the twenty-first century have seen much discussion about the intricacies of sovereignty among scholars such as Vine Deloria Jr. (Standing Rock Sioux, sovereignty in community); Robert Warrior (Osage, intellectual sovereignty); Craig Womack (Creek-Cherokee), Simon J. Ortiz (Acoma Pueblo), and Gerald Vizenor (Anishinaabe, literary sovereignty); Jace Weaver (hermeneutical sovereignty, communitism); Mark Rifkin (erotics of sovereignty), and others, especially in relation to the written word. Scott Richard Lyons (Ojibwe/Dakota) and Amanda J. Cobb (Chickasaw) have succinctly summarized how the etymology of "sovereignty" grounds the concept in the rhetoric of the nation-state and its relation to power—particularly, a "locatable and recognizable power" (Lyons, "Rhetorical Sovereignty" 450). As recognized nations located within the borders of the United States, Indian tribes have long been treated as internal foreigners, as *domestic* aliens. The double entendre of *domestic* is locating bodies within the borders of a sovereign nation *and* within the walls of a single-family home. Therefore, to read texts written by Native women about domesticity in the sentimental mode is to read assertions of domestic sovereignty, or sovereign domesticity.

Sovereignty is about representation as much as it is about power—how a nation represents itself to other nations and how a writer represents personal and/or tribal self-governance in language. "Discursive strategies" are "key," Joanne Barker (Lenape) argues, to international policy on peoples' rights of self-determination (19). "Rhetorical sovereignty," Lyons writes, is the "guiding story" in pursuing this self-determination, and, if Native American literature is "the colonized scene of writing: a site of contact-zone rhetoric in its fullest sense," then rhetorical sovereignty is also "the inherent right and ability of peoples to determine their own communicative needs and desires in this pursuit, to decide for themselves the goals, modes, styles, and languages of public discourse" (449–50). Literary domesticity, as I discuss it in this book, is a crucial rhetorical contact zone. As white writers use it, domesticity is a tool for colonizing Indian women. As Indian writers use it, domesticity is a tool for asserting Native sovereignty. Engaging Euro-American rhetoric and rituals of domesticity does not threaten Indianness, then, but instead becomes the very site of sovereignty, the very places where we live:

> And so, "what" does sovereignty mean? Self-governance, recognized by others, for the purpose of peoplehood—the continuation of a community's way of life. "How" does sovereignty have meaning? In living. Placing emphasis on the "how" of sovereignty underscores the ability of dynamic cultures to find pragmatic ways to appropriate elements of a new ideology or system into their own belief systems and practices. (Cobb 125)

The power of sentimental and domestic rhetoric has always been twofold: it is both mimicry and mimesis. It calls for the material emulation of habits of living and it interpellates the emulator into an ideology played out in discourse. As such, the literature of sentimentality and domesticity is inherently colonial. Homi Bhaba asserts that "what emerges between mimesis and mimicry is a writing, a mode of representation, that marginalizes the monumentality of history, quite simply mocks its power to be a model, that power which supposedly makes it imitable" (125). The colonialism of sentimental literature, therefore, makes it a perfect platform for colonized women to stand on to speak back to colonial powers. Further, sovereignty is about recognition as much as it is about representation and power. If others must recognize sovereignty, then colonial domesticity is a deliberate *mis*recognition on the part of white women writers—not only of Indian sovereignty but of Indian women's domesticity. Sovereign domesticity, then, is what emerges when colonized women use the conventions of sentimentality to represent, in writing, the materiality and ideology of indigenous ways of living.

As chapter 2 discusses more fully, some scholars—including myself—posit that Mexican American iterations of domesticity might be read more accurately as claims to whiteness than as assertions of precontact indigenous lifeways. For example, Rosaura Sánchez, Beatrice Pita, and José David Saldívar describe María Amparo Ruiz de Burton's *The Squatter and the Don* (1885) as dramatizing a struggle between conquered *Californios* and Anglo settlers. But José F. Aranda Jr. argues that we cannot read the novel as (or written by) a subaltern mediator because Ruiz de Burton is more concerned with claiming the landedness (and whiteness) of Californios than she is with critiquing colonialism from the perspective of the conquered indigenes ("the people") or even from the more recently conquered Spanish colonials. Jesse Alemán pushes on Aranda's discussion of Ruiz de Burton's depictions of "competing colonialisms at work in California after 1848" ("Returning California" 13) to assert that, while it is tempting to read her work as part of Chicana literary history, her narratives actually "claim white racial identity for Californios at the expense of nonwhite racial Others, Native Americans and blacks in particular" ("Citizenship Rights" 5). In *Manifest Destinies: The Making of the Mexican American Race,* Laura E. Gómez explores the historical period Ruiz de Burton uses as the backdrop for her novels, highlighting how "the central paradox was the *legal* construction of Mexicans as racially 'white' alongside the *social* construction of Mexicans as non-white and as racially inferior" (4). Because of this paradox, I interpret the writings of Mexican American women writers who, though certainly writing from positions more privileged than that of many indigenous Mexican or Native American women, still had less power (i.e., they were subaltern) than Anglo women who were more safely "white."

I begin this introductory chapter with a passage from McLean and Williams's missionary report, titled *Old Spain in New America,* juxtaposed against a passage from Jovita González's *Caballero,*[3] to argue that González's writings, like all the non-Anglo texts I examine in this project, directly write back to the colonizing forces of these historical and literary Anglo-American women who were their new neighbors in the southwestern states. If Indian writers use domesticity as a tool to assert sovereign domesticity and white writers use it to colonize Indian and Mexican women, Mexican American women use domesticity as a tool to negotiate their positions as both colonizers *and* colonized. When the Chicano/a literary recovery effort began to gather steam in the late 1970s and early 1980s, critics generally tended to categorize the found writings as "resistance literature." Major scholars in this initial recovery and critical labor were Tey Diana Rebolledo, Genaro M. Padilla, José David Saldívar, Ramón Saldívar, Rosaura Sánchez, Beatrice Pita, and José E. Limón. During the 1980s and 1990s, scholarly work on the writings of María Amparo Ruiz de Burton, Cleofas M. Jaramillo, Nina Otero-Warren, Fabiola Cabeza de Baca, and, after her recovery in the late 1990s, Jovita González, focused heavily on the lives of the writers and the resistance of their narratives.[4] Of course, this makes sense in the contexts of both the academic and the political goals of the Chicano movement: to create a sense of nationalism that would fuel a revolutionary change in the way texts by Latin American writers were perceived as equal to the "great American canon" and were received in literature classrooms and journals across the country. Categorizing this literature as resistant makes sense academically because it makes sense politically; early scholars in the Chicano movement wanted a literature apart because they wanted a nation apart—to establish a nationality and a homeland that bore little resemblance or had little relevance to the United States as both an ideological and a geopolitical construct. Reading Chicano/a literature as resistant is also attractive because the westward expansion that brought Anglo settlers to Texas, New Mexico, and California throughout the nineteenth century and into the twentieth century was fueled and sometimes funded by colonizing federal agencies, Christianizing Protestant churches, and "civilizing" boarding schools. Chicano/a historians and literary scholars look for moments of resistance to these overwhelming institutional colonialists to find and imagine ancestors who did something more than roll over during the maelstrom that grade school history books tell us is how the West was won.

Constructing a literary genealogy comprised of resistance literature is another trend in Chicano/a literary scholarship whose impulses are both easily respected and ultimately insufficient. Though I do not make much of this argument in chapter 2, I nod toward this literary and critical history here to reveal my own leanings when reading Chicano/a literature; I cannot justify, for example, reading María Amparo Ruiz de Burton's 1872 novel, *Who Would Have Thought It?*, as having the same political or cultural agenda as Felicia Luna Lemus's 2004 novel, *Trace Elements of Random Tea Parties* (which I discuss in the epilogue). The separatism and presentism that has, at points, characterized the Chicano/a literary movement limits the work of literary critics who would read early texts by Mexican Americans in light of the historical encounters these writers had with the Anglo settlers who steadily and permanently moved into their ancestral lands. Elizabeth Jacobs, for example, gathers Jaramillo's and Cabeza de Baca's writings into her discussion of modern-day Chicana writings that resist patriarchy and Julie Ruiz echoes Sánchez and Pita to write that "Ruiz de Burton is a forerunner of Chicana/o writers" despite her "vacillations between colonizer and colonized positions" (114).

Other scholars have written against the critical trends of appropriating literary ancestors and reading narrative resistance. Carol Jensen reads syncretism in the marriage customs Jaramillo describes in *Romance of a Little Village Girl* and Gloria Velasquez-Treviño argues that the writings of Jovita González and other early Mexican American women writers are characterized not by resistance but by "cultural ambivalence" (140). Margaret Garcia Davidson cautions against categorizing post-1848 Mexican American literature as primarily resistance literature because "the literature of the late nineteenth and early twentieth centuries often reveals a complex and tangled duality of politics rather than an unambiguous statement of resistance" (180). She also argues that the terms *US Hispanic* and *Chicano/a* are "not necessarily interchangeable terms when applied to literature" (181). José F. Aranda Jr. also questions the quest for literary genealogy, arguing that Ruiz de Burton's work challenges the "usefulness of resistance theory when applied to writers who preceded the Chicano Movement" ("Contradictory Impulses" 553). María Carla Sánchez takes up the question of literary genealogy, and her work also exemplifies a more recent trend in scholarship on these five writers: questioning the claims to whiteness from these writers and their characters. Sanchez writes that "whiteness operates as symbolic shorthand for genealogical connection to imperial Spain and its colonizing projects. Thus, the further back that Chicano Studies extends its reach, the more and more it finds writers unfamiliar (in all senses of the word) with the indigenous identifications and working-class ethos of the Chicano movement" (65). Further, in her discussion of Jaramillo, Otero-Warren, and Cabeza de Baca, Sánchez stridently critiques Chicano studies for its willingness to turn a blind eye to racism and classism in these early texts in order to concentrate on moments of resistance so as to identify ancestors: "Early writings are simply not resistant in the same ways as post-1960s writings; they're not Chicano" (78).

Reading the claims to whiteness in the texts of Ruiz de Burton, Jaramillo, Otero-Warren, Cabeza de Baca, and González dominates much of the more recent critical scholarship on these writers. In response to Saldívar's assertion that Ruiz de Burton's *The Squatter and the Don* "begins to offer a subaltern literature of the U.S.-Mexican borderlands" (*Border Matters* 168), Aranda argues that the novel does not support a reading that makes it qualify as resistant or subaltern ("Returning California" 15) and Marcial González argues that to focus on the potential subaltern aspects of the text risks missing what Marxist theories of class might help us observe. Pascha A. Stevenson argues that Ruiz de Burton's "racial bargaining" "compels us to problematize the tired conceptualization of ethnic rhetoric as the gesture of the subaltern" (64). Stevenson urges readers to consider that Ruiz de Burton's texts illustrate "the real diversity of ethnic authors" and warns against critical tendencies that can inscribe "yet another stereotype, that of the ethnic subaltern" (71). Lázaro Lima historicizes Ruiz de Burton's claims to whiteness in the aftermath of the Mexican-American War to argue that "whiteness and racial passing, not romance, serve as the organizing principle around which citizenship can be fully articulated" (54). And Peter A. Chvany argues that Ruiz de Burton and her *Californiana* characters should be read as white because of her "identification with (and as) the 'white woman'" and that in her novels "racism is misdirected at certain people who really should be regarded as white" (106, 108). Vincent Perez offers readings of whiteness that compare the displaced, post-1848 Californios with displaced post–Civil War southern plantation owners, and many other scholars read the interracial marriages in Ruiz de Burton's and González's novels as variations on the theme of claims to whiteness. Intermarriage might signify the union of Mexico and the United States; it might symbolize interethnic cooperation among Americans; it might argue for the cultural assimilation of Mexican Americans; or it might theorize how collaboration with white women and their social roles can be a means for *Tejana*,

Californiana, or *nuevomexicana* liberation from Mexican patriarchal tradition.[5]

As we see, then, in the epigraphs to this chapter, McLean and Williams and González all insist that the home is the central site where women assert and negotiate culture. Writing in 1916, McLean and Williams read Spanish American homes as vacuous spaces lacking the characteristics that define a "real home"; this vacuity allowed room for Anglo women—"Bible women, . . . district nurses, and . . . settlement workers"—to move in and fill this empty space with their Anglo-American version of domesticity. Written in the late 1930s, González's assertion that Mexican homes are full of beautiful treasures and culture can be read as if it were a direct response to McLean and Williams's assertions to the contrary. These passages are written through the voices of a Christian churchman and a churchwoman. McLean was a Presbyterian minister and the superintendent of Presbyterian missionary efforts in the American Southwest; Williams was a missionary and teacher who worked among Mexican women and children of the Southwest. The character speaking the passage from González's novel is Padre Pierre, a French Catholic priest who lives and works among the Spanish American landowning community in South Texas. The fact that these speakers are clergy not only shows how domesticity was an ideological by-product of American versions of Christianity, it also fleshes out the Protestant/Catholic tensions that were inevitable products of westward expansion.

Ruiz de Burton exposes the hypocrisies of American Protestants who stole land and livelihood from their Californio Catholic neighbors. As I discuss in chapter 2, Ruiz de Burton lampoons the so-called benevolence of white women reformers in her 1872 novel, *Who Would Have Thought It?*, and *The Squatter and the Don*. In 1939 Cleofas M. Jaramillo published a memoir-style cookbook, *The Genuine New Mexico Tasty Recipes*, with the express goal of correcting the errors of Elizabeth DeHuff, a white woman who published recipes for "Intriguing Mexican Dishes" in *Holland's Magazine*. Gertrude Simmons Bonnin, publishing in the *Atlantic Monthly* under the name Zitkála-Šá, wrote her now well-known accounts of her days at Carlisle Indian School to belie the Christianity behind the domestic education she received there. Other Indian women—while still students at Carlisle, Chilocco, Haskell, and other federal boarding schools—wrote numerous essays, stories, and poems that indicated their struggle to integrate their lessons in Euro-American domesticity with their families' domestic rituals and habits. More women than I could include here—and many more after the end date for this project, 1950—wrote about their encounters with Euro-American domesticity and used their writing to synthesize multiple domestic ideologies. For example, Kay Bennett wrote *Kaibah: Recollection of a Navajo Girlhood* and Polingaysi Qoyawayma wrote *No Turning Back: A Hopi Indian Woman's Struggle to Live in Two Worlds*; both were published in 1964 and both focused on the challenges of reconciling federal, domestic educations with their tribal, home cultures.

This project is organized dialogically—that is, the next four chapters form two pairs of textual conversations between Euro-American women, Mexican American women, and American Indian women. Contextualizing my readings within these writers' publication records at *Woman's Home Companion* and other popular magazines, I argue in chapter 1, "Delegating Domesticity: White Women Writers and the New American Housekeepers," that the apparently benign waldorf salad recipes and better-babies contests reproduce malignantly racist and eugenicist undertones in the Progressive Era's pop-culture scientific housekeeping movements. Willa Cather and Pulitzer prize–winning Edna Ferber seemingly abandoned domestic roles in their own lives in favor of the new woman or the adventurous, primitivist woman free from patriarchal expectations. But neither writer abandoned domesticity in her writing: white characters allocate it to Indian and Mexican American characters. In a post-emancipation America where blacks cannot be remanded into slavery, women of color are drafted to do the housekeeping so white women characters can have public lives.[6] Similarly, Elinore Cowan Stone—whose popular fiction has never received extended analysis—draws a white teacher who teaches Mexican American children (and their mothers) how to be American through the new "scientific" methods of housekeeping and hygiene. The writings of Cather, Ferber, and Stone show how the work of white women reformers hinges on an underlying Anglo fiction: that Native and Spanish-Mexican cultures lack domestic sensibilities.

Chapter 2, "Dialoging Domesticity: Resisting and Assimilating 'The American Lady' in Early Mexican American Women's Writing," considers writers who confute the idea that Mexican American women need to be taught anything at all about domesticity. María Amparo Ruiz de Burton ridicules the supposedly Christian domesticity of her white characters yet still describes the domestic space as a *mexicana*'s primary sphere of influence. Jaramillo writes a cookbook to correct Anglo recipes for "Mexican Dishes." Jovita González seems to respond directly to claims by Presbyterian missionaries who write that the Spanish American "home has never been a sacred place, and family relations have not been held sacred" (McLean and Williams 138). González, by contrast, writes that Texas Mexicans have "beautiful homes filled with many treasures, ordered households where courtesy reigns. . . . We are not the ignorant people they take us to be" (54). Ruiz de Burton, Jaramillo, González, Cabeza de Baca, and Otero-Warren resist Anglo assertions that Mexican American culture lacks domesticity and modernity, but they also argue for inclusion in national platforms of feminine authority, sometimes through collaboration with white women and sometimes *as* or *in place of* white women.

In chapter 3, "Regulating Domesticity: Carlisle School's Publications and Children's Books for 'American Princesses,'" I begin by showing that prominent anthropologists and "experts" on the "Indian problem" believed that "savage tribes can now be elevated chiefly through their women" (Mason 238).[7] Moses Friedman, superintendent of the famous Carlisle Indian Industrial School, used its magazines as documentary evidence to assure the reading public that Carlisle Americanized Indian students by converting them to Anglo styles of housekeeping and dress and as primers for Indians to read and learn the Americanizing habits of Anglo domesticity. Further, chapter 3 offers the first extended analysis of Evelyn Hunt Raymond's novels about white girls' "friendships" with Indian and Mexican girls in the West—*Monica, the Mesa Maiden* (1892), *A Daughter of the West: The Story of an American Princess* (1899), *A Yankee Girl in Old California: A Story for Girls* (1901), and *Polly, the Gringo: A Story for Girls* (1905)—which duplicate the "civilizing" work of Carlisle's publications. Drawing on Victorian-era theories of children's literature, I show how these texts presume that white female readers will acknowledge and fulfill their responsibility for uplifting Indian and Mexican women through domesticity and that nonwhite female readers will cooperate with and assimilate into Anglo domesticity. But nonwhite female readers did not always cooperate or assimilate indiscriminately.

In chapter 4, "Practicing Domesticity: From Domestic Outing

Programs to Sovereign Domesticity," I again take up Carlisle school publications, along with newspapers and magazines from the Phoenix, Haskell, and Chilocco Indian schools and the Cherokee Female Seminary, rereading and recovering writings on domesticity by female Indian students. Because these schoolgirls wrote under the direct instruction of their domestic education teachers, some scholars might dismiss their writings as too coerced to be of any cultural or literary value or see the domestic themes as contaminated. But their domestic educations introduced Indian girls to more than Euro-American housekeeping rituals: while learning to practice colonialist models of domesticity, Indian girls also learned to *write* about domesticity. Unknowingly, white domestic educators at the federal schools initiated Indian girls into the traditions of literary domesticity, providing a shared rhetoric that Sarah Winnemucca, S. Alice Callahan, Zitkála-Šá, Mourning Dove, and Ella Cara Deloria eventually used to speak back to white women reformers who worked to elevate Indian women. Domesticity does not contaminate Indian women's writing but instead provides a common language that these women writers manipulate to expose the hypocrisy of reformers and assert the syncretic traditions of their own sovereign domesticity.

The archive I assemble and interpret in this project exposes the fictions of American domesticity: contrary to what we may find in typical narratives of literary history, many modernists cared deeply about sentimentalism, modernist domesticity relied heavily on gendered colonialism, and colonized peoples manipulated colonial tropes and conventions for their own purposes. In an epilogue to these chapters, I close the book with a comparison of the rhetorical and visual postcolonial and postmodern survivance strategies of Ora V. Eddleman Reed and Leticia, the main character in Felicia Luna Lemus's *Trace Elements of Random Tea Parties*. Comparing images that circulated through popular mainstream magazines with Reed's *Twin Territories: The Indian Magazine*'s "Types of Indian Girls," and following Leticia's self-fashioning patterned after cultural icons such as La Malinche, La Llorona, La Virgen de Guadalupe, and Dolores del Río, we see that the patriarchal, colonial contest to define American femininity continues into the twenty-first century. Nonwhite female bodies are still figured as lands under contestation by the clashing constructions of American and Americanizing femininity.

CHAPTER ONE

Delegating Domesticity

White Women Writers and the New American Housekeepers

History shows us that Edna Ferber and Willa Cather abandoned conventional domestic roles. They did not marry, did not set up house, did not have children. But neither abandons domesticity in her writing: white characters delegate it to Indian and Mexican American characters. In early twentieth-century America, where slavery has been abolished, and in the western states with few free black domestic servants, white female characters recruit Other nonwhite women to do the housekeeping so the white characters can pursue public lives. Similarly, Elinore Cowan Stone draws a white teacher who teaches Mexican American children (and their mothers) how to be American through the new "scientific" methods of housekeeping and hygiene. Popular magazines like *Woman's Home Companion* (*WHC*) serialized such stories alongside advertisements for household products, further normalizing and gendering the racist and eugenicist ideologies of the so-called Progressive Era.

The novels I discuss in this chapter—Ferber's *Cimarron*, Cather's *Death Comes for the Archbishop*, and Stone's *The Laughingest Lady*—were serialized in magazines before appearing as novels. *Woman's Home Companion* published *Cimarron*, most installments of *The Laughingest Lady*, and several stories by Cather. *Good Housekeeping* and *Collier's* issued a few episodes of Stone's novel. The *Forum* distributed *Death Comes for the Archbishop*. Early in her writing career, Cather also worked for two women's magazines, the *Home Monthly* and *McClure's Magazine*. Regardless of the writers' personal politics or individual preferences, Ferber, Cather, and Stone participated in a popular print culture that sought to create and perpetuate a homogenous American society. Aleta Feinsod Cane and Susan Alves assert that many white women writers have used periodicals to reinforce prevailing models of American femininity and "to expand the opportunities for American women within the context of the dominant social norms" (11). Jennifer Scanlon contends that *Ladies' Home Journal* (*LHJ*) (1883–present), one of America's longest-running women's magazines, is among many "vehicles" that transported definitions of "what it meant to be an American" to readers who made up a developing notion of "mass or popular culture" that "leaves out significant numbers of people, since 'mass' is often associated with race, the white race, and with class, the middle class" (4, 5). Women's magazines such as *Ladies' Home Journal* and *Woman's Home Companion* and self-consciously highbrow magazines such as the *Century* and the *Forum* "promoted a narrow definition of the true American, who was both Protestant and native-born" (Scanlon 18). Perhaps, as Gayatri Chakravorty Spivak argues, white American women's fiction often works "as an allegory of the general epistemic violence of imperialism, the construction of a self-immolating colonial subject for the glorification of the social mission of the colonizer" ("Three Women's Texts" 251). That is, the white woman writer/character fabricates a helpless, self-destructive (because ignorant) nonwhite woman character that she can save with her (self-)edifying message of colonial domesticity.

In his foundational history *Magazines in the United States*, James Playsted Wood extensively discusses the production and reception of *Ladies' Home Journal*, covering the history of *Woman's Home Companion* in only a few brief paragraphs. No scholar has dedicated a full-length critical study to *WHC*, but Wood's work, in addition to an entry on the magazine in Kathleen L. Endres and Therese L. Lueck's biobibliography of American women's periodicals, provides an overview of its lifespan (1873–1957). Endres and Lueck write that *WHC* was one of the original Seven Sisters of women's magazines that shared "huge circulations, long lives, and service editorial orientations" (444). The Seven Sisters still in circulation today, with their initial publication dates, are *McCall's* (1873), *Ladies' Home Journal* (1883), *Good Housekeeping* (1885), *Redbook* (1903), *Better Homes and Gardens* (1922), *Family Circle* (1932), and *Woman's Day* (1937) (Endres and Lueck xiii–xiv). Gertrude Battles Lane edited *Woman's Home Companion* from 1911 to 1940, and under her leadership it "crusaded" for "packaged groceries," started the *Companion*'s Better Babies

Bureau, and initiated a program that solicited editorials from readers (Wood 123). Lane's direction spurred circulation, which grew from 727,000 to over 3,500,000 (123). *WHC* offered housekeeping advice and escapist fiction, but, more than the other Sisters, it "extensively covered women's reform activities" and "offered profiles of strong women who made a difference, practical advice for succeeding in business or going to college, and unusual adventures or travels by women" (Endres and Lueck 446). Endres and Lueck note that the magazine's "departments reflected a diversity in the readership" (446). Columns geared toward clubwomen, working women, and, primarily, wives and mothers showed a strong commitment to "social improvements" (446). With Lane as editor, *Woman's Home Companion* began to take on more controversial topics, and by the 1950s, under later editors, the magazine's treatment of such topics as "divorce, abortion, breast cancer, childbirth, birth control, and dieting" likely contributed to its demise (450). Like other women's magazines then and now, *WHC* presented fiction, essays, and how-to articles on topics ranging from health to homemaking, fashion to fund-raising, parenting to self-pampering. Also like other magazines, *WHC* featured writers who developed into the most renowned authors of the early twentieth century, including Sherwood Anderson, Pearl S. Buck, Dorothy Canfield, Willa Cather, Edna Ferber, F. Scott Fitzgerald, Zona Gale, Edna St. Vincent Millay, Kathleen Norris, Carl Sandburg, and others. In 1933 the magazine also featured a series of essays by Eleanor Roosevelt—"Mrs. Roosevelt's Page"—that directly addressed American women and their roles as homemakers, consumers, mothers, and moral advocates against such wrongs as exploitive child labor.

If, as Endres and Lueck suggest, *Woman's Home Companion*'s departments "reflected a diversity in the readership," they seem to define this diversity only in terms of the range of choices white women might make about their daily habits and routines. Additionally, although the magazine instilled the moral responsibility in its white women readers to right social wrongs, *WHC* still perpetuated racism. Scanlon writes that *Ladies' Home Journal* and other ladies' magazines "made deliberate choices about how they handled race and class as well as gender. African-American and immigrant women found their way into the pages of the *Journal* in one of two ways: as the subject of jokes or as domestic help featured in advertisements or editorial discussions; otherwise, they were ignored" (16). Popular magazines—particularly in fiction and advertising—treated Mexican American and American Indian women in much the same ways Scanlon argues *LHJ* treated black and immigrant women. Popular periodicals ignored Native women and Latinas; implicitly addressed supposedly ignorant Indian and Mexican American women through didactic advertisements for domestic and hygienic products; drew exoticized caricatures of Indians and Mexicans in advertisements for everything from travel companies to tapioca cereal; and fictionalized Natives and Latinas as a primitive labor force who could learn the Americanizing rituals of domesticity from and perform domestic tasks for white men and women.

Peyote in the Kitchen: Colonial Domesticity in Edna Ferber's *Cimarron*

Ferber's *Cimarron* is a study in the gendered machinations of the colonial project in the United States.[1] Initially serialized in *Woman's Home Companion* from November 1929 to May 1930, *Cimarron* reinforces and reinvents popular cultural ideas that white American women have not only the privilege but the responsibility to make Americans out of the indigenous women of North America. As Peggy Pascoe, Jane E. Simonsen, Margaret D. Jacobs, Amy Kaplan, Cathleen D. Cahill, and others show, historical Euro-American women and fictional white female characters used domesticity to colonize American Indian women as white women moved west to perform the roles of field matrons, missionaries, and members of racial uplift groups such as the Women's National Indian Association. Additionally, Shari M. Huhndorf, Brigitte Georgi-Findlay, Donna Campbell, Philip J. Deloria, and others argue that American colonialism is also a story of synthesis and exchange, a two-way street where the colonizer and the colonized influence each other. Through the imperial domesticity of Sabra Cravat and the cultural exchanges between the Cravat family and the Osage people, Ferber's *Cimarron* implicates American feminism for its colonial underpinnings. Moreover, the novel probes the complexities and costs of the relations between the colonizer and the colonized. Ferber narrates the price of white women's colonizing movement into the West, displaying both the desirability of cross-cultural exchange and white women's resistance to exchange. Jane Tompkins argues that one cultural effect of the Western genre is that its heroes' stories "have influenced people's beliefs about the way things are" (*West of Everything* 6). But *Cimarron* exposes the fallout of cultural synthesis, for in this novel, Ferber undermines cultural security about "the way things are." In *Cimarron*, border crossing and boundary blurring demystify staid beliefs about American femininity and masculinity, class distinction and work ethic, and biological markers of racial difference.

Set in Oklahoma Territory and the state of Oklahoma between the 1889 land rush and the 1920s oil gush, *Cimarron* tells how the West was won through the lens of the Cravat family. Sabra Venable Cravat, a belle from a transplanted and dilapidated southern family, grudgingly moves from Wichita to Oklahoma Territory to discover that her inherited racism, absentee husband, and domineering personality make way for her roles as a pioneering newspaperwoman and congresswoman. Yancey Cravat, Sabra's husband and a dashing figure from mysterious origins, moves his family to the territory with the triple motivation of escaping the decaying Venables, building his law and newspaper businesses, and championing the rights of the Indians displaced by US policies. Along the way, Sabra goes from despising Indians to using Indians as a political platform. Yancey goes from seldom following through on his ostentatious platforms for Indians to "going native" in the way, Huhndorf argues, that white Americans characteristically adopt American Indian cultural practices for ulterior motives. Cim Cravat, their son, also goes native, marrying an Osage and living on the reservation; and Donna Cravat, their daughter, goes capitalist, marrying the first oil millionaire she can snare. Ferber purchases the feminist agenda of the novel—arguably the driving agenda in all her work—at a hefty cost. Sabra's dubious growth from domestic maven to political mastermind comes at the expense of a disturbing racism that exposes the destructive quality of attitudes toward what many Americans see as the internal foreigner: the Indian.

On the surface, Sabra evolves from the traditional true woman, whose primary sphere of influence is her home and family, to the modern new woman, whose influence extends beyond the walls of the home and into the public world of men and politics. In this way, *Cimarron* might be read as a triumphant feminist novel. Initially, Sabra is bound to the model of republican motherhood Linda Kerber describes: where a mother's primary service to the nation is to raise good-citizen sons and daughters. Ultimately, she rises to a seat in the US Congress and thus literally services the nation. During her ascension, Sabra fulfills one of Sarah Grand's criteria for new women—that they become mothers of men—when her husband and son seem too irresponsible to provide for the family, and she steps in to do their work and teach them how to be men.

But reading *Cimarron* primarily as a triumphant feminist novel misses the colonialism that taints Sabra's new womanhood. Sabra's presence in Oklahoma and her exchanges with her Osage housemaid, Ruby Big Elk, are fitting illustrations of what Kaplan calls "Manifest Domesticity." Sabra's treatment of Ruby also smacks of what Simonsen calls "imperial domesticity" and Jacobs calls "maternal colonialism," terms they use to describe the historical phenomenon of white women moving west across the North American continent and using the Anglo version of home and family to colonize and subjugate the indigenous women they encountered. Despite the preponderance of androcentric histories of the West—histories that often let white women off the hook, as it were, of colonial violence—"the great irony is, of course, that women were the practical impetus behind frontier expansion. It was they who actually fashioned the wilderness into a garden" (Smyth 117). Of course, women did not transform the entire wilderness into a garden, nor did they drive western expansion all by themselves. Yet Yancey Cravat recognizes this irony, asserting that if the history of the United States is "ever told straight you'll know it's the sunbonnet and not the sombrero that has settled this country" (Ferber, *Cimarron* 19). Sabra tries to wield both colonial domesticity and maternal colonialism to subjugate not only Ruby Big Elk but also her own son and husband and the entire town of Osage. In the end, Sabra's only success is her rise to the House of Representatives, where she can make maternal colonialist decisions at the level of national and state policy. Sabra's efforts to exert colonial power over Ruby Big Elk, Cim, and Yancey are ultimately thwarted when Cim learns Osage, Cim and Ruby marry, Yancey "goes native," and the town memorializes Yancey instead of Sabra. The cultural exchanges between the Cravats and Osages transform both the colonized and the colonizer.

While perhaps "more impressive for its feminism than for its treatment of Osages" (R. Parker, *Changing* 197n5), *Cimarron* takes up the debate about the "Indian problem" by criticizing not only federal policies concerning Indians but cultural assumptions about gender, nation, race, and work in relation to being Indian. Ferber herself claimed that the novel "malevolent[ly]" satirizes "American womanhood and

American sentimentality" (*Peculiar Treasure* 330) and laments "the triumph of materialism over the spirit in America" (Gilbert 312). Indeed, Sabra Venable Cravat, the "heroine," is the embodiment of institutionalized racism and the protector and disseminator of all things American against the flood of all things foreign that threatens to wash over those whites who live in close contact with the Osage of Oklahoma Territory. Though written about sentimental fiction of the antebellum period, Kaplan's influential article, "Manifest Domesticity," can help characterize Sabra Cravat. Kaplan asserts that domesticity is not a "static condition" but a "process of domestication." In this sense, "the home contains within itself those wild or foreign elements that must be tamed," so domesticity must patrol the external borders between civility and savagery and must control any internal indications of savagery (582).

In this context, "home" has a double meaning: house as home and nation as home. *Cimarron*'s interpretations of civilization and savagery in Oklahoma Territory play on both of these meanings. Shortly after her family's move to the territory, Sabra finds the borders of their tumbleweed town and the walls of their stick-built house inadequate boundaries between the civilized and the savage. Georgi-Findlay argues that white-Indian relations in western women's writing reflect "a sense of insecurity accompanied by an emphasis on domestication and control (over self and others)" (xiv). Sabra anxiously (and quickly) realizes that her physical and cultural boundaries are not fixed margins at all; in Oklahoma Territory, everything—notions about gender, nation, race, work, and the land itself—is up for grabs.

Sabra's self-perception as the domesticator of Indians stems from conversations she overhears between her father and other men and from her childhood education at a Catholic school in Wichita run by the Jesuit Sisters of Loretto. As she reflects on what she knows about Indians, Sabra remembers that "she had heard of them at school" and that "their savagery and trickiness had been emphasized; their tragedy had been glossed over or scarcely touched upon" (41–42). Sabra's school started as a mission school, and her teacher, Mother Bridget, taught at the mission as a young nun who came along with the Jesuit priests "to convert the Indians" (42). When Sabra returns to the school to tell the now-elderly Mother Bridget that she is moving to Oklahoma Territory, Mother Bridget tells Sabra of her own early days at the mission school, when "she had taught the Indian girls to sew, to exchange wigwams for cabins, and to wear sunbonnets. . . . These things they did with gratifying docility for weeks at a time, or even months, after which it was discovered that they buried their dead under the cabins . . . and then deserted the cabins to live outdoors again, going back to the blanket at the same time" (43). Mother Bridget tells Sabra they cycled through this routine with the Indian girls over and over again until "the Indians were herded on reservations in the Indian Territory" and the mission turned to teaching "ladylike accomplishments to the bonneted and gloved young ladies of Wichita's gentry" (43). Mother Bridget prays for Sabra as she leaves for Oklahoma Territory but not before charging her with the role she must take on when she lives among the Indians who live in the territory as if they'd never been taught by whites: "here in this land, Sabra, my girl, the women, they've been the real hewers of wood and drawers of water. You'll want to remember that" (45). Sabra's response is to tell Mother Bridget the domestic trappings she's bringing to Indian Territory—china, linens, silks, mantel sets—presumably as talismans against the "blanket" contagion, as teaching tools for her civilizing mission, and as comforting objects to soothe the terrifying anxiety that grips her as she contemplates a life in the wilderness.

Having heard Mother Bridget's tale of failed attempts at domesticating Indian women, Sabra should be prepared for the permeability of cultural borders in Indian Territory. On the contrary, as Georgi-Findlay suggests, this knowledge heightens Sabra's anxiety about her role imposing Anglo culture on Indians, especially after she begins to realize that this role is two-sided: she must also protect Anglo culture from Indian culture. But since she grew up believing Indians were no more than "dirty and useless two-footed animals" (42), it is no wonder she is surprised that the Osage have a powerful, transmittable culture too. The narrator addresses Sabra's anxieties in a scene fairly late in the novel. Ironically, the scene occurs when Sabra finds peyote in her own kitchen, a space venerated in nineteenth-century sentimental white culture as the sanctuary of true womanhood, the domestic space where mothers of the Republic can feed their citizen sons and daughters a steady diet of American values.

It slowly dawned on Sabra that young Cim was always to be found lolling in the kitchen, talking to Ruby (their hired Osage girl). Ruby, she discovered to her horror, was teaching Cim to speak Osage. He seemed to have a natural aptitude for a language that whites found difficult to learn. She came upon them, their heads close together, laughing and talking and singing. Rather, Ruby Big Elk was singing a song of curious rhythm, and (to Sabra's ear, at least) no melody. Cim was trying to follow the strange gutturals, slurs, and accents, his eyes fixed on Ruby's face, his own expression utterly absorbed, rapt.

> "What are you doing? What is this?"
>
> The Indian girl's face took on its customary expression of proud disdain. She rose. "Teach um song," she said; which was queer, for she spoke English perfectly.
>
> "Well I must say, Cimarron Cravat! When you know your father is down at the office—" She stopped. Her quick eye had leaped to the table where lay the little round peyote disk or mescal button which is the hashish of the Indian. . . .
>
> Like a fury Sabra advanced to the table, snatched up the little round button of soft green.
>
> "Peyote!" She whirled on Cim. "What are you doing with this thing?" (291–92)

The peyote physically desecrates Sabra's domestic altar—her kitchen table—and undercuts any idea that home equals a safe haven from the lurking evils of Indianness (figure 1.1).

Ruby's very presence has already transgressed the physical boundaries of domestic space—an Indian girl is working in the white woman's kitchen, albeit in the position of a servant who at once collapses and reinforces boundaries between whiteness and Indianness, between haves and have-nots. This is part of Ferber's satire of domesticity, of course, but the peyote is also a metonym for broader cultural matters at stake here, such as gender roles, class distinction, and language acquisition. Cim's learning Osage from Ruby is one trigger of Sabra's anger in this scene. Not only are class and gender roles reversed—a young white man is acting the part of the submissive student of the female Indian hired help—but so is the cross-cultural exchange; under the federal policy of assimilation, Indians are supposed to be learning English, not the other way around.

The scene that Sabra witnesses between Cim and Ruby Big Elk stings a bit more sharply after the experience Sabra had with her first Osage housemaid, Arita Red Feather. When Yancey increasingly shirks the

FIGURE 1.1 Sabra's conversation with Cim shows that she misunderstands peyote's role in Osage culture. Illustrated here in the serial version of the novel, Sabra's kitchen table functions as the stage where her family emphasizes her ignorance of the Osage. Illustration by N. C. Wyeth and Charles S. Chapman, *Now Listen, Sabra, Woman's Home Companion* 57 [1930]: 32. Courtesy Illinois State Library, Springfield.

actual labor of producing his newspaper, the *Oklahoma Wigwam*, Sabra increasingly takes responsibility for it. Sabra cannot do both the paper work and the housework, so she hires Arita Red Feather because Arita had already been to the Indian school, where she "learned some of the rudiments of household duties: cleaning, dishwashing, laundering, even some of the simpler forms of cookery" (210). In a turn of events that Sabra does not foresee, Arita Red Feather falls in love with the Cravats' longtime servant, Black Isaiah, which sparks a huge controversy in both the town and the Osage community. When Isaiah and Arita run away together, have a child, and are brutally murdered by the local Osage, Sabra needs another house servant. So she, "in common with the other well-to-do housewives in the community, employed an Indian girl" because "there was no other kind of help available. After the hideous experience with Arita Red Feather she had been careful to get Indian girls older, more settled" (288).[2] Sabra chooses Ruby Big Elk because she is twenty-two and, as it turns out, twice widowed.

Sabra sets about domesticating the town and her Indian house servants using several methods: directly teaching her Indian girls how to perform domestic tasks; decorating and maintaining her own house in exemplary Victorian fashion; organizing and running women's clubs; and using the *Oklahoma Wigwam* to spread mainstream American women's culture. She teaches Ruby Big Elk how to make "grape jell"—"to let it get thoroughly cool before you pour on the wax" (289). When Yancey suggests they build their house in "native style," Sabra retorts, "Native! What in the world! A wickiup?" And Yancey backpedals, "Well, a house in the old Southwest Indian style—almost pueblo, I mean. Or Spanish, sort of, made of Oklahoma red clay—plaster, maybe. Not brick" (286–87). In keeping with his character and his mysterious origins, Yancey takes a more syncretic approach to making a life in Osage. But true to her character, Sabra builds "a white frame house in the style of the day, with turrets, towers, minarets, cupolas, and scroll work" (287). The novel meticulously describes the out-of-place Victorian house Sabra builds in the middle of Osage, symbolizing her refusal to be influenced by the landscape or the people of Indian Territory. Sabra's house also stands as a manifestation of her efforts to civilize and domesticate even the other white women of Osage. In her Victorian house she holds meetings of the clubs she organizes, the women's "defense against these wilds" (171): the Philomathean Club and the Twentieth Century Culture Club (figures 1.2 and 1.3).

Sabra's house also operates as the hub of Osage society because of the influence she exercises through popular print culture. Even before she begins organizing clubs, "Sabra's house became sort of a social center following the discovery that she received copies of *Harper's Bazaar* with fair regularity" (167). The town women glom onto all the how-to advice in *Harper's* and, following Sabra's example, commence a "beautifying process" in their homes (167). "It was the period of the horrible gimcrack" (167), so the women adorned everything that could be adorned, painting gold leaf on frying pans and sewing velvet covers for their toasters. After seeing how quickly and uncritically the women follow the advice in *Harper's*, Sabra soon begins using the *Oklahoma Wigwam* to reprint articles from *Harper's* and other national magazines that represented the women's culture she wants to replicate in Osage. Her women's interest stories in the *Wigwam* prove so popular that "Sabra was, without being fully aware of it, a power that shaped the social aspect of this crude Southwestern town" (233). Much like the pages of *Women's Home Companion*, where the novel was first published, magazines and newspapers in *Cimarron* convey a supposedly dominant culture, reinforcing the idea

FIGURE 1.2 "Leading Doctors Recommend Karo for Growing Children." *Woman's Home Companion* formatted *Cimarron*'s serials alongside advertisements for products that civilized women used to fulfill their most important domestic duty: raising healthy children. Read together, the advertisement and Ferber's story suggest women's magazines, culture clubs like Sabra's, and products like wallpaper and Karo Syrup provide layers of defense against the wilds of Oklahoma Territory. Courtesy Main Library, University of Illinois at Urbana–Champaign.

that people can and will accept and mimic cultural, material, and even linguistic habits without contributing some aspects of their old habits to combine with the new. Of course, this idea does not hold up, as we see Osage customs change Yancey and Cim Cravat at least as much as Euro-American habits change Ruby and Chief Big Elk.

Sabra starts to learn that cultural encounters change people on both sides of the equation. Just as Sabra uses the printed word as a tool in her civilizing project, the kitchen scene with the peyote comes directly after an extended narration about spoken language. Osage chief Big Elk refuses "to speak a word of English, though he knew enough of the language. . . . It was his enduring challenge to the white man. 'You have not

FIGURE 1.3 A close-up inspection of the Karo Syrup advertisement in figure 1.2 highlights Karo Syrup's mascot, a dehumanized caricature of an Indian woman. With a corncob body and a cornhusk gown, her natural healthiness argues that children who ingest Karo will acquire the same strength and vigor that Euro-Americans ironically associated with the very peoples—American Indians—they sought to exterminate. The Karo ad in figure 1.2 claims that the syrup is "quickly" and "easily digested," just as Sabra laments that her son, Cim, can so easily ingest peyote and Osage culture and Yancey can so convincingly "play Indian." Courtesy Main Library, University of Illinois at Urbana–Champaign.

defeated me'" (290–91). "Nothing so maddened" Sabra as coming home to find Yancey "squatting on the ground with old Big Elk, smoking and conversing in a mixture of Osage and English, for Big Elk did not refuse to understand the English language, even though he would not speak it" (291). Sabra sees language as the final frontier to conquer before the Osage will be assimilated into white society.[3] She is infuriated as much by Big Elk's refusal to speak English as by the fact that he understands it. White culture, through spoken English, is legible to Big Elk while Indian culture, through spoken Osage, remains unintelligible to Sabra. Yancey's attempts to understand and speak Osage reveal Sabra's paradoxical attitude toward Indian culture; she chooses to remain ignorant and is frustrated by her ignorance, yet she insists that Indians have no culture to interpret anyway because, after all, Indians are subhuman at worst (40) and "bad people" at best (60). Sabra enacts the colonialist assumption that only the colonizers have culture and can assimilate the colonized; she realizes her miscalculation when she sees that Indian culture is assimilating her husband and her son. That peyote—a sacrament of the syncretic Native American Church that draws on both Christian and pan-Indian traditions—precipitates this realization is ironically fitting. In the kitchen scene, Ruby's unusually "Indian" dialect—"Teach um song"—mocks Sabra's assumption that she had Ruby's English (and thus Ruby) well under control, and Cim's "natural aptitude" (292, 293) for learning Osage causes Sabra to question her son's essential whiteness.

Sabra already interprets language as a marker of cultural destiny, but, as she mentally processes Cim's ability to learn Osage, she also sees language as a marker of biological destiny. After she listens in "horror" to Cim sing the "eerie song" Ruby taught him, Sabra watches him leave the room and "realized she hated his walk, and knew why. He walked with a queer little springing gait, on the very soles of his feet. . . . She remembered that someone had laughingly told her what Pete Pitchlyn, the old Indian scout . . . had said about young Cim: 'Every time I see that young Cimarron Cravat a-comin' down the street I expect to hear a twig snap. Walks like a story-book Injun'" (293). It is easier for Sabra to suppose learning Osage and walking like an Indian is symptomatic of Cim's already being genetically Indian than to suppose that he would choose Indian culture over white culture, or at least allow himself to be interpellated by Indian culture. As Georgi-Findlay argues, narratives of encounter such as Sabra's often "disrupt [white] women's visions of control—of the self and others"—by "presenting Indians as speakers, commentators, and actors who assert power over their own lives" (xv). Sabra is a witness to the blurred boundaries of cultural and biological demarcation; but even after her nascent recognition of this blurring and realization that she lacks control over others' responses to her colonizing, she resists accepting these realities.

Sabra's anxiety heightens when she realizes Yancey too has used peyote "many times," provoking her raid on a peyote ceremony in one last attempt to rescue Cim from acculturating Indianness. As Sabra prepares pineapple and marshmallow salad for her afternoon reception of the

FIGURE 1.4 This illustration, included with an installment of the novel in *Women's Home Companion*, dramatizes how Sabra is no longer the prime influence in Cims's life. Her hand on the wagon wheel cannot impede the cultural exchanges inside the buggy. Illustration by N. C. Wyeth and Charles S. Chapman, *She Knew She Must Not Lose Her Dignity*, *Women's Home Companion* 57 [1930]: 29. Courtesy Illinois State Library, Springfield.

Twentieth Century Culture Club, she watches helplessly as Cim prepares to take Ruby out to the reservation for a "Mescal Ceremony." Much like the white female photographers that Susan K. Bernardin, Melody Graulich, Lisa MacFarlane, Nicole Tonkovich, and Louis Owens examine in *Trading Gazes: Euro-American Women Photographers and Native North Americans, 1880–1940*, Ferber captures a snapshot of colonial gazes that betray as much about the watchers as they do about the watched. As Sabra looks on, she sees Ruby (who is dressed in the stereotypically eroticized Indian garb of a fringed doeskin dress and moccasins with beading and embroidery) and thinks she "almost looked beautiful" in her "robe of a princess" and notices that "her dark Indian eyes were alive," as opposed to the dead, black Indian eyes that Sabra usually sees when she looks at

Ruby. Cim's "eyes shone enormous" when "he saw the Indian woman in her white doeskin dress," and Sabra, recognizing the physical attraction between them, "ran across the yard" to stop the buggy with "one hand . . . at her breast, as though an Indian arrow had pierced her" (303) (figure 1.4). Their souls bared through their eyes, Cim and Ruby's physical attraction to each other troubles Sabra more than Cim's impending participation in the peyote ceremony.

Sabra's raid on the peyote ceremony exposes the duality of her approach to Indian culture; her words reveal the colonialist impulse to deny that the colonized have an organized culture, but her actions betray her fears that Indian culture could assimilate and is assimilating her son. After finishing her domestic duties entertaining the ladies' club and feeding her husband dinner (after which Yancey leaves again), Sabra can no longer resist driving out to the reservation to retrieve Cim. Leaving town at 1:00 a.m. with her friend Sol Levy (the Jewish town merchant, another racialized figure), Sabra listens to "barbaric sounds, wild, sinister," which she realizes are "the savage sound of the drum" as she approaches the reservation. "A drum in the night," Sabra says to Levy. "It sounds so terrible, so savage." Levy responds. "Nothing to be frightened about. A lot of poor ignorant Indians trying to forget their misery" (311). Again, the non-Indian characters view the use of peyote as a mindlessly gloomy response to and an escape from white culture, not a spiritually vital element of contemporary Indian culture. But Sabra's actions in this scene contradict the emptiness her language attributes to the peyote ceremony. Strengthened by her resolve to reclaim her son for the cause of Americanness, she barges into the tepee that houses the ceremony and finds Cim asleep under a striped Osage blanket, presumably passed out from his dose of peyote. Sabra thinks, "'This is the way I should look at him if he were dead.' Then, 'He is dead'" (314). Cim's choice to participate in Indian culture makes him dead to Sabra; nevertheless, she and Levy drag him out of the tepee and, with the help of an Osage man, lift him into the buggy for the long ride back to town. Think what she might, Sabra's actions reveal her anxious belief that Indian culture is indeed an organized yet fluid entity, capable of influencing and assimilating members of the dominant Euro-American culture.

Sabra's anxiety about Indian and Euro-American cross-cultural exchange, which reaches its boiling point when Cim and Ruby marry and have children, could be read as nativism, a popular concept in 1920s

American thought. Campbell brings together the scholarship of John Higham, Walter Benn Michaels, and others to argue that Ferber criticizes the idea of nativism in *Cimarron* and her other regional novels. Michaels quotes Higham's foundational definition of nativism—"intense opposition to an internal minority on the grounds of its foreign (i.e., 'un-American') connections" (2)—only to build his own, albeit controversial, term from it: *nativist modernism.* "In nativist modernism," Michaels explains, "identity becomes an ambition as well as a description. Indeed, it is only this transformation of identity into the object of desire as well as its source that will make the dramas of nativism—the defense of identity, its loss, its repudiation, its rediscovery—possible" (3). In *Cimarron,* Yancey and Cim make finding identity an ambition; they both distance themselves from white culture through words and actions, and they sample Indian culture to varying degrees, from Yancey's frequent disappearances into nature and using peyote "to escape into a dream life" (295) to Cim's marrying an Osage and fathering so-called half-breed children. On the other hand, Sabra makes "the dramas of nativism possible" (Michaels 3). In her defense of white culture (the other side of the coin that is her degradation of Indian culture), she initiates the identity cycle that Michaels describes. Yancey tells Sabra that she is to blame for Cim's decision to participate in Indian culture, which also implies that she is responsible for Yancey's own ventures into Indianness.

In her defense of white identity, Sabra sets herself up for a loss of identity and the eventual rediscovery of identity through Cim and Ruby's children, her Indian grandchildren. As Richard Slotkin notes, people often suppose that "romances involving white men and Indian 'princesses' have the saving grace of preserving the political and moral hierarchy of a male-dominated ideology" (371). The irony, of course, is that such romances rarely, if ever, offer such "saving grace." If Cim and Ruby's romance reinforced existing hierarchies, Sabra would have little need for anxiety. Instead, Sabra realizes that her son's marriage to an Indian can weaken, if not destroy or even invert, the American hierarchy where whites males dominate. Campbell asserts that "in *Cimarron,* intermarriage is recast as sound eugenics, an infusion of fresh blood to strengthen the pioneer stock," again quoting Michaels as saying that "'no event in the nativist canon was more common than sex with an Indian,' an act attempted so that children could be 'as native as their native American parent'" ("Written" 33). Campbell describes Cim's marriage to Ruby as an example of "cross-racial 'hybridity'" and says that "their relationship goes beyond Michaels's 'sex with an Indian' paradigm to include cross-cultural exchanges" that include the wedding, as well as the peyote scenes that I have already described (34). Putting quotation marks around the word *hybridity* signals Campbell's awareness of the vexed status of the term, though she continues with the concept, concluding her discussion of the novel by congratulating the way that "Cim Cravat's matter-of-fact adoption of Osage ways demonstrates that cultural reciprocity and pride in identity, not assimilation, is the fulfillment of Yancey's dream" (35), that Cim and Ruby's union will produce "such stuff as Americans are made of" (Ferber, *Cimarron* 357).

Hybridity theory often risks assuming that both cultures being hybridized are discreet, concrete, and unified against the other culture. Further, it assumes that the product of hybridization is a new species that abandons the old genetic and cultural tendencies. While this may work for growing stalks of corn, reading Cim and Ruby's marriage as hybridity poses problems. Not only is hybridity theory's underlying assumption misleading in general—one culture is never truly and purely isolated from another—but it also contradicts the racial scenario Ferber sets up in the novel. Ferber narrates Yancey and Cim as Indian *already*, before the peyote scenes, before Yancey's back to nature/back to the blanket wanderings, and before Cim's marriage to Ruby Big Elk. As Deloria writes, "Much has been made of the . . . notion of an American synthesis, of the 'wilderness marriage' that joined Indian and European and thus resolved the dialectic of civilization and savagery in the form of a new product. . . . Playing Indian offered Americans a national fantasy—identities built not around synthesis and transformation, but around unresolved dualities themselves" (185). Ruby and Cim exemplify these unresolved dualities—or rather, their dualities are resolved in a nondualistic way; even though they live as Indians after their marriage, their home is a large, government-built, oil-funded brick house garishly decorated in "*mongrel* Spanish" style (Ferber, *Cimarron*, 358, italics added), showing that cultural enmeshment is the norm, not the exception.

In *Cimarron*, Ferber accentuates relations between whiteness and Indianness, masculinity and femininity, and the domestic and the foreign, incorporating the raced, classed, and gendered question of essential American identity into a broader modernist, overtly feminist project.

While Yancey and Cim Cravat may embody Ferber's dreams for a new American identity that includes the internal foreigner, they are overshadowed by Sabra Cravat's strong maternal colonialism and imperial domesticity. Campbell wants to see Sabra's movement from innocent pioneer girl to savvy political woman as character growth, noting that she goes from disparaging Indian culture to accepting it through Cim's marriage to Ruby and their children (34). While this may be, when Sabra displays her acceptance of her daughter-in-law and her grandchildren at a ball in Washington DC (371), she makes her so-called acceptance of them seem to be *only* a display. Sabra parades her Indian family to the Washington politicians, showing that she has reclaimed control over the "savage within" her own family—and her own nation—after the peyote in her kitchen sparked her desperate desire for separation. She is the defender of American borders throughout the novel. Even at the end, when it might seem the boundaries have blurred so as disappear entirely, Sabra seems to emerge victoriously as the venerable American new woman-as-congresswoman. But Ferber ultimately critiques American imperial domesticity—and Sabra's role as a maternal colonialist—by showing how Sabra's control over her domestic space and her family unravels throughout the novel. The peyote in the kitchen symbolizes the continued and enduring presence of Osage and American Indian peoples within the geopolitical boundaries of the United States, a presence that continues to speak back to, resist, and influence American colonizers like Sabra Cravat.

"To make these poor Mexicans 'good Americans'": Paternal Domesticity in Willa Cather's *Death Comes for the Archbishop*

Literary critics from every corner of the discipline have wrangled over Willa Cather's placement in the canon since she began writing.[4] Early reviewers of *Death Comes for the Archbishop* argued over its generic categorization. An anonymous writer for the NEA Book Survey and Lee Wilson Dodd, among others, argue that the book is not a novel but is historical biography, or maybe "biography in the guise of fiction" (Dodd 316). Edwin Francis Edgett and Lillian C. Ford assert that it is historical fiction, a "straightaway historical novel" (Edgett 324). Some contemporary reviewers seemed completely befuddled about the book's genre; Francis Talbot and Frances Lamont Robbins are not sure if *Archbishop* is a novel, a biography, or a historical narrative. James Schroeter narrates a history of Cather criticism where twentieth-century literary scholars claim Cather as the poster child for their particular methods of reading. "Coming-of-Age" critics (Schroeter 21), New Critics, Modernists, Marxists, Realists, Naturalists, New Historicists, traditionalists, those who read Cather's work through her biography, and those who attend to the universal themes and mythic, archetypal patterns in her work have all declared that "Cather is ________" and have filled in the blank with their own readerly preferences. By the end of the twentieth century, literary critics were asking Cather's work to be increasingly pliable, continuing to read her as critics did in the early years of the century but adding new methods.

William R. Handley, Marilyn C. Wesley, Joseph R. Urgo, and Janis P. Stout claim Cather's work for the library of travel narratives and novels about the American West. Elizabeth Ammons, Guy Reynolds, Christopher Schedler, J. David Stevens, and Urgo critique Cather's novels through the lenses of race and empire studies. Danielle Russell, Anne E. Goldman, Handley, and Deborah Karush focus on gender roles and domesticity in her work. Mark J. Madigan, Charles W. Mignon, and John J. Murphy, Stout, Urgo, and M. Catherine Downs write about Cather's stint in journalism and her works' circulation in print culture. Since the turn into the twenty-first century, critics read Cather's work through the paradigms of queer theory (Marilee Lindemann, Heather Love, Jonathan Goldberg, Christopher Nealon, and Scott Herring) and ecocriticism (Susan J. Rosowski, Patrick K. Dooley, Mary R. Ryder, and J. Gerard Dollar). Perhaps most enduring among all the critical readings of Cather and her work are the ideas that "prove" Cather was "removed from her time": she was anti–mass culture, anti–traditional gender roles, and antiracism. But recent critics have shown, and as I discuss in this section, the opposite is true. Cather was firmly grounded in her historical moment. The publication history of *Death Comes for the Archbishop*—as well as the novel's treatment of women, Mexicans, and Indians—shows that, despite her sometimes critical relationship to pop culture and mainstream ideologies, Cather's fiction does not escape the destructive power of the colonial American mindset.

Death Comes for the Archbishop was first serialized in the January–June 1927 issues of the *Forum* alongside advertisements for exotic travel—ads that stem from and feed colonial ideology. The first two images I include here are printed within a travel-advertisement essay by Henry H. Kinyon, "South America, Land of Contrasts": "whatever may be the individual reasons for travel, whatever the chief source of delight, South America possesses such a diversity of scenery and wonder and magnificence that even the most cross-grained globe-trotter can hardly help feeling abundantly satisfied with a visit there" (figures 1.5 and 1.6). Kinyon highlights the foreignness of South America but at the same time familiarizes it in terms of domesticity, encouraging tourists to visit "our great continental neighbor" (Kinyon, Illustrated Section 38). The name of the travel line in one advertisement, the "Great White Fleet," recalls the Great White Hunter of the same period (mid-nineteenth to early twentieth centuries) (figure 1.7). These "great white" titles signify more than just the color of the ships or the hunter; the people who can afford such luxurious travel and sport are, of course, white people. Teddy Roosevelt popularized exotic game hunts, and the United States appropriated more and more western territories and displaced more and more indigenous peoples. Set in and written during the same time period, *Archbishop*'s Navajo-hunting (184) and soul-hunting (206) reproduces and naturalizes pop culture's colonial, racist, exploitive ideology that white people can use and abuse the world, its peoples, and its natural resources. The *Forum* also advertised domestic travel, using images and slogans that exoticize Indians as the internal foreigner. A Maine ad features a wizened "Indian Chief" who wisely approves of his "white brothers" making a "playground" out of his ancestral lands (figure 1.8). A New Mexico ad features an "enchanted land" belonging not to the pictured Indian but to Coronado; the Indian is a foreigner, a sideshow "detour" for a now-American destination (figure 1.9). Caroline M. Woidat reads *The Professor's House* and *The Song of the Lark* in relation to "Indian-detour" advertisements like the one I include here to "reevalute Cather's position as a woman writer and a tourist" in relation to the ways "the Indian-detour responds to the complex and often contradictory desires of Americans in confronting racial difference and the legacy of a pre-Columbian past" (24).

Other ads in the January 1927 issue are for specific travel companies and banks (that could finance the travel). The magazine also promoted self-help books such as "How to Work Wonders with Words" to turn the shy man into a brilliant public speaker and "Scientific Mind Training" to turn the insecure man "with his tail between his legs" into a confident trailblazer who can "do something about yourself" and "make others

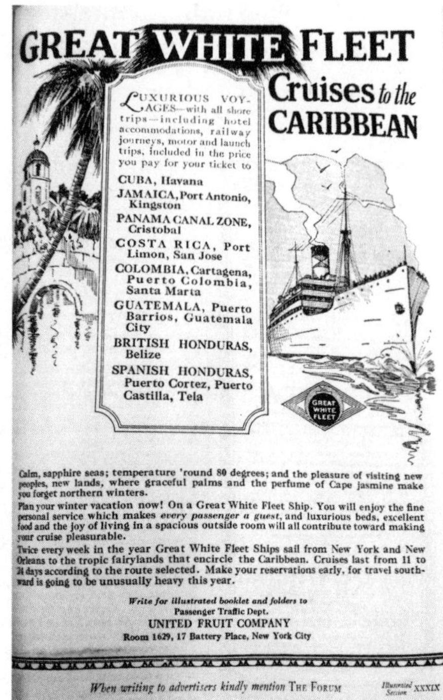

FIGURES 1.5 and 1.6 (*left*) Two travel advertisements published with Cather's *Death Comes for the Archbishop* in the *Forum* promote the habit of white people traveling to tropical places populated by "exotic" people of color (West Indies, South America). Courtesy Main Library, University of Illinois at Urbana–Champaign.

FIGURE 1.7 (*right*) The "Great White Fleet" not only evokes thoughts of the Great White Hunter, an American ideal for masculinity made popular by Teddy Roosevelt, but also recalls the Great White Hope, the hoped-for white boxer who could beat the best black boxers—most famously, Jack Johnson. Courtesy Main Library, University of Illinois at Urbana–Champaign.

rich and happy" (Kinyon, Illustrated Section 5, 9). Intellectual fare also graced the *Forum's* ads, such as *Encyclopedia Britannica*, *The Lost Books of the Bible*, and for the autodidact armchair traveler, a collection of Balzac's "masterpieces" that would "let Balzac show you Paris!" (Kinyon, Illustrated Section 11).

In this self-consciously highbrow print culture, the *Forum* presents *Death Comes for the Archbishop* as a travel narrative about an exotic place (New Mexico Territory) and exotic peoples (Indians and Mexicans). But contemporary reviewers received and recirculated *Archbishop* as history

FIGURE 1.8 (*left*) Travel advertisement for Lucerne-in-Maine. "Old Chief Nicolar" may in fact be, or be related to, the historical Joseph Nicolar, who wrote a history of his people, the Penobscot. Courtesy Main Library, University of Illinois at Urbana–Champaign.

FIGURE 1.9 (*right*) This advertisement assures readers of the *Forum* that they can view the "ancient" and "prehistoric" peoples and places of New Mexico from the modern comfort—and safe distance—of their Harveycar. Courtesy Main Library, University of Illinois at Urbana–Champaign.

and biography—as a real and true representation of these "foreign" places and peoples. By reading the novel, one could be transported to another time and place, just as the *Forum* ad suggests that by reading Balzac one could visit Paris. If the autodidact could learn about the Bible, Paris, and anything in the world by reading books and encyclopedias, then readers could also learn about Mexicans and Indians by reading Cather's novel. Similarly, Scanlon argues that "turn of the century magazines . . . educated people to exercise prejudices against difference in general, and against racial, ethnic, and religious difference in particular" (18). In addition to the travel and autodidactic advertisements, the *Forum* also published several essays concerning (white) women's roles. Where magazines like *Woman's Home Companion* glorified domesticity and featured ads where white women were vacuuming or washing dishes, the *Forum*'s essays and advertisements featured alternative amusements and preoccupations for women. In the *Forum,* white women traveled, worried about whether they should wear pants or short skirts, and weighed in on what it meant to have the perfect child. Or, in Cather's case, they wrote about Indian and Mexican women who performed domestic labor for Catholic priests. Like Ferber's *Cimarron,* Cather's *Archbishop* not only encourages white Americans to stereotype nonwhites, it also reinforces the common idea held by white reformers that Indian and Mexican women need training in Euro-American domesticity and are the ideal workers to whom whites could delegate domestic labor.

At first thought, it might seem like a stretch to claim that the *Forum*'s serialization of *Archbishop* is an instance of the mainstream culture's imposition of Euro-American domesticity on Indian and Mexican women. But like the *Forum*'s advertisements, the novel circulated among white female readers who often delegated domesticity to racial others. Moreover, the very plotline of the novel—Jesuit priests set up house among Mexicans and Indians of New Mexico—is an exercise in domestic colonialism. Additionally, women's magazines printed some of Cather's other stories that promoted traditional roles for women, even though in the early days of her career Cather lampooned the *Ladies' Home Journal* for publishing fluff fiction that bore little resemblance to anything that could be called "literature" (Slote 188). For example, Park Bucker writes about the *Woman's Home Companion* publishing "Neighbour Rosicky" to show how Cather's story is complicit in the magazine's presentation of material culture as the inevitable state of modernity and the "kitchen as a physical site of family happiness, stability, and morality" (67). Cather herself worked at two women's magazines, *Home Monthly* and *McClure's.* Jennifer L. Bradley asserts that *Home Monthly*'s goals were "often at odds with [Cather's] own literary ideals." When the "readers' desire for instruction on social propriety, home, and family" was combined with Cather's advertisers' need to sell products, Cather found herself in conflict (38). But Urgo concludes the opposite in his examinations of issues of *McClure's* that published Cather's writing. He finds a "cohesive quality between Cather's writing and the salient issues and ideas of the magazine" and asserts that "Cather's literary concerns were consistent with its social and political agenda" ("Willa Cather's" 61).

Making an argument similar to Terence Whalen's about Edgar Allan Poe's financial need for popular readers who insulted his artistic sensibilities, Robert Seguin discusses Cather's ambivalence about working for and publishing her stories in popular magazines. He asserts that a "tension was inherent in the very project Cather self-consciously set herself, which was, on one hand, to reach a wide popular readership (and her novels were in fact consistent best-sellers, and continue to sell well today) and, on the other hand, to be considered an uncompromising literary artist of the first rank" (77). As Ellen Gruber Garvey points out, fiction does not emerge from some "pure sphere of literature," where it avoids the "commercial nexus" its writers inhabit. On the contrary, "fiction constantly if uneasily reflects on its place within commerce" (5). Cather's uneasiness with how her writing circulated in the marketplace contributes to scholars' historical tendencies to read her work as a retreat from the crass commercialism of modern life. Stevens argues that, "despite the critical tendency to read Cather as 'high art' . . . the impulses, biases, and events of *Death Comes for the Archbishop* can be understood together if the book is read as a thematically straightforward, if slightly amended, version of the popular frontier novel" (135). Whether or not Cather's personal politics, beliefs, or preferences were at odds with the periodicals that employed her or the market that received her work, her writing cohered with the racist and colonial overtones of popular magazine fiction and advertisements during the first few decades of the twentieth century.

In *Death Comes for the Archbishop*, Cather uses both traditional and modernist conventions that show her simultaneous distaste for modernity and inability to escape it. On the other hand, as Downs critiques Cather's modernist journalism, "while twentieth-century modernism tried to break with its past, it dragged the past into the future" (30). In her desire to escape the racism and colonialism that helped found American life, Cather drags some of it into the present. In *Archbishop*, Cather's desire to provide an escape from domesticity for herself and for her female characters translates into a fusion of two imperial constructs, reinscribing colonial domesticity onto nonwhite female characters. Such contradictory Janus-vision is part of her experimentation, part of what makes her a modernist writer. Joan Acocella suggests that reading racism or colonialism in Cather is not about labeling Cather herself a "racist" but rather about showing how her work participates in a vast, dominant cultural apparatus that defines "American" as "of or adapting to European descent and culture." Writing about Cather's "domestication of empire" in *The Professor's House,* Karush asserts that Cather takes a dual approach to writing about American imperialism. By setting her novels in centuries past, she relegates American imperialism to the past, narrating it as a past event. Second, this relegation, combined with what Karush sees as Cather's emphasis on the ways that "continental expansion keeps the United States figuratively at home," shows how her "ambivalent treatment of imperialism reveals her embeddedness in" it (146). By focusing on Cather's portrayals of race, women, and domestic culture, *Archbishop* is also caught up in two historical moments: the time when Cather *writes* it and the time when Cather *sets* it.

In the first section of the novel, "At Rome," when the cardinals are deciding whom to send to the New Mexican people to replace the retiring Father Ferrand, Cather sets up a preoccupation with nationality and ethnic identity that will permeate the novel. The very first line of the novel reinforces this preoccupation too, setting the novel in the year—1848—that the United States signed the Treaty of Guadalupe-Hidalgo with Mexico to take the territory that would become New Mexico and other western states. The bishops want to send a French priest because the French "are the best missionaries. Our Spanish fathers made good martyrs, but the French Jesuits accomplish more. They are the great organizers" (8). From the outset, Cather asserts that a French priest is the best candidate "to deal with [the] savagery and ignorance" (8) of the Indians and Mexicans of New Mexico. The novel's narrative structure does, in fact, take on the tone and form of the (in)famous Jesuit Relations that early French priests wrote and sent back to the crown as reports on their progress in the New World. From these letters, Europeans got some of their first—and lasting—misinformation about indigenous peoples in North America, though Cather's cardinal sees the letters as efforts to "discover the logical relation of things" (9).

In this first section, Cather also sets up a fine distinction between which characters essentialize Indians and which "really know" Indians. The cardinal admits, "My knowledge of your country is chiefly drawn from the romances of Fenimore Cooper, which I read in English with great pleasure" (10). He relates a story that his great-grandfather used to tell of another missionary to New Spain who begged for an El Greco painting, a portrait of "a young St. Francis in meditation" (12), even though the great-grandfather protested that "some picture of the Crucifixion, or a martyrdom, would appeal more strongly to his redskins. What would a St. Francis, of almost feminine beauty, mean to the scalp-takers?" (12). The cardinal reflects on his great-grandfather's story, asking that this new French priest keep an eye out for the El Greco during his missionary journeys: "of course the painting may have been ruined in a pillage or massacre. On the other hand, it may still be hidden away in some crumbling sacristy or wigwam" (12). Father Ferrand respectfully corrects the cardinal: "Down there the Indians do not dwell in wigwams, your Eminence" (13). The cardinal dismisses Ferrand's attempt to correct his misunderstanding of Indians and insists on believing the sensationalized image of Indians circulated through mainstream American culture: "No matter, Father. I see your redskins through Fenimore Cooper, and I like them so" (13). With this conversation about real Indians and fictional Indians, Cather sends a message to readers—that is, she distinguishes her portrayal of Indians in *Death Comes for the Archbishop* from Cooper's portrayal of Indians in *The Leatherstocking Tales*. Cather leads readers to believe that she will present a more accurate, or at least a more sympathetic, picture of Indian life. But just as the cardinal dismisses Ferrand's insistence on a fact about Indians in favor of a fiction, so the novel ultimately dismisses its sympathies with the Indians and Mexicans of New Mexico.

As Mary Austin points out, Cather's sympathies lie with the colonial powers in the novel: "Miss Cather used my house to write [*Death Comes for the Archbishop*], but she did not tell me what she was doing. When it was finished, I was very much distressed to find that she had given her allegiance to the French blood of the Archbishop; she had sympathized with his desire to build a French cathedral in a Spanish town. It was a calamity to the local culture. We have never gotten over it" (*Earth Horizon* 359). It is worth highlighting that Austin aligns herself with the Spanish even as she scolds Cather for siding with the French. Neither writer seems concerned with the local Indian cultures that lived in New Mexico before either the Spanish or the French. Both women writers exploit the region and its peoples for their own purposes. Cather writes about "how I happened to write *Death Comes for the Archbishop*" (quoted in Mignon 373): "The longer I stayed in the Southwest, the more I felt that the story of the Catholic

Church in that country was the most interesting of all its stories. . . . The story of the Church and the Spanish missionaries was always what most interested me" (374–75). Cather writes of learning about Jean Baptiste Lamy, the first bishop of New Mexico (and, later, the first archbishop of Santa Fe), and says she wished she "could learn more about a pioneer churchman who looked so well-bred and distinguished, . . . something that spoke of race. What I felt curious about was the daily life of such a man in a crude frontier society" (375). Early critics Edward A. Bloom and Lillian D. Bloom note that while Cather drew on her visits to New Mexico as source material for *Archbishop*, she relied on and "manipulated" colonial narratives of the Southwest (written by Charles F. Lummis, Ralph Emerson Twitchell, J. B. Salpointe, Hugh H. Bancroft, Adolph Bandelier, George Parker Winship, and Francisco Paulo) "to fuse a relatively sophisticated Catholicism with the ancient paganism of Indian rites on one hand, and with primitive Mexican devotion to Catholicism on the other" (336). The Blooms' binary has some problems of its own—implying, for instance, that Catholicism is sophisticated but indigenous spiritualism is ancient and primitive" and thus unsophisticated—but their assertion is on point. Cather prioritized these nineteenth-century colonizers' perspectives on Indians and Mexicans over what she likely saw with her own eyes. Her own musings suggest that *Archbishop* is less concerned with the indigenous side of this colonial history; instead, it is a novel about how well-bred Europeans and Euro-Americans finally civilize the Mexicans, Indians, and outlaws who make up a crude frontier society.

Given the scarcity of white women in New Mexico during this time, the priests teach Indian and Mexican women Euro-American domesticity in the novel. But the novel as a whole can be read as an exercise in colonial domesticity if we imagine, as does Cathryn Halverson, Cather's "use of the male housekeeper [as a way] to moderate the seeming incongruity of the West and the domestic" (28). As a white woman from America's eastern and midwestern states, Cather relocated to New Mexico and wrote a novel about French Catholic colonial mission work in the region. By focalizing her narrative through European characters who work to bring about a French revival of Catholicism in a historically Spanish-Catholic and indigenously spiritual place, Cather writes a colonizing text about colonialism. By setting so much of the narrative in a series of domestic spaces—kitchens, dining rooms, and living rooms—and by populating these settings with narratively and culturally marginalized Indian and Mexican women workers, Cather's novel hinges on the apparatus of colonial domesticity. The only significant white woman in the novel, Doña Isabella, performs no domestic labor; the white woman who wrote the novel—Cather—constructs a fictional world where white women wile away the hours being pretty and frivolous and situates herself as a new woman of privilege who can write about brown and red women performing domestic labor without performing it herself.

Throughout the novel, Bishop Latour and Father Vaillant partially recognize Mexican and Indian domesticity even as they equate true domesticity with being civilized, European, and Euro-American. Though she uses *The Professor's House* as her primary example, Goldman's assertions about Cather's fictional domesticity apply to *Archbishop* as well. Goldman compares the United States' renaming its conquest of Mexico ("annexation") to Cather's recasting "domesticity as a civilizing force, that is, to simultaneously justify *and* cover imperial relationships" ("All in the Family?" 113). During one of his first missionary journeys, Latour eats at the "mother-house" of the Mexican settlement called Hidden Water, where the widower Benito lives with Josepha, his daughter, who "was his housekeeper" (25). The bishop describes what he sees as their primitive supper consisting of frijoles and meat served with bread, goat's milk, cheese, and apples. Detailing their dinner might be just a simple element of plot except for Latour's continued description, which shows that Latour forms his opinion of Benito's family based on his impressions of the home's interior:

> From the moment he entered this room with its thick, whitewashed adobe walls, Father Latour had felt a kind of peace about it. In its bareness and simplicity there was something comely, as there was about the serious girl who had placed their food before them and who now stood in the shadows against the wall, her eager eyes fixed upon his face. He found himself very much at home with the four dark-headed men who sat beside him in the candlelight. Their manners were gentle, their voices low and agreeable. When he said grace before meat, the men had knelt on the floor beside the table. (25)

The simple decor and food make Latour feel peaceful in Benito's home, but their dinner conversation does nothing to make him feel "at home." On the contrary, Cather highlights the differences between Benito's family and the newly arrived Americans, with whom Latour identifies. Benito and his family "had no papers for their land and were afraid the Americans might take it away from them" (26). José, Benito's oldest grandson, tells Latour, "They say at Albuquerque that now we are all American, but that is not true, Padre. I will never be an American. They are infidels." Latour corrects him: "'Not all, my son. I have lived among Americans in the north for ten years, and I found many devout Catholics.' The young man shook his head. 'They destroyed our churches when they were fighting us, and stabled our horses in them. And now they will take our religion away from us. We want our own way and our own religion'" (27). This conversation between Latour and José introduces another domestic site where national and ethnic identity are defined: the church.

In his visits to the Indian missions at the western pueblos, Latour contrasts the churches at Acoma, Isleta, and Laguna, using the churches' interiors as measures of the pueblos' cultural identity and progress toward civilization. Latour appreciates the fact that the Laguna people "prepared" for his visit: "the church was clean, painted above and about the altar with gods of wind and rain and thunder, sun and moon, linked together in a geometrical design of crimson and blue and dark green, so that the end of the church seemed to be hung with tapestry" (89). But Latour is unsure whether this church, which reminds him of a "Persian chieftain's tent he had seen in a textile exhibit in Lyons" (89) can be a marker of the Laguna people's progress toward Catholic Euro-Americanness. Though he assumes that the Indians cleaned the church for his arrival, his mental comparison of the church's interior with a Persian interior he had seen in France also makes him assume that the Indians could not have decorated the church. He seems bothered enough by this cultural composite to have asked about the decor, but "whether this decoration had been done by Spanish missionaries or by Indian converts, he was unable to find out" (89). To Latour, cultural enmeshment seems to be a marker of civilization in Europe—prompting his memory of Persian domesticity at a French fair—but here in Laguna, he cannot quite accept that the Laguna people would have the agency or ability to produce such evidence of cultural fusion. Indeed, though Latour seems not to know this, the history of the Lagunas is already all about fusion among Pueblo cultures.

When Latour arrives at Acoma, though, the Laguna Indians seem highly civilized compared to the Acoma Indians, who "were all unreclaimed heathen at heart" (83). Latour bases this judgment, in part, on their church's interior. The church at Acoma "depressed the Bishop as no other mission church had done," with its "gaunt, grim, grey . . . nave rising some seventy feet to a sagging, half-ruined roof, it was more like a fortress than a place of worship" (100). But just as he is hesitant to credit the Laguna people with the culturally sophisticated interior of the church at Laguna, Latour is hesitant to blame the Acoma people for the decaying interior of the church at their pueblo. For "the more Father Latour examined this church, the more he was inclined to think that Fray Ramirez, or some Spanish priest who followed him, was not altogether innocent of worldly ambition, and that they built for their own satisfaction, perhaps, rather than according to the need of the Indians" (101). Cather digresses from the narration to tell the story of Fray Baltazar, who lived at Acoma in the early eighteenth century and who made the Indians carry materials over long distances so he could build the church and maintain the grounds. He was also "able to grow a wonderful garden, since it was watered every evening by women,—and this despite the fact that it was not proper that a woman should ever enter the cloister at all. Each woman owed the Padre so many *ollas* of water a week from the cisterns, and they murmured not only because of the labour, but because of the drain on their water supply" (104). Latour is amazed and dismayed when he realizes that all the adobe and timber for the church was carried forty or fifty miles from the San Mateo Mountains "on the backs of men and boys and women" from Acoma (101). Latour does not see the church at Acoma as a marker of the Acoma people's domesticity—represented by the descriptions of the women's work—or as a marker of their syncretism or as an achievement of which the community can be proud. Latour misses these things correctly, yet sees this church only as a monument to colonial vanity and the colonial exploitation of natural and human resources.

But while Latour can recognize colonialism in the way Fray Baltazar took advantage of Acoma women over a century earlier, he does not recognize the domestic colonialism he and Vaillant act out during their tenure in the New Mexico diocese. And while the two priests at times recognize and appreciate Mexican domesticity (they rarely, if ever, recognize Indian domesticity), they usually impose European or

Euro-American domesticity on the Mexican and Indian women who work for them. Other priests in the region do the same thing. At Isleta, Father Jesus has an Indian girl who "cooked his beans and cornmeal mush for him" (85). Despite his instruction in the kitchen, "the girl was not very skillful, he said, but she was clean about her cooking. When the Bishop remarked that everything in this pueblo, even the streets, seemed clean, the Padre told him that near Isleta there was a hill of some white mineral, which the Indians ground up and used as whitewash. They had done this from time immemorial, and the village had always been noted for its whiteness" (85). Father Jesus is surely commenting on the literal whiteness of the town, for the cleanliness of the Isleta people predates his arrival; their "whiteness" seems not to be a result of his efforts to domesticate the Indian girl. She was already "clean" and she feeds him indigenous foods—beans and corn—because she has not learned enough from his instruction to cook Spanish foods.

The cultural exchange via food at Father Jesus's house also transpires at Latour and Vaillant's home. Latour and Vaillant, though, seem well aware of their syncretic domestic choices and use of domesticity to Americanize the Mexicans and Indians who perform the household labors. An extended meditation on domesticity at the Episcopal residence is but one example of how cooking, architecture, and gardening relate to national identity and degrees of civilization in *Archbishop*. Additionally, the syncretic domestic spaces and decor at the priests' home—a blend of traditional and modern, indigenous and European—indicate Cather's modernist experimentation. The decor is a collage, an "*original bicultural composite composition*" (Krupat, *For Those* 31), a signal of Cather's attempt, both in *Archbishop* and elsewhere in her writings, to craft something new out of the literary and cultural heritage of the United States in the 1920s.

When Father Vaillant moves into the old adobe rectory, local carpenters and Mexican women help him arrange it. He receives bedding, blankets, and furniture from Yankee traders and the military commandant at Fort Marcy. When Bishop Latour moves in, he chooses for his study a secluded room where "thick clay walls had been finished on the inside by the deft palms of Indian women, and had that irregular and intimate quality of things made entirely by the human hand" (33). Russell generously reads Latour's descriptions of indigenous women's work, asserting that "it is literally a 'feminine touch' which humanizes the building; intimacy is derived from the distant yet ever-present feminine presence" (146–47). Indeed, actual indigenous women are distant in this novel; usually only the results of their labor are ever-present. Latour eventually appreciates the Mexican women's domestic gifts: "the Mexican women, skilled in needlework and lace-making and hem-stitching, presented him with fine linen for his person, his bed, and his table" (226). Apparently, Mexican women have more nimble fingers for daintier domestic work, but Indian women work with their palms to perform tougher tasks that are associated, in Europe and most of America, with masculinity. Cather further describes the interior of the priests' residence with painstaking detail. The study features a ceiling coffered with cedar and aspen and an earthen floor carpeted with Indian blankets. The bishop's books and religious objects rest on tables, shelves, and chairs hand-hewn by "native carpenters," but his desk "was an importation, a walnut 'secretary' of American make" and the silver candlesticks that illuminate his writing were an ordination gift from his aunt in France (34–35).

In this domestic scene, Latour sits at his desk to write a letter to his brother in France about his early experiences in New Mexico. Like the letters of the many Jesuit missionaries that came before him, Latour's letter reflects his own perspective on his purposes in the New World and betrays his alliance with colonial powers: "the kindness of the American traders, and especially the military officers at the Fort, commands more than a superficial loyalty. I mean to help the officers at their task here. I can assist them more than they realize. The Church can do more than the Fort to make these poor Mexicans 'good Americans.' And it is for the people's good; there is no other way in which they can better their condition" (36). Latour's limited, perhaps self-limiting, perspective on American colonialism in the Southwest echoes the Jesuit Relations that notoriously misread North American indigenous cultures. It also presages modern historical works that take as truth European missionary letters and reports. For example, Ramón A. Gutiérrez's *When Jesus Came, the Corn Mothers Went Away: Marriage, Sexuality, and Power in New Mexico, 1500–1846* sensationalizes sex and violence among southwestern Indian groups, and Richard White's *The Middle Ground: Indians, Empires, and Republics in the Great Lakes Region, 1650–1815* meliorates the violence of European colonialism by relying on a French interpretation of cooperative, power-balanced trade relations with Great Lakes Indian groups. Audrey Goodman writes that, in *Archbishop*, this colonial "history of perception [is] inextricable from the Southwest's history of conquest" (154). Stevens asserts that to Latour the Indians' "presence as actual humans is far less important . . . than the Christian metaphors they suggest. To be blunt, he dehumanizes them, thereby echoing the imperial logic which held that Indians should be either assimilated (through religious conversion, for instance) or destroyed by men like [Kit] Carson" (148). It might be impossible to know if Latour's seemingly blind cooperation with colonialism is grounded in a naiveté that Cather drew into his character or if, as John Murphy suggests, Cather herself was unaware of the physically and culturally violent history of the Catholic Church and the US government in the Southwest (348). Either way, the novel aligns itself with Latour's belief that the federal and Catholic presence in New Mexico is ultimately benevolent.

Latour's goal of Americanizing Mexicans is shared by white missionaries, teachers, federal agents, and female reformers. As I show in chapter 4, federal officials believed that getting Indian and Mexican women to change their indigenous domestic habits to Euro-American habits would be the most efficient means of assimilation. Though Latour's primary method for "making good Americans" is Catholic conversion, he measures this conversion through the concrete habits of domesticity. After this statement about making Mexicans good Americans, Latour's letter immediately switches to a discussion of Father Vaillant's cooking and cooking instruction: "Father Joseph has sent away our Mexican woman,—he will make a good cook of her in time, but to-night he is preparing our Christmas dinner himself" (36). Latour describes how Vaillant "has been in the kitchen all afternoon. There is only an open fire-place for cooking, and an earthen roasting-oven out in the courtyard. But he has never failed me in anything yet; and I think I can promise you that to-night two Frenchman will sit down to a good dinner and drink to your health" (36). After finishing his letter, Latour "carried the candles into the dining-room, where the table was laid and Father Vaillant was changing his cook's apron for his cassock" (37). In this apparently traditional domestic setting, with the same extended focus on the national value of domestic rituals that we see in nineteenth-century domestic novels, Cather makes an unexpectedly modernist move. The two people at the dining table are not a man and wife but two male priests; the cook changes *his* apron for a cassock instead of changing *her* apron for a dinner gown. Cather may change the gender of these domestic actors, but she does not move away from the theme of traditional domestic novels: that domestic rituals equal national identity. While enjoying their Christmas dinner, Latour tells Vaillant that, in the whole United States, "'there is probably not another human being who could make a soup like this.' 'Not unless he is a Frenchman,' said Father Joseph. 'I am not deprecating your individual talent, Joseph,' the Bishop continued, 'but, when one thinks of it, a soup like this is not the work of one man. It is the result of a constantly refined tradition. There are nearly a thousand years of history in this soup'" (38). During this brief conversation, the subject seems to change from a history of nationalism—disguised as a history of soup making—to the history of colonialism in the Southwest.

As the novel progresses, we see that Vaillant cooks as often as he teaches cooking, even when he is a guest in someone else's home. Evidently their "Mexican women" are not adopting the art of French-American cuisine quickly enough. When Vaillant stops at Santa Domingo on his journey to Santa Fe, he rests and dines at the home of Señor Lujón. When Vaillant finds that a lamb has been killed for their dinner, he is disappointed when Lujón says they plan to cook the lamb in their usual fashion: as chili with onions. Saying he has had too much stewed mutton, Vaillant asks, "Will you permit me to go into the kitchen and cook my portion in my own way?" Lujón replies, "My house is yours, Padre. Into the kitchen I never go—too many women. But there it is and the woman in charge is Rosa" (57). When Vaillant tells Rosa he wants to roast a leg of the lamb, the exchange between them shows how completely domesticity is bound up in one's cultural and national identity and proves that barbarism is in the eye of the beholder:

> "But Padre, I baked before the marriages [earlier today]. The oven is almost cold. It will take an hour to heat it, and it is only two hours till supper." "Very well. I can cook my roast in an hour." "Cook a roast in an hour!" cried the old woman. "Mother of God, Padre, the blood will not be dried in it!" "Not if I can help it!" said Father Joseph fiercely. "Now hurry with the fire, my good woman." When the Padre carved his roast at the supper-table, the serving-girls stood behind his chair and looked with horror at the delicate stream of pink juice that followed the knife. Manuel Lujón took a slice for politeness, but he did not eat it. Father Vaillant had his *gigot* to himself. (57–58)

Food and culinary practices are sites of cultural exchange throughout the novel. Vaillant, intimating that by the end of his life (and the end of the novel) he will understand that such a cultural exchange can change both the colonized the colonizer, says, "I have almost become a Mexican! I have learned to like *chili colorado* and mutton fat. Their foolish ways no longer offend me, their very faults are dear to me. I am *their man!*" (208). Even though Vaillant and Latour are both influenced by the Mexicans and Indians, Vaillant's statement shows not only the relationship between food and culture but also the colonial idea that a colonized culture can be reduced to its food. The Mexicans have not changed their food or their "foolish ways," but these "faults" that they cling to are to Vaillant no longer offensive but endearing.

Even though Latour and Vaillant perform most of the domestic education for the Mexican and Indian women who work for them, a few white women populate *Archbishop*, and, as the novel progresses, their domestic instruction parallels that of the priests. Just as they did in the Wichita of *Cimarron*, the Sisters of Loretto start a mission school in Santa Fe. Near the end of his "Missionary Journeys" in book 2 of the novel, Bishop Latour travels east to attend the Provincial Council at Baltimore. He brings "five courageous nuns" out west with him so they can "found a school for girls in letterless Santa Fe." Whether this school is for Mexican girls or American girls Cather does not say, but the bishop brings an abused and broken young Mexican woman, Magdalena, to live with and work for the sisters. Magdalena "became housekeeper and manager of the Sisters' kitchen. She was devoted to the nuns, and so happy in the service of the Church that when the Bishop visited the school he used to enter by the kitchen-garden in order to see her serene and handsome face. For she became beautiful, as [Kit] Carson said she had been as a girl. After the blight of her horrible youth was over, she seemed to bloom again in the household of God" (77). The domestic haven of God's house is a blessing for Magdalena: she escapes an abusive white husband. But Magdalena's labor is also a blessing for the sisters: a Mexican girl does their housework so they can attend to more important spiritual duties. While protection from physical abuse is a genuine benefit for Magdalena, she trades one objectifying captivity for another. Instead of being a punching bag for her white husband, now she is a bloom in the white sisters' garden. She is simultaneously a pretty addition to their household; an example of their converting, cultivating, and domesticating efforts; and their labor force.

Señora Isabella Olivares also uses Mexican and/or Indian women as a labor force. Despite her Spanish-sounding name, she was born in Kentucky, raised in New Orleans, and educated in a French convent. She married wealthy Mexican ranchero Don Antonio Olivares during one of his visits to New Orleans and moved to New Mexico with him. Isabella is Olivares's "American wife," and "she had done much to Europeanize her husband" (175, 176). Señora Olivares always makes the French priests welcome at her home, where, like a true American woman, "she had made a pleasant place of the rambling adobe building, with its great court-yard and gateway, carved joists and beams, fine herring-bone ceilings and snug fire-places. She was a gracious hostess, and though no longer very young, she was still attractive. . . . She spoke French well, Spanish lamely, played the harp, and sang agreeably" (176). The priests, "who lived so much among peons and Indians and rough frontiersmen," enjoyed their opportunities "to converse in their own tongue now and then with a cultivated woman and sit by that hospitable fireside, in rooms enriched by old mirrors and engravings and upholstered chairs, where the windows had clean curtains and the sideboard and cupboards were stocked with plate and Belgian glass" (176). Here, as in the church at Laguna, culturally composite interiors speak of European cosmopolitan inhabitants; in the mid-nineteenth century, Old World accoutrements spoke of well-traveled wealth. During the modernist period, cosmopolites and their eclectic interiors signaled trendy American artists. The fact that "all sorts of stories went out from the kitchen" about Dona Isabella indicates that she does not work in her kitchen but that her servants—implicitly Mexican or Indian—do the domestic labor (178). Indeed, in a typically Eurocentric, insular-upper-class interpretation of this fact, Isabella believes that "the gossip did not mean that her servants were disloyal, but rather that they were proud of their mistress" (178).

While domestic servants at the Olivares house might have a kind mistress worth their pride, Cather provides a contrast with the Smith family and their Mexican servant, Sada. On one particularly dark, cold night, Latour sees her sneaking into the church. Sada

> was a slave in an American family. They were Protestants, very hostile to the Roman Church, and they did not allow her to go to Mass or to receive the visits of a priest. She was carefully watched at home,—but in winter, when the heated rooms of the house were desirable to the family, she was put to sleep in a woodshed. . . . The Smiths, with

> whom she lived, were Georgia people, who had at one time lived in El Paso del Norte, and they had taken her back to their native State with them. Not long ago some disgrace had come upon this family in Georgia, they had been forced to sell all their Negro slaves and flee the State. The Mexican woman they could not sell because they had no legal title to her, her position was irregular. Now that they were back in a Mexican country, the Smiths were afraid their charwoman might escape from them and find asylum among her own people, so they kept strict watch upon her. They did not allow her to go outside their own *patio*, not even to accompany her mistress to market. (214)

In Sada's case, Cather—and Latour—seems well aware of the damaging effects of colonial domesticity, even equating Sada's servitude with black slavery. But through the rest of the novel, Latour and Vaillant consciously use domesticity as but one tool in their mission work of making good Americans out of the "poor Mexicans" in New Mexico. Similarly, though Latour can see vanity, pride, and colonialism in the church buildings constructed by previous priests, he cannot see how his own building project requires the same imposition of colonial domesticity.

As Latour reflects on his work in New Mexico at the end of his life, he uses a metaphor from the New Testament to compare evangelism to domestic architecture. He feels that "his work seemed superficial, a house built upon sands. His great diocese was still a heathen country. The Indians traveled their old road of fear and darkness, battling with evil omens and ancient shadows. The Mexicans were children who played with their religion" (211). Even though it is the Indians and Mexicans who hear the Word but do not obey it, Latour believes himself to be the foolish man in Matthew's Gospel who built his house on sand and saw that house washed away when the rains came. Evidently determined to become the wise man who builds his house on rock—a house that will withstand the storms of life—Latour decides to carve a French cathedral out of Santa Fe rock. Life in New Mexico and cultural exchanges with Mexicans and Indians may have influenced Latour's interior design, but in the end, his ultimate act as archbishop of the New Mexican diocese is to impose Euro-American ideals—via architecture—onto the people and landscape. Latour thinks, "It was the Indian manner to vanish into the landscape, not to stand out against it. . . . They seemed to have none of the European's desire to 'master' nature, to arrange and re-create. They spent their ingenuity in the other direction; in accommodating themselves to the scene in which they found themselves" (233). And then, to assert his European identity, to maintain his non-native identity, Latour carves his Mount Rushmore–esque cathedral out of a cliff outside Santa Fe. Latour claims the actual landscape for himself, telling Vaillant, "That hill, *Blanchet*, is my Cathedral" (239). Latour's house of God subsumes nationality, identity, and domesticity as the two priests talk about all the English, Roman, French, American, and Ohio German (but not Indian, Mexican, or Spanish) cathedrals that now punctuate the North American continent (240–43). As Urgo writes, "The archbishop's cathedral is an emblem of an American conception of home" (178). When his cathedral is finally finished, Latour thinks critically of the "incongruous American building" that typified buildings in Santa Fe in 1880 but gazes adoringly at his French cathedral that he carved out of the Indian/Mexican rock: "Wrapped in his Indian blankets, the old Archbishop sat for a long while, looked at the open, golden face of his Cathedral. How exactly the young Molny, his French architect, had done what he wanted! Nothing sensational, simply honest building and good stone-cutting,—good Midi Romanesque of the plainest" (268–69). For Latour, building good Americans out of poor Mexicans requires literal and metaphorical constructs of imperial domesticity.

Cleanliness Is Next to Americanness: Elinore Cowan Stone's *The Laughingest Lady*

Although she has fallen into obscurity, Elinore Cowan Stone wrote many romance, mystery, and adventure stories that ran in popular magazines and newspapers across the United States during the 1920s and 1930s. She also wrote one children's book (*Binks, His Dog and His Heart*) and one mystery novel (*Fear Rides the Fog*), both published in 1937. According to a biographical article by Victor Berch, the Cowans moved east during Elinore's childhood, where she went to Brighton High School and Emerson School of Expression in Boston and Mt. Holyoke College. Elinore did graduate work at the University of California, Sacramento, and in an English class she met the man who became her husband, Clarence Arthur Stone. They married in 1915 and by 1917 were living in New Mexico, where Elinore "taught in a one-room school on an Indian reservation" and where her first novel, *The Laughingest Lady*, was inspired and named. Jan Rider, a journalist who interviewed the Stones on Elinore's ninetieth birthday, quotes Elinore as saying that "the book's title was the name many of her Indian pupils called her." The setting of the book is actually in a New Mexican mining town near the Mexico border, not on an Indian reservation, and the fictional students are Mexican American, not Indians. It's hard to know, then, if the reporter bungled the facts or if Stone actually saw her students as Indians. Details in the novel support the latter idea, as Katherine Nevin, the fictional teacher, implicitly conflates Mexicanness and Indianness. After living in New Mexico for a short time, the Stones moved to the Midwest, where Elinore taught at another one-room school on a ranch. They moved again, to Pittsburgh, where she wrote a column for the *Pittsburgh Post Gazette*. Berch writes that after living in Pittsburgh for thirty years, the Stones retired to Morehead City, North Carolina, where Elinore died in 1974.

The Laughingest Lady did not receive many contemporary reviews. Instead, marketing marked the record of its early production and reception—that is, publishers and reviewers presented it as one of various types of books that readers could purchase for their personal libraries. Ostensibly, the novel is a romance chronicling the ups and downs of the stormy courtship between fiercely independent schoolteacher Katherine Nevin and Alexander Firth Kilkenny, the macho "big boss" of the Santa Anita Mining Company. Thus, when the D. Appleton division of Grosset & Dunlap first published the novel in 1927, the publishers included a list of "if you liked this book, you'll love these" romance novels by Tempe Bailey, Margaret Pedler, and Grace Livingston Hill. In other advertisements, Appleton presented the novel as something of an adventure story, publishing a list of "Books You Want to Read and Own" in the *Chicago Daily Tribune*. Edith Wharton's *Twilight Sleep*, "the best selling novel in America," tops the list at the cost of $1.50 and Stone's *The Laughingest Lady* appears as well, billed as "a delightful story of an American school teacher on the Mexican border" that could enhance one's collection for $2.00. In addition to the list of books, the advertisement also offers a year's subscription to the company's *Illustrated Monthly Guide to New Books* for the small sum of fifty cents (6).

Other reviewers presented *The Laughingest Lady* as realistic, didactic fiction that student readers could model their behavior after. In 1938 the *English Journal* includes Stone's novel in a "Bibliography of Occupational

Fiction for Junior High School Readers." Ruth Bynum, compiler of the bibliography, notes that the "list contains only books which are reasonably acceptable as literature," assuring her audience—presumably teachers and maybe parents—that the books "do not simply contain a character who engages in a certain work, but they give some authentic information about the work or the preparation for it" (678). Organizing the list around careers as diverse as "Artist," "Explorer and Archaeologist," and "Florist," Bynum places *The Laughingest Lady* in the "Teacher" section (681). In what I believe to be the only modern reference to Stone's novel, Nina Baym gathers these diverse categorizations of the novel—romance, adventure, and pedagogic realism—and briefly presents it as one of the few novels by whites about nonwhites that grant the nonwhites some degree of respect and agency (243–44).

Perhaps critics reserved comments on *The Laughingest Lady* because most of its chapters had already run serially in magazines and garnered critical and popular reviews. Indeed, I focus here on how Stone's texts circulated in multiple contexts, arguing that while the novel itself can be read as an ideological tool of Americanization efforts typical of Progressive Era reformers, reading the chapters' original manifestations as serials in popular magazines exposes how they participated in broader, mainstream efforts to homogenize American culture. With its overarching tale of a white woman who moves from Rhode Island to New Mexico to teach the "Third Grade, Mexican" (as opposed to the "Third Grade, American"), Stone's novel already engages the history of reformers, teachers, missionaries, nurses, and other workers in newly feminized professions who moved West to instruct Indian and Mexican women in the tripartite colonial discourse of domesticity, religion, and education. But comparing specific events of the novel—particularly the Third Grade, Mexican Indian Pageant, Americanization Exercises, and Better Baby Show—to the context where the original stories were published shows how these magazines used stories, advertisements, contests, and how-to articles to preach a gospel of eugenics and domestic science that sought to put white women and nonwhite women in their supposedly proper places.

In the opening pages of *The Laughingest Lady*, the scene Katherine witnesses when she steps off the train in southern New Mexico sets up a series of binaries that characterize the town of Santa Anita and its white and Mexican inhabitants. This scene also sets the novel squarely within the discourse of domestic colonialism that permeated women's magazines and fiction.

> Squatting on one side of the track, a square box of a station flouted the heat in a new coat of passionately red paint; on the other some half dozen de-wheeled and domesticated freight cars drowsed in a squalid dooryard. Before these, shapeless rags flapped in the desert wind, and sparsely clad brown babies left their games to stare solemnly at the train that had jerked to a sudden, sliding stop, as if falling to its haunches in wonder and alarm before the newly-painted splendor of the station.
>
> The wonder was reflected in the eyes of the small, cool, blue and gold lady who had stepped from the single passenger coach—wonder, and some dismay. So this was what Martha Winters' letter had described as the "most delightfully different place in the world." Well, it was different. And for this, the blue and gold lady reflected, she had rashly signed away the next eight months of her life on the unbalanced representations of a single-track public health nurse, who would call anything "delightful" which afforded limitless scope to her tiresome propensity for cleaning up and making things over. Katherine Nevin glanced at the slatternly hovels before her, sniffed the odors that drifted from them, and turned with a shiver from the tobacco-splotched platform. The blithe sense of adventure with which she had applied for a leave of absence from that smoothly oiled, perfectly running mechanism, the Model School of Providence, to follow Martha into her land of romance, suddenly ebbed before this squalid, unpicturesque reality. (2–3)

This is but one example of how the novel describes and categorizes the people in Santa Anita by color. Katherine is always cool blues, shimmering golds, and rosy pinks, while the Mexicans—both adults and children—are always dull shades of brown and black. As we see in this scene, the novel also visibly segregates Santa Anita's man-made structures. The train station—which literally and metaphorically marks Anglo movement across the continent—shines with a fresh coat of paint. On the other side of the tracks, the train company's cast-off freight cars house a Mexican family. In marked contrast to the station, this home is filthy.

Farther from the train station, in Santa Anita proper, the Mexican homes' exteriors are not as "squalid" as in the passage above. But their interiors apparently are, and they look vastly different from the white people's homes. As Katherine walks home from her first day of school, through the "narrow, rocky streets of the Mexican quarter," she glimpses the houses painted with

> fascinating flashes of color, . . . pastel patches of blue, salmon, and mauve that were the walls of small houses peeping through luxuriant draperies of wild cucumber and hop vines; here illuminated by the morning sun against the gray crumbling plaster wall just opposite an open door, a gorgeous image of the Virgin, in crimson and blue and gold—the one bit of brightness of a squalid interior; there—mauve-gray against the emerald of the willows that bordered a little stream—a square adobe house, hung with yellow gourds and strings of gleaming pepper. (26)

Even though the novel paints the Mexican people in dull hues, the landscapes of the Mexican quarter are all color and vibrance and lushness. Katherine's perspective that reads the quarter's landscapes as both natural and old, with its crumbling, viney, rocky, and winding pathways, evokes Anglo ideas that Mexicans are less civilized. In Katherine's view, instead of taming the wild landscapes, the community has adapted to its environment, as do other animal societies. The novel contrasts the wildness of the Mexican quarter to the more civilized white part of town, with its neat, orderly command of shapes and nature. Katherine believes when just "crossing the tracks, one stepped into another world":

> The town itself kept to the level streets, in demure rows of low, square white cottages, identical to the windowpane, and shaped with geometrical precision in the centers of square lots. Each yard was surrounded by a barbed wire fence with a white picket fence; each house had a neat gravel walk leading to its front door and a coal shed in the extreme left corner of the back yard. One passed four such rows of white roofs, gleaming dazzlingly in the afternoon sun, before one came upon a row of still smaller cottages with tiny square porches set in one corner. At this final outpost the town seemed to halt abruptly to peer with distrust at the sweep of the open mesa beyond. In one of these last cottages Katherine and Martha Winters were to live. (27)

The "white" part of town—literally and figuratively white—is tellingly not named the "white quarter" or the "American quarter" but is the town itself. The planned community, with its precise grid and tidy gravel sidewalks, stands out against the wild, unwieldy organic paths through the named Mexican quarter. And though its outer edge allows vistas of the vast mesa, the town does its best to protect itself from vandals and vermin that might come from the deserts or the Mexican quarter. Barbed wire reinforces quintessential picket fences to secure a new, modern, civilized life against threats natural, disorderly, or uncivilized.

Several American institutions color Katherine's gaze: colonialism, domesticity, social Darwinism, Christianity, education, journalism, advertising, and consumer capitalism. Studying advertising campaigns across a wide swath of history, from early modern European peddlers to twentieth-century American corporations, Jackson Lears narrates "the story of how advertising collaborated with other institutions in promoting what became the dominant aspirations, anxieties, even notions of personal identity, in the United States" (2). Most relevant to Katherine's view of Santa Anita, and the circulation of Stone's stories in popular magazines, Lears discusses mimetic advertising and its links to domestic sentimentalism as a means of maintaining moral authority. He argues that "mimetic doctrines were most effective as a stabilizing force when they were invoked in the service of ethnocentrism—as part of the set of binary oppositions that separated the bourgeois self from the exotic Other. . . . A literalist concept of mimesis allowed Anglo-Saxons to assume . . . that they could enjoy the lure of the exotic without descending to the level of the 'sensual, degraded' Other" (85). As we see in Katherine's comparison of the Mexican quarter and the white section of Santa Anita, Lears asserts that, in advertising of the period, "imperial primitivism gave way to imperialism, a dualistic rather than a dialectical relation with the nonhuman world and with humans supposedly 'closer to nature' than the Anglo-Saxons" (163). Lears links this phenomenon to Darwin's theories, arguing that the "resulting cultural pattern, at least as expressed in advertising iconography, was less an attempt to extract regenerative secrets from mysterious interiors than an effort to impose civilized values on 'inferior' native populations" (163).

Both scenes quoted above offer reasons for Katherine's and Martha's presence in Santa Anita—reasons that support Lears's argument. The narrator tells us that Katherine moved to New Mexico in search of adventure and romance. Superficially, she might be read as one of the independent new woman types who, with newfound professional status and freedom of movement, bobs her hair, travels west, and supports herself by her own specialized labor. Several characters, including her students, comment on Katherine's less-than-ladylike choices. One day after school, as they watch her mount a horse for the ride home, the children are shocked to see that she's wearing trousers—"A ticher in pants!"—and two of them squabble (as always, in heavily accented English) about whether that's acceptable behavior. Pedro Gonzalez "insisted primly" that "the leddies—the leddies doss not wear the pants," drawing Angela Robles's blunt retort: "Doss she not got two laigs—joost lig you awthers? *Bueno*! To poot on the pants one doss not need no more" (77). The children may have inherited this modesty from their own patriarchal Mexican culture, but they may also have picked it up from white women in town. This same afternoon, as Katherine stops at the company store on her way home, one of the mining wives, Mrs. Taylor, mistakes Katherine for a boy.

Another white woman—the creamy-complexioned, aptly named transplanted southerner, Carrie Belle Clayton—implicitly compares her own highly elaborate femininity to Katherine's apparent lack: "South'n guls of ouah class live such ridiculously protected lives, you know, Miss Nevin, that we just nevah learn to take care of ouahselves lak you-all. Of cose it's foolish, but ouah men just can't bear to think of ouah exposin' ouahselves to the world. They say a woman's paht is just to help make life beautiful, not to get out and hustle lak men" (81). Katherine's new woman affectations hinder the romance plot that frames her novel. Even though Kilkenny shows romantic interest in her, Katherine hears from Carrie Belle that Kilkenny "was saying only yesterday that it's positively restful to meet a gul who's satisfied to just stay in huh home, instead of cheapenin' huhself by hustlin' out into the world to compete with men" (83). Katherine also knows that the town needed her to fill the Third Grade, Mexican teaching position because the previous teacher got married, an action that evidently necessitated her retirement. Her worries about keeping her teaching post, along with Carrie Belle's words echoing in her mind, make Katherine resist initial advances by Kilkenny, romantic or otherwise. As she leaves the company store on horseback and eventually struggles to control her high-spirited mount, Kilkenny appears out of nowhere to calm the horse and rescue her from certain peril. She takes offense at his help, thinking, "Let him try that high-handed, masterful stuff on his helpless little Carrie Belle. She'd probably conciliate to him by doing a sweetly pretty faint. But he needn't think he can steam roller me, even if I am a masculine working girl with bobbed hair and no time to make life beautiful" (89).

While Katherine might tell herself she simply does not have time to perform acceptably feminine tasks, she is also not "satisfied to just stay in huh home" as Carrie Belle preaches. Stone sets Katherine's actions in her schoolroom, in the company store, at a barn dance, outside, on her front porch, and in other spaces, but Katherine rarely speaks or acts from the interior of her home. She and Martha spend most of their evenings on the front porch, and when she is inside the house, she's either lying in bed fretting about Kilkenny or sitting at her desk feverishly writing a letter to him. And in these times, "the stillness of the house shut down on Katherine like a trap" (222). On the surface, then, Katherine is not in New Mexico to spread the doctrine of domesticity. She seems to be a new woman who is more at home in her workplace than in her house.

In contrast to Katherine, Martha Winters comes to New Mexico with the express purpose of "cleaning up and making things over" (3). As Santa Anita's public health nurse, Martha spends most of her time at the Mexican school, striving—usually in vain—to keep the children clean and teach their mothers cleanliness. When Katherine calls Martha to examine a student who shows signs of illness, Martha focuses not on José's "dull" eyes or "flushed" face but on his poor hygiene. "'Say, *hombre*,' she wanted to know, 'did you ever have your ears washed—*washed*—with soap and water?' 'Mees, no ma'am,' hastily disclaimed her horrified patient. 'My mama tells too mooch water no good.' 'I'll bet she does,' agreed Miss Winters calmly. 'Well, you come along with me. We're going to give your mama the shock of her life'" (39). Martha treats José's illness as if his symptoms of headache and fever could be caused by the dirt build-up behind his ears. Moreover, she blames a supposedly ignorant Mexican mother for both the dirt and the illness; the only way José's dirty ears and feverish face could shock his mother, presumably, is if she's learning for the first time that the two symptoms have a cause-and-effect relationship. This scene in the novel was originally published in *Women's Home Companion* under the title "José the Onlucky." One of the story's illustrations, drawn by Frederic Dorr Steele, reinforces the idea that José's mother knows nothing about the preventive medicine that is modern hygiene, repeating José's protest as the caption: "Mees, no ma'am, my mama tells too mooch water no bueno" (Steele, *Too Much Water* 13) (figure 1.10). An advertisement for Watkins' Mulsified Cocoanut Oil Shampoo, printed on the same page as the ending of "José the Onlucky," seems to address the same ignorant mothers Stone addresses in the story (figure 1.11). Overtly didactic even by the standards of early twentieth-century advertising, the ad's headline—"The Beauty of Children's Hair Depends upon Shampooing"—is obvious to the point of condescension (Mulsified 48).

Later, Miss Winters gets hold of Abundio Lopez, who holds the dubious honor of being the dirtiest kid in the Third Grade, Mexican. Even the other children notice how dirty he is: "'That Abundio Lopez—he does not lig veree good the soap and water,' Maria Sanchez observed superfluously" (225). Maria's observation sets off a series of pronouncements among those "enlightened" members of the class "who knew that people of nice sensibilities profess, at least, an ardent devotion to soap and water" (226). Jesus Estradilla, "complacently smoothing an impeccably clean frock," echoes, "Oh, that Abundio Lopez, Ticher! He iss joost too awful onclean!" (226). Anita Perez adds, "Joost to smell heem mags me seek a-bed. Sooch large smells!" (226). Catching Abundio in the hallway, Miss Winters interrogates him about his hygiene:

> "When did you wash [your hands] last, Abundio?" demanded Miss Winters.
>
> Abundio grinned and raised a deprecatory shoulder.
>
> "Mees," he answered piously, "*Dios sabe.*"
>
> "He must have a good memory," muttered Miss Winters. "Well, will you wash them now, or shall I have to do it for you?"
>
> "Mees, but yess ma'am," Abundio assured her with desperate alacrity, and scuttled toward the washroom. Indeed Abundio did not wish Miss Winters to do it. Too well he remembered an earlier occasion when Miss Winters had forced valet service upon him and several unhappy classmates. Was there not, even yet, just over his collarbone, an aenemic [*sic*] patch of skin which three weeks of jealous shielding had failed to weather to the rich, seasoned hue of other, unprofaned surfaces? (225)

Stone delivers these stories humorously, and indeed the stories were circulated and received as good humor. In his commentary on the

FIGURE 1.10 (*left*) Nurse Winters, whose mission is to clean up and make over Mexican families, closely inspects José's hygiene while Katherine Nevin and the curious third-graders watch; José's body performs an object lesson for hygienic education. Illustration by Frederic Dorr Steele, *Too Much Water, Woman's Home Companion* 52 [1925]: 12. Courtesy Main Library, University of Illinois at Urbana–Champaign.

FIGURE 1.11 (*right*) "The Beauty of Children's Hair Depends upon Shampooing." People in the 1920s did not shampoo as often as people do in the 2010s. But this advertisement for Mulsified Cocoanut Oil Shampoo, printed alongside Stone's story about white teachers instructing Mexican children in personal hygiene, partipates in a domestic colonialism that, Stone's story suggests, assumes nonwhite people are uncivilized and unclean. Courtesy Main Library, University of Illinois at Urbana–Champaign.

"Good—Better—Best Short Stories" of 1924, Gerald Hewes Carson includes Stone's "One Uses the Handkerchief" in a list of "humorous" stories that won an O. Henry Memorial Award that year (350). Reviewing "The American Short Story in the First Twenty Five Years of the Twentieth Century," the novelist Frances Newman counts Stone among such promising writers as Edith Wharton, Henry James, Sarah Orne Jewett, and F. Scott Fitzgerald. Newman notes that "the stories concerned with the Americanizing of little aliens which Elinore Cowan Stone began to write a year or two ago—stories like 'One Uses the Handkerchief'—differ from Myra Kelly's 'Little Citizens' only in a New Mexican instead of a New York scene" (192). As will become more apparent as I discuss "One Uses the Handkerchief," Stone purchases this humor at the hefty cost of a racism that is dead serious. In this scene, Nurse Winters not only cleans the dirt from Abundio's skin but attempts to scrub the brown right off the kid, evidenced by the hidden spot on his skin that she scrubbed to an "aenemic" white. Indeed, reading the stories in their original publication formats alongside advertisements and essays heralding the American virtues of domestic hygiene and healthy babies might make us wonder if Stone were commissioned to write these particular stories that would turn into her novel.

In addition to scrubbing the Mexican children and teaching their mamas the importance of such scrubbing, Martha has also contributed to the broader domestic education of the Mexican mothers. The mother of Angela Robles, one of Katherine's third-grade students, does the laundry and cleaning at the house Katherine and Martha share (17). Whether Martha herself taught Señora Robles Anglo domestic rituals is unclear, but the narrator implies that Martha has been in Santa Anita long enough to have been instrumental in the town's process of cleaning up and making over. And if Martha has no trouble marching a kid home from school to shock the mother with a hygiene lesson, she would certainly not hesitate to tell a hired domestic how to clean the house she herself inhabits. Like Martha, several other white women in Santa Anita hire Mexican domestics and, presumably, teach them to keep house in Anglo ways. If the "American section" of town boasts "trim cottages gleaming under the sun like little white pastries, all cut out with the same mold, iced, and set in neat rows to dry," the town maintains its gleam through the labor of "prematurely withered" Mexican women (79). Despite statements like Carrie Belle's that a woman's proper place is in her home, none of the white women in *The Laughingest Lady* actually keeps her own home, nor do they often keep to their homes. The white women are either working in public—like Katherine and Martha—or they are shopping, gossiping, and planning and attending town gatherings. Carrie Belle Clayton takes pride in being a "helpless creature" (81), so that when her mother's "Mexican girl" leaves, the Clayton household gets "rather complicated" with no one to do the chores (85). When Katherine holds the classroom

FIGURES 1.12 and 1.13 These images suggest laundry methods are a marker of cultural evolution. In figure 1.12, Mama Habanera's laundry looks slightly more evolved. Her laundry is piled neatly in a basket and she is indoors, though she still carries the basket on her head in a "primitive" fashion. Illustration by Frederic Dorr Steele, *Mama Habanera, Woman's Home Companion* 52 [1925]: 18. In the Ivory ad, the white woman who does the laundry inside at her sink illustrates the most culturally advanced method among these caricatures. In figure 1.13, Piute "Johnny Pine" becomes "Johnny Soap" when he uses Ivory to do the wash. Coincidentally, Ivory's slogan about the purity of their soap—99.44% pure—echoes the blood quantum rhetoric that supposedly quantifies and qualifies "authentic" Indianness. Such percentages are equally confusing, whether applied to soap or to people. Johnny Soap uses Ivory, but he still does the wash outside in a rough barrel. Courtesy Main Library, University of Illinois at Urbana–Champaign.

Better Baby show, many of the Mexican mothers come from their cleaning jobs. One mother, Mama Habanera, visits the show in between jobs. She arrives carrying "a mound of clean white clothes which she bore in a huge basket on her head" and has to leave early to return the "wash off one leddy" and then go to another home to "clean a Señora" (presumably, white readers are supposed to laugh at Mama Habanera's broken English, envisioning a Mexican woman literally cleaning the body of a white woman) (274) (figure 1.12). Once again, the narrative humor—here using incorrect or missing prepositions in a Spanish-English dialect to conjure ridiculous images of a Mexican woman actually washing the body of a white woman—masks the colonial domesticity at work in this scenario.

Another third-grade student, Maria Sanchez, has a mother who takes in wash for a white woman. Yet another student, Soledad Quintar, lives with her "wizened, worried little grandma" who "must work so hard in the houses of the American ladies" because Soledad's "heart-broken little mama" died of grief when her outlaw father was run out of town (64). But even though Grandmother Quintar has learned how to keep house as the Anglos want, that knowledge does not translate to keeping her own house in Anglo style, suggesting that one of colonial domesticity's methods of indoctrination is not highly effective. The Carlisle Indian Industrial School ran an "outing program" that placed Indian schoolgirls in the homes of white families in town so they could learn firsthand the rituals and values of Euro-American domesticity (see chapters 2 and 3 for more on the outing program). These programs operated on the assumption that Indian girls would internalize Anglo domesticity and teach it to their mothers and grandmothers when they returned home and that the Americanization efforts of Carlisle would change Indian communities across the continent. An Ivory Soap advertisement tells the story of how Ivory might have helped these endeavors; transforming Paiute Indian "Johnny Pine" into "Johnny Soap" illustrates the desire of such Americanization efforts (figure 1.13). Lears discusses a similar Ivory ad that features a Plains Indian who testifies in verse to the civilizing qualities of Ivory Soap. Since at least the 1850s, he writes, "a preoccupation with cleanliness, often carrying racial overtones, had been a central theme in bourgeois culture" (164), a phenomenon explored more broadly by Mary Douglas in her influential *Purity and Danger: An Analysis of Concepts of Pollution and Taboo*. By the turn into the twentieth century, "soap had begun to imply not cleanliness per se but a certain kind of cleanliness, purged of any decadent, hedonistic associations, oriented toward productive activism and a broader agenda of control" (Lears 164). That the Johnny Soap ad ran in the same issue of *Woman's Home Companion* that published Stone's "A Question of Precedence" (included in the novel as chapter 35, "Comes the Substinoot"), speaks to this activism and social control that Lears describes. Certainly, regardless of Stone's personal beliefs or agenda, her stories circulated in a textual milieu that promoted white women's role as the Great White Hope who—with the aid of such useful products as the great white soap—could whitewash Mexicans and Indians living within US borders. In reality, the Indian girls' return home did not often include a transfer of domesticity's doctrines, just as the Mexican mothers of Santa Anita do not automatically clean their own homes (or their children) the way they keep house for white ladies.

Several reasons could explain why the Mexican women do not immediately apply their knowledge of Anglo domesticity to their own lives, most of which would lead into theories of cultural acquisition that I will not engage here. *The Laughingest Lady* offers its own logic for the disconnection between a Mexican woman's domestic labors in a white woman's house and her labors in her own home, and that logic largely rests on issues of social class and access to adequate resources. Some Mexican families have more access to capital than others. At the Quintar home, supported only by an elderly grandmother, clean floors and clothes are not priorities and perhaps not possibilities: "On the dirt floor of the Quintars was no gay, warm rug as made cheerful the houses of the Villas and the Martinez [*sic*]; and while Anita Perez might deck her braids with wonderful bows of pink or blue ribbon, Soledad must satisfy herself with bright scraps of wrapping cord" (64). Even though Angela Robles's mother keeps house for Martha and Katherine and knows the rituals of Anglo domesticity, that knowledge does not translate to the domestic or personal habits of the Robles family. Angela is a "wildly disordered little figure" who often "bore the appearance of having been [the] storm center of some peculiarly enterprising whirlwind" (17). Perhaps such dishevelment could be typical of any high-spirited and energetic young girl, but in other descriptions we learn that Angela's clothes are completely inadequate. She "seemed always to be clutching to place some portion of her scanty apparel. Now, as she spoke, she struggled with one hand to cover an angular shoulder with the shift-like garment that was her dress, while with the other she dragged at a dangling stocking" (35). With this description, Angela's slipshod appearance becomes more than a symptom of a rough-and-tumble little girl. Worn-out, ill-fitting clothes are symptoms of poverty; Angela's mother does not have money to buy materials to repair this dress or make a new one, nor would she likely have the time even if she did have the money. Domestic laborers are typically short on both commodities. Further, we know that the Robles family struggles to survive when Angela cannot buy a ticket to go to the circus with her class. Angela reflects on the family's financial struggles: "This was Thursday; for three meals the Robles family had dined simply on *tortillas*, and the papa would not get any money until Saturday. Perhaps—who could tell?—it would have been different had they not last week sold the rug to buy beads, that Domatilla, the pretty big sister of Angela, need not go to the *fiesta* unadorned. Now there was nothing left to sell" (100). However well-intentioned the efforts, Americanization through domestication fails in Santa Anita—and in many communities like it—because domestic colonialism misunderstands an economic system that privileges privilege and punishes poverty.

Katherine also misunderstands the economics of her own students' families. She decides that the class will raise money to support orphans in Russia and asks the students to bring contributions for the fund. One student, Emilia, asks, "The Rooshian chiltren, Ticher, of wheech you tell us last day that they have always the beeg hole in the e-stomach?" When Ticher responds, "Yes, Emilia, the poor little children of Russia, who have to go without bread and milk, while we all have more than we can eat," (91–92) the students "showed faces a shade dubious at what seemed to them a slightly over-enthusiastic picture of the local situation" (92). After awkward moments, when the students silently dared each other to correct Ticher's naiveté, the brave Mateo Gomez says, "My mama tells she iss mooch sorry for thoss hongry chiltren, but she tells also that in our house iss not always the bread to eat and the milk to drink. I thing I did not bring anytheeng." And Anita Perez adds, "My papa—she say too mooch geev and not mooch get. I thing I did not bring anytheeng, also" (92). The students are relieved when Ticher kindly agrees to give up the orphan project and work on something else—"How fortunate that Ticher was so reasonable!"(93)—but there is no hint that Katherine feels any remorse or embarrassment at having assumed that all the children are well-fed and that their families have extra cash and food available to feed hungry kids on the other side of the world.

Instead of learning from this awkward moment with her students and trying to understand their families more, Katherine charges ahead with her own agenda of Americanizing the Third Grade, Mexican. On the surface it appears that Katherine came to Santa Anita for adventure and romance and Martha came as the colonial domesticator, but as the novel progresses, Katherine's teaching programs expose her own participation in the mainstream discourses of race-based domestic science, eugenics, and Americanism. Even though Martha and Katherine have escaped the private sphere and work in the public sphere, their domestic curricula betray the duplicity of modern American domesticity: white women can preach domesticity instead of practice it as an acceptable performance of American femininity, but nonwhite women must prove their American femininity by performing domestic labor. While Martha and Katherine work at the school, the Mexican mamas work in their homes and in the homes of other white ladies in Santa Anita. Katherine's distinctions between the Mexican quarter and the white town betray the fact that her perspective indirectly and presumably unwittingly informs the white women's mission: to clean up, make over, and transform the Mexicans' current living conditions so they can become Americans. While Martha is more literally involved in teaching Mexican women and cleaning Mexican children, Katherine joins the effort by holding three major Americanization events in her classroom—an Indian pageant, "Americanization Exercises," and a "Better Bebbies Contest"—and encouraging the Mexican mamas to attend.

Just as Katherine sees the differences between the train station and the Mexican dooryard—between the Mexican quarter and the town itself—she also sees her third-grade students as binary opposites to white Americans. Free indirect discourse shapes much of the narration around Katherine, implicitly evoking her thoughts and words. She continually notes their "brown faces" and "black eyes," and even though they are labeled "Mexican," she sees them as Indians. On their first day of class, Katherine surveys the students, and "stolidly as little totem poles they stared back" (19). When she has to work harder than she thinks necessary to entice the children into laughter and make-believe play, Katherine thinks to herself, "The poor, solemn little Indians. I wonder if anything would make them forget their dignity and be natural" (24). Ironically, the children react after she announces, "'I'll tell you,' she cried. 'We're going to play that you are Indians—all of you. We'll have an Indian show'" (24). Katherine is relieved to see the children laugh and smile at this suggestion, but she misses the joke completely:

> Of course the real humor of the suggestion appeared first to Ramon Sedillo . . . [who] halted in mid-stride and cocked an appreciative

> bright eye at his friend. Indians—they! But that was too delicious! Of course, José Setrada, in the second grade, might be of Indian extraction, or any one of a number of others they might mention. One might even have his own private suspicions of some of his own classmates, but as for oneself—of course one was Spanish. Secure in his ten percent of Caucasian blood, every Third Grader grinned delightfully. They—Indians!
>
> Bewildered, Miss Nevin stared as the grin grew to a titter, the titter to a cackle of rich amusement.
>
> Emilia Villa was the first to see the surprise in Ticher's eyes. Suppose she should think they were laughing at her! Emilia scrambled to her feet.
>
> "Ticher—but yes ma'am," gasped Emilia. "I thing we lig to mag-believe Indian. Eet weel be joost too awful fonny."
>
> Katherine Nevin sat back with a huge sigh of relief.
>
> "Well thank heaven!" she murmured. "Thank heaven, there's something that's funny to you. You're human, then, after all." (24–25)

The students' reaction to Ticher's request that they play Indian signals their awareness that doing so could jeopardize their already precarious position in a racial hierarchy that is exclusive rather than inclusive. As Philip J. Deloria discusses in *Playing Indian*, it is safe for white children to play Indian through dress or behavior because no one will mistake them for actual Indians. The August 1925 cover of *Woman's Home Companion* shows how culturally acceptable it was for white children to represent "The Wild Indian" (figure 1.14). Despite their misgivings, most of the students are willing to "mag-believe Indian" as long as everyone agrees it is a joke, but one critically thinking student, Ramon Sedillo, refuses to participate. Even after Ticher appeals to his sense of importance and says, "I am counting on you, I want you to be one of the Indians. You make such a nice Indian," Ramon firmly replies, "Ticher, no, . . . I do not weesh for be Indian. . . . I weesh be American, Ticher" (51–52). Ticher seems to approach the casting and planning of the Indian pageant with varying, contradictory levels of verisimilitude. She sees the Mexican students as Indian, so her insistence that they all play Indians is typecasting. But she chooses the student who appears the "least white" to play the lone white character; "the only Anglo-Saxon role, that of the American scout, was played by chocolate-colored Pedro Gonzales, whom

Ticher suspected of African antecedents" (69). Katherine casts Pedro as the "only Anglo-Saxon" (69), implying an appeal to the sense of white supremacy among the Anglo-Saxons of Santa Anita: Pedro is not trying to pass as white because Pedro is clearly nonwhite, maybe even black. Likewise, an Anglo-Saxon audience would not think the Mexican children are trying to pass as Indian because, like Katherine, they see the children as Indian already. The Third Grade, Mexican Indian pageant, then, encapsulates the contradictory, seemingly erratic workings of the American racial hierarchy, particularly as it operated in the early twentieth-century West.

Enthusiasm for playing American quickly replaces the Third Grade, Mexican's discomfort with playing Indian when Katherine suggests they hold Americanization exercises that, like the Indian pageant, the town can attend. The belief in their Spanish heritage that made them want to disassociate from their Mexican Indian heritage explains their eagerness to prove their Americanness—to play up that security in their "ten percent of Caucasion blood" (24)—and accounts for their wholehearted participation in the classroom's Americanization exercises. Some students, especially Ramon Sedilla, quickly understand that one's appearance and hygiene matter greatly when defining Americanism. Other students learn it more slowly, or more intuitively; by the end of Katherine's classroom Americanization events, every child has had ample exposure to the traits of true Americanness. The novel's portrayal of these exercises participates in a racialized pseudoscience of housekeeping and hygiene that claims cleanliness is the path to Americanization. Moreover, the magazine version—"One Uses the Handkerchief," serialized in the *Women's Home Companion*—works alongside advertisements and "scientific" essays to convince both white and brown female readers that keeping clean houses and clean, well-fed children is *the* measure of American femininity. In the same issue of *Woman's Home Companion* with Stone's story, an advertisement for Minute Tapioca cereal contextualizes the students' hesitancy to play Indian and their keenness to play American (figure 1.15). In the ad, a clearly Caucasian boy eats his tapioca while wearing a feathered headdress, and the headline reads: "Another redskin bit the ——." Presumably, the word *dust* would fill in the blank, implying that a strong, well-fed American boy conquers Indians. When presented with what seems like an identity choice, and inundated with pedagogy and advertisements that tell them Indians are destined for

Figure 1.14 Maybe the third-grade Mexican students, or their nonfictional analogues, see magazine covers like this at local stores or among their mamas' possessions. Their discomfort with "playing Indian" may stem from their knowledge that they are not as "white" as this blue-eyed, curly-headed toddler. Viewers might know that playing Indian was one of the most American identities a white child could peform (à la the twisted logic of nativism and playing Indian that Philip Deloria describes), but the third-graders worry that viewers might mistake their *playing* Indian for actually *being* Indian (and thus un-American). Illustration by Dorothy Hope Smith, *The Wild Indian, Woman's Home Companion* 52 [1925]: cover. Courtesy Main Library, University of Illinois at Urbana–Champaign.

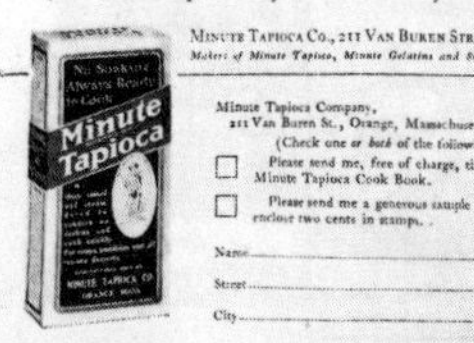

FIGURE 1.15 The opening lines of this advertisement seem at odds with the headline and image: "A moment ago he was a ruthless savage, devastating a paleface settlement. Now he's only a rosy little boy—but he's more than devastating that big bowl of tapioca cream!" Courtesy Main Library, University of Illinois at Urbana–Champaign.

extinction and that Americans will cause that extinction, it is no wonder that Stone's Third Grade, Mexican students are willing to sacrifice indigenous identity to become American. And this is exactly the response white female teachers and missionaries, a Eurocentric advertising industry, and the US government wanted.

In "One Uses the Handkerchief" and its related scenes in the novel, a new student, Rafael Arcienega, announces his presence with an uncovered sneeze, and the students dissolve into paroxysms of outcries about the impending doom that will certainly be theirs for breathing the now-contaminated classroom air. Miss Nevins reprimands the students, noting that "perhaps no one has ever told him that one uses the handkerchief when he coughs or sneezes. I am sure that if we explain kindly to him why it is necessary to do so, he will try to remember after this. Who would like to tell him about some of the things we are trying to do here as good Americans?" (138–39). Ever ready to prove his own Americanness and overall superiority, Ramon Sedilla volunteers an answer. "'Here we try to be the good American, Ticher,' began Ramon easily. 'To be the good American,' he explained, 'one doss not fight weeth the knife or throw the stone or shoot the crap in the yard of the school'" (139–40). Ramon continues, "To be the good American, one keeps clean the body and the clothes. One breathes by hees nose weeth the window open, always the fresh air. To breathe the bad air iss lig to drink the dirty water. Eet is full of thoss bug that call heemself 'my—my—my—cubs.'" After Ticher interjects with the correct term—"microbes"—Ramon finishes his lecture: "Ticher yes ma'am. Eet is heem [the microbe] that makes us seek. And to cough and sneeze without to cover the mouth is to fill weeth thoss my—my—weeth thoss dirty bug the clean air. . . . [T]hey get inside off us and eat on us" (141). This event between Rafael and Ramon inspires Ticher to set up a program of Americanization exercises: "There were to be songs and speeches, and there would be people there, she told the Third Grade, many people, to see and hear them. And—ultimate thrill—there would be a prize, offered by the big boss of the Company, himself, for the pupil who proved himself the most truly American" (143). The class begins rehearsals, and Rafael thrills to learn that he will play an important role in the exercises. Eleven third graders "were to recite in chaste and lofty verse the merits of hygienic and wholesome living. Each individual verse was a separate unit with a theme of its own, and the initial of each them was one of the letters that spell 'Health First'" (143). Rafael's "tremendous responsibility" is to distribute, to each of the eleven children, a placard displaying the letters that spell the slogan so that the children can hold them as high and proudly as Old Glory herself (144).

When the day of the Americanization exercises arrives, the Third Grade, Mexican students are highly practiced and terribly excited. Rafael and all the other children "hysterically" vie for Miss Nevin's attention, each eager to show that he or she is "the good American" (155). In addition to distributing the placards, Rafael's regular classroom duty is to maintain the classroom's stock of handkerchiefs. In hilarious prose, the narrator details Rafael's antics as he checks the hankie cabinet, finds that it is empty, and, in a panic—because "the good American does not sneeze or cough without using the handkerchief!" (159)—decides to cut his own shirt into handkerchiefs to prepare for the likely disaster of a coughing and sneezing epidemic. No one notices when Rafael leaves the classroom, but Miss Nevin notices when he sneaks back in wearing his heavy overcoat. Thinking he must be cold, she asks another student to turn up the heat. This, of course, turns Rafael into a sweaty mess, but he insists that he is cold when Ticher tells him to take off the coat. He finally obeys, miserably shirtless and having "shocked with his nakedness the delicate sensibilities of the Third Grade's gentle public" (163). Flustered and mortified, Rafael is utterly humiliated when he distributes the placards incorrectly, so that the children's lofty standard spells "Healf Thirst" instead of "Health First" (163) (figure 1.16). It took a few minutes for Katherine and the other adults in the room to connect Rafael's half-nakedness with the fact that every handkerchief in the classroom was cut from the same red and white polka-dotted cloth, but they understood what happened in time to adjust the prizes for the best American. Even though Ramon Sedilla wins the best American award medal, as everyone predicted he would, the big boss gives his very own pocket watch to Rafael Arcienega in reward for his "distinguished service in the cause of Americanism"—that is, for giving the shirt off his back to keep the "circumambient air" in the third-grade classroom free of menacing microbes (166).

Humor barely masks the racism implicit in the early twentieth-century impulse to make scientific the age-old duties of cleaning a home and raising a family. The domestic science, or domestic economy, movement that materialized as Americanization exercises, such as Katherine Nevin's in the Third Grade, Mexican, is based in the nineteenth-century rhetoric of domesticity. As Marilyn Irvin Holt writes, the domestic economy movement between 1890 and 1930 "expected to dilute ethnic and racial traditions, creating *American* homemakers" (8). Literary and historical scholars such as Mary Kelley, Linda Kerber, and Ann Douglas have shown that white women used both Christian and scientific discourse to give public value to their private work in the domestic sphere. Catherine E. Beecher's *Treatise on Domestic Economy for Use of Young Ladies at Home and School*, published in 1841, was one of the first comprehensive how-to manuals for young housewives and new mothers. Beecher partnered with her famous sister, Harriet Beecher Stowe, to write *The American Woman's Home, or*

FIGURE 1.16 Katherine coaxes Rafael out of his coat as the children line up with their placards. Illustration by Frederic Dorr Steele, *Health First, Woman's Home Companion* 51 [1924]: 20. Courtesy Main Library, University of Illinois at Urbana–Champaign.

Principles of Domestic Science; Being a Guide to the Formation and Maintenance of Economical, Healthful, Beautiful and Christian Homes (1869), what "might be called the Sears, Roebuck catalogue of domestic and moral standards of a century ago" (Van Why 1). Beginning with the conceit that women workers at home should be trained for their duties just as men workers at offices or factories are, Beecher and Stowe cover domestic topics from religious training to home decor to first aid. The first two chapters lay the foundation for a proper American home ("The Christian Family" and "A Christian House") and the third and fourth chapters build the ground floor ("A Healthful Home" and "Scientific Domestic Ventilation"). In Beecher and Stowe's home manual, cleanliness is literally next to godliness. The chapters include illustrations of floor plans and closets, kitchen arrangements and window treatments that will not only allow for optimal health through cleanliness and ventilation but will also inspire Christian devotion. As the title of chapter 1 implies, the very arrangement of household space can be or become Christian.

The authors also include chapters that instruct American women to turn their godly attentions outside their homes. In "Giving in Charity," Beecher and Stowe rehearse the New Testament story of the Good Samaritan to point out that the wounded man who needed the Samaritan's help "was not only a stranger, but he belonged to a foreign nation, peculiarly hated. . . . [F]rom this we learn that the destitute of all nations become our neighbors" (242). Beecher and Stowe argue that Christians should meet the physical needs of humanity because so doing "is often the easiest way of touching the moral sensibilities of the destitute" (243). In this view, moral and spiritual destitution is a more serious lack than physical poverty. The authors highlight the foreignness of the Good Samaritan's roadside patient, implying a parallel between Anglo-Americans (the moral and physical haves) who have a duty to uplift non-white Americans (the moral and physical have-nots). This logic only thinly veils the ulterior motives behind this gospel of charity; in short, they argue, we will feed, clothe, or educate people not because humans need those things, but because in providing those things, we can manipulate them into thinking, believing, and living like white Protestant Americans.

Many more such how-to manuals were published during the nineteenth and early twentieth centuries. Mary Pattison's *Principles of Domestic Engineering: Or, the What, Why and How of a Home* (1915) is much like Beecher and Stowe's only with more focus on scientific management of household spaces, bodies, and budgets and less focus on Christian regulation. In 1929 Helen W. Atwater contributed a short, thirty-nine-page volume on domestic science to the Reading with a Purpose series of courses published by the American Library Association. Atwater's *Home Economics: The Art and Science of Homemaking* is a summary of six full-length books on the various aspects of housekeeping that Beecher, Stowe, and Pattison discuss. Skimming any of the books in this series, a reader could find basic information on a variety of topics from the short introductory books like Atwater's; true autodidacts could read all the books in a given course. A few years earlier, in 1925, Christine Frederick's *Efficient Housekeeping, or Household Engineering: Scientific Management in the Home* was published as a correspondence course for the American School of Home Economics in Chicago. The sixth edition of this treatise on domestic science moved away from Beecher and Stowe's Christian model of housekeeping. Frederick's version of domestic science focuses on helping privileged (that is, white) women harness modern technology—and a not-so-modern staff of servants—to save themselves time and labor.

Frederick includes a chapter on "The Servantless Household" and suggests that, at least during the early days of her homemaking years, she did not have servants and so "faced the problem which confronts many young mothers—how to do my housework and care for two small children, and yet have any time for myself or outside interests" (7). But Frederick also includes a chapter on the "Management of Houseworkers," where she reproduces a photo of her own children with their "housekeeper-nurse" (418), so she undoubtedly writes from a position of class privilege. Frederick also writes from a position of race privilege, for in this chapter, a connection surfaces between domestic science and its coeval discourse, eugenics. Here Frederick makes a list of workers whom she organizes by country of origin and describes with sweeping generalizations based on contemporary stereotypes. She writes that,

> while there are exceptions, it seems to be true that workers of these nationalities have the following characteristics: Irish (good hearted but often untidy, inefficient, little responsibility). Scotch-English (great dependability, sense of duty, well trained). German (thrifty, hard-working, capable of much manual work). Scandinavian (self-reliant, sometimes tricky, often extravagant, excellent as laundresses and cleaners). Polish-Lithuanian, etc. (emotional, little responsibility, inefficient, but frequently good cooks). Italian (not dependable or take responsibility, sloppy at work, but thrifty and excellent cooks). French (very neat, thrifty cooks and sewers, sometimes unreliable or looking to their own interest, but excellent managers; not capable of heavy work). (447)

Frederick also notes it is "wisest to secure workers of all one nationality, or one religion, so that there will be more harmony" (446–47). Curiously, the workers in Frederick's list are now considered white; the history of whiteness in the United States, however, shows that whiteness does not define itself by skin color alone. Class status and national origin barred many ethnic groups from the full privileges of whiteness well into the twentieth century.

Stone's characterization of the Third Grade, Mexican students who are so concerned about "my-cubs" in "One Uses the Handkerchief" loses some of its humor when read contextualized within this history of domesticity and domestic science that racializes difference and stereotypes workers based on their national, ethnic, and racial origins. Just as Frederick categorized household servants based on stereotypes about which nation puts out the best workers for various tasks, Alexandra Minna Stern writes that

> Mexicans were simultaneously racialized and medicalized, sometimes in competing directions. Whereas eugenicists claimed that Mexicans needed to be placed under an exclusionary immigration quota because they constituted a mongrel—half Southern European and half Amerindian—"race," agricultural growers contended that this same biological composition endowed Mexican laborers with remarkable "stooping abilities" and the capacity to work long hours in the fields. From 1917 until the late 1930s, Mexicans entering the United States along the southern border were subjected to aggressive disinfection rituals that were based on exaggerated, nearly hysterical perceptions of them as dirty and diseased. Associations of Mexicans with typhus, plague, and smallpox solidified in the 1920s and were fused with stereotypes of Mexican women as hyperbreeders whose sprawling broods of depraved children threatened to drain public resources. Furthermore, more than in any other region in the country, the racialized public health measures implemented in the American West were initially devised and assayed in the U.S. colonies. From the 1890s on, the cities, towns, and inhabitants of the Philippines, Cuba, Puerto Rico, Hawai'i, and the Panama Canal functioned as laboratories for the elaboration of modern modalities of epidemiological surveillance and disease control that in short order were transposed to San Francisco's Chinatown or El Paso's Chihuahuita barrio. (21)

Katherine's Americanization exercises, then, are not only based in the Progressive Era's pseudoscientific housekeeping movement but are also enmeshed in the eugenics movement of the same period. With the relatively recent demarcation of a border between Mexico and the United States, early twentieth-century eugenicists pushed for heightened patrols of the border and, as Nancy Ordover writes, intensified "their scrutiny of Mexicans and Mexican-Americans (regardless of their immigration status or country of birth), watchful and laudatory of what was unfolding in Germany, and ready to launch new organizations in the United States" (32). For eugenicists, Mexicans in the American Southwest posed threats to the American body politic because of unique diseases they supposedly carried and because they were seen as "the embodiment of interracial unions" (38). In both cases, Mexicans could seriously undermine the "eugenic health of the United States" (37). Wendy Kline notes the importance of ideologies of motherhood and the family to the preservation of the Anglo-Saxon race, particularly the idea among birth control advocates of the early twentieth century that reproduction should be limited to the "eugenically fit" (4). Because Anglos viewed Mexican and Mexican American women as prolific, but "unfit" breeders (Stern 21), people of presumably Mexican descent who lived in the American Southwest became prime targets of eugenics-fueled birth control campaigns and, as Stone so aptly illustrates in another episode from *The Laughingest Lady*, a nationwide breeding-improvement program known as the Better Babies Contests.

One afternoon at school, Nurse Winters gives the third-grade girls a lesson on the proper way to bathe and dress a baby. Displaying the now "immaculately groomed—and acutely indignant—brown baby" for the girls' inspection, Martha declares that that he is "fine enough for any baby show" (253). She immediately regrets her pronouncement because the girls—who have already displayed their affinity for pageants and programs—talk her into running a classroom "bebby show" (253) complete "weeth prices [prizes]" and "jawdges" (254). As on the day of the Americanization exercises, the Third Grade, Mexican is in a frenzy of excitement to show off their baby brothers and sisters. Also as before, the narrator focalizes on the comic exploits of one hapless third grader. This time, Pedro Gonzales worries because he does not have a baby brother or sister to bring to the show, so he takes to the streets of Santa Anita to look for a spare baby. As luck would have it, he finds a baby playing unattended in the dooryard of a small adobe house, and, since the baby "had both eyes and was sound of limb" (277) Pedro figures this is his chance. Pedro makes it out of the yard and back to school with the baby, whom he names Jack Demps.[5] Once at school, Pedro hands Jack over to classmate Maria Sanchez, who is in charge of bathing and prepping the babies for the judges' examinations. Freshly cleaned, Jack Demps is "deliciously pink and dewy," with surprisingly blue eyes, fair skin, and light brown hair tinged with gold (279). After carefully weighing, measuring, and examining each baby and marking up each baby's score card, the judges—a pink-faced male doctor and a "pretty American lady" with "white jeweled fingers" (273)—choose their winner: Pedro's baby brother, Jack Demps. Only after the contest does truth unveil itself: for not only is Jack Demps not Pedro's baby brother, Jack Demps is also not a boy. The girls who bathed the baby knew this, but in the hullabaloo of the contest they apparently did not tell anyone and the babies wore their diapers during the judges' exams (figure 1.17 illustrates a diaper-free baby). In an amusingly dramatic scene of losing and finding, Señora Habanera is relieved to discover her daughter, Rosita, sleeping in the basket of clean laundry she had yet to deliver to her white lady (see figure 1.12 and the surrounding discussion). Initially furious with Pedro for kidnapping her daughter, Mama Habanera declares that everything is "all nize" when she realizes Rosita won the contest (286). Rosita, the twin sister of the "black-eyed Carlos" (283), presumably takes after a distant white relative, but no explanation of her fair coloring is given. Regardless of where Rosita's whiteness comes from, the "white" baby wins the contest.[6]

As included in *The Laughingest Lady*, the Third-Grade, Mexican's "better bebbies" show is another example of Martha Winters's and Katherine Nevin's efforts to Americanize this New Mexican border town. In its original publication context, as a story—"Better Bebbies"—in the *Woman's Home Companion*, these Americanization efforts are caught up in the broader cultural-historical movements of eugenics and white women's work to claim authority in the pseudosciences of domestic health and hygiene. It is no coincidence that *Woman's Home Companion* published most of the novel's episodes, including "Better Bebbies." In 1913 *Woman's Home Companion* launched the Better Babies Bureau. Evidently inspired by Mrs. Mary de Garmo's baby contest at the Louisiana State Fair in 1908 and a contest at the Iowa State Fair led by Mary T. Watts in 1911, the Bureau organized and standardized Better Babies Contests as perennial events at state and county fairs and urban settlement houses across the country until 1952 (Engs 2005).

Chronicling the history of the Better Babies Contests, Annette K. Vance Dorey notes that a central motive behind the contests was decreasing infant mortality rates and reducing the terribly high numbers of mothers

PAGE 18

mad exhilaration. This was immediately swamped in a rush of dismay even as he negligently pocketed the coin and turned away. Now he had done it! Of course he could not wager his mother's hard-earned fifty cents upon a purely hypothetical baby. Yet a single glance at the ring of grim faces about him showed Pablo that he would not be allowed lightly to forget that mad bet.

The simple expedient of avoiding the issue by absenting himself from school that afternoon naturally occurred to him. This plan might have served nicely had he not fallen afoul of Mr. Sawyer, the young officer who patrolled the Mexican section of Mesa with a pitiless eye for truants. Salvador Calaveras or Ramón Sedillo, now, would have been ready with some apt bit of fiction to meet the crisis, but Pablo's was not a facile wit. He did manage a conciliatory smile and the hasty assurance, "I—go—e-school." But the very look he had cast about him at the officer's approach was incriminating.

"You bet you do, general," genially agreed Mr. Sawyer.

Pablo's ignominious entry before the shocked but delighted eyes of his schoolmates, dangling like a draggled kitten in the firm grasp of Mr. Sawyer, only served, of course, to direct toward him the very suspicions he had so feverishly hoped to divert; so that when, at the end of the afternoon session, he would have slithered unobtrusively out of sight Ramón transfixed him with a stern stare.

"Where do you go, Pablo?" Ramón wanted to know. And behind Ramón gathered a suspicious phalanx of Third Grade sportsmen.

Pablo, head on one side, offered a conciliatory but hopeless grin, and mentally threw up his hands.

"Bebby," he assured them desperately, "get bebby heawther," and strode from the yard in a panic.

Outside he paused and scratched his head in rueful consideration. Not that Pablo failed to grasp the fact that he was in for it. He had definitely committed himself to a baby. *Bueno!* by fair means or foul he must produce a baby, or life would not be worth living hereafter.

THE Third Grade room, meantime, was assuming a delightful air of festivity. Large clusters of cosmos appeared magically to star a background of blue bunting with rose, white and maroon. Ticher, very intent and pink-cheeked, was spreading a white cloth over her desk and setting out ravishing little plates of wafers, while Jesús and Anita switched to and from the cupboard on mysterious errands. Miss Winters was getting ready a set of scales. Miss Winters was to be one of the judges; Ticher's part was to lend social luster to the occasion. Hortensia Valdes bustled up, all frowning importance.

"Ticher," Hortensia wanted to know anxiously, "you thing mebbie better now we poor on the glawves—eh?"

"Gloves, Hortensia!" gasped Ticher. "Mercy, no!" Then as disappointment made the plain little face wan, she finished weakly, "That is, unless you have some here that you brought to wear."

And now the rest of the judges arrived. The company doctor puffed in, mopped his genial pink face and began taking important-looking objects from his black bag and ranging them on the table. A pretty American lady appeared hurriedly, loosening her wraps with white, jeweled fingers and smiling curiously about the room as she apologized for being late.

"The *Señora* Taylor," whispered Hortensia—Hortensia was inordinately proud of her conversance with the Mesa social register—"Oh, a awful swelled lady! My *mama*—she washes heem."

As for the Third Grade, they were conspicuously "swelled" this afternoon, themselves. There was Anita, for instance, with a sophisticated, if a bit moth-eaten, piece of summer fur completing a costume of gay print; there was Maria Sanchez, her brisk competence reinforced tenfold by a crackling paper cap and apron—like Miss Winters'; and there was Hortensia, whose hands and arms, ostentatiously folded across her bosom, were encased in gloves, long silk gloves of an intriguing black, only a little too large, and hardly worn out at all—except for the finger ends.

MAMA HABANERA was among the first three to arrive. *Mama* Habanera affected a plaintive manner that accorded oddly with her stalwart frame and rather gruff voice. Her right hand steadied a mound of clean white clothes which she bore in a huge basket on her head. From her left arm peered shyly a small rose and tan person with laughing black eyes.

"My Carlos twin—my boy," announced Mrs. Habanera, with a glance of complacent pity toward the two other hopeful *mamas* with their hopelessly commonplace offspring. "The wash off one lady," she further explained the hamper, as she deposited it on a desk. "*Mas tarde* I come and take. Very far to my 'ouse."

"Why, surely, Mrs. Habanera," Ticher told her. "We'll put it in the vacant room across the hall where it will be quite safe. But where is Manuelo this afternoon?"

"Mees, you mus' pleass excuss. My Manuelo, he minds my awther twin, my leetla Rosita. Sooch a nize boy, my Manuelo—too nize—eh?" Mrs. Habanera was pensively hopeful.

If Ticher had reservations, she veiled them studiously.

"And oh, so nize that leetla Rosita that you do not leave to come," pursued Mrs. Habanera plaintively. Under her reproachful glance Ticher began to make futile, apologetic little sounds. But Mrs. Habanera had not finished.

"*Bonita!*" She fixed the group with eyes that despaired of appreciation as she touched here the small Carlos' delicately embroidered yoke, there his lacy skirts. "Nize! All nize! Everything too nize!" she told them proudly.

Mama Habanera was among the first three to arrive

WOMAN'S HOME COMPANION

It developed that Mrs. Habanera could not stay; she went to "clean a *señora*." At the five she would return for the *chiquita* and the "wash off the lady." Even as she turned toward the door Mrs. Habanera paused to consider. She put her head first on one side, then on the other, frowning in an agony of indecision.

"You may pin the price," she determined finally, pointing to the embroideries on the little Carlos' stalwart chest, "'ere."

AND now things happened rapidly at the Third Grade baby show. Babies began to pour in—a confusion of babies—and were assigned numbers and positions about the bunting-hung walls of the room.

In a gorgeous blue and gold carriage lolled superciliously Number One, Juan Romero, the perfectly groomed young stepbrother of Maria Sanchez. Mrs. Romero had sent regrets. Maria was quite frank as to the reason.

"She sells shees shoes to get thees boggy," was Maria's matter-of-fact explanation.

Next to the Romero exhibit Ramón Sedillo importantly stood guard by a shiny red express wagon in which smiled Number Two, a small, bright-eyed replica of the round-faced Ramón himself.

For babies not so luxuriously equipped Miss Winters had provided such accommodations as she could beg and borrow from her friends. Number Three—the young Enriqueta Villa—enraptured with the beautiful green and orange paint of the high chair allotted to her, lost no time in attacking it with ravenous pink tongue and four sharp teeth. Number Four, the *Señorita* Nita Quiterrez, promptly deserted her well-padded packing box to clamber into that of her neighbor, the young Domingo Estradilla, who retreated to the farthest corner in horrified consternation before her distinctly sticky caresses. Number Six, Jesús Arcienega, viewed the world with one distrustful black eye from the stronghold of his mother's arms; his button of a nose buried in her neck, two fat hands clutching the bosom of her dress. Maria Valdes slept the sleep of utter indifference, sprawled indecorously among the blankets which lined her clothes hamper. Over Number Eight, the young Luis Florida, Sister Concha hovered frantically, wet handkerchief in hand. The enterprising Luis had discovered an ink bottle, left recklessly open on a desk at his elbow, and by dint of fast and skillful work had managed to adorn his small person lavishly with its contents before an agonized sister could anticipate his ambition.

"ALL over he iss bath thees morning," wailed the distracted Concha, "*all over*—weeth the peenk soap! And now you may loog!"

It was a make-up well worth a look. An artistically blackened eye and a jaunty, if unsymmetrical, mustache of ink lent rakish charm to an already captivating smile.

Number Nine, Benito Gonzalos, in a purple-faced passion that threatened apoplexy, called the heavens to witness the outrageous invasion of his sacred privacy which he was suffering at the hands of the judges. For already the all-important business of weighing, measuring and examining was under way. And still Pablo Talamentes had entered no candidate.

Repeated discouragements had seen Pablo's jaunty confidence wilt to a despairing doggedness. It was away down by the big dam at the edge of town that hope again stirred in his heart. Here, close to the railroad track, squatted a small adobe house, literally roofed with vivid red peppers. About the house was a little enclosed space, sandy, with tufts of coarse grass. And on the ground within this yard sat an utterly unchaperoned baby, happily rubbing [CONTINUED ON PAGE 61]

Babies began to pour in—a confusion of babies

"He's a beautiful baby"

FIGURE 1.17 These drawings illustrate Stone's "Better Bebbies" story as it appeared in the November 1925 issue of *Women's Home Companion.* Illustration by Frederic Dorr Steele, *Baby Show, Woman's Home Companion* 52 [1925]: 18. Courtesy Main Library, University of Illinois at Urbana–Champaign.

who died during childbirth (14). While Dorey also notes that maternal education—not necessarily scientific intervention—improved these mortality rates (15), the presence of doctors at the contests and the physical statistics included on the scoring cards suggest that contest organizers imbued a degree of medical science into the contests (figures 1.18 and 1.19). For example, in 1922 the Illinois Department of Public Health issued a pamphlet about the state's Better Baby Conference. Written by Superintendent Dr. C. W. East for public health officials, the pamphlet provides the rationale behind the contests and a curriculum to implement during a conference. East asserts that "the Better Babies contest is a popular yet scientific movement to insure better babies and a better race" and "makes for a better race of Americans because it teaches parents how to improve the physical condition of children already born and to protect those yet unborn" (2). Moreover, East notes, "by means of a uniform score card [the

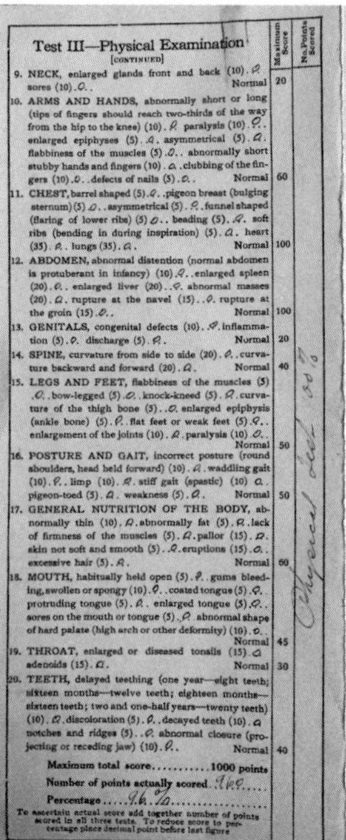

Test III—Physical Examination [CONTINUED] | Maximum Score | No. Points Scored

9. NECK, enlarged glands front and back (10). 0 sores (10). 0. . Normal 20

10. ARMS AND HANDS, abnormally short or long (tips of fingers should reach two-thirds of the way from the hip to the knee) (10). 0. paralysis (10). 0. . enlarged epiphyses (5). 0. asymmetrical (5). 0. flabbiness of the muscles (5). 0. . abnormally short stubby hands and fingers (10). 0. clubbing of the fingers (10). 0. . defects of nails (5). 0. . Normal 60

11. CHEST, barrel shaped (5). 0. . pigeon breast (bulging sternum) (5) 0. . asymmetrical (5). 0. funnel shaped (flaring of lower ribs) (5) 0. . beading (5). 0. soft ribs (bending in during inspiration) (5). 0. heart (35). 0. lungs (35). 0. Normal 100

12. ABDOMEN, abnormal distention (normal abdomen is protuberant in infancy) (10). 0. . enlarged spleen (20). 0. . enlarged liver (20). . 0. abnormal masses (20). 0. rupture at the navel (15). . 0. rupture at the groin (15). 0. . Normal 100

13. GENITALS, congenital defects (10). . 0. inflammation (5). 0. discharge (5). 0. Normal 20

14. SPINE, curvature from side to side (20). 0. . curvature backward and forward (20). 0. Normal 40

15. LEGS AND FEET, flabbiness of the muscles (5) . 0. . bow-legged (5). 0. . knock-kneed (5). 0. curvature of the thigh bone (5). . 0. enlarged epiphysis (ankle bone) (5). 0. . flat feet or weak feet (5). 0. . enlargement of the joints (10). 0. paralysis (10). 0. . Normal 50

16. POSTURE AND GAIT, incorrect posture (round shoulders, head held forward) (10). 0. waddling gait (10). 0. . limp (10). 0. stiff gait (spastic) (10) 0. pigeon-toed (5). 0. weakness (5). 0. Normal 50

17. GENERAL NUTRITION OF THE BODY, abnormally thin (10). 0. abnormally fat (5). 0. lack of firmness of the muscles (5). 0. pallor (15). 0. skin not soft and smooth (5). . 0. eruptions (15). 0. . excessive hair (5). 0. Normal 60

18. MOUTH, habitually held open (5). 0. . gums bleeding, swollen or spongy (10). 0. . coated tongue (5). 0. protruding tongue (5). 0. . enlarged tongue (5). 0. . sores on the mouth or tongue (5). . 0 abnormal shape of hard palate (high arch or other deformity) (10). 0. . Normal 45

19. THROAT, enlarged or diseased tonsils (15). 0 adenoids (15). 0. Normal 30

20. TEETH, delayed teething (one year—eight teeth; sixteen months—twelve teeth; eighteen months—sixteen teeth; two and one-half years—twenty teeth) (10). 0. discoloration (5). 0. . decayed teeth (10). 0 notches and ridges (5). . 0. abnormal closure (projecting or receding jaw) (10). 0. . Normal 40

Maximum total score . . . . 1000 points

Number of points actually scored. 960 . . .

Percentage . . . . . 96 % . . . .

To ascertain actual score add together number of points scored in all three tests. To reduce score to percentage place decimal point before last figure

Physical 1st 300

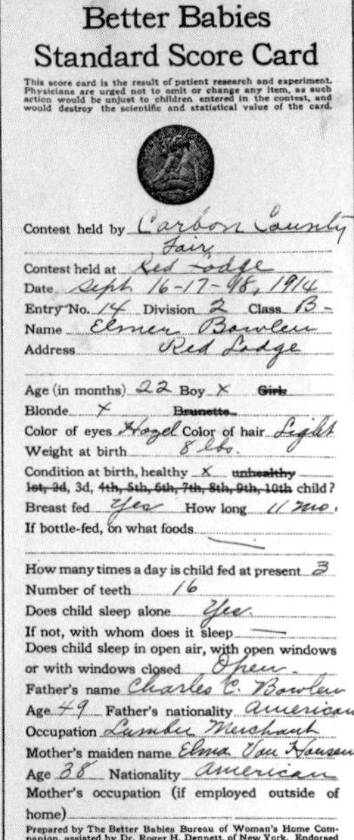

Better Babies Standard Score Card

This score card is the result of patient research and experiment. Physicians are urged not to omit or change any item, as such action would be unjust to children entered in the contest, and would destroy the scientific and statistical value of the card.

Contest held by Carbon County Fair

Contest held at Red Lodge

Date Sept 16-17-18, 1914

Entry No. 14 Division 2 Class B-

Name Elmer Bowlen

Address Red Lodge

Age (in months) 22 Boy X ~~Girl~~

Blonde X ~~Brunette~~

Color of eyes Hazel Color of hair Light

Weight at birth 8 lbs.

Condition at birth, healthy X ~~unhealthy~~

~~1st, 2d,~~ 3d, ~~4th, 5th, 6th, 7th, 8th, 9th, 10th~~ child?

Breast fed Yes How long 11 mo.

If bottle-fed, on what foods

How many times a day is child fed at present 3

Number of teeth 16

Does child sleep alone Yes

If not, with whom does it sleep

Does child sleep in open air, with open windows or with windows closed Open

Father's name Charles C. Bowlen

Age 49 Father's nationality American

Occupation Lumber Merchant

Mother's maiden name Elma Van Hausen

Age 38 Nationality American

Mother's occupation (if employed outside of home)

Prepared by The Better Babies Bureau of Woman's Home Companion, assisted by Dr. Roger H. Dennett, of New York. Endorsed by the New York Milk Committee, Dr. Godfrey R. Pisek, Medical Director.

For use at Better Babies Contests
With the compliments of WOMAN'S HOME COMPANION
Copyright 1913 by The Crowell Publishing Company

FIGURE 1.18 (*top*) Charles and Elma Bowlen of Red Lodge, Montana, saved this scorecard measuring the health of their son, Elmer. Author's collection.

Test I—Mental and Developmental

IMPORTANT NOTE. No specific figures can be given for separate tests; perfect development counts 100 points. Defects reduce the score. The examining physician will mark "x" for "yes" and "o" for "no" after each individual test, and before dismissing the child will write in the second column the total number of points scored in the entire test (on a basis of 100 points for a perfect test) according to his judgment.

	Maximum Score	No. Points Scored
SIX MONTHS. Sits alone. . . . plays with simple objects like a pencil or spoon. . . . grasps for watch. . . . hears (looks in the direction of unexpected noises) . . . . sees (follows objects moving about). . . . irritable . . . . highly nervous. . . . Normal	100	
ONE YEAR. Stands with support. . . . walks with support. . . . plays with toys. . . . listens to the ticking of a watch. . . . hears (looks in the direction of unexpected noises). . . . sees (follows objects moving about) . . . . says one or two words. . . . knows the mother (cries when taken away from her). . . . plays with children. . . interested in surroundings. . . . irritable. . . . highly nervous. . . . bad temper. . . . Normal	100	
ONE AND ONE-HALF YEARS. Stands and walks without support. . . . says a few words. . . . knows mother (cries when taken away from her). . . . interested in surroundings. . . . hears. . . . sees. . . . irritable . . . . highly nervous. . . . bad temper. . . . unmanageable. . . . Normal	100	
TWO YEARS. Runs. X. joins words to make short sentences. . X speech defects. 0. interested in pictures . . X. can point to eyes, nose, ears, etc.. X. sees X. hears. X. irritable. 0. highly nervous. 0. bad temper 0. unmanageable. 0. Normal	100	100
THREE YEARS. Talks normally. . . . speech defects . . . . repeats six syllables perfectly "It rains. I am hungry". . . repeats two figures "6, 4," "3, 9". . . . enumerates objects seen in pictures. . . . knows the names of the various members of the family. . . . good vision. . . . good hearing. . . . irritable. . . . highly nervous. . . . bad temper . . . unmanageable. . . . Normal	100	
FOUR YEARS. Knows sex. . . . can name familiar objects. . . . repeat three figures "2, 7, 1," "4, 8, 5,". . . comparison of two lines (which is the longer). . . . enumerates objects seen in pictures. . . . good vision. . . good hearing. . . . irritable. . . . highly nervous. . . bad temper. . . . unmanageable. . . . Normal	100	
FIVE YEARS. Comparison of two weights (which is the heavier). . . . copy a square (satisfactory if one can recognize it). . . . visiting card cut diagonally can be put together again. . . . can count four pennies. . . . can describe a picture. . . . good vision. . . . good hearing. . . . irritable. . . . highly nervous. . . . bad temper . . . . unmanageable . . . Normal	100	

Test II—Measurements

The examiner should insert actual measurements only. Later the scorer will reckon the score from these measurements

Weight 29 . lbs. . . 0 . . oz. (20) . . 0 . . height. 36 . in. (20). 20. circumference of head 20½ in. (15). 0. . circumference of chest 20½ in. (15). 15. circumference of abdomen 20½ in. (10). 10 lateral diameter of chest taken with calipers at level of nipple line (5). 6½. . diameter of chest from front to back taken with calipers at level of nipple line 5 . in. (5) . 5 . . length of arm from tip of acromion process to tip of middle finger. . 13 . in. (5) . 5 . . . length of leg from greater trochanter to the sole of the foot. 16½ in. (5). . 5 . Normal | Maximum Score 100 | No. Points Scored 60

Table of Standards

Age in months	Weight	Height	Circumference of head	Circumference of chest	Circumference of abdomen	Lat. Diameter of chest	Chest front to back	Length of arm	Length of leg
	lbs.	in.	in.	in.	in.	in.	in.	in.	in.
6	17	27	17¼	17¼	17¼	5	4¼	10	10
9	19	28	18	18	18	5	4¼	11	11
12	20	29	18½	18½	18½	5	4¾	12	12½
16	23	30	18½	18½	18½	5½	5	12½	13½
20	24	31	18½	19½	19½	6	5	14	15
24	25	32	19	20	19½	6	5	14½	15½
28	27	33½	19	20	19½	6	5	14½	15¾
32	29	35	19½	20½	19½	6¼	5½	14½	15¾
→36	32	36½	20	21	20	6½	5½	15	16½

Test III—Physical Examination

IMPORTANT NOTE. In this examination the examiner should place either "x" or "o" in each space that contains a figure in parentheses. "x" signifies "yes", "o" signifies "no". When the score is finally reckoned each "x" represents a penalty and the sum placed in parentheses will be deducted from the total which is found in each division after the heading of "normal"

1. FEATURES, irregularities (5). 0. Normal 5
2. HEAD, abnormally small (10). 0. . abnormally large (10). 0. abnormally square (box shaped) (10). 0. . asymmetrical (5). 0. Normal 35
3. FONTANEL, (normally open until the eighteenth month) delayed closure (5). 0. . abnormally large (5). 0. . Normal 10
4. HAIR AND SCALP, poor condition of scalp (5). 0. bald spots (5). 0. . scanty hair (5). 0. brittle (5). 0 Normal 20
5. EYES, pale color of mucous membranes (5). 0. quivering of eyeballs (nystagmus) (10). 0. position (too near together, too far apart or slanting) (10). 0. lids (abnormality in shape or inflammation) (5). 0. squint (10). 0. discharge (5). 0. . Normal 45
6. EARS, abnormally large (5). 0. abnormally small (5). 0. protruding (5). 0. abnormal shape (5) 0. discharge (not wax) (10). 0. . Normal 30
7. NOSE, depressed bridge (5). 0. deviation one side (5). . 0. obstruction in breathing with mouth closed (10) 0. . discharge (5) . 0. Normal 25
8. LIPS, poor color (5). 0. cracks or fissures (5) 0. abnormally thick (5). 0. Normal 15

FIGURE 1.19 (*bottom*) The other side of baby Elmer Bowlen's scorecard from the Carbon County Fair (Montana) Better Babies Contest. Author's collection.

contest] will supply to the medical profession what it has long been wanting—scientific data concerning the normal child" (3). The remainder of the pamphlet walks readers through organizing and implementing a contest, down to which measurements to take during physical exams of the children, which movies to run in the demonstration halls, and how to use lifelike dolls arranged in museum-like tableaux to demonstrate hygienic issues such as proper ventilation and "swapping germs" (21). And as Nurse Winters teaches the third-grade girls the proper care of infants, East includes a "Little Mothers' Day—School Day" in his suggested weeklong conference, where nurses would produce "plays bearing upon child welfare" for the "teaching of infant hygiene to school girls" (24), thus reinforcing the idea that child welfare is women's work, and that women must be trained early.

Anna Steese Richardson built her career off the contests, serving as the first head of the magazine's Better Babies Bureau (Dorey 170). In addition to *Woman's Home Companion*'s heavy involvement with the contests, several other popular magazines printed advertisements, photos of babies, and various magazine-specific contests and prizes (79–82) (figures 20 and 21). *Woman's Home Companion* capitalized on the contests, printing the long-running Better Babies column, creating and circulating the Better Babies Standard Score Card, and insisting on certain conditions that user groups had to meet. Chiefly, *Woman's Home Companion* held any publishing rights to stories or photographs featuring contests, prizewinners, and even leaders in education or reform (172). In 1914 Richardson published *Better Babies and Their Care*, a guide for new mothers that included chapters on everything from "Preparation for Motherhood" to "How the Normal Baby Grows" to "Diet for Older Children." Richardson presented herself as a parenting expert, identifying herself on the title page as the National Chairman of the Department of Hygiene, Congress of Mothers and Parent-Teacher Associations. *Woman's Home Companion* editor Gertrude Lane vouches for Richardson's professional expertise in the preface, noting that after "a little more than one year of hard work, the Better Babies Bureau of the *Woman's Home Companion*, under the directorship of Anna Steese Richardson, has become a tremendous machine for aiding in the reduction of infant mortality, and for raising physical, mental, and moral standards among children" (viii). Perhaps more importantly for the book's target audience—young mothers—Lane also vouches for Richardson's personal expertise, for "the woman who writes [this book] has had not only the actual experience of bearing and rearing her own children, but she has had the rare privilege of corresponding with mothers from every point in the United States, of witnessing many of the Better Babies Contests, and of studying not only what is the matter with the sick baby, but the baby who is well" (ix). Lane and Richardson had grand visions of how many consumers would buy into their message of better babies, through the ongoing magazine columns and the book itself. Richardson dedicates the book

> [t]o the one hundred thousand babies, the one hundred thousand mothers, the one hundred thousand helpers who have taken part in better babies contests this book is dedicated by a mother who knows what better babies, better mothers, better helpers mean to this and future generations. (v)

The first line of the first chapter also elevates motherhood—and by extension, professional writing about motherhood—as a woman's ultimate labor of moral and intellectual service: "Maternity is woman's exclusive profession, the only one of which progress and science cannot rob her. It is also her highest profession, for, compared to motherhood, art and science dwindle into insignificance" (1).

Richardson, Lane, and Better Babies Contest organizers circulated the idea that motherhood is an American woman's highest calling, but their own careers—and Katherine Nevins's and Martha Winter's careers in Stone's novel—perhaps made an even stronger case that teaching supposedly less American women how to be better mothers was, in fact, an American woman's highest duty. Dorey discusses the "missionary approach" (6) of the contests as white female reformers brought them to poverty-stricken urban areas and later to rural areas. She writes that "less fortunate, 'ignorant' lower-class others and children were identified as needing intervention" and "baby health contest volunteers and supervisors often interacted with many foreign-speaking mothers and ethnically diverse babies" (7). As with most reform programs, middle-class whites were in charge of the Better Babies Contests, which coalesced with the eugenics movement. White reformers imposed their own values on large groups of immigrants and indigenous populations, as Dorey explains, "in an effort to help them achieve a better life. The movement's leaders were primarily native-born, white, upper-middle

Page 50 WOMAN'S HOME COMPANION

THE LITTLEST COWBOY
A Better Babies Prize-Winner
This is Jasper M. Bellinger who won first prize at the Better Babies contest at the Oregon State Fair at Salem. Jasper lives on a ranch near Lebanon, Oregon. The Better Babies movement has reached the western cowboy country. Has it reached your town?

How healthy are the babies in your town?

IF ALL the little tots between six months and three years of age were weighed and measured and tested, would their average score be above standard—or below? That is the question that is now being asked in hundreds of towns in the United States. And these towns are going to find out. They are going to hold Better Babies contests to determine, scientifically, just where their babies stand. In every town the WOMAN'S HOME COMPANION is going to help.

How healthy are the babies in your town? A Better Babies contest this summer will give the answer, and you can be certain of this: however high your home town babies score this summer, they will score higher next summer. This, of course, is what the Better Babies contest is really for—*to show each baby's parents how to make that baby better.*

As a reader of WOMAN'S HOME COMPANION you have an obligation in this matter. You owe it to your town to show it how to hold a Better Babies contest. This will be very easy when you remember that the WOMAN'S HOME COMPANION will supply all necessary information.

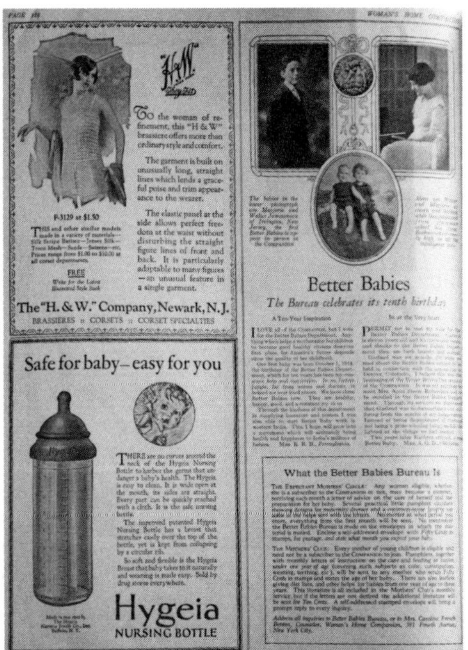
"H.&W." They Fit

To the woman of refinement, this "H & W" brassiere offers more than ordinary style and comfort.

The garment is built on unusually long, straight lines which lends a graceful poise and trim appearance to the wearer.

The elastic panel at the side allows perfect freedom at the waist without disturbing the straight figure lines of front and back. It is particularly adaptable to many figures—an unusual feature in a single garment.

F-3129 at $1.50

FREE

The "H. & W." Company, Newark, N.J.
BRASSIERES :: CORSETS :: CORSET SPECIALTIES

Safe for baby—easy for you

THERE are no curves around the neck of the Hygeia Nursing Bottle to harbor the germs that endanger a baby's health. The Hygeia is easy to clean. It is wide open at the mouth, its sides are straight. Every part can be quickly reached with a cloth. It is the safe nursing bottle.

The improved patented Hygeia Nursing Bottle has a breast that stretches easily over the top of the bottle, yet is kept from collapsing by a circular rib.

So soft and flexible is the Hygeia Breast that baby takes to it naturally and weaning is made easy. Sold by drug stores everywhere.

Hygeia
NURSING BOTTLE

Better Babies
The Bureau celebrates its tenth birthday

What the Better Babies Bureau Is

FIGURE 1.20 (*left*) *Woman's Home Companion* printed this advertisement for the Better Babies Contests in their own pages and sold the ad to other magazines. Courtesy Multnomah County Library, Portland, Oregon.

FIGURE 1.21 (*right*) This Better Babies column features a "where are they now?" story about two babies examined at the first Better Babies Contest ten years prior. Editors strategically placed the column beside ads for products presumably indispensable for new mothers—brassieres, corsets, and baby bottles. Courtesy Main Library, University of Illinois at Urbana–Champaign.

class professionals and community leaders who nurtured their own employment opportunities in programs focused on perceived needs, ignoring the rights of those served" (19). Further, "The gospel of better babies promoted the 'genuinely eugenic baby'—the hope for a purer future race. Proponents of eugenics preached loudly about starting a child's life 'right,' *before* parents choose marriage partners. The welfare and future of children were bound to the ideal known as 'race betterment'" (23). "Better babies' beginnings in Iowa made a strong connection between crops of livestock and babies in an effort to awaken the public mind to the value of 'human stock'" (25).

Holt also briefly discusses the domestic economy movement's involvement with "better babies and rural health," noting that the "Indian Agricultural Fair on the Potawatomi Reservation in Kansas simply awarded prizes to the best male and female babies under eighteen months, and the Kickapoo Indian Produce Fair in Horton, Kansas, considered its few better baby candidates as a group" (113). She writes that these fairs likely used the Better Babies Standard Score Card created and circulated by *Woman's Home Companion* for use at state and regional fairs (112). Dorey also writes about Native American and Mexican involvement in the Better Babies Contests, particularly in the western states. American Indian families often attended state fairs. Even though Indians were usually "featured as entertainment" at the fairs, one unnamed Hopi baby earned a red ribbon at the Arizona State Fair in 1913. In the same year, where the Washington State Fair included "Indian dances, races, councils of chiefs, and powwows," a Nez Perce "papoose" named Hilbert Johnson earned a score of 94 percent in the Better Babies Contest. At the same fair, Agnes Wildshoe, from the Coeur d'Alene tribe, scored a 91.5 percent (Dorey 145).

Lisa E. Emmerich writes about the Save the Babies campaign that the Bureau of Indian Affairs (BIA) organized and implemented from 1912 to 1918 in the western states. She discusses a baby show for Cocopah and Quechan women and babies held at the Fort Yuma Indian Reservation in November 1916 as one example of "a national health campaign that focused exclusively on American Indian women in their roles as mothers. The Save the Babies campaign worked toward the wholesale redefinition of native family life according to Euro-American standards and values" (395). Like the priests in *Death Come for the Archbishop*, Sabra Cravat in *Cimarron*, Katherine Nevins and Martha Winters in *The Laughingest Lady*, and *Woman's Home Companion*'s Better Baby Contests, the Save the Babies campaign "reinforced the standard assimilationist beliefs: Tribalism was a retrogressive force; traditional native family patterns and medical practices were antiquated and dangerous; and Indian women had to accept sole responsibility for the health and welfare of their children" (399). Emmerich writes about the ways Indian women would have heard about the message of the Save the Babies campaign. The BIA put out several pamphlets, including the 1914 *Indian Mothers: Save Your Babies* and the 1916 *Indian Babies: How to Keep Them Well*, but Emmerich notes that many Native women would have already heard the same message through *Woman's Home Companion*—either by reading the magazine or by attending a baby show, depending on the community and the region (402). Moreover, she discusses how publications from federal Indian schools made their way to western reservations, "carried back by returning students who also brought with them firsthand training in scientific motherhood" (401). A student-written article in the *Carlisle Arrow* encourages Indian mothers to "Save Your Baby" with the latest public health rhetoric. Field matron Elsie E. Newton guest wrote a similar column, "What an Indian Girl Should Know," in the *Indian School Journal*, the student newspaper at the Chilocco Indian Agricultural School in Oklahoma (401). Regardless of the ways Indian and Mexican women learned about the tenets of scientific motherhood, Euro-American campaigns and characters, doctors, and editors—the enforcers and perpetuators of colonial domesticity—all overlook one simple but culturally threatening truth: American Indian and Mexican American women have been raising children and keeping house on this continent far longer than any Euro-American women have. As the next chapter shows, whether or not white women recognize it as such, Latina women exercise and fictionalize rituals and values of domesticity to belie white assumptions that nonwhites are culturally and morally depraved and to claim authority over their own lives and families.

CHAPTER TWO

Dialoging Domesticity

Resisting and Assimilating "The American Lady" in Early Mexican American Women's Writing

In others chapters I argue that Anglo-American women used their newly acquired freedom of mobility during the first decades of the twentieth century, at the height of westward expansion, to colonize Mexican American women with Anglo-American domesticity. In this chapter, I interpret writings by Mexican American women who belie the idea that Hispanic women need to be taught anything at all about domesticity.[1] Cleofas M. Jaramillo writes a cookbook to correct Anglo recipes for "Mexican Dishes." María Amparo Ruiz de Burton lambastes the hypocritical Christian domesticity of her white characters yet still describes the domestic space as a *mexicana*'s primary sphere of influence. Jovita González corrects claims by Presbyterian missionaries who write that the Spanish American "home has never been a sacred place, and family relations have not been held sacred" (McLean and Williams 138). Ruiz de Burton, Jaramillo, González, Fabiola Cabeza de Baca, and Nina Otero-Warren resist Anglo assertions that Mexican American culture lacks domesticity and modernity, but they also argue for inclusion in national platforms of feminine authority, sometimes through collaboration with white women and sometimes *as* or *in place of* white women.

While other scholars have compared these writers in pairs or trios or have briefly mentioned all of them in an extended analysis of one, no scholar has brought all five together for extended analysis, as I do here. I will show how domesticity gathers into itself two other cultural institutions: religion and education. Matters of religion in general and assertions of Catholicism in particular are part of cultural negotiations that these five Mexican American writers perform in their novels and memoirs. Religious matters overlap educational efforts; as the McLean and Williams epigraph to the introduction shows, whites educated Mexican Americans to domesticate and proselytize them, making education central to the work of these five writers. Even though these discourses of domesticity, religion, and education are almost inextricably bound together, for clarity's sake I separate them into two sections here. I argue in this chapter that these five writers responded to the historical and literary presence of the Anglo woman in the West; nearly all scholars of this literature write about the writers' relations (as the colonized) to the encroaching American colonizers, but here I flesh out this colonizing force by arguing that these writers respond specifically to the actual Anglo women who lived and wrote among them. Colonialism has taught us not to think of subalterns as readers, but these five writers were adept at reading texts and extratextual signifiers, as their own writings prove.

I contend that these narratives do not simply resist or assimilate Anglo encroachment. Rather, they constantly negotiate with and even collaborate with Anglo women to claim space in national rhetorics and narratives about women's roles that historically excluded Mexican American women in particular and women of color in general. Charlotte J. Rich argues that during the 1890s and 1910s, "the rhetoric of American feminism as articulated by its largest constituency—middle-class white women—seemed emancipatory yet upheld the hegemonic constructions of American culture. Much Progressive feminist discourse preached equality yet was exclusive, leaving little room for those outside the white middle class" (4).

Rich argues that the writings of S. Alice Callahan, Mourning Dove, Pauline Hopkins, Sui Sin Far, and María Cristina Mena suggest possibilities for female authority that stand apart from white, middle-class standards yet draw "syncretic characters" who are equally competent in both "hegemonic American culture and their own ethnic traditions" (36). The five writers that I consider here, like those Rich studies, do feature syncretic female characters who move easily between Anglo and Mexican American cultures. But these writers, and my readings of their work, differ from Rich's analyses in that Ruiz de Burton, Jaramillo, Otero-Warren, Cabeza de Baca, and González are not necessarily looking for cultural authority *aside from* middle-class female norms. On the contrary, their claims to whiteness—claims that critics have repeatedly and convincingly proved—can be read as claims to the platforms and freedoms that American women's rhetorics, in their various incarnations from the 1850s through the 1950s, allowed white women. That is, through their narrative engagements with domesticity, religion, and education, these women write themselves into the rhetorics of republican motherhood, true womanhood, and new womanhood. As such rhetorics evolved into the twentieth century—as part of the Progressive movement—these five women directly responded to Anglo women who historically and literarily colonized Mexican American women's spaces and asserted that Mexican American women's customs are compatible with Anglos' customs and with modernity.

Chicana feminist scholars such as Gloria Anzaldúa, Cherríe L. Moraga, and Sonia Saldívar-Hull have argued since the early 1980s that American feminism has a history of blindness to issues of race, class, and sexual orientation and that, in most instances, American feminism only addresses the needs and concerns of white, middle-class heterosexual women. Consequently, they theorize a field of "Chicana Feminisms" (Saldívar-Hull 2000) that would more adequately address the needs and concerns of women of color—and particularly Chicana women—than does mainstream American feminism. Saldívar-Hull, while acknowledging the crucial contributions of Euro-American feminism, urges a critical "color consciousness" among literary scholars rather than the well intentioned but ultimately still restrictive "color blindness" practiced by earlier varieties of liberal scholars (36). While I do not argue with their positions—in fact, I agree that American feminism can be terribly tunnel-visioned—I depend on the work of these scholars while also believing that practicing a Chicana-feminist reading of these five Mexican American writers remains insufficient. Their lives and writings predate the social circumstances that allow modern Chicana feminists to insist—and rightfully so—on a broader vision among American feminists. Further, in their claims to whiteness, these women are themselves less concerned with race or ethnicity in and of itself than with class and social privilege. While I have no desire to follow a critical template that would always weigh class over race, these works, and the ways that these writers see their works, call attention to the ways that race concerns are subsumed by—and even manipulated by—gender and class concerns. María Eugenia Cotéra argues that Jovita González's writings collaborate with Anglo women and Anglo feminine ideals. This is particularly true with her novel, *Caballero,* which González coauthored with an Anglo—Margaret Eimer—and as such is "a collaborative text about collaboration that self-consciously enacts the politics of its production" ("Recovering" 169). Whether or not they are as explicitly collaborative with Anglo women and ideals as is González, all five writers blend moments of resistance to Anglo hegemony with lifetimes of assimilating the platforms of white feminists in order to gain initial freedoms from the Mexican patriarchal order.

A growing body of scholarship about how domesticity functions in these authors' works provides the conversation my work will engage; there is far more scholarly work done on Ruiz de Burton and González than on Jaramillo, Otero-Warren, and Cabeza de Baca. My readings of the latter three writers also argue that they deserve far more sustained literary attention than they have received to this point. Further, pushing scholarship on all five authors in new directions, I focus on how religion and education work in these texts as extensions of domesticity and as public platforms for female authority.

Domesticity on Display

All of the five Mexican American women writers in this chapter, in some way or another, use the rhetoric of domesticity to resist Anglo definitions of femininity and negotiate a space in US national narratives regarding womanhood. This contradiction, this impulse to resist and assimilate, is inherent to the very conception and structure of González's *Caballero* and her other writings, and the same is true of the other texts I work with in this chapter: the memoirs by Cabeza de Baca, Jaramillo, and Otero-Warren and the novels by Ruiz de Burton. All these works are written in English, a fact that alone tells at least a personal history of contact between Anglos and these Hispanic writers. Some of the writers had careers with the federal government; all moved away from strictly traditional roles for Hispanic women and worked instead as teachers, politicians, women's club/society figures, and writers, and not primarily as homemakers. The most important commonality for this study, though, is that, in their personal lives and in their narrative characters, whether the narratives be fiction or memoir, these writers came in contact with Euro-American ideals and habits of domesticity through the shape and consequence of their contact with Anglo women. One can look to government and church records to see that, yes, Anglo women came to the Southwest in droves, bringing with them American ideologies of domesticity, religion, and education. But one can also read references to contact with these Anglo women in the writings themselves. Sometimes these references take the form of proselytizing, maternalistic Anglo female characters, as in Ruiz de Burton's novels. Sometimes they are a present absence just off the page, as in Cabeza de Baca's *The Good Life.* And sometimes, Anglo women's writing directly called forth Hispanic women's textual production, as with Jaramillo's writings. In these ways and others, contact with Anglo women spurred these Hispanic writers to write—for preservation, for resistance, for assimilation, for survival, and for complicated combinations of these purposes and others.

Both of María Amparo Ruiz de Burton's novels—*Who Would Have Thought It?* (1872) and *The Squatter and the Don* (1885)—feature domestic Anglo matrons as main characters. Of the writers I interpret in this chapter, Ruiz de Burton is the only one who draws fully realized Anglo female characters such as Mrs. Norval and Mrs. Darrell; they represent Ruiz de Burton's satiric argument that the rhetorics of republican motherhood and true womanhood are, at best, racially exclusive and culturally colonial and, at worst, fundamentally hypocritical and ultimately inferior to the morality and gentility of her own Spanish American domestic traditions. Suzanne Bost argues that Ruiz de Burton's "racializations of true womanhood and true Americanness suggest that Mexico and *mestizaje* must be brought into discussions about race, gender, and nation in the nineteenth-century United States" (656). *Who Would Have Thought It?* is about a Mexican orphan named Lola Medina, a young girl rescued and brought back east by Dr. Norval, a geologist on an expedition to the American Southwest. The doctor's wife, Jemima Norval, is every bit the wicked stepmother in her "mothering" of Lola, who is every bit the fairy-tale princess with a heart of gold and an actual treasure chest full of it. In their introduction to the 1993 edition of the novel, Rosaura Sánchez and Beatrice Pita argue that it is, in part, a parody of the earlier popular forms of the sentimental novel and the domestic novel (x). Kate McCullough argues that the novel not only revises the eligibility criteria for true womanhood but that "Othered" women fulfill these criteria better than New England ladies do (151). Beth Fisher pushes on this idea, showing how Ruiz de Burton's portrayal of Jemima Norval as "the source of savage desires that transform Lola's residence in the

Norval home into an experience of captivity" ultimately "indicts domestic womanhood as a discourse of class and racial dominance" (60). That Ruiz de Burton questions and demystifies the ideals of Anglo domesticity in this novel is undeniable; her creation of the evil Mrs. Norval shows that Anglo "women are also implicated," along with the men we read of in history books, in the racial and cultural colonialism that characterized westward expansion (Fisher 61).

Like the New Mexican writers who argue that Spanish-Mexican womanhood is far superior to Anglo womanhood and claim the rights and privileges of whiteness, Ruiz de Burton contrasts "the hatred of the Christian matron" (92)—Mrs. Norval—with Lola's kindness to argue that Lola's "characteristic modesty is both an essential trait of Mexican womanhood and a sign of her natural superiority as a white, European aristocrat" (Fisher 62). Ruiz de Burton also contrasts Mrs. Norval's flawed womanhood with Lola's mother's saintlike womanhood. Lola's mother dies a martyr, believing that by enduring ten years of captivity among the Apaches rather than succumbing to the temptation of suicide, she has "purchased for my child, my husband, and my father, the happiness that was denied to me" (202). Margaret D. Jacobs notes that Ruiz de Burton exposes Mrs. Norval's deviation from the "sexual norms of true womanhood" ("Mixed-Bloods" 224) to show how Lola and her mother, Doña Theresa Medina, more faithfully adhere to the standards of true womanhood (225). Julie Ruiz argues that Mrs. Norval's inability to domesticate the "alien" within herself and her home is a metaphor for the United States' anxieties about its internal foreigners—Mexicans, Indians, and Africans (120). Of course, Mrs. Norval's savagery not only reverses the stereotypes Anglos held about Mexican or Indian women, but, as Amy Kaplan has argued about domesticity, her hypocrisy and hatred mirror how the United States treats indigenous people living within its borders.

Mrs. Norval is not the only Anglo woman who serves as a foil for Lola and Doña Theresa. The novel opens on a scene where two Anglo reverends—humorously dubbed Hammerhard and Hackwell—discuss the plight of the Californians and the sympathy Dr. Norval has for them. Before meeting Mrs. Norval we meet (through the reverends' conversation) Mrs. Cackle, whose racism matches Mrs. Norval's and who is confounded by Dr. Norval's interest in California "natives": "to me they are all alike—Indians, Mexicans, or Californians—they are all horrid" (11).

Mrs. Cackle conflates Californios with Indians and Mexicans, parroting the rhetoric of Manifest Destiny, claiming that God will help the Americans acquire all the land from these "native Californians [who] are savages" (12). Later, the narrator sardonically describes Mrs. Cackle, who, "as she was a good American woman, believed firmly in 'MANIFEST DESTINY,' and that the Lord was *bound* to protect the Union, even if to do so the affairs of the rest of the universe were to be laid aside for the time being" (159). With this characterization, as Fisher points out, *Who Would* foreshadows contemporary criticism such as Kaplan's, which traces a literary motif of "womanly cultural dominance that she terms 'Manifest Domesticity'" ("Precarious" 189).

Kaplan's idea of Manifest Domesticity, which locates in nineteenth-century American literature the metonymical rendering of home-space as nation-space, and vice versa, can also inform a reading of Ruiz de Burton's second novel, *The Squatter and the Don*. This novel opens as *Who Would* does, with two Anglos—in this case, Mr. and Mrs. Darrell—discussing the dispossession of landowning Californios. But this time, the roles reverse; where Dr. Norval was sympathetic to the plight of the Californios, Mr. Darrell—the squatter the title refers to—is the land-grabbing capitalist-colonialist. And where Mrs. Norval is the racist wicked witch of the East, Mrs. Darrell is the perfect picture of moral conscience and cultural sensitivity. This one-hundred-eighty-degree difference between Ruiz de Burton's characterizations of these two Anglo women might be the result of her attempts to recoup white female readers she may have offended with Mrs. Norval, as Fisher notes (66). The change may also signal Ruiz de Burton's awareness of the sentimental reform efforts driving Helen Hunt Jackson's enormously popular *Ramona*, published in 1884, just a year before *The Squatter and the Don*. A third possibility regarding this change, and an aspect that I will highlight later in the chapter, is that Mrs. Darrell was raised Catholic, only becoming Protestant at her marriage, which allows Ruiz de Burton to draw her more sympathetically than Mrs. Norval, whose Protestant hypocrisy she blames for Mrs. Norval's downfall. Whatever the reason—most likely, a combination of all three of these ideas—Ruiz de Burton's constant constructions of domestic scenarios show "her awareness of the rhetorical power" of domesticity (Fisher 66).

Indeed, *The Squatter and the Don* opens in the domestic space of the Darrells' living room, and Mrs. Darrell has the first lines of the novel, as she argues for the rights of the Californios who are being dispossessed of their land by squatters and settlers backed by the US government. Mr. and Mrs. Darrell discuss the rights of the homestead claims, a narrative that runs throughout the plot of the novel. Mrs. Darrell is the novel's moral conscience, constantly speaking on behalf of the Californios, Mexicans, and Indians and encouraging her son, Clarence, to pay Don Maríano for his land behind Mr. Darrell's back. This connects Mrs. Darrell to the line of historical white women who make it a moral mission to proselytize the indigenes of the American West. In this case, she is sympathetic to the Californios and respects their culture, customs, and claims to the land. Ruiz de Burton is much more generous by creating this kind of white female character than is Sarah Winnemucca, for example, who describes the white women she encounters as viperous and treacherous. Mrs. Darrell is nearly the exact opposite of Sabra Cravat in Edna Ferber's *Cimarron*, who takes it as her duty to civilize the Osage through domesticity; and Mrs. Darrell is indeed the total opposite of Mrs. Norval, whose rampant racism ultimately leads to her own undoing. Mrs. Darrell is acting out a maternalism that ties her to writers like Harriet Beecher Stowe and the sympathetic white women of *Uncle Tom's Cabin*, as well as to Helen Hunt Jackson.

The political rhetoric that Mrs. Darrell voices in the novel's opening chapter might seem out of place because its setting is not in the public arena of, say, a town square, but is rather in the private space of the living room. On the other hand, the living room is, traditionally, the most public space of a house. As Kaplan argues about other nineteenth-century women writers, Ruiz de Burton configures the home as a stage on which national dramas play out. But in placing Mrs. Darrell in the public rooms of the house she is also making a distinction between this Anglo woman, who has a voice to speak and presumably has an audience to listen to her concerns about the fallout of Manifest Destiny, and the Californiana matron of the novel, Doña Joséfa, who readers first glimpse in the private space of her bedroom. In chapter 2, Doña Joséfa witnesses through her bedroom window the conversation between her husband, Don Maríano, and Mr. Darrell, as he lays claim to land that is rightfully the Maríanos' through a Spanish land grant. That Doña Joséfa views the thievery of her land from the most private, intimate, even sexualized space in the house does more than equate the Californio dispossession with rape. By placing Doña Joséfa inside her house as an observer of events taking place outside of her house, Ruiz de Burton also suggests a passivity in Spanish womanhood that is made sharper by the contrast with Mrs. Darrell's actions: when Mrs. Darrell enters this public, masculine world of economics and pays Don Maríano for his land without her husband's knowledge.

At the same time, though, Ruiz de Burton makes a case in this novel, as in *Who Would Have Thought It?*, that Californianas are actually better examples of true womanhood than Anglo women. Placing Doña Joséfa in the feminine space of the bedroom could also highlight that she "knows her place," and as such, is another example "of how Spanish women wholly deserve the crown of true womanhood" (M. Jacobs, "Mixed-Bloods" 225). McCullough points out the dark side of this assertion, arguing that *The Squatter and the Don* "uses gender to locate the Californios as part of the white elite, representing the Californio women as 'American,' for instance, by revealing the model of American True Womanhood as regionally inflected and by disturbingly displacing outsider status onto the California Indians" (11). In this way, whereas she draws the Anglo women in *Who Would Have Thought It?* as outsiders to their own feminine ideals, in *The Squatter and the Don* Ruiz de Burton takes a threefold approach to Anglo women and their public domesticity as something to aspire to and transcend and someone to collaborate with against the oppression of Spanish-Mexican patriarchy.

Even though Jovita González does not draw any fully realized Anglo female characters, she echoes Ruiz de Burton's ruminations on the passivity of Spanish American womanhood by contrasting Tejanas with Anglo women who, at least in the world of her folklore and fiction, enjoy a relatively wide field of action and influence. Trained as a folklorist under J. Frank Dobie at the University of Texas at Austin, González published a master's thesis and articles that explore the gender roles in South Texas Mexican patriarchal culture. She continued to wrestle with the oppression of Tejanas in *Dew on the Thorn*, a collection of folkloric vignettes about South Texas border communities, and *Caballero: A Historical Novel*, between the late 1920s and the early 1930s, though neither was published until the late 1990s as part of José E. Limón's recovery scholarship. That González chose an Anglo coauthor for *Caballero*—Margaret Eimer— still sparks debate among Chicano/a literary critics and can inform the way we read González's texts; as Cotéra argues, González's collaboration with Eimer represents the ways her writings argue for potential collaboration between Tejanas and Anglo women against the oppression of Mexican patriarchy.

González's writings use domesticity to serve a double purpose: to show how Texas Mexican domesticity is more about patriarchal control than female influence and to argue that Anglo domesticity can allow Tejanas a freedom they could not achieve by remaining loyal to Texas Mexican social/gender norms. Anglo women in González's writings, then, highlight Texas Mexican patriarchy and offer Tejanas an alternative gender role. In one of her earlier published ethnographic pieces, "America Invades the Border Towns" (1930), González describes how older generations of Texas Mexicans view Anglo girls:

> The Texas-Mexican families do not want social intercourse with Americans, but they do demand the privilege of attending the same public places as Americans do. They are very conservative, have kept the Spanish traditions in regard to the position of women and look down upon American customs as free, loose and immoral. . . . According to their ethics, woman was made for the home, her duty in life is to create a home and to bring children into the world. In the freedom which American girls enjoy, Mexican parents see the beginning of all social evils. . . . "I am told that becoming Americanized means being progressive," said a leading citizen of Rio Grande City, "but if that means that my daughter will bob her hair, disobey her parents, chew gum, smoke, drink, and be out with boys until late at night, and finally elope, and get a divorce at the end of one or two years of married life, I do not want progress. Our customs may be of the Old World, but they suited our parents and they suit us now." (476)

González follows this with the assertion that "if the older generation feels that way about Americanization the young people do not" (476). In *Dew on the Thorn* and *Caballero*, she draws Tejana characters who "have the blood of one [race] and have acquired the ideals of another" ("America" 477) and who, in scenarios with endings that range from disastrous to hopeful, test the waters of Anglo feminine roles in order to escape Texas Mexican patriarchy.

The scenes of Tejana domesticity we read in *Dew on the Thorn* and *Caballero* are fraught with contradictory commentaries on male-female relations at the characters' haciendas. In *Dew on the Thorn*, González imbues Doña Margarita with calm authority. Her husband, Don Francisco de los Olivares, "lived like a feudal lord" and was a "tyrant by inheritance and breeding, . . . but though he was a master of many he was the slave of one—Doña Margarita, his wife. And as he thundered through the rooms of the house, his spurs echoing through the tile floors, one look from his wife was sufficient to calm him" (12–13). But while Doña Margarita enjoys some authority in her own house, González draws other Tejanas in *Dew* who meet disastrous ends when they try to make lives for themselves outside of marriage. Lucita, who wants to go to college rather than marry, goes mad; she "became as a wild beast" and "died crouched on the floor like a sick lamb" (112). González includes the legend of Santa Lucia, who wanted to remain an unmarried virgin so she could serve the poor. When a persistent suitor would not relent, he "was horrified on receiving the eyes which the maiden had plucked out with her own hands. The good god put them up there [as stars] in the sky as a reward for her sacrifice" (114). Don Francisco's daughter, Lucia, ends up being the lucky one when he tries to sell her in marriage to the rich old Anglo, Mister Luis, for a pair of earrings (118). Lucia lets her parents plan the wedding and then escapes through the window the night before to run away with Marcos, "her mate, the Indian peón" (119).

González draws different scenarios for the Tejanas in *Caballero*. Several scholars argue that the Mendoza y Soría homesites are not spaces for feminine influence but are for patriarchal control. Monika Kaup argues that *Caballero*'s Rancho La Palma, the hacienda of Don Santiago de Mendoza y Soría, "is in fact a man's house," and the women who live there are nothing more than part of Santiago's collection of patriarchal artifacts and symbols, similar to the religious icons hanging above his fireplace (582). Rosemary A. King argues that the hacienda is actually more a prison than a home with Santiago as guard and warden (25), and B. J. Manriquez notes that it is the quintessence of feudal and patriarchal thought (176). Marci McMahon similarly argues that *Caballero* "reveals the precarious roles of the female characters who do not follow the prescribed gender roles of Spanish colonialism and patriarchy" (238). González figures this hacienda as entirely within Santiago's control in the opening scene of the novel: "Such was Don Santiago, lord of land many miles beyond what his eye could compass, master of this *hacienda* and all those that would soon gather before him" (3). Of course, figuring the home as the man's domain is completely opposite from the way Anglo women writers of the same period—and the preceding century—drew homes as spaces where female influence reigned supreme; in this way, González makes her subtle argument that Anglo domesticity, though not without its own oppressions, offers more female authority than does Texas Mexican domesticity. Andrea Tinnemeyer offers a more complicated reading of how domesticity works in *Caballero*. She argues that González and Eimer use

> this nineteenth-century litmus test [that is, the cult of domesticity] for national inclusion for women from both angles: they display the interior of the Mendoza y Soría household to reveal how domestic science is aptly applied to the *tejana* home and thus prove the worthiness of the family's female membership for symbolic U.S. citizenship, yet they also denounce the cult as oppressive to women by depicting the tyrannical hold Don Santiago and Alvaro have over every member of the hacienda, regardless of gender or rank. (42)

Kaup highlights this irony when she contrasts the masculine domesticity of Rancho La Palma with the feminine domesticity Don Santiago's daughter, Angelina, obtains when she marries the Anglo soldier, McLane. Kaup argues that the house Angelina and McClane set up together in San Antonio shows that the "American home is an architectural and symbolic antithesis to the Mexican *hacienda*" (585). And even though Don Santiago's daughters escape Mexican patriarchy only to marry into the "legal subordination" of Anglo patriarchy (582), Susanita and Angelina use their newfound freedom in their marriages to Anglo men not only to enjoy the social calendar of officer's wives but also, in Angelina's case, to act on her charitable impulses like helping the Tejano poor in San Antonio (*Caballero* 328). And while Kaup describes the daughters' marriages as little more than a medieval transfer of property between two patriarchs, Angelina makes an informed, intellectual decision to marry McLane as a means of achieving more social authority. In a courtship letter to McLane, Angelina asks him about living in San Antonio: "[W]hat kind of dresses did the women wear, how did they do their hair. . . . Was it true that they had a voice in how the household should be run?" (210). McLane's answer represents González's hope that collaboration with Anglos, and inhabiting a role that Anglo women enjoy, will free Tejanas from Mexican patriarchal oppression and allow them social freedoms otherwise unavailable to them:

> Think of yourself in such a home . . . that will be wide in its entertaining, that will have seated at its table men who hold power and position. That will be my home, being built now in San Antonio. . . . Consider, then, the good you can do your people. Many will be homeless and will need comfort. The good *padres* at the church will need money and encouragement in this their task, and it will be you who can organize groups to help them. You can go to the humble homes of the poor, there will be the sick to visit and comfort. We will see that there is a school, you and me, to teach those who wish to learn. The *padres* will have true friends in us when they need friends. (211)

McLane offers Angelina inclusion in the national progressive movement that widened a woman's sphere of influence from the narrowness of her hearthside to the vastness of the continent where she could move more freely as a teacher, missionary, or social worker. By creating this scenario, González claims a space in progressive rhetoric that had previously been excluded to any but middle-class Anglo women.

Domestic rhetoric functions in the texts of Nina Otero-Warren, Cleofas M. Jaramillo, and Fabiola Cabeza de Baca in at least three main ways: first, it corrects ideas among Anglo women that Spanish American women are without their own traditions of domesticity and that Anglo women can be reliable interlocutors of Spanish American domesticity; second, it asserts a domestic ideology that is both centuries-old and that they see as superior to Anglo versions of domesticity; and finally, it encourages a more collaborative domesticity that fuses Spanish Mexican traditions with Anglo-American modernity to posit a Spanish American modernity. All three women wrote memoirs/autobiographies in the cultural preservation mode, and two of them—Jaramillo and Cabeza de Baca—wrote cookbooks of Spanish/New Mexican recipes to correct recipes for Mexican dishes published by Anglo women and teach Mexican American women how to fuse Spanish Mexican traditional food preparation with scientific nutritional knowledge and modern cooking methods and technologies.

Early critics of these writers, such as Tey Diana Rebolledo, Genaro M.

Padilla, and others, read their writings as resistance narratives, arguing that they assert Spanish Mexican domesticity in order to resist cultural appropriation (at best) or eradication (at worst) by demonstrating that home and family are long-held values of Spanish and Mexican cultures. Later critics—such as McMahon, María Carla Sánchez, and others—have argued that these assertions of domesticity, while surely resisting Anglo ideals, also serve as racist class posturing that separates these wealthy, landowning Spanish Americans from the Indian and Mexican laborers who have no property and thus, in the newly formed American capitalist system, have no claim to space or privileges. I argue that these writings do some of all these things—resist Anglo culture, assimilate to it, and distinguish between Spanish and Mexican/Indian—and, moreover, argue for inclusion in national women's rhetoric of their time period. Indeed, by the time these women are writing in the 1930s, 1940s, and 1950s, to use the rhetoric of domesticity as a vehicle for asserting culture and assigning value is to participate in a nearly century-old rhetoric about a woman's social and cultural influence. And because this rhetoric—whether its current incarnation is dubbed republican motherhood, true womanhood, or new womanhood—was initiated and sustained by Anglo women (particularly white women writers), using it is in itself an act of cultural negotiation.

Because the writings of Otero-Warren, Jaramillo, and Cabeza de Baca straddle the genres of autobiography, memoir, folklore, and cooking, much of the scholarly work on their writings and lives tends to be biographical, at least in part. This is particularly true with Otero-Warren, likely because she published only one book. Most historians, including Charles Montgomery and Maurilio E. Vigil, highlight her position as the first female national politician of Spanish Mexican descent. Anne M. Massmann's biography of Otero-Warren frames her as a "cultural broker" (877) or a go-between, intermediary, and border dweller who spent her life and career negotiating the Spanish and Anglo-American cultures in New Mexico and was recruited by Anglo women politicians to be a "Hispano voice" (885), just as Cabeza de Baca would later be recruited by the Cooperative Extension Service (CES, also known as the Agricultural Extension Service) and the country life movement to be a literal Hispano voice, a Spanish speaker for federal programs (Jensen and Miller 208). With her book, *Old Spain in Our Southwest* (1936), Otero-Warren, like Jaramillo and Cabeza de Baca, uses domesticity as a primary lens to view "the old days" when "the great Spanish families lived in haciendas" (Otero-Warren 9). She carefully describes both the architectural arrangement of the buildings within a hacienda and the physical arrangement of rooms and objects within a particular house of a hacienda. Although she opens the chapter "An Old Spanish Hacienda" with an apologetic disclaimer about noble poverty—"the Spanish descendant of the *Conquistadors* may be poor, but he takes his place in life with a noble bearing, for he can never forget that he is a descendent of the Conquerors" (9)—Otero-Warren describes an interior with expensive objects such as "great high beds with feather mattresses" and "a gilt-framed mirror which hung over the washstand, which had a marble top" (10). While she mentions that the peónes who worked the hacienda often had their own houses, her narration centers on wealthy patrónes and doñas who own and manage the haciendas. This contradiction could reflect that, as Massmann notes, she "never lived the Hispano communal family life in Northern New Mexico which she often was writing about" (894). On the contrary, born into a wealthy, landowning, and politically well-connected family, Otero-Warren lived quite a cosmopolitan life, traveling the world and being educated in New York and Germany (Massmann 881).

This contradiction between the opening line that focuses on the rural Hispanic poor and the narration that focuses on the Hispanic aristocracy, as well as the discrepancy between her own life and the collective memory she is trying to evoke, makes Otero-Warren's rhetoric of domesticity all the more constructed; she was not simply recording a lived past full of warm memories. Rather, as Massmann argues, her "book continued the practice of mediating Hispano respect for its history and culture with a romanticized language that an Anglo audience could understand and appreciate" (893). Further, even though the book was published in 1936, its setting could be almost a century earlier—a time before or shortly after 1848, when the Treaty of Guadalupe-Hidalgo changed the future of the hacienda system forever. Using a mid-nineteenth-century time setting allows Otero-Warren to engage the rhetorics of republican motherhood and true womanhood that are, historically, Anglo- and Eurocentric, when she highlights the role of "the *Doña* of the hacienda [who] was the dominant head of the family, for she was in complete charge of the house and the children" (13). In fact, by claiming that the fictionalized doña and her customs descend directly from the conquistadors, as in that opening line, she not only argues that Spanish American women should be included in national ideals for womanhood but that, chronologically speaking, Spanish American domesticity predates Anglo-American domesticity by at least a hundred years. Moreover, Otero-Warren indirectly addresses her Anglo female readers and the domesticating impulses of Anglo missionaries, teachers, and writers who live in the Southwest to assert that Anglo women misread Spanish American domesticity—or perhaps don't even see it at all:

> "Strangers do not understand our hospitality," said Don Antonio's brother-in-law. "A young attorney from 'the States' came to the hacienda a short time ago on business. He brought his wife. My *señora* received her guest in her usual courteous manner. The shutters of the guest room had been opened, the room well aired, the bed, with its feather mattress, was made ready. A silver basket, filled with fruit, was placed beside the candle on the bedside table. On retiring for the night, my wife told the American lady: 'My house, all that it contains, is yours.' She did not know that this phrase, perfectly sincere, is our way of making a guest feel at ease. One hardly accepts a house and its belongings! My *señora* had left a set of jewelry, a brooch, a bracelet and ear-rings on the dresser of the guest room. The American lady took these away with her, thinking it was a gift to her. It was her understanding of our hospitable, 'My house is yours.'" (33)

Beyond merely illustrating a misreading of Spanish American domesticity, with this anecdote Otero-Warren indicts Anglo women as cultural opportunists who justify their greedy impulses by refusing to see a civilization that differs from their own. In this way, stealing the jewelry becomes metonymic for westward expansion and the Anglo appropriation of lands that already legally belonged to Mexican landowners—and before them, of course, to Indian nations. In addition, with this anecdote she reverses the stereotype held by Anglos that Mexican Americans are primitive simpletons; in this case, the "American lady" dons the guise of a simpleton (which masks her opportunism) who takes literally a common phrase spoken metaphorically as a gesture of hospitality. Under this guise, the American lady can excuse her theft to her host and rationalize it to herself.

If setting her book in the past allows Otero-Warren to use the rhetoric of true womanhood to claim space for Hispanic women in American ideals of femininity, then publishing it in 1936 allows her to engage the rhetoric of new womanhood and draw on the ideals of the Progressive movement that provided her the opportunity for a highly public career as a national politician. Massmann notes that after her husband died, Otero-Warren never remarried or had children but her life's work was, on one hand, "typical of the female Progressive reformer. She tried to bring the 'feminine virtues' from the private sphere of looking after the welfare of children and families into the public sphere, such as women's issues, education, and social welfare work. But because of her background as a Catholic Spanish-American, Otero-Warren was also in a decidedly unique position from which to view this work" (885). Otero-Warren's roles as national politician, superintendent for Indian schools, and educator in the Works Progress Administration's (WPA) adult literacy programs signal her participation in, but not completely resisting, the roles and values that Anglo-American women brought to the Southwest. Indeed, Otero-Warren uses the same social platforms to modernize and further Americanize the women she sees as Other to herself. Like the other New Mexico writers I interpret here, she continually separates the Spanish characters in her book from the Indians—who she almost always sees as raiders and savages and only sometimes recognizes as distinct peoples such as the Apache or the Comanche. Her life's work, in addition to her writing, was also characterized by this racial distinction. As Massmann notes, Otero-Warren's platforms echoed those of Progressive Era reformers in the ways she contended that "teaching Indian mothers hygiene and modern methods of caring for babies was a particularly important component of reform" (892). Much like the American lady Otero-Warren addresses in her anecdote—the lady who comes to the Southwest and misreads Spanish Mexican domesticity—Otero-Warren's life and writings are characterized by a similar impulse to assert her own power and culture by misreading as primitive the civilizations she sees as beneath her.

Cleofas M. Jaramillo's writings can also be read as a response to the misreading American lady in her upper-class New Mexican milieu. In her memoir, *Romance of a Little Village Girl* (1955), she mentions her relationship with well-known Anglo writers of the Southwest such as Willa Cather (28) and Ruth Laughlin Barker (118). But she also writes that her organization of *La Sociedad Folklorica* (1936) and her book *The Genuine New Mexico Tasty Recipes* (1939) shared the goal of correcting popular (mis)representations of Hispanic culture by Anglo women:

> While calling upon and taking one of my Spanish recipe cookbooks to one of my neighbors, our conversation for the moment centered around Spanish recipes. "Have you seen the article in *Holland's Magazine* written by Mrs. D?" she inquired. I had not seen it, so she gave me the magazine to take home to read it. It was a three-page article, nicely written and illustrated, but very deficient as to knowledge of our Spanish cooking. In giving the recipe for making *tortillas* it read, "Mix bread flour with water, add salt." How nice and light these must be without yeast or shortening! And still these smart Americans make money with their writing, and we who know the correct way sit back and do nothing. (173)

The article Jaramillo sarcastically refers to here is "Intriguing Mexican Dishes" by Elizabeth Willis DeHuff, which appeared in *Holland*'s in March 1935. The very title of the article is exoticizing, and the opening lines imbue Mexican cooking with a mysticism and religiosity that must be

FIGURE 2.1 Though Jaramillo did not design the colorful cover of this 1981 reprint of her cookbook, she certainly chose its title, with emphasis on the "genuine." Author's collection.

FIGURE 2.2 The title pages to the original edition of Jaramillo's cookbook—including the portrait of her in an "old-fashioned gown"—argue that the recipes and customs in the book are "old" and "Spanish" (not new, Mexican, Indian, or American). Author's collection.

demystified: "To read a menu of Mexican dishes is like chanting a hymn of praise. The musical syllables, with their decided accents, scan themselves joyously to one's ear. There are *empanadas, enchiladas, ensalada, sopapillas,*" and so on (34). It appears that Jaramillo was offended by DeHuff's playing with Spanish words and her method of making tortillas, as she insinuates in this passage. She likely was even more offended by DeHuff's use of dialect to characterize a "Mexican American housewife" as she shops the market for chili peppers for cooking: "'I got no use for thees kind of chile,' she will say. 'Ees no gude! Ees very bad for the e-stomark!'" (34). DeHuff goes on like this for several more lines, with no reason other than to, presumably, add local color to her piece. Jaramillo's response to this Anglo woman's (mis)representation of her Spanish culture characterizes her entire body of work (figures 2.1 and 2.2).

More than the other New Mexican writers I study here, Jaramillo uses domesticity to glorify an irretrievable past, resist Anglo appropriation of Spanish Mexican lands, and assert a pre-Anglo Spanish American culture, as both Anne E. Goldman and Maureen Reed point out. She begins her introduction to *Shadows of the Past* (1941) with nostalgia: "As a descendant of the Spanish pioneers, I have watched with regret the passing of the old Spanish customs and the rapid adoption of the modern Anglo customs by the new generation" (1). This wistful recollection characterizes the domestic scenes she describes in *Romance* too. Moreover, as McMahon notes, Jaramillo's domesticity "demonstrates that public displays of Spanish Mexican homes are a powerful strategy of survival because they ultimately enabled women to resist certain aspects of their colonization" (252). This passage from the memoir, where she reflects on the simplicity of her childhood, encapsulates Jaramillo's perspective on the sharp contrasts between Spanish tradition and Anglo modernity:

> Children fed with simple food raised on their lands, and housed in neat little whitewashed houses with large sunny yards, were healthy and happy, too. But they were quiet and respectful, not spoiled by too much liberty and by the bold example they learn now from television and movies. Juvenile delinquency?—No one knew what it meant. People's lives radiated between church and home. Mothers stayed home taking care of their children, satisfied to live on their husband's earnings. They were not buying new clothes all the time nor visiting beauty shops. No one was ever late for church, although some of them lived two and three miles distant and rode in slow wagons or even walked. How nice it would be if people now would live thus! (14)

The modernity she lives with in her old age frames Jaramillo's views of her childhood, and in this passage she blames technology, feminism, secularism, and consumerism for the loss of the old Spanish customs she refers to in *Shadows of the Past.* Of course, all these social phenomena are also examples of "the modern Anglo customs" that she herself participated in during her adulthood, a fact she belies in her memoir when describing her relatives' large two-story homes, rare in that region (54), and all the finery that filled those homes (59). Jaramillo's autobiographical characterization of herself resembles any spoiled socialite character that Edith Wharton drew. For example, during the stress of Jaramillo's wedding planning, her husband-to-be asks her what is wrong: "'Nothing, but I want my own home,' I said, and burst out crying. 'You shall have it,'

Ven answered soothingly" (89). The home she and Ven built could also be straight out of Wharton and evokes Thorstein Veblen's theory of conspicuous consumption:

> My eight rooms finished, Ven thought of adding a second story. Seeing him so determined, I resigned myself to his wishes and showed the builder a picture I had of a house built with a balcony running all around the second story. Four bedrooms and a flower room were added upstairs, opening onto this balcony. That left the large reception hall in the center opened to the ceiling of the second story, in the style of some of the hotel lobbies I had seen. (90)

One might read consumerism and conspicuous consumption in descriptions of her travels to Chicago, New York, and Washington, DC (where she attended President William McKinley's inauguration), as well as in her southern tour to Mexico. One could also read consumerism and modernity in the fact that her winter home in Santa Fe "had all the conveniences that save time and work" (123). Jaramillo seems aware of the duality of her position—that she pined for simpler times even as she enjoyed modern conveniences—for she holds her "progressive husband" responsible for wanting the bigger house (90) and for their reliance on and enjoyment of something so modern as an automobile (122).

Jaramillo need not apologize for choosing which elements of tradition and modernity she will or will not keep and use in her personal life. Most cultural anthropologists and cultural historians would argue that all of us make such choices every day, as did our ancestors before us. Gayatri Chakravorty Spivak writes about "worlding" to indicate that everyone is worlded, that the colonized participate in the contemporary international world as much as the colonizers, even though the colonizers try to define the contemporary as if it consisted only of *their* contemporary. Jaramillo writes that the people of her world are "still untouched by modern progress" (35), showing that, on one hand, she buys into the colonialist, nostalgic romanticization of the subaltern past even as, on the other hand, she distances herself from her indigenous heritage. What Jaramillo sees as duality, then, is in fact syncretism; she rewrites modernity in ways that claim space for a particularly feminine, Spanish

American modernity. Similarly, Reed argues that Fabiola Cabeza de Baca's life and work show her to be a "living agent" of Elsie Clews Parsons's theory of "cultural borrowing": cultures must *not* either "stay the same or die out: they are always undergoing processes of change, borrowing from other cultures especially when doing so will help to strengthen cultural identity" (64). We see such cultural borrowing in the work of all five Mexican American writers featured in this chapter. And of the three New Mexican women writers, perhaps the life and writings of Fabiola Cabeza de Baca best portray the complicated and conflicted ways that Mexican American women responded to Anglo women and their domesticity.

In her memoir, *We Fed Them Cactus* (1954), Cabeza de Baca writes that she learned how to cook while she lived with white homesteaders as the local schoolteacher; "If today I can fry chicken, make sour milk biscuits and cornbread, I owe it to the friends of my youth on the Llano," and "with all my home economics training, I could not compete with them" (151). We might trace the centrality of domesticity in *The Good Life: New Mexico Traditions and Food* (1949), her book of New Mexican customs and recipes, to the ideals of the country life movement and other programs of the federal Cooperative Extension Service. By 1914 the CES had reached New Mexico and established the country life movement, a rural component of Progressive Era reform programs. At their heart, the country life movement and the CES had goals of reinvigorating the farming way of life, encouraging farm families to stay put and city families to return to farming. Joan M. Jensen and Darlis A. Miller write about Cabeza de Baca's role as a home demonstration agent for the federal CES in New Mexico beginning in 1929; she was the first Spanish-speaking woman to hold this position, and she held it for ten years. Jensen and Miller note that the leading participants in these movements were "primarily white Protestant professional groups dedicated to an orderly transition to industrial capitalism" (201–2). "Country lifers" used domestic reforms to train farmworkers—both men in the fields and women in the homes—to work more efficiently. As part of this program, the federal government sent demonstration agents to rural-area homes to perform, as their title implies, demonstrations on how to better implement domesticity: cooking, sewing, canning, cleaning, child-rearing and so on. Jensen and Miller assert that the program of teaching women on reservations in New Mexico to can food, for instance, was "part of the national program to replace traditional skills of the Indian woman with skills that would make them more dependent upon the Euro-American culture and occupy the place women were assigned in that culture" (205).

With her writings, Cabeza de Baca directly responds to these federal efforts to replace traditional Indian skills with modern Anglo ones. Goldman writes that, in the work of Jaramillo and Cabeza de Baca, "home economics . . . serves as a suitable genteel forum for theorizing about the social and political economy" ("I yam" 16). This is certainly true, and I would frame Goldman's abstraction about social and political theory as a more concrete dialogue with physical, fleshed-out speakers: Cabeza de Baca is speaking back to the Anglo women of the country life movement and the Cooperative Extension Service who taught her what she knew about being a home economist with a voice that at once hearkens back to an idealized past and looks forward to a future where traditional Spanish New Mexican lifeways are included in the future of a progressive America. Suzanne Forrest writes about the country life movement in New Mexico and the "Janus-faced model for the future of American society" (36) that it represented—a model that both looked "backward to a largely mythical arcadia, and forward to an industrialized world increasingly concerned with efficient business practice and monetary gain" (41).

Cabeza de Baca's writings might also be characterized as Janus-faced, and the mechanism that allows her to look backward and forward at the same time is the rhetoric and practices of domesticity. And while Chicana studies scholars such as Rebolledo and María Camino Bueno-Alastuey read her work as an act of resistance to the cultural domination of Anglo hegemony, I argue that her writing evinces a syncretism that combines tradition with modernity, Spanish (and Mexican and Indian) with Anglo. Indeed, as Reed argues, "like their female counterparts in the Progressive movement at large, New Mexican women involved in this early and mid-twentieth century movement for Hispanic equality found an opportunity to bring the strength of traditional female roles as nurturers into the wider realm of the public sphere" (122). In the preface to *The Good Life*, Cabeza de Baca writes that the recipes in the book "have been a part of the lives of Hispanic New Mexicans since the Spanish colonization of New Mexico" and that they were taught to her by her paternal grandmother, who helped her father raise her and her three siblings after their mother died when she was four years old. Raised on the family ranch "by my grandmother's side in her home at La Liendre and outdoors by my father's side," Cabeza de Baca says this early apprenticeship began her knowledge of "the good life" (v). Establishing this maternal heritage validates Cabeza de Baca's qualifications as a home economist; working among both Hispanic New Mexicans and Anglo settlers, she seems aware that she is moving in and through a culture of domesticity generated and tended by women.

After having rehearsed her own biographical information, Cabeza de Baca comments briefly on the good life in the rest of the preface. "Life as I grew up and as I knew it as a home economist was rich but simple," she writes, and "people drew their sustenance from the soil and from the spirit. Life was good, but not always easy" (v). The fictional Turrieta family, whose annual family life cycle Cabeza de Baca records in the handbook portion of this book, "could have been any Hispanic family in a New Mexico village during my work as a home economist. The same pattern of life is followed today in many isolated New Mexico villages" (vi). The recipes in the book describe foods she ate in her grandmother's home and that were prepared with the women whose homes she visited during her work. Cabeza de Baca notes that she has altered the recipes "from 'un poquito de . . . y un poquito de . . . ' [a little of this and a little of that] to more workable measures. Otherwise, they are the same as those used by our Spanish forebears and those adopted from their Indian friends" (vi). In the preface, Cabeza de Baca identifies—both directly and indirectly—the various peoples who influenced the formation of New Mexican village culture as she finds it during her upbringing and her three decades as a home economist. Using food and recipes as her exemplary cultural artifact, she acknowledges the dual influences of both Spanish and Indian culture on the foods of New Mexican culture, which she offers as the stable or primary culture. She also identifies Anglo culture as having influenced both her own life and the lives of the Hispanic New Mexicans among whom she worked.

Cabeza de Baca's perception and promotion of herself as a "home economist/nutritionist" and her references to the "kitchen laboratory of my own home" (vi) internalizes the Anglo tenets of domestic science that came out of the East Coast–based Progressive movement and migrated west with the country life movement. Her compulsion to record the recipes in *The Good Life* with "more workable measures" instead of the "a little of this and a little of that" measures of one who has prepared the recipes habitually also nods to the efforts of these movements to make household chores more systematic and scientific. Cabeza de Baca's description of the fictional Turrieta family's pattern of life as exemplary of a family that might still live "today in many *isolated* New Mexico villages" (vi, italics added) betrays her belief, as conflicted as it may be, that contact with Anglos has changed traditional New Mexican life forever.

If contact with Anglos changes traditional life, then, following Cabeza de Baca's logic, New Mexicans can best keep tradition and custom in isolation from Anglo culture. Ina Sizer Cassidy, who wrote the introduction to *The Good Life*, continues with this idea of isolation and contact: "The family around which this book is written is an old family, living in a isolated village, carrying on the traditions of the early Spanish colonizers, living the life as it was in those days among the early New Mexicans of Spanish and Indian extraction. In a straightforward and entertaining manner THE GOOD LIFE brings the fascinating life of the Conquistadores from the dim past into the every day light of now" (3). So if contact with Anglos brings change and modernity, and isolation from Anglos allows for continuation of custom, then writing about the past in a book such as *The Good Life* crafts a contemporary space to preserve the "dim past" using the modern methods of the "every day light of now" (3). Even though this dim past is more likely a nostalgic and falsely stabilizing fantasy, Cabeza de Baca was apparently thinking about such contrasts between past and present, tradition and modernity, isolation and contact. Cassidy quotes her as saying, "As a home economist I am happy to see modern kitchens and improved diets, but my artistic soul deplores the passing of beautiful customs which in spite of New Mexico's isolation in the past, gave us happiness and abundant living" (4). But there is some contradiction between the ways Cabeza de Baca characterizes her happiness as a modern home economist and the "happiness and abundant living" that has been lost with the passing of New Mexico's customs. And by deeming her nostalgia for this lost past "artistic," she echoes the sentiments of Anglo women artists such as Mary Austin or Mabel Dodge Luhan, who moved to New Mexico to recover this kind of traditional, pure way of living that can never be recovered if contact with Anglos (or removal from isolation) is what finally relegated it to the past. But just like Jaramillo's writings, Cabeza de Baca's life and writings exemplify the syncretism that valorizes tradition *and* embraces modernity, despite sentimental reveries of days gone by.

Cassidy translates the Euro-American concept of the "housewife" not only into traditional New Mexican culture but also back to a pre-Spanish, pre-Anglo, precontact past that incorporates this modern female role into the ancient mythology of the New Mexican people. "Who knows," she wonders, "whether the crudely drawn circles so commonly found on our cliffs, styled by the archaeologists as the 'sun symbol,' might not in truth be a picture of one of the first *tortillas* patted out by the brown hands of one of our early Basket Maker housewives? Who is there to say?" (1). This concept of "housewife" is surely something that Anglos taught Hispanic women during the country life movement. But housewife, as traditionally defined in more urban, upper-class settings, was not a role that a southwestern farmer's wife could perform if she was to help keep the family farm going. Jensen and Miller write,

> Agents assumed a woman's place was in the home being a skilled, efficient homemaker. In doing so, however, agents provided a model of work for girls and women that was not functional for poor women and farm families if they were to survive on the land. In providing this model of "domesticity," agents undermined the very goal they had of keeping families on the farm. Farm women could not both meet the needs of survival and the ideals for women of the Country Life Movement. (220)

But by making this fantasy housewife a basket maker and tortilla patter who has brown hands, Cassidy, along with Cabeza de Baca, argues for the inclusion of Mexican American women in the modern rhetoric of progressive womanhood.

Readers soon realize that the Turietta family is not as isolated from Anglo contact as Cabeza de Baca and Cassidy make it seem in their introductory remarks. The central housewife in *The Good Life* is Doña Paula, the matriarch of the Turietta family. Cabeza de Baca describes in great detail the cyclical events and traditional celebrations that the Turietta family enacts in a given year. In chapters entitled "Autumn Harvest," "Winter's Plenty," "Christmas Festivities," "The Wedding," "Lent," and "The Wake," the Turietta family, led by Doña Paula, dries peppers, makes cheese, picks piñons, turns sugarcane into molasses, butchers hogs, and prepares feasts for Christmas, a wedding, and a funeral. In the last chapter, "The Cookbook," Cabeza de Baca includes recipes that are

"New Mexican in character; an amalgamation of the different influences which have been evident in the state since and before the Spanish conquest" (45). While the chapters preceding the cookbook highlight traditional customs, the customs she describes are, like the cookbook, still more of a "bi-cultural composite composition" (Krupat, *For Those* 31) than a pure preservation of life before contact with Anglos. In a few telling incidents, Doña Paula's actions betray how their family has indeed come in contact with Anglos. In chapter 5, "The Wedding," Doña Paula's son, José, gives his fiancée, Panchita, a diamond ring to seal their engagement, although "his mother would like to have given her the *memoria*, the intertwined puzzle ring which Don Teodoro presented her at her betrothal but it was old-fashioned and her children were of another age and generation" (32). And when Tilano, the Turiettas' goatherd, follows tradition and celebrates the engagement by firing gunshots into the air, José tries to stop him and complains, "Mother, we are living in the modern age. What will the neighbors think of us?" (31). These "neighbors" José worries about could very likely be Anglo-Americans, who would not be used to such displays, yet even the tradition of firing celebratory gunshots has to be a postconquest custom. The fact that José gives a diamond ring instead of a puzzle ring also suggests that the Turiettas have met Anglos; giving diamonds as engagement rings grew more widespread after 1888, when the DeBeers family discovered diamond mines in South Africa, and this custom had spread from Europe to America by at least 1938, when the N. W. Ayer & Son advertising company made a deal with DeBeers to market the trend in the United States (B. Kaplan). This squares with the time period Cabeza de Baca uses for the setting of *The Good Life* and shows that Anglo/European modernity had indeed found its way into this isolated New Mexican village.

In chapter 2, "The Herb Woman," modern domesticity also sneaks into a section of the narrative that most celebrates traditional New Mexican customs. The titular herb woman, or *curandera*, is Señá Martina, the village's medicine woman. In a conversation with her about cooking herbal remedies, Doña Paula plays the role similar to José's in chapter 5 when Señá Martina tells her, "You young people believe too much in doctors and you have no faith in plants" (14). After a discussion of whether modern doctors and dentists know better than curanderas how to treat diseases like diphtheria and gingivitis, Doña Paula tells Señá Martina, "We have to keep up with the times," to which Señá Martina replies,

"Not with the times, Doña Paula, with your neighbors, or they will laugh at you. They have laughed at me, but I am too old to care so I laugh at them too'" (16). This passage not only dramatizes the typical and mutual suspicion between practitioners of modern medicine and herbal remedies, it provides another suggestion that the Turiettas may well have Anglo neighbors—neighbors who would laugh at the idea that plants can heal disease better than medicine can. Another reference to neighbors in *The Good Life* actually comes earlier in the narrative and is the most compelling indication that, despite Cabeza de Baca's and Cassidy's romance of isolation, Anglo modernity had already reached this New Mexico village. This reference to neighbors takes up the paired subthemes of domesticity that run through all the writings of these five writers: responses to Anglo versions of religion and education.

The Five Rs: Reading, 'Riting, 'Rithmetic, Religion, and Resistance

In this chapter, we have seen how Mexican American writers negotiate Anglo-American domesticity. In this section, I show how Ruiz de Burton, González, Otero-Warren, Jaramillo, and Cabeza de Baca negotiate the anti-Catholic religious and educational efforts of Anglo women. I conflate religion and education because history and literature already conflates them, as can be seen in the following examples. And although, for the sake of clarity, I separate religious and educational activities from my broader discussion of domesticity, they both operate as crucial modes of influence within the discourses and activities of feminine domesticity. Some of these writers describe their own religious customs and educational experiences in detail, as do Otero-Warren, Jaramillo, and Cabeza de Baca. Some stage conflicts between Catholic and Protestant female characters, as does Ruiz de Burton. Some, like González, argue that Mexican Americans must participate in the American educational system so as to have the knowledge to both engage and subvert hegemonic culture. Though Audre Lorde has argued that using the master's tools to dismantle his house of oppression never brings true freedom, all five of these women engage the closely entwined rhetorics of education and religion for just such purposes. They write to correct Anglo assumptions that Hispanic culture is a religious and educational tabula rasa; to resist the encroachment of Anglo Protestantism as yet another colonizing force; and to claim for Mexican American women the religious and educational authority that Anglo women attained as both true women/republican mothers and new women/progressive reformers. That is, even while these writers resist the domination of Anglo culture (domesticity, religion, education), they assimilate these aspects of culture *as platforms* on which to stage their own assertions of culture and claims to female authority in the public, national sphere.

Before turning to Cabeza de Baca's third reference to neighbors in *The Good Life*, I present a passage from McLean and Williams's *Old Spain in New America* to show an example of common Anglo modes of religious and educational colonialism against which these five Mexican American writers push back. In addition to their assumptions about Mexican American homes, McLean and Williams argue that the "marked difference between Saxon and Latin America cannot be due wholly to climate or to race" but rather to a "fundamental lack in their [religious] system. . . . It seems legitimate to ask whether the form of Christianity introduced long ago has not proved itself inadequate to create a civilization that would develop the best qualities of those who accepted it" (xiii). McLean and Williams respectfully acknowledge and commend the work of the early Roman Catholic missionaries who arrived with the first Spanish explorers but point to their supposedly

> fatal error of adapting Christian worship to the beliefs and practices of pagan tribes. Instead of Christianizing paganism, they allowed their Christianity to become paganized. In the place of patiently teaching right thinking and right living to the Indians, the more expeditious method was adopted of having the converts conform mechanically to a system differing slightly from that they had always practiced. (xiii)

McLean and Williams then fall back on the conservative-nationalist rhetoric that still echoes through right-wing evangelical-political speeches of the twenty-first century by asserting that "the Protestant founders of this nation brought with them high ideals and a true knowledge of spiritual things" (xiv). Further, they assert that "the mission of the Protestant Church is not to destroy the Roman Catholic Church, but to bring it into cooperation with all Christian forces on the one foundation Christ Jesus" (xiv). With the goal, then, of taking advantage of the "wonderful opportunities" that are offered by the mission field of "Spanish-Americans" (xiv) who are out there waiting to be converted, these Protestant missionaries trained workers and reported on the progress of the churches' work in four major branches: evangelistic, educational, medical, and social.

Of these four branches of mission efforts, white women were certainly involved with the educational and social (including domesticity) work among the Mexicans of the southwestern states. Peggy Pascoe historicizes the ways that white Protestant women were active in efforts to assimilate Other women such as Chinese Americans, Mormons, American Indians, and even unwed mothers. These "home mission women . . . interpreted the 'home' as the ideal Christian home of Victorian rhetoric," so that by the end of the nineteenth century, "Protestant evangelical women engaged in 'woman's work for woman' all over the country" (6). By instituting and running home missions in western cities with large non-Anglo populations, these women strove for public power by enforcing the private morals of Victorian domesticity on the women whom they Othered. Sarah Deutsch, writing more specifically than Pascoe about Mexican American/Anglo-American encounters, notes that "by 1900, churches in the United States had come to think of mission fields as frontiers of Christian civilization and missionaries as a vanguard. Anglo Protestants spoke in one breath of Americanizing and 'Christianizing' New Mexico, of conquering this frontier" (63). In fact, between 1900 and 1914, more than two hundred mission women came to New Mexico and southern Colorado (64), women who were "firmly rooted in America's Victorian ideology of domesticity" (72) and who, in their work in New Mexican communities, "determined to take over the direction of the entire village and to reshape it, in a brand of miniature empire building. If male empire builders evinced paternalism, then this was maternalism" (73). Deutsch also notes that another outcome of reform work was that "the Presbyterian education produced an elite corps of Hispanics who succeeded in the Anglo context, but at a price. . . . [T]he new religion could distance its adherents from old neighbors as well as old customs" (28).

In *The Good Life*, Cabeza de Baca dramatizes this potential for drift between neighbors when contact with Anglo Protestants threatens the customs of the Turietta family. Though she says in the preface that the Turiettas are like any family she worked with as a home economist and, like any family that might still live in isolation from Anglos, Anglos have indeed made contact in El Alamo, New Mexico, the village the Turiettas live near. Cabeza de Baca indirectly refers to Anglo evangelists in the opening scenes of the book. It is harvest time, and Doña Refugio Garcia and her family, as well as Doña Petra and Don José and their two sons, have come to the Turietta household to help Doña Paula and Don Teodoro string red peppers into *ristras* to dry in the sun. Tilano, the Turietta family's goatherd and storyteller, has recently returned from town and wants to share the latest gossip. He initiates a discussion on the religious controversy of the day by asking the family,

> "What is happening in the village, are we all going to join the *Aleluyas*?"
>
> Doña Refugio without raising her head and tying chile pods as fast as her fingers could move answered,
>
> "Do you think we have all lost our minds? Don't you know that we already have a religion?"
>
> Doña Paula joined in saying, "We have a good religion we do not need to seek another. Our faith has guided us through many bad years. God has seen that we do not want."
>
> "Yes," chimed in Don Teodoro. . . . "Has God not been good to us? Why should we forsake the teachings of the church which has guided us through the years?"
>
> Tilano with bowed head replied, "The *Aleluyas* say that there is no future in being a Roman Catholic and they told me if I joined them I would not have to herd goats for you for such low wages, Don Teodoro."
>
> "What do they offer you in place of herding goats, Tilano?" asked Don Teodoro. "They didn't say, but I think I shall try the *Aleluyas.* I like their singing with the guitar accompaniment and I could play for them."
>
> "Why don't you play the guitar for us Tilano," said Doña Paula. "Go into the *sala,* the living room, the guitar is hanging in there."
>
> Tilano did not need coaxing. No sooner had Doña Paula spoken than Tilano was playing familiar strains. Some of the young folks joined in by singing which made Tilano so happy that he forgot all about the *Aleluyas.* (6–7)

Roberto R. Treviño (74) and Marta Weigle (99) define the Aleluyas as Mexican Americans who have converted to Protestantism. In the online community newspaper *El Defensor Chieftain,* Richard Melzer and Francisco Sisneros write about nineteenth-century La Joya, New Mexico, and its religious culture, also discussing the cultural context of the Aleluyas:

> Other residents of La Joya became divided on issues of religion. Thomas Harwood, an active Methodist missionary in the Rio Abajo, had established a Methodist church in Socorro in 1871. Starting with eight adults and two young girls, the church gradually grew to include members of extended families in several surrounding communities. While a majority of the families in La Joya remained Catholic, some joined the Methodist faith. But there is little evidence of friction between Methodist families and their Catholic neighbors, as had occurred in other towns in New Mexico. In Peralta, for example, Father Jean B. Ralliere was said to ring his church bells to drown out Sunday sermons delivered by Methodist missionaries preaching in their nearby church. Farther north, Bishop Jean B. Lamy [the model for Willa Cather's archbishop] told Catholics in Santa Fe that they would suffer excommunication if they even looked at a Methodist missionary who had arrived to preach in the territorial capital. Some families later joined the Pentecostal Church. Locally called the "aleluyas," these people were best known for the loud gospel music they often played outdoors.

Defining and contextualizing the term *Aleluyas* confirms that, despite Cabeza de Baca's nostalgic fantasy about an isolated New Mexican village, the Turietta family and their neighbors have indeed made contact with the Anglo Protestants. Further, including this exchange about the Aleluyas in her folkloric vignettes shows not only her anxiety or sadness about changes in custom but also her speaking back to the Anglo Protestant women who assume that the Mexican American family is without a religious or moral center: "We have a good religion we do not need to seek another," Doña Paula argues.

Indeed, we can read this same assertion in the folkloric memoirs and autobiographies of all three New Mexican writers. As we have seen, in *The Good Life,* Cabeza de Baca takes readers through a year of festivities closely tied with the Catholic calendar. Jaramillo and Otero-Warren structure their books in similar ways. Otero-Warren includes several Catholic-themed folksongs and stories, as well as three chapters specifically dedicated to religious customs: "Old Churches in New Spain," "Saints' Days and Feasts," and "Holy Week Processional." She conflates domesticity and religiosity in the first full chapter, "An Old Spanish Hacienda," and describes in great detail the architectural situation of the chapel within the walls of the hacienda and the women's work as they prepare for the mission priest's arrival (10–11). Otero-Warren also touches on the issue of corrupted Aleluya neighbors: when the priest performed mass at the hacienda, "it was always noticed if a neighbor did not come and he was considered a savage who did not know the Catholic belief or else did not abide by his Christian teaching" (12). In her description of a christening service she suggests that raising a child in the Catholic tradition was first and foremost the responsibility of the women. After the priest baptizes the child, he hands the child to his godmother, who recites a verse of dedication and then hands "the new little Christian to his mother," who takes the child and responds by reciting another verse committing the child to Christ and the Catholic Church (18). Otero-Warren does not mention men, except for the priest, in this transaction. Christian education, she implicitly argues, is mainly the province of Mexican American mothers, an argument which directly contradicts McLean and Williams's assertion that the "Spanish-American" "home has seldom been a sacred place, and family relations have not been held sacred" (138). Home is indeed a sacred place, both literally and figuratively: the chapel is inside of the home, and, as both Cabeza de Baca and Otero-Warren assert, Mexican American mothers take it as their sacred duty to instruct their families in the Catholic tradition.

Jaramillo also stresses this conflation of domesticity, religion, and education. *Shadows of the Past*, like *The Good Life*, takes as part of its structure the calendar year of the Catholic Church, with chapter titles like "La Funcion (Feast Day)," "Holy Week at Arroyo Hondo," and "Noche Buena and Religious Dramas." In the chapter "The Penitente Brotherhood," Jaramillo defends the controversial religious sect against Anglo writers who misrepresent their practices: "due credit is given to the English writers who come to New Mexico and write such interesting books from second-hand information, but I wish here to contradict some of their statements. One author starts his article on the *penitentes*: 'Are they lunatics or murderers?' They are neither. The members that live according to the brotherhood's rules are the best, most sincere religious people" (64). Here we read the same tart tone Jaramillo takes when she responds to DeHuff's misinformed recipes for Mexican dishes—she sarcastically punches holes in the credibility of Anglo writers who claim authority on a custom they have not practiced by using sources who are not practitioners. She ends this discussion of the penitentes by saying that the Catholic Church "has condemned this order for years," excommunicated the most extreme members, and predicted an end to the order in just a few years' time (65), which shows that her motive for discussing the order is really not to defend their practices at all but rather to take advantage of the chance to point out another way that Anglos are wrong about Mexican American cultural practices and to claim the authority to speak to such things for herself. In *Romance of a Little Village Girl*, Jaramillo also takes pains to show Anglos that Mexican American women are serious about making home a sacred place: "In our hidden nook, isolated from the outside world and still untouched by modern progress, people were content to live their simple lives. Religion was the most important to them" (35); "like all the Spanish ladies in her time, my aunt was very faithful in attending the church services every day, sometimes getting there so early, the church was not open" (51); and "religious tradition ruled" in Grandma Melita's home (95).

Elizabeth Jacobs notes how Cabeza de Baca's female characters in *We Fed Them Cactus*—and, I would add, *The Good Life*—perform feminized rituals and espouse feminized values to transmit culture in their households (5). Working through Ann Laura Stoler's theory of the intimacies of empire, Jacobs argues that the female characters in Jaramillo's and Cabeza de Baca's memoirs "represented and projected the most effective form of colonialism. . . . That their daily habits, including household and social etiquette as well as religion, can be translated in this context as the conscious and planned reproduction of fundamental colonial values" (5). Jacobs further argues that in Cabeza de Baca's writings women had "to sustain religious orthodoxy" when priests and churches were not on the llano and that "in supporting the church and orthodoxy in these ways, Cabeza de Baca and other women of the *hacienda* elite played an active role in colonization, particularly during the social ruptures that unsettled the community's economic, religious, and cultural context" (6, 60). Jacobs speaks here to the complicated position these and other Mexican American women inhabited as products of Spanish colonialism and patriarchy who, by perpetuating Spanish colonial religious and domestic customs, actually reinforce this earlier brand of colonial (Spanish) dominance. While these writers reinforced Spanish patriarchal colonialism with their assertions of culture and subjugated the other peoples of the Southwest they viewed as beneath them—namely, Mexicans and Indians—I argue that these assertions also signify complicated maneuvers to resist being colonized yet again by a new force: Anglo Protestantism.

If the New Mexico writers used their autobiographical folklore to insist that Mexican American mothers do indeed play a central role in making home a sacred place, then Ruiz de Burton can be said to explore what happens to a Mexican American girl when she is removed from the nurturing Catholic influence of her mother's home and displaced to the hostile Protestant environment of a white woman's home. In *The Squatter and the Don*, Mrs. Darrell cares about Doña Joséfa and the other Californios because she herself was raised Catholic, only becoming Protestant at her marriage to Mr. Darrell. David Luis-Brown argues that "the narration implicitly compares the restraint, manners and Catholicism of Mary [Darrell] and the white South she represents to similar qualities in Don Maríano, . . . contrasting these traits with the Protestant, violent temper of William [Darrell] and the northeast" (60). In this way, Mrs. Darrell has a colonial, patriarchal experience in common with the Californios: her marriage conversion echoes the ideological colonialism that characterized westward expansion. She actually *is* Catholic by tradition, and her coerced Protestantism is actually a marker of her oppression and a link between her and the oppressed Californios. Similarly, if from the opposite angle, McCullough argues that "Catholicism here becomes the site of another link between the Dons and the Anglos and a link specifically forged and embodied by Doña Joséfa and Mary Darrell. For the Californio and Anglo women share not just a common religion but also a common maternal function: the transmission of this religion to their children" (175). But before drawing Mrs. Darrell, Ruiz de Burton drew Mrs. Norval in *Who Would Have Thought It?*, a character whose Protestantism does not make her an ally with the colonized but instead makes her the epitome of colonial racism and capitalist greed.

In this earlier novel, Ruiz de Burton sets the theme of Catholicism versus Protestantism on the very first page, when the two reverends are discussing the plight of the Californios. But she zeroes in on the twin issues of religious education and a parent's right to choose that education in chapter 4, where Mrs. Norval, a staunch Presbyterian, asserts that "her duty as a Christian woman" is to raise Lola to "learn to work and earn her living" and "go to our Sunday school" (23). The doctor insists Lola be educated with the Catholic catechism, as her own mother requested, which appalls Mrs. Norval. She asks caustically, "and pray who is to teach her that abominable idolatry here? And who is to pay for her magnificent education?" (24), questions that insinuate that the payer for and provider of education has the right to choose a pupil's curriculum, regardless of parental concerns or wishes. Ruiz de Burton returns to this conversation between Dr. and Mrs. Norval again in chapter 15, contrasting the wishes of Mrs. Norval and Lola's mother for Lola's education:

> "Unless you yourself think that the idolatry of the popish rites is religion, I don't see how you can conscientiously send the girl to be brought up to believe in such mummeries," said the lady.
>
> "That is not the point. [Lola's] mother did not leave it to my conscience to choose the child's religion. I shall be abusing her confidence if I force upon her child other than the faith she designated. If you had died, leaving your children young among Catholics, would it not be your last and most earnest injunction before dying that your children should be brought up Protestant?"
>
> "Of course I would, but my religion is a rational one, not an absurd belief in images, and saints, and relics, and holy water."
>
> "I am not defending the Catholic image itself. . . . What I am holding is, *the right to choose our religion*—the freedom which Mr. Hackwell lauded the Pilgrims for defending. Parents choose it for their children. . . ."
>
> "The point is this, you say that parents ought to choose religious faith for their children. You occupy the place of Lola's parents; you ought to choose her religion."
>
> "That would be a better argument if the child's own mother had not most positively chosen it herself." (66)

Even though *Who Would Have Thought It?* was published in 1872, decades before McLean and Williams published *Old Spain in New America*, this passage can be read as a direct response to the rhetoric of a text like that of McLean and Williams. Historically speaking, this reading is not a stretch; since Presbyterian missionaries were working in the Southwest as early as 1850 (McLean and Williams 39), Ruiz de Burton had no doubt encountered their opinions about Catholicism, even though she would not have read their publications before writing *Who Would Have Thought It?*. Of course, anti-Catholic sentiment in the United States did not require missionaries; some non-missionary Protestants could say the same things. In this passage, Mrs. Norval represents the myopia of the early Presbyterian missionaries and Protestant Americans who only saw meaningless paganism in Catholic rituals (McLean and Williams xiii). Dr. Norval's insistence that every American has the constitutional right to choose his/her own religion might be a direct response to Protestant rhetoric about the religion of the "founding fathers" being the only true pathway to spirituality (McLean and Williams xiv). Further, this conversation about parents' roles in their children's education engages the history of Catholic and Protestant mission schools in the American West and federal programs, such as those concerning education out of the Office of Indian Affairs, that removed indigenous children from their homes and families and took them miles away—if not across the continent—to boarding schools where they could be educated, Protestantized, and Americanized. In this way, Ruiz de Burton anticipates the work of Jane E. Simonsen, who writes about field matrons; Peggy Pascoe, who studies white women's searches for moral authority; Margaret D. Jacobs, who sees maternal colonialism in the historical phenomenon of child removal; and other historians, who argue that white women wield like colonial weapons the discourses of domesticity, religion, and education when they meddle with indigenous family life and choices about indigenous children's futures.

As seen in this example from Ruiz de Burton's novel, Anglo reformers fuse religious rhetoric and educational aims between the mid-nineteenth century and the mid-twentieth century, if only for the historical reason that federal and church expansion programs often combined the two. Besides the references to religious education, Jaramillo, Cabeza de Baca, and Otero-Warren also concern themselves more singularly with education. Jaramillo writes in *Romance* of her own education in Catholic day schools and boarding schools, arguing for a Spanish colonial history of educational endeavors that predates colonial Anglo history; to this end, she claims that her ancestors as far back as the conquistadors were interested in educating the young—particularly in the fine arts—and that one of her distant cousins was actually the first public schoolteacher at Taos, New Mexico (5). She says that the sisters at her convent school quenched her "great thirst for learning" (31) and that the explorer Juan de Oñate "started a culture of religion, arts, and science in New Spain, even before the Atlantic seaboard was settled" (49). In contrast to her usual harsh criticisms of Anglo representations of Spanish American or New Mexican customs, she praises Cather's *Death Comes for the Archbishop* for its characterization of Bishop Lamy as "an authentic picture of his noble, energetic life" (28). Jaramillo notes that this "smart vicar saw at once how sadly neglected education had been and set to work to remedy it" (28).

Otero-Warren dedicates a chapter of her book to education: "Early Schooling in New Mexico." She writes that the Franciscans who first came to New Mexico were not satisfied with the vast practical knowledge of the Indians they found, for "their desire was to educate the Indian in the Christian faith" (104). She writes that in 1781, "when the Spaniards finally settled peaceably as neighbors with the Indians, it became necessary to instruct the Spanish, as well as the Indian youth" (105), and by 1822, when Santa Fe was under control of Mexico, local government organized the first public schools (106). Otero-Warren writes of a practical education for boys, who were taught methods of farming and carpentry, and for girls, housekeeping. "An education was a living thing," she writes. "It was knowing how to live and how to produce a living by one's own efforts" (106). In her description of this early curriculum, which sounds similar to those of the federal boarding schools for Indian children, Otero-Warren asserts that Mexican Americans already have a practical, domestic educational program in place and do not need the intervention of Anglo missionaries and social workers to teach them "right living." Of course, what Otero-Warren writes in her folkloric memoir reflects her own work as a federal agent for education. As I have noted, she worked for the WPA's adult literacy programs in New Mexico and Puerto Rico (Massmann 891). So even while she asserts in her writing that Mexican Americans do not need Anglos to intervene and educate their youth, she herself is participating in federal programs developed by Anglos and designed for Spanish speakers. Further, Otero-Warren performs at least one kind of maternalism Anglo women enacted upon both Indians and Mexican Americans: teaching indigenous mothers modern habits of hygiene and childcare, as if Native women were ignorant of such matters (Massmann 892).

Duality—or syncretism—also characterizes Cabeza de Baca's written references to education and her own experiences as both a student and an educator. For example, she was educated in Anglo schools populated by students, faculty, and administrators of various racial and ethnic backgrounds that were no doubt started by white Americans as part of federal programs. She graduated from New Mexico Normal/New Mexico Highlands University and New Mexico College of Agriculture and Mechanic Arts/New Mexico State University. She studied home economics, a role that was part of the Cooperative Extension Service and the country life movement—programs conceived primarily by white Protestant capitalists who wanted to Americanize and industrialize the rural, mostly Spanish-speaking inhabitants of the American Southwest (Forrest; Jensen and Miller). Yet for all her involvement in federal education programs, both as student and teacher, nostalgia still characterizes Cabeza de Baca's writings: longing for a past where New Mexican communities were self-sufficient in matters of domesticity, education, and religion.

Of all five writers discussed in this chapter, Jovita González's writings might express the most concern with Mexican American participation in the American educational system. Perhaps the centrality of education springs from her own life experiences, as she was the first Hispanic woman to graduate with a master's degree from the University of Texas, and, as Limón points out, one of the first Hispanic academic scholars in the field of folklore. For González, education can accomplish three tasks for Mexican Americans: it can be a site of resistance to patriarchy, it can be a site of resistance to Anglo values, and it can be an opportunity to collaborate with Anglos—particularly Anglo women—against various forms of cultural subjugation.

In *Dew on the Thorn*, as we have seen, Lucita wants to go to college instead of marry and play the traditional role of wife and mother expected of her under Mexican patriarchal custom. While Lucita's resistance meets crushing opposition, education remains a domain of hope where women can escape patriarchy. González's own life exemplifies the potential freedoms education offers, as her education and training allowed her a profession as a teacher (even if she was still bound by the patriarchal standards of her day). Aside from her own life story, though,

González constructs another textual space where education and, particularly, writing, offer freedom from patriarchy and the opportunity to pursue such freedom with the collaboration of Anglo women. In "Shades of the Tenth Muses," apparently her only non-folkloric story (Reyna 108), González characterizes a Tejana writer who is visited, or perhaps haunted, by the ghostly figures of Sor Juana Inés de la Cruz and Anne Bradstreet. Known as the "Tenth Muse" in their communities of New Spain and New England, both writers act as companion muses to the writer who, in a Virginia Woolf–type "room of her own," writes in her garage to elide her "family's efforts to have me work in the house" (108). Cotéra argues that the muses' discussion implies a "shared epistemological orientation that traverses the boundaries of the nation-state and gestures towards a transnational feminist imaginary, potentially rewriting the foundational narratives of both Mexico and the United States" (2–3). That de la Cruz, Bradstreet, and González are able to write only when their "duties permit" ("Shades" 110) speaks to the patriarchal culture all three live in, but it also suggests that such collaborations among women of different ethnic or racial backgrounds share a resistance to patriarchy.

Finally, González also argues for using education as a space where assimilation is necessary to resist Anglo hegemony. In "America Invades the Border Towns," she argues for the kind of assimilation-as-resistance strategy that Lorde criticizes in her famous statement about the "master's tools":

> There is a group of advanced progressive Texas-Mexicans who, realizing that their future depends upon their getting an American education, are sending their sons and daughters to American colleges and universities. And when those girls are among typical American college girls they are not going to sit in their rooms and uphold family traditions. When in Rome they will do as the Romans do. All of these girls are in the process of receiving their education. What their reaction will be when they go back home after four or five years of complete freedom is yet to be seen. Many of the boys are studying the professions: law, medicine, pharmacy, engineering. When this crop of American-educated young men returns to their respective towns, will they submit to the racial distinctions in the border towns? That also is a future problem. (477)

González dramatizes this idea in chapter 13 of *Dew on the Thorn*, first by drawing a scenario with the opposite philosophy. She describes a school for Mexican boys in South Texas where the teacher is "paid by the parents to make good Mexicans out of these boys" (144); many of these boys, she writes, returned to Mexico at the age of twenty-one to become influential citizens. The teacher, Don Alberto, is described as having "tolerated the United States as a nation of blue-eyed barbarians who were the born enemies of anything Mexican or Spanish" (144) and is apparently effective at producing young men who go back to live successfully in Mexico. So for Don Alberto and the parents of these boys, education is a means of preserving culture, of transmitting values, of maintaining the status quo. But Don Alberto cannot be pigeonholed as a cultural purist or preservationist; his critique of traditional Spanish-Mexican culture—and particularly of the caste/feudal class system that characterizes its economy—permeates his education-for-all slogan. Traditionally, the children of peónes did not go to school, as the upper class held to the belief "that learning spoils them for work" (145). Don Alberto held classes for the children of the peónes outside of school hours. In addition, rather than teaching the *hidalgo*'s children only about their aristocratic Spanish ancestors, he taught them of "the past greatness of the indigenous races," the heritage they share with the Aztecs, and how a "mestizo, Don Porfirio Díaz, directs our destinies" (146). González laces this acceptance of racial and cultural mixing throughout the stories in *Dew*, as in this next example about education and culture from chapter 14, which also serves as an example of assimilating to American education as a means of resisting American hegemony. González's writings indicate that she understands cultural truths Ruiz de Burton, Jaramillo, Cabeza de Baca, and Otero-Warren never acknowledge. That is, cultural exchanges move both ways between colonizer and colonized. And this mimicry, as Homi Bhaba discusses it,

> is the sign of a double articulation; a complex strategy of reform, regulation, and discipline, which "appropriates" the Other as it visualizes power. Mimicry is also the sign of the inappropriate, however, a difference or a recalcitrance which coheres the dominant strategic function of colonial power, intensifies surveillance, and poses an imminent threat to both "normalized" knowledges and disciplinary powers. (123)

As we see most clearly in González's work, cultural exchanges almost inevitably produce cultural syncretism on both sides of a colonial divide (a divide that is never as structurally sound as the colonizer would want); and what can look to the colonizer like the colonized's assimilating is actually the colonized's synthesizing dominant ideals and practices in ways that redistribute power to the disenfranchised members or the oppressed group.

In chapter 14 of *Dew,* Fernando de Olivares is a product of the system of sending educated Tejanos back to Mexico for their careers. Though he has established himself in a threefold career as a "businessman, a ranchman, and a politician" (152), he decides that the border Texans need a leader who will encourage Texas Mexicans "to exercise their rights as American citizens." He says, "It is our duty to learn English, to send our children to American schools. Not that we are ashamed of our Mexican traditions, but because this will make us know how to protect ourselves against them" (152). By "them," Fernando refers to the *Americanos* who, in ever-increasing numbers, are invading the border country and wresting the land from the rancheros.

This tactic seems like espionage assimilation, a way for the oppressed group to infiltrate majority culture to defend itself against further encroachment or domination. For Ruiz de Burton, Jaramillo, Cabeza de Baca, Otero-Warren, and especially González, domesticity, religion, and education are a tripartite rhetoric that challenges, preserves, transmits, assimilates, negotiates, and synthesizes cultural performances of national and cultural identity. Anglo-American federal officials also recognized these triangulated discourses as primary voices to transmit cultural ideals, but, curiously (or perhaps just confidently, with the arrogance of any colonial power), many white Americans did not understand that culture is not only transmitted but exchanged. As the next chapter shows, officials of federal Indian boarding schools, such as Richard Pratt, saw Indian education—and particularly the domestic education of Indian girls—as perhaps *the* most effective method for forcing the assimilation of American Indians to Euro-American ideals. Espionage assimilation apparently never entered the minds of Pratt or any other federal official; they assumed that the schools would convince Indian students to assimilate, and then Indian students would go home and convince their families to assimilate. Besides the obvious method of indoctrinating Indian students via classroom instruction, Pratt and others used the boarding schools' newspapers and magazines, often featuring essays and articles written by the students themselves, to inculcate Euro-American domestic values in the students and their parents, who might read the publications, as well as to prove to a white reading public that the Indian boarding schools were doing their American duty—that is, to "kill the Indian, and save the man."

CHAPTER THREE

Regulating Domesticity

Carlisle School's Publications and Children's Books for "American Princesses"

Home life like that which with us lies at the core of everything social is practically unknown among the Indians in their primitive state. They live together in families, it is true, all the members of a family sharing a dwelling. . . . [B]ut of a subtler kind of enjoyment which the Caucasian finds in his home, the Indian is ignorant. . . . Until a spirit of emulation was stirred among Indian women by the missionaries and government matrons, there was none of the pride of good housekeeping which we find among even the humblest white wives and mothers. A great deal has been accomplished in this direction by tribal fairs [where the women] . . . contest for prizes offered for the neatest tepee, the most palatable cookery, the best appointed dinner-table, and the most sensibly dressed children. In their wholesome rivalry we can detect the initial glimmerings of a home-making ideal like that which we find among the best women of our own race.

—Francis E. Leupp, *In Red Man's Land: A Study of the American Indian,* 1914

We have seen how federal boarding schools and female agents of various institutions used domestic education and the tenets of domesticity inherent in the Victorian ideals of true womanhood to colonize American Indian women by systematically replacing indigenous ways of life with European American domestic habits. In this chapter, I read texts and images produced by European Americans and published in Carlisle's publications and girls' novels to argue that these sites of cultural production supported and extended the regulatory efforts of boarding schools and female agents and reinforced colonial assumptions that Indian women needed to be domesticated and that white women were their ideal domesticators. In chapter 4, I read essays written by female Indian students and published in boarding school magazines, but in the first section of this chapter I interpret essays written by and photographic images chosen by white boarding school officials, which share a focus on domesticity and the school's domestic education programs. In the second section of this chapter, I interpret four once popular but now nearly unknown girls' novels by Evelyn Hunt Raymond, published around the turn of the twentieth century, as another site for regulating the domestic behavior of both white girls and Indian/Mexican girls. I use the slash to merge my reference to Indian and Mexican girls because, as I will show, the nonwhite characters in Raymond's novels are often ambiguously racialized, and the narrator is often unclear about who is Indian or Mexican. Because virtually no literary criticism has been published on Raymond's novels, I use the history and theory of children's literature to argue that Victorian ideas about child readers make children's novels ideal tools for inculcating colonial attitudes and behavioral codes in both white and Indian readers.[1]

Carlisle School's Publications and Domesticating Indian Girls

Moses Friedman, superintendent of Pennsylvania's Carlisle Indian Industrial School and editor of its publications, reprinted an article from the *Sunday Magazine* in the November 1909 issue of the *Indian Craftsman* that distills the stories of civilizing progress Carlisle presented to readers:

> There is no more interesting or remarkable development in American life today than the evolution of the squaw of reservation and ranch into the modern Indian girl. . . . The unique evolution of the "real American girl" has been due to the educational advantages offered her by the Government in its non-reservation schools. The largest of these is at Carlisle, Pa. Here the Indian woman is seen at her best. . . . The Indian girl enters Carlisle when a child—before she has become a part of reservation life, with its constant tendency to shiftlessness. At once she comes into contact with Indian women of the nobler mold—women who see in their own energy and development the hope of the Indian race. . . . When the school term is over, the Indian girl is placed in some well-recommended household in the Eastern United States. . . . When she doffs her

> graduation gown and steps forth to face the world she is a woman in every sense. . . . [T]he Indian girl herself believes that her greatest work is in elevating her own people. . . . It is her function to arouse [the Red Man] from his lethargy. ("Modern Indian Girl" 23–25)

Carlisle's domestic education and outing programs—where the "Indian girl is placed in some well-recommended household"—strove to transform Indian girls into Indian women by "rescuing" them from the reservation that would turn them into squaws. In the passage above, squaws apparently do not qualify as women, and Indian girls do not become Indian women until they have graduated from Carlisle's program. After graduation, Indian women were to perform the critical work of returning home and Americanizing their communities. I argue here that Friedman used Carlisle's publications to reproduce and reinforce the domesticating work of Carlisle's programs. The programs domesticated Indian girls during their years at school; the publications served not only as textbooks on domesticity for students at school but also as dictatorial, do-it-yourself domestic manuals for students who had returned home.

Amelia V. Katanski argues that the publications served, in part, to show the general population that the institution inculcated Americanness. She notes that, in 1893, Carlisle circulated *Indian Helper* to nine thousand subscribers each week (48). In this way, the publication functioned as evidence assuring the general population that the "Indian problem" was under control. Further, Katanski argues that Carlisle used its publications as didactic tools for student readers. As I discuss in chapter 4, Katanski shows how Carlisle officials created "paper Indians" that populated the pages of the publications as examples of assimilated Indians and "to establish and reinforce hegemony over the students, who were expected to conform to a unified, assimilated, 'American' identity without question or resistance. . . . At Carlisle, education was a process of imprinting, and those who controlled the printing process—who were also both literally and figuratively the educators—deeply believed in their power to edit and rewrite Indian identity through use of newspapers as disciplinary tools and rhetorical weapons" (47–48). In this section, I read Carlisle's publications alongside Katanski but with a focus on how Carlisle officials used these pages to show that Indian adaptation of Euro-American ideals and habits of domesticity tangibly and materially measured how "American" Carlisle Indian students could or had become.

The May 1909 issue of Carlisle's the *Indian Craftsman* includes the commencement address given by George E. Reed, then president of Dickinson College. Reed focuses on Indian women as markers of Indian progress, and this extended section of his address touches on many of the issues in this chapter:

> I think this is the finest commencement I have ever witnessed since I have been to Carlisle, and that is twenty years. . . . It shows the splendid progress you are making, and I learn a great deal every time I come out here as to the progress of the Indian. I was delighted to see a young lady, and other young ladies with her, with her hair dressed ala [*sic*] pompadour, and of the most pronounced character, and I also noticed that these ladies were wearing the latest directoire gowns. These are the representatives of the Indian race, and I am absolutely sure that no young lady who parades around here today with a directoire gown on will ever go back to the Indian blanket. I heard one of the young ladies say that the ambition of her life was to be a neat housekeeper, and then she added,—"I wish to be economical," and I thought what a sense of relief must pass over the minds of these Indian braves when they heard a woman absolutely state that she desired to be economical. I watched with considerable interest the process of making that bed over there. . . . You are learning all these beautiful arts of housekeeping here, and all about the economies of life, and I am sure you will put into splendid practice by and by the lessons you have here acquired. . . . We want you to become good citizens of the Republic; that is what the whole school is for—to train young men and young women to become good citizens, and we hope every one of you will become a good citizen of the United States, and that you will be manly men and womanly women. (19–20)

Several of Reed's statements reinforce the school's position that domesticity signifies an Americanized Indian woman, and they betray how much Euro-American popular culture influences his measure of gender roles. Reed assumes that the Indian woman who has felt the joys of Euro-American fashion—wearing a pompadour hairstyle and a

Directoire gown—would never abandon such fashionable attire for the so-called garb of blanket Indians. His assertion that he overheard an Indian girl say her life's ambition was to be a neat and economical housekeeper not only underscores the girl's internalization of the school's dogma but echoes the sentiments found throughout popular women's magazines of the period. Finally, that he jokingly refers to the "Indian braves" who will be relieved that their potential mates value neat and economical housekeeping also shows Reed's assumptions that assimilated Indians—though he assumes Indians will only marry Indians—will appropriate the Euro-American gender roles modeled in magazines that, by 1909, had already become go-to guides for American consumer culture.

The inclusion of Reed's address in this issue of the *Indian Craftsman* was but one of many such editorial decisions Friedman made with the apparent goal of reiterating the school's dogma of domesticity. Reed says that "he watched with considerable interest the process of making that bed over there," undoubtedly referring to the "industrial talks" that the school included in the commencement program to demonstrate what the students had learned. Figure 3.1 reproduces a photograph that appeared a few pages after Reed's address. The photo captures the commencement demonstration that was meant to prove the domestic assimilation of female Indian graduates to those who attended the commencement, which no doubt included community members, Carlisle students, and faculty, and perhaps even family members of the graduates. The intended effects of these performances would be threefold. Community members might watch this performance and be moved to participate in what Carlisle called the outing program by hosting students in their own homes. Underclass students in the audience might watch it and look forward to the day when they too could participate in the outing program. And if there were family members in attendance, they would see what their children had learned and what habits they might bring back to their tribal communities. Publishing a photograph of this demonstration would have had similar intended effects, with the added benefit that everyone who received the publication could be influenced by the commencement demonstration. If, as Katanksi argues, we can assume that Carlisle students and nine thousand households around the United States read the Carlisle publications, then thousands of people might have seen this photograph of Indian women wearing

FIGURE 3.1 Female Indian students at Carlisle act out Friedman's "Industrial Talks—Benefits of the Outing System" on the commencement stage, performing their newly acquired skills in Euro-American domesticity. *From left to right,* the rooms each show different tasks mastered: fluffing pillows in the bedroom, dressmaking in the living room, setting tables in the dining room. Each room is also neat, tidy, and decorated with Euro-American furnishings, and the whole "house" is flanked by gigantic American flags. *Indian Craftsman* 1 [1909]: 23. Courtesy Special Collections Division, J. Willard Marriott Library, University of Utah.

Directoires and pompadours while making beds, sewing clothes, and setting tables. Initially, these photographs might be viewed as a novelty—"look at the Indian women dressing and acting like white women!"—but eventually these photographs could lose their impact. I would argue that this is exactly what Friedman and other producers of the Carlisle publications counted on: that reading essays and seeing photos about Indian women and domesticity would be both normalizing and routine to Indian and white gazers alike and that whites can be secure in the knowledge that Indian women would always be "*almost the same, but not quite*" (Bhaba 122).

Ultimately, then, the photographed Indian students—willingly or not—would turn into regulatory agents of Euro-American femininity and domesticity to each other, as seen in figure 3.2. As the original caption on the image implies, Friedman uses this photograph to tell a story of Carlisle's success: the Indian students dressed in Euro-American clothes are not anomalies but represent the appearance of the student body at large. The visiting Blackfeet, in their traditional regalia, recognize the students' style of dress as a material product of their education and that it is good, a "benefit." Quite literally, the subjects in the photograph are "trading gazes," as Susan K. Bernardin, Melody Graulich, Lisa MacFarlane, and Nicole Tonkovich discuss. In turn, 1913 readers who view the photograph would notice the contrast between the American and the Indian costumes. Two of the three Americanized girls are literally standing a step above the Blackfeet people, figuratively signaling the superiority of both white culture and Americanized Indians. If the Blackfeet are the "old Indians," then the gowned girls are the "new Indians," the federally educated Indians who blend into Euro-American culture.[2] And let it not be overlooked that these new Indians in the photograph are all women, despite the fact that they are supposed to represent the general students of Carlisle. From the 1880s to the early 1900s, white reformers thought that they could most efficiently assimilate American Indians by first converting Indian women to Euro-American habits of fashion and domesticity. Otis T. Mason, a famed anthropologist, wrote in *Woman's Share in Primitive Culture*, "savage tribes can now be elevated chiefly through their women" (238). The *Sunday Magazine* passage I opened this section with, as well as figure 3.2, echoes Mason's belief: "the Indian girl

FIGURE 3.2 "Blackfeet Indians Visiting the Carlisle Indian School." *Red Man* 5 [1913]: 429. Courtesy Special Collections Division, J. Willard Marriott Library, University of Utah.

herself believes that her greatest work is in elevating her own people. Clear-visioned, she sees that his indolence and his innate desire to resist the encroachment of civilization have resulted almost in the annihilation of the Red Man" ("Modern Indian Girl" 25).

To this regulatory and normalizing end, the *Indian Craftsman*, and its later incarnation, the *Red Man*, contains essays and notes about Indian women and domesticity; and nearly every issue between 1909 and 1912 includes dozens of photographs of Indian domesticity and the homes of Carlisle's ex-students. Many of the essays and photos concerning domesticity focused on Carlisle's outing program, as shown in figure 3.1. In the February 1909 issue of the *Craftsman*, Friedman writes an update about the outing system, arguing that for years it "has been one of the most important features of the school's work" and that, because of Carlisle's geographical position in the East, it is likely to be more successful than outing programs in schools in the West "because of the prejudicial attitude and the impatience which is manifested toward the Indian" in the West ("Improvements" 15). The irony of this statement is, of course, that prejudice toward Indians was alive and well in the East as well, especially considering Richard Pratt's motive behind founding the Carlisle school in the first place: "kill the Indian, and save the man." But to Friedman and other Carlisle officials, their work was philanthropic, not racist, and the Pennsylvania families who opened their homes to Indian students were providing firsthand experience with Euro-American domesticity, not hiring domestic slaves. According to Friedman, the outing program provided multiple benefits:

> Then, too, those into whose homes our young people go, take such a personal interest and do so much towards bringing the boys and girls into active touch with the highest type of civilization, and with the best methods of living, that if nothing else were done, this character training would be a sufficient excuse for the outing system.
>
> The industrial training which our girls receive in the country home is incomparably superior to any domestic science which has ever been taught in any Indian school. They learn by doing, and when they return to the school after an extended experience in a Pennsylvania home, they know how to cook, to housekeep, and to wash and iron in a way which would shame many of our graduates from some of our expensively maintained domestic science departments in the service. ("Improvements" 15–16)

FIGURE 3.3 "Educating the Indians—A Female Pupil of the Government School at Carlisle Visits Her Home at Pine Ridge Agency." In addition to publications at the boarding schools, mainstream publications circulated images that perpetuated the idea that Indian women, transformed by their domestic and fashion educations at government schools, would go home and "civilize" their communities. *Frank Leslie's Illustrated Newspaper* [15 Mar. 1884]: cover. Courtesy Library of Congress, Prints and Photographs Online.

Publishing essays such as this one served multiple purposes. They challenged schools in the western United States to implement outing programs (albeit using a kind of reverse psychology), encouraged students to see the benefits of participating in the programs, fostered pride among the families who housed these students, and reinforced the school's legitimacy and progress in solving the "Indian problem."

Figure 3.4, a collage of photos originally published in the May 1910 issue of the *Craftsman* and reprinted in the September 1911 issue of the *Red Man,* depicts Indian girls performing a series of tasks associated with Euro-American domesticity. The two images on the left-hand side show the girls engaging in modern, mechanical methods of doing laundry and processing milk. The girls perform both tasks outside in a conspicuously manicured lawn contained by a quintessential white picket fence. The placement of these Indian girls in such artificially natural settings might resonate with contemporary readers who, prior to Carlisle's

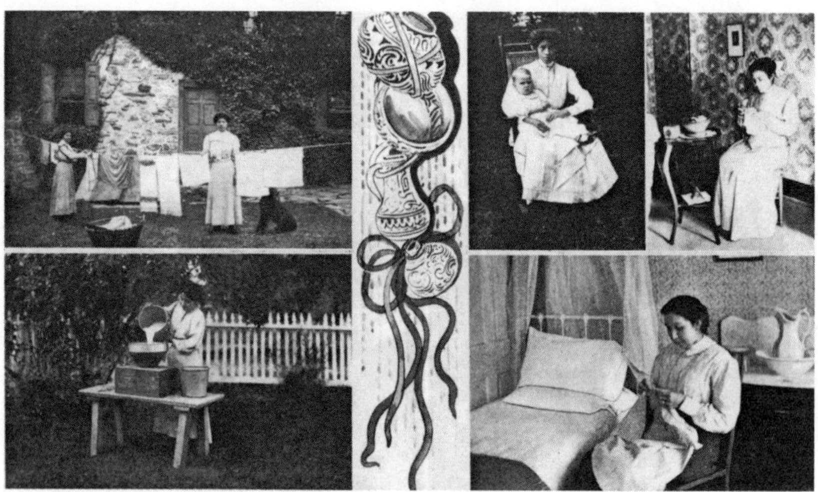

FIGURE 3.4 "Girl Students of Carlisle in Pennsylvania Households under the School's Outing System." *Red Man* 4 [1911]: 11. Courtesy Special Collections Division, J. Willard Marriott Library, University of Utah.

civilizing efforts, were more used to seeing Indian girls photographed or illustrated in wildly natural settings. The two images on the right-hand side show the girls performing the indoor woman's work of child-care, embroidery, and needlework. That all the girls are wearing white dresses, that one is rocking a presumably white child, that two are working near a whitewashed picket fence, and that one is sewing near a starched white bed tells the viewer that these Indian girls have been whitewashed, literally and figuratively. As before, these photographs serve several functions: to assure the reading public that Carlisle is in the business of Americanizing Indians, to remind student readers of their proper places and performances, and to advertise to Pennsylvania homeowners and potential employers the tasks they could expect Carlisle Indian girls to perform.

To reinforce the domestic outing program for their female students, the Carlisle publications also reprinted brief articles about the program from mainstream newspapers and magazines. The September 1910 issue of the *Red Man* reprinted "Carlisle Commencement as Seen by *Collier's Weekly*," wherein J. M. Oskison writes that "scores of housekeepers in Jenkintown, Wilmington, and less important centers of good living, prepare to take in Indian girls who want to supplement, with practical household work, their school training in sewing and cooking" (18).[3] Friedman would have had two motives for reprinting this article by Oskison. It reiterates to *Red Man* readers the popularity and usefulness of the school's outing program, but Oskison's identity as a Cherokee and a well-known magazine writer would have sent another message to Indian readers: adult Indians who are successful in the white world also endorse domestic assimilation for Indian girls. Indeed, other Indian writers such as Marie L. Baldwin argued, at the first meeting of the Society of American Indians in 1911, that the tenets of Euro-American domesticity are not all that different from the duties Indian women performed for millennia and should be adapted as a means of survival.

Friedman reprinted two other such articles in the November and December 1910 issues of the *Red Man*. In the November issue, he included a brief article that originally ran in the popular women's magazine *Good Housekeeping* under the title "The Indian Girl." The piece essentializes artistic Indian girls as anomalies and argues that most are best fit to be housekeepers:

> Indian girls make splendid needlewomen. They inherit the skill their grandmothers put into bead work or basket making. They have excellent taste and an intuitive idea of good coloring. You may find among them good musicians; they excel as teachers of their own people and many have achieved a high place as workers in the arts and crafts. As often as possible art is taught in the schools by an Indian woman, with a high regard for all that is best in native handiwork.
>
> It is possible, however, to make artists, musicians, teachers and nurses of only a small minority of Indian women. Carlisle has a system which aids materially toward making the Indian girl self-supporting. Its outing agents place hundreds of students each summer in homes throughout the Eastern states. The girl becomes a guest as well as a helper, becomes one of the family, and while receiving the sensible training that a good mother gives her own daughter, she also enjoys the social life of a country home. (136)

Publication in such a widely circulated magazine as *Good Housekeeping* meant that this article would have been read by thousands of women and would have reinforced stereotypes among whites about Indian women even as it attempted to compliment Indian girls. Republishing the article in the *Red Man*, a magazine that was all but required reading for Carlisle students, would have reproduced those stereotypes among Indian readers, the very people being characterized by said stereotypes. To argue that Indian girls with specialized skills are the exception buttresses the second idea in the article that Indian housekeepers are the norm and could produce the effect in readers that Friedman surely desired and encourage cooperation with the domestic training and outing program at Carlisle: Indian women can become "*almost the same, but not white*" (Bhaba 128).

The December 1910 issue of the *Red Man* also reprints an article about the outing program, ominously titled "Eradicating Tribal Distinctions." Originally published in an unnamed Detroit newspaper, this article provides statistics about ex-students and graduates of Carlisle, arguing that "of all the work which it is doing, the school is quietly proud of the fact that it is wiping out tribal distinctions among Indians. . . . If the condition of the race of first Americans is improving, and those in close touch with it say it is, undoubtedly a large measure of credit is due to the influence of the school at Carlisle" (156–57). The writer provides evidence of this improvement by listing professions that ex-students have taken up and specifically emphasizes that "especially beneficent has been the training afforded the Indian girls" (156). Of the 514 living graduates, "142 are housewives, and they are the mistresses of modern, well-furnished homes, too, not squaws in tepees and wigwams" (156). That Carlisle was "quietly" proud of its role in breaking down tribal affiliations is arguable, especially since Friedman chose to reprint this article in his own publication. But by now the point is clear: Carlisle used its publications to reinforce, reproduce, and redistribute its domestic education and outing programs for Indian girls to inculcate the idea among its Indian and white readers that Indian women belonged in Americanized domestic spaces.

Several historians of other Indian boarding schools—such as Brenda J. Child, K. Tsianina Lomawaima, and Myriam Vuckovic—have argued that the domestic education programs were only designed to train girls to be laborers in white homes, despite some insistences by federal officials that part of the value of this domestic education was to train Indian girls in the values of true womanhood. While this may have been the case for the majority of female boarding school graduates—that they went on to work as domestic laborers, not necessarily becoming wives and mothers working in their own homes—at least a minority of students were not house servants but went on to be housewives or homeowners, teachers or nurses, and, at least in some performative way, seem to have come close to achieving the status of the middle-class American.

The *Indian Craftsman* and the *Red Man* also include several notes and photos about ex-students and graduates of Carlisle who seem to have established themselves as keepers of their own homes. For example, Friedman excerpts a letter in the "Graduates and Returned Students" section of the September 1912 issue of the *Red Man* wherein Georgia Bennett Pierce, Class of 1909, writes, "I am married and keeping house. I am happy and doing all I can to keep our home nice and pleasant. I am thankful for what the Outing System has done for me in the line of housework and cooking, for it has helped me a great deal" (42). An article reprinted in the September 1911 issue of the *Red Man* from a Bangor, Maine, newspaper argues that the graduates of Carlisle are going back to their tribes and "building good houses" and that the "girl graduates are mistresses of their homes and are living up to their educations" ("Progress of the Indian" 39). In the November 1913 issue, Friedman published a piece called "Able Indian Girls" as an installment in an editorial that spans multiple issues titled "Indian Progress; Remarkable Advancement Made by Education and Training." In one of his most concentrated arguments for the material benefits of the domestic training programs at Carlisle, Friedman writes,

> Most of the Indian girls at Carlisle specialize in domestic science. Most of the girls marry educated Indians, and their homes, on reservations, on farms, or in cities, are found to be models of skillful domestic management. The successful Indian is never a slum dweller. The educated Indian has graduated from the rude shack. The good house with modern conveniences is what the modern, educated Indian demands and gets these days when he settles down to raise children who will be educated in the arts of civilization from the time of their birth.
>
> That is the way in which the educated Indian of to-day is solving the perplexing Indian problem. In this scheme of advancement, the Indian woman is as important as the Indian man. The Carlisle

> male graduate does not pick the uneducated, tepee-trained Indian maiden to be his housewife and the mother of his children. Rather, he picks the Indian maiden whose ideals are the same as his, and who has absorbed the ways of civilization in a training school such as Carlisle. These educated Indians, men and women, are succeeding in rejuvenating the Indian race. They have been taught to avoid degenerating practices which have been killing off by the thousands the slovenly reservation Indians who have not embraced sanitary living. The educated Indians do not abuse drink. Their lives are clean, and they have ideal home lives, so ideal that they are greatly respected in the communities which they settle. (126)

To illustrate the points he makes in this argument that Carlisle Indians are models of modern, sanitary, house-proud citizens, Friedman includes many photographs across several issues of the *Red Man* that feature named ex-students standing in front of their "good" homes, only a few of which I include here.

Figure 3.5 shows six houses built and inhabited by six families of Carlisle ex-students. The Carlisle publications contained many such collages. Friedman writes that, as one of many efforts aimed at "educating the Indian to the need of better homes," his magazine has "printed scores of illustrations showing the present residences of Indians in various parts of the country, as a means of inspiring those who are not yet living in good homes to improve these conditions at the earliest date possible, and own a good home built within their means" ("Encouraging Home Building" 172, 171–72). Figure 3.6 is unique among these photos in that it is a collage of one family's home and includes glimpses into the home's interior and a close-up portrait of the family who lives there. Figure 3.7 shows several more Indian families living out the expectations of Carlisle's domestication programs.

Viewed together, these images perform more functions than simply providing illustrations of ex-student residences to encourage home building among Indians who have not moved into Euro-American houses. First, these images anticipate modern-day critics who argue that the domestic education programs were just machines for turning out domestic workers. Perhaps Friedman fielded such criticisms in his own moment, but these photographs challenge the claims of scholars such as Lomawaima, Vuckovic, and Child, who argue that officials at the

FIGURE 3.5 “Homes of Indians Educated at Carlisle—Abner St. Cyer, Winnebago, Winnebago, Neb. Joseph Dubray, Sioux, Revinia, S. D. James Waldo, Kiowa, Anadarko, Oklahoma. Mrs. Laura Pedrick, Kiowa, Anadarko, Oklahoma. Leti St. Cyr, Winnebago, Winnebago, Neb. Wm. Springer, Omaha, Walthill, Neb.” *Red Man* 5 [1913]: 430. Courtesy Special Collections Division, J. Willard Marriott Library, University of Utah.

Figure 3.6 “Home and Family of Mr. Benjamin Caswell and Leila Cornelius, Cass Lake, Minnesota. Carlisle, Class 1892 and 1896—Chippewa and Oneida.” *Red Man* 3 [1911]: 381. Courtesy Special Collections Division, J. Willard Marriott Library, University of Utah.

Figure 3.7 "Homes of Carlisle Ex-Students; Upper—Louise Provost McNutt, Omaha, St. Joseph, MO. Lower—Mrs. Ida Warren Tobin, Class 1894, Chippewa, White Earth, Minn." *Red Man* 3 [1911]: 284. Courtesy Special Collections Division, J. Willard Marriott Library, University of Utah.

Chilocco and Haskell schools never intended for Indian girls to go on to be housewives and mothers in their own homes. Figure 3.6 especially challenges these claims, as the photographer and the editor have taken care to show how fully the family of Benjamin Caswell and Leila Cornelius are living out the ideals of Euro-American domesticity. Not only is the exterior of their house typical of a Victorian American farmhouse, complete with a wide front porch and gingerbread gable ornaments, but the interior furnishings display a certain degree of American consumerism. The editor did not include photographs of the more practical features the house must have had—a kitchen, a bedroom, a common living space—but rather the spaces that could be considered luxurious. The photo on the far left that includes the bookcase could be but a corner of the family's common living room, but its arrangement suggests a separate, well-appointed library. The bookcase is not rough-hewn but is a barrister bookcase with glass-plated doors and the walls are decorated with landscapes and what might be a school pennant. Similarly, the center photo focuses on a wooden china cabinet, also with glass-plated doors. The objects arranged on the serving surface of the cabinet are not rough containers made of metal or pottery but look to be made of delicate glass.

Most importantly, the portrait of the family indicates their assimilation of Euro-American ideals of family and domesticity. Not only are all six family members dressed in typically American fashions, but the fact that they are photographed as a single family unit speaks to their assimilation as well; they appear to have adopted the concept of the nuclear family, living away from tribal kinship connections. Moreover, the fact that Caswell, a Chippewa, and Cornelius, an Oneida, have married outside of their own tribal affiliations exemplifies Carlisle's success at "eradicating tribal distinctions." Indeed, many of the home photographs indicate tribal intermarriages, as figure 3.7 also shows: William and Josephine Smith are a Digger and an Oneida, respectively. Though these images argue that Carlisle Indians achieved some measure of American middle-class status, today's scholars should view these photographs with a healthy dose of skepticism, acknowledging that, as Katanski argues, the Carlisle publications were didactic propaganda.

The perspectives of these images also suggest that the most important subjects in the photographs are the houses, not the people who live in them. In all but figure 3.5, the houses dominate the frame, and the people standing in front of them are not much more than hazy figures. Without the photographer's captions, viewers would not recognize the human subjects, and they might not even notice them at all. Granted, any photograph of a house with a person standing in front of it will be scaled in this way: to photograph an entire house, a photographer has to stand at some distance, dwarfing anyone standing in front of it. But seeing this series of photographs over and over, in issue after issue of Carlisle's publications, would doubtless send the message that individual identities are less important than architectural styles. In these photographs, Indian identity is literally minimized and figuratively subsumed by Euro-American domestic space.

Finally, that these photographs were published in Carlisle's magazines confirms the regulatory purposes of the publications. As Katanski has argued, the student body was the main group that the publications sought to regulate. Students were to read the monthly magazines and learn, by seeing themselves and their peers written in the pages, how to be civilized Americans. The general population outside the school was also a target audience. Friedman wrote that he hopes the photos will inspire other Indians to build and live in "American" homes. But when we consider the logistics of securing these photographs, we realize that these regulatory practices actually followed the students home after they left Carlisle. The photographs evince the policing of a parole officer providing documentary evidence to his/her superiors that the parolees are abiding by the rehabilitative guidelines set up by the correctional institution. The families photographed in front of their homes were apparently keeping to the indoctrinated tenets of domesticity in their adult lives on the outside. The families who were not photographed, but who perhaps saw old classmates in current issues of the *Red Man*, might have been motivated to keep up with Carlisle's lessons in domesticity in their own homes (or, on the other hand, they might have resented those classmates who "got with the program"). In this way, Carlisle's publications serve as an Orwellian Big Brother or, as Katanski also discusses, a literary version of Foucauldian panopticism. Carlisle followed its students home to watch how they kept to the rules, but it mattered just as much that ex-students believed they *could* be watched by the larger, cultural regulatory eye that Carlisle embodied and represented.

Evelyn Hunt Raymond's Fiction for "American Princesses"

These regulatory photographs of the homes of ex-students of Carlisle offer evidence that the federal Indian schools shared the conviction that if Indian students could be converted to the habits of Euro-American domesticity, then white reformers might hope that tribes could be disbanded and Indians subsumed into the general population as American citizens. However the historical statistics played out for the actual students who returned home, fiction from the period—produced by the schools and in popular culture—shows a preoccupation with the idea that domesticity could civilize American Indian communities. Marianna Burgess's didactic novella, *Stiya, A Carlisle Indian Girl at Home: Founded on the Author's Actual Observations*, produced by and circulated at the Carlisle school, features a returned-home heroine, Stiya, who transforms her family's way of life to be a model of domesticity. We know Stiya is successful because, like the photographers who followed Carlisle students home, her teachers visit her home and approve of the tea-table spread with a white tablecloth and the rooms appointed with modern furnishings. Amy Goodburn calls *Stiya* "conduct fiction," a "primary form of education for girls that participated in the cultural and social production of 'girlhood' more broadly" (83). Just as *Stiya* circulated at Carlisle, Goodburn writes that it, and similar books, were also used at the Genoa Indian Industrial School (GIS) in Nebraska for "reinforcing GIS assimilationist ideologies" and remaking Indian "girls' identities through the reading of literary texts explicitly written for Indian youth" (85, 84). The idea that domesticity could Americanize Indian women also circulated through the popular press—in children's novels and women's magazines—not just in texts written especially for Indians.

Carlisle superintendent Friedman's comments that readers of the *Red Man* would see the home photographs and make material changes in their own ways of living based on what they read betray a belief about reading: that readers consciously or unconsciously connect their material lives and the fantasy life of a text and are willing to change their lives based on what they see in those texts. Friedman asserts that these photos are "educating the Indian to the need of better homes," "inspiring those who are not yet living in good homes to improve these conditions at the earliest date possible, and own a good home built within their means" ("Encouraging" 171–72). In addition, the overtly didactic quality of the *Red Man* and *Stiya* implies similar common beliefs about reading—that readers, and particularly child readers, can be taught lessons and values through a text. In this way, Indian readers are equated with child readers: they need to learn the lessons of the text, but they also need to be taught that they need to learn these lessons in the first place. Discussing *Stiya* and S. Alice Callahan's *Wynema: A Child of the Forest*, Janet Dean argues that sentimental novels taught Indian readers to "feel right by reading right" as part of their domestic educations (202).

Directing what Indian students read, then, is another way that federal educators practiced indoctrination and attempted ideological control. Vuckovic notes that administrators at the Haskell Institute in Kansas held beliefs about reading similar to Friedman's. At Haskell, "reading was encouraged as a great civilizing force," and Haskell officials "made sure that the school library held books and magazines promoting Anglo values and culture"—particularly, the values and culture comprising the Victorian tenets of true womanhood found in novels such as Louisa May Alcott's *Little Women* (102–3).[4] Similarly, Laura Wexler asserts that guiding student reading at the federal boarding schools would "accomplish what the entire U.S. Cavalry had tried and failed to do: to persuade the western tribes to abandon their communal, nomadic way of life; adopt the prizes, mores, and values of consumer culture; and turn their little girls into desirable women on the middle-class commodity plan" (*Tender Violence* 112–13). Like *Little Women*, Raymond's books for girls contain lessons for both white and Indian female readers about the proper roles for American women.

Whether we look at the self-consciously didactic children's literature of the Puritans or the moral-lesson-hidden-behind-a-pleasurable-story children's literature of the Victorians, all children's literature is founded on an adult belief that children are influenced by what they read. Although some scholars of children's literature argue that didacticism had gone the way of the dinosaur by the early decades of the twentieth century, Raymond's books suggest the opposite, and most scholars in the field proceed from the premise that children's literature instructs children in some way. Several scholars historicize this belief in the instructional power of children's literature. Peter Hunt asserts that children's writers are particularly positioned to transmit "cultural values" through their storytelling (3). John Morgenstern explains how, near the turn into the nineteenth century, children were seen as "pre-readers" and thus as "some kind of primitive Other" (2). "On the one hand," Morgenstern argues, "the pre-literate child is endowed with a spiritual presence, an innocence that unfortunately must be abandoned, must be allowed to die so the adult can be born. On the other hand, the pre-literate child is a savage that must be trained, an uncivilized emptiness that must be supplemented with adult experience in the form of a constantly expanding series of steps or 'grades'" (21). Morgenstern writes about a moment in the history of children's literature a century before Raymond's novels. But he suggests the double or even triple work that children's books with Indian characters could perform: first, if all children were seen as savage preadults who could be civilized by reading, then this metaphor actualizes when the novel includes white characters who instruct and civilize

Indian savages. Further, if these savages can also be tamed by their own reading, then Friedman's assumptions about Indian readers can be and are replicated by writers like Raymond who draw model encounters between white and Indian characters.

Analyzing the historical shifts in children's literature from the early nineteenth century to the early twentieth centuries, Anne Scott MacLeod, Leonard S. Marcus, and Mary Lystad link the changes from didacticism to delight to broader concerns in the American public about morality, nationalism, gender roles, and an increasingly diverse American population. Writing about Victorian instruction children's books, Lystad notes that the books generally appeal to white Protestant readers and only infrequently appeal to minority readers. And "when minorities do appear in books, they are represented as difficult to instruct because of their uncivilized" ways of life (57). As I will show, Raymond's moral teaching in her novels combines incidental hints with explicit didacticism, perhaps because the lessons she teaches address two questions that weighed on the hearts and minds of nineteenth-century citizens of the United States: the "woman question" and the "Indian question."

Scholars of children's literature subdivide the field into many categories, or subgenres, of study (and debates about the subdivisions are almost numerous enough to make up another subgenre). Perhaps the most basic subdivision, though, is gendered: these are books for girls and those are books for boys. Jeffrey Richards writes that the goal of children's fiction in the mid-nineteenth century "was both to entertain and to instruct, to inculcate approved value systems and acceptable gender images, in particular gentlemanliness for the boys and domesticity for the girls" ("School Story" 2). R. Gordon Kelly argues that children's literature was used to reveal and stabilize these very systems of value and gender roles, so that while literature socialized child readers, the producers of children's literature circulated it to revive their own dedication to these social systems (xvii). MacLeod asserts that writers and publishers used children's literature to safeguard and sustain the centrality of the home in American society so as to pass domestic customs on to their children (*American Childhood* 17). In *Behold the Child: American Children and Their Books, 1621–1922*, Gillian Avery proposes that children's books that focus on home and hearth present a particularly American brand of success, security, and achievement and that the American mother character was almost singularly responsible for this notion of success. Discussing the mid- to late nineteenth-century categories of domestic, family, or home stories for girls and adventure stories for boys, Morgenstern asserts that "the girl's domestic novel, like the boy's adventure story, encourages more identification with the protagonist than does the pure children's novel. This is also why they are potentially more insidious in inculcating gender roles" (102). He also argues that "the adventure story encourages boys to leave home while the domestic novel encourages girls to stay home," where "the adventurous perversity of young girls must always be tamed in order to produce proper wives and mothers" (125), since these wives and mothers—republican mothers, that is—perpetuate the American domestic dream.

However, Raymond's novels combine the domestic novel with the adventure novel. And the white heroines' adventures, somewhat ironically, become the act of domesticating savage Indian and Hispanic girls. Gwen Athene Tarbox writes that "the American girl became what might be called 'the little educator'" (36) in nineteenth-century children's literature, a role that certainly fits Raymond's heroines. She also notes that, even though young American heroines were often drawn as the "selfless provider" and "domestic expert," many girls—especially those who "grew up on the frontier"—escaped "the domesticity that was glorified in girls' books" (37). Raymond's heroines seem to escape domesticity in this way. Because they are living in or touring the Wild West, free from close parental supervision, they go off on all kinds of adventurous excursions—rescue missions, treasure hunts, even ostrich races—and sometimes behave like what Tarbox calls tomboys. But Raymond's tomboys do not really escape domesticity after all, and their stories exemplify what Tarbox terms "taming narratives," where "the tomboy heroine experienced increasingly acute societal pressure to bring herself indoors and to leave the public life of adventure" (38). Tarbox discusses Susan Coolridge's 1872 bestseller, *What Katy Did*, as the ultimate taming narrative in which the heroine is paralyzed—literally tamed—by her tomboy ways and eventually transforms into the perfect domestic young lady. Raymond's novels feature young white heroines who are teenagers on the cusp of adulthood and need to retire from their adventures. Moreover, they are taming narratives in that these white heroines must tame not only themselves but Indian and Hispanic girls, compelling them to assimilate to acute societal pressure and become true women. In this way, Raymond offers a way for her heroines and readers to have their domesticity and their adventure too, mirroring the real life of the American girl-turning-woman.

Raymond's young white heroines, then, can be read as caricatures of the historical female missionaries, teachers, and reformers who lived among Indian and Hispanic women of the West in efforts to civilize and Americanize them and as representations of female reformers at the turn of the century who left the confines of domesticity but brought it with them and enforced it on the Other women they encountered in their travels. Louise Michele Newman writes about "one of the most profound ironies of this history": while the white woman's movement vigorously critiqued "patriarchal gender relations, it also called for the introduction of patriarchy into those cultures deemed 'inferior' precisely because these cultures did not manifest these gender practices" (7–8, 8). The great irony here is that, even though early white feminists viewed the cult of domesticity as too restraining and repressive for themselves, they saw domesticity as the primary means of civilizing progress for "primitive" women (8). Female activists would be well known to Victorian writers of children's literature, making them ideal role models to offer new or modern American (white) girl readers because of their multiple focus on domesticity, philanthropy, and racial uplift. In other words, the sense of Manifest Destiny that fueled the United States' westward expansion also motivates the activist-heroines of late nineteenth-century children's writing.

Indeed, Marcus suggests that we see Manifest Destiny in children's literature of the period because it was one of the few ideals shared by the national consciousness in the bitter aftermath of the Civil War (35). Raymond capitalizes on these activist figures in her fiction, and her novels substantiate Kaplan's Manifest Domesticity; she also offers Indian and Hispanic girl readers models to emulate, for her nonwhite heroines learn their lessons well: cooperate with white people, be domestic, and then you will be allowed to survive. In Raymond's Western novels, then, the adventure story combines with the domestic story to present a new American heroine for a new colonial relationship, where kindness and friendship between white girls and Indian/Hispanic girls produce an Americanized but still racialized nonwhite American. And when read in the context of Victorian beliefs about child readers, the number of girls who might be the targets of these taming narratives—the tamees, if you will—could multiply if the novels also tame the white girls and the

Indian/Hispanic girls who read about white girls who tame Indian/Hispanic girls.

Of course, discussions about children's literature often lead to circular and perhaps unproductive questions about authorial intention, how children actually read, and how they are influenced by what they read. My point is not to belabor such debates here but to acknowledge the fraught territory and to spell out thoughts that underpin my readings of Raymond's novels. First, as I have shown, most scholars of children's literature agree that most writers of children's books, for most of children's literature's history, write to instruct child readers in their cultural mores.[5] This is especially so for scholars of children's books who lived in the Victorian period, and Victorians were particularly concerned about books for girls. Writing in 1886, for example, Edward G. Salmon asserts, "there is a wide and splendid field for the display of humanizing and elevating literature among girls." Salmon admonishes adults, "if in choosing the books that boys shall read it is necessary to remember that we are choosing mental food for the future chiefs of a great race, it is equally important not to forget in choosing books for girls that we are choosing mental food for the future wives and mothers of that race" (523, 526).

Second, adults believed that children would emulate what they read, as evidenced by Eveline C. Godfrey's worry, in 1906, that naughty characters will damage child readers (105). Friedman's comments about Indian readers of the *Red Man* also signal a belief that readers emulate characters, along with the accompanying assumption that Indians were like children in need of the Great White Father's care and instruction. One only needs to Google "banned books" to find that twenty-first-century adults still believe that children can be changed by what they read; the fear that their children might try to become sorcerers if they read the *Harry Potter* series sounds ridiculous to most adults when spelled out, but it betrays a common, deep-seated belief in the power of reading and a fear of relinquishing control of a child's formation to some unknown writer or set of beliefs. Children's literature scholar Maria Tatar answers the question of whether books can change us by considering how words function as "souvenirs of reading" (her term for psychologist D. W. Winnicott's "transitional objects") that help readers "construct their identities" (90). If reading can indeed help readers "construct their identities," it is little wonder that adults have been anxious for centuries about what children read. Of course, this is not only a question of *if* but also a question of *how* books change us; and how do we know when we ourselves are changed by a book, let alone how do we know when a book changes someone else, especially when that someone else is a child who might have limited capacity to articulate those changes?

In general, adults assume that reading makes a difference. Janice A. Radway's groundbreaking study about adult readers of popular book-of-the-month-club books, for instance, initiated an entire body of reader-response criticism. More to the point, adults assume that children are more impressionable than adults and thus more vulnerable to the difference that reading makes. When we combine this assumption with our larger sense of a need to protect, guide, or control children, we end up with adult writers who cultivate certain patterns of response to children's literature. Some scholars have worked to assess responses among child readers, such as Elizabeth Segel, who writes that choices in reading material among boys and girls are "governed by early experiences" and a "polarization of gender roles" (165, 170). Jean Ferguson Carr argues that many social "institutions depended on girls' literacy to further moral and political agendas" in the nineteenth century, so "girls were encouraged to use literacy for the social good, for temperance reform, or to extend domestic values into the public arena" (52). Writing about series books such as *Nancy Drew* and the girls that read them, Sherrie A. Inness argues that such books created communities of girls with shared responses to the books and so contributed to the socialization of girls by reinforcing "cultural ideologies" (1). Nancy Tillman Romalov studies the marginalia that girl readers inscribed in early twentieth-century series books and asserts that "librarians' fears seem to have been confirmed: young females indeed showed a penchant not only for relating life to fiction but also for behaving like fictional characters" (93). Dean shows how Burgess's *Stiya* and Callahan's *Wynema* are about Indian girls learning to "read right" (203) and Goodburn notes that a lack of written responses to fiction by Genoa Indian School girls makes it difficult to assess how fiction changed girls' worldviews (88). But my point here is not to explore reader-response theory or to reconstruct historical readers of the texts I interpret.

Regardless of how historical girls read Raymond's novels, or of how American Indians read Carlisle's publications, Victorian American writers shared the belief that published texts had a powerful potential to affect moral, spiritual, psychological, intellectual, and even material change in their readers. Raymond's novels can be read in this context of literature believed to alter materially the lives of readers, not least because the publishers explicitly market them as novels for girls that contain moral lessons. An advertisement in the back of Raymond's *A Yankee Girl in Old California* titled "Best Books for Boys and Girls" boasts that this book is part of Penn Publishing's series of books for children that "are not only told in an interesting and charming manner, but most of them contain something in the way of information or instruction, and all are of a good moral tone. For this reason they prove doubly good reading; for, while the child is pleasantly employing his time, he is also improving his mind and developing his character. Nowhere can better books be found to put into the hands of young people" (389). Indeed, Raymond's books were often touted as such beacons of morality, for each book's publication solicited a new onslaught of advertisements and reviews in newspapers, magazines, and book catalogs across the United States. I have included a list of such notices as an appendix to show the widespread circulation of Raymond's books; indeed, most girls, from Massachusetts to Montana, would have had opportunity to find a Raymond book at a bookseller or public library. Though she is all but unknown to today's audiences, Raymond's books enjoyed a wide circulation.[6]

As far as I can tell, the only modern literary critics who discuss her are Emily Honey in her unpublished dissertation and Nina Baym in her 2011 recovery-bibliography, *Women Writers of the American West, 1833–1927*.[7] I will show how Raymond's novels join the US effort to Americanize American Indians at the turn into the twentieth century by engaging the discourses of domesticity, education, and general reformism—discourses that were, by and large, the distinct domain and responsibility of white women. Furthermore, I interpret Raymond's books with the underlying assumption that they circulated self-consciously *as texts* written for young girls and argue that, like the Carlisle publications—like most children's literature—they contain lessons to be learned and emulated by readers. In the case of these Raymond novels, the lessons are geared toward both white and Indian/Hispanic female readers: domesticity and education are ways to perform one's civility and Americanness. White girls bring domesticity and education to Indian/Hispanic girls. Indian/Hispanic girls cooperate with and learn from these white girls. And in most cases, if threads of kinship or bonds of friendship can be discovered or forged, then the Americanized Indians/Hispanics can achieve their goals. As will be clear as I move through my interpretations of the novels, my use of the slash to separate yet link Indian and Hispanic girls stems from the way Raymond racializes her characters ambiguously and unevenly. I again use the census term *Hispanic* instead of more culturally specific terms such as *Chicana, Latina,* or even *Mexican* for similar reasons. Raymond often presents her "native" Californian characters as having Spanish descent—even pure Castilian—when they historically would have also shared a genetic heritage with Mexicans and Indians. But, typical of a white writer from this period, Raymond's distinctions between who is Indian, who is Mexican, and who is Spanish are stereotypically racist, classist and, to a modern-day critic, fluid.

The four novels I interpret here—*Monica, the Mesa Maiden* (1892), *A Daughter of the West: The Story of an American Princess* (1899), *A Yankee Girl in Old California: A Story for Girls* (1901), and *Polly, the Gringo: A Story for Girls* (1905)—share similar plotlines and characteristics. Typical of many children's books, all the novels feature teenaged heroines who are remarkably free from the close supervision of parents or other guardians, a position that allows them a freedom of movement and adventure. *Monica* presents two such heroines. One is the Hispanic Monica Rivera, who lives with her elderly grandmother and her lazy father and brother. Reinforcing such stereotypes as the lazy Indian or Mexican man and the squaw drudge, she shoulders the responsibility of providing for her family and keeping house, but she abandons these duties to look for her beloved yet good-for-nothing brother who has disappeared. The other heroine is the white Christine Dana, who is touring California with her parents. Christine has the freedom to explore on her own because her mother is ill and her father has already seen all the sights. She discovers Monica's house and family and eventually goes in search of Monica, who has gotten lost while searching for her lost brother. *A Daughter of the West* also has two heroines. Patience Eliot (white) lives in California with her father. Because her mother died long ago and her father is busy running their sprawling ranch, Patience is free to explore the village and surrounding "wilderness," thus enabling her friendship with the novel's second heroine, Tulita. Patience's task is to lift Tulita from the mires of living as a California Indian and Tulita's task is to rescue Patience who, in classic captivity-narrative fashion, is kidnapped by a rogue and rakish Indian man.

In *A Yankee Girl*, orphan Edith Hale leaves the care of her grandfather and great-aunt in Sissimit, New Hampshire, and travels alone, by train, to San Diego, California, to live with her mother's people, the "pure" Spanish Garcelon family. Edith's challenge is to restore the Garcelon family and their home to its former grandeur. When hope is nearly lost, Edith finds "liquid gold"—water—on the family land, providing irrigation for the crops and financial resources to renovate the family mansion to acceptable Spanish American standards. In *Polly, the Gringo*, Polly is virtually an orphan who lives in Maine with an overbearing aunt. Her mother is dead and her seaman father is often absent. Polly is angry that her father takes her weakling brother along on his latest voyage instead of her, and she pays for passage to California on a stranger's ship so she can catch up with him. Remarkably, Polly makes it to the San Diego ranch of her father's friend, Doña Delores Ysidro, where her task, among many, is to save the family from raiding Indians. The novels all argue, to various degrees and in differing circumstances, that the domesticity and education, mores, and fashions brought west by the white girl have the power to civilize and Americanize Indians, Mexicans, and Spaniards.

Domesticity characterizes *Monica, the Mesa Maiden* from the opening scene, when we see Monica's great-grandmother, Señora Ynez Padilla, sitting in a rocking chair by the hearth of her adobe house, and we begin to learn about Monica's "quaint housekeeping notions" (17). These "quaint" methods are soon subjected to the gaze of Christine, who, out on a solitary tourist excursion, happens upon the house on the mesa. The house enraptures Christine, who gazes at it as if it were there just to satisfy her tourist curiosity:

> "Oh! It is all so quaint! So—so just what I dreamed!" cried Christine. . . . This house upon the *mesa* was an old adobe structure with a curiously tiled roof. Once it had been very spacious and had sheltered many inmates; for, though greatly in decay, its broken wall still stretched both far and wide; with an irregularity of architecture not common to the time of which it was a remnant. The open court in the centre, surrounded on three sides by walls which were yet firm, was, at that season, bright with roses and hibiscus, and carpeted by sea-apple and nasturtium vines, whose dazzling crimson and orange blooms were shadowed by the mighty palms which stood like guardians at the entrance. To Christine Dana, fresh from school

> in a Northern city, the scene was a revelation. Her love of nature was strong; and nature enriched by this bit from a historic past enchanted her. She would have been surprised to know that those who dwelt within it had never thought of admiring their home, though they certainly loved it with all the warmth of their Southern natures. (27–28)

Several contemporary reviewers praised the novel's descriptions of such "genteel picturesque poverty," which fulfilled Anglo expectations of "the dreamy idyllic atmosphere of Southern California" ("Story for Girls" 167). The beginning of this selection is presumably a description of the home as Christine sees it, and in the latter portion, the focalization switches from Christine's view to the narrator's description of Christine's blinkered gaze. The narrator distinguishes between past and present, between northern and southern natures, and between the inhabitants of the house and Christine's understanding of them. To the narrator—and perhaps, by extension, to Christine—the Rivera home is but an antiquated remnant of a historic past, out of place in the present except for its physical connection to the landscape around it. It seems the Rivera family has the presence of mind to love their house with, the narrator implies, some kind of gratefulness, but their mindset is not modern enough to admire their home in the way that practitioners of Euro-American domesticity do. Finally, the narrator judges that Christine would assume the Riveras would admire their home in the way she does, as exemplified by the initial conversation she has with Benito Jaume, Monica's cousin. When Christine first arrives at the house she exclaims, "Do you know, little boy, that this is the loveliest house I have ever seen?" Benito replies, "The loveliest—house? What dost thou mean? Art thou not teasing me? Because Gabriel says we are very poor" (25).

This mismatch in the ways Christine and Benito see the house suggests more than a difference between their supposed northern and southern natures. Even as Christine admires the house, she romanticizes it and naïvely assumes, according to the narrator, that its inhabitants share her luxurious position of seeing a house as an artistic opportunity rather than a structure that meets the necessity of shelter. That the narrator intervenes to say Christine is wrong in her assumption to stress that, in fact, the inhabitants of the house are not like Christine at all, suggests the cultural work that this novel self-consciously performs. The novel's main task is to help white girls understand that nonwhite families do not have the proper relation to or regard for their domestic spaces and that it is white girls' responsibility to teach them this domesticity.

Christine is in a moment of transition from childhood to adulthood, a place where she must move from the naïve "personality of childhood to take on the characteristics of an adult woman," a transition that MacLeod argues is common in children's books from this period. Further, Macleod notes that children's writers likely "saw this transition as a dramatic event in a girl's life; certainly they saw it as the supremely fitting moment for a didactic message defining the obligations and limitations of a woman's future" (*American Childhood* 14). MacLeod uses Alcott's *Little Women* to exemplify this point, but Raymond's novels show it as well. The horizons of Raymond's heroines are wider than the horizons of Alcott's March girls; Raymond's girls combine domesticity with adventure to carry on the work of woman reformers. But Macleod's message still applies: American girls—especially white girls—could anticipate a future defined by domesticity, even if they managed to make that domesticity portable.

Another scene shows Christine's tendency to romanticize the Rivera house instead of properly criticizing it, as would a teacher, missionary, or other female reformer. After she has talked with Benito and met the great-grandmother, Bisabuela, outside the house, Christine gains access to the interior. Bisabuela has not eaten breakfast yet because Monica is still at her job of guiding tourists around on burros, so she allows Christine to go inside and get her food. Christine is happy to comply, both to help Bisabuela and to satisfy "her own curiosity concerning the interior of this strange house. So she hurried into the living-room and looked eagerly about her," seeing sparse spaces with few objects, including "some faded pictures of saints and a mat of coyote skins," which "were the only attempts at decoration." She notices that "most of the walls were whitewashed, and in spite of a bareness which spoke of great poverty, Christine thought she had never seen any house so daintily clean, nor any outlook so charming" (34–35).

Christine's romanticizing the Rivera house anticipates the movement of primitivist women writers and artists such as Mary Austin and Mabel Dodge Luhan, who would move to the Southwest and spend their lives romanticizing and appropriating Indian and Mexican cultures. Her equating of bare walls with poverty also anticipates Veblen's *The Theory of the Leisure Class* (1899), betraying her position in a society that values ornament, decoration, and other material markers of conspicuous consumption. Though Christine and Monica eventually rescue each other from various scrapes and forge a friendship, Christine never teaches Monica domesticity. Rather, domesticity frames the novel and punctuates certain chapters—for instance, when a bitter relative, to whom Monica's father is indebted, kidnaps Monica and forces her to perform his housework until she escapes one day—and sets the backdrop against which the white girl can engage the Hispanic girl, laying the groundwork for Raymond's future novels, where the young white heroines are much more active domesticators. Contemporary readers apparently made this connection between Raymond's novels and white women reformers; Nathan Haskell Dole noted that "from its name [*Monica*] might be thought to be akin to Mrs. Jackson's 'Ramona.' But Mrs. Raymond scarcely touches on Indian life; her aim was evidently to picture an idyll with a happy ending" (2). Siobhan Senier shows that Helen Hunt Jackson's best-selling *Ramona* and her activism on the part of California Indians "reveal how the desire for self-authorization erupted into the political projects of white women reformers who claimed to speak for Indians" (*Voices* 30). Even though Dole reads Raymond's aim as different from Jackson's, that he associates one with the other suggests that he reads similarities between the two. I argue here that they are, in some ways, the same. And if *Monica* does not have enough Indians to qualify as an activist novel in Dole's estimation, he might have changed his mind about Raymond's intentions if he read the next novel she wrote about western girls.

In *Daughter of the West*, published seven years after *Monica*, Patience Eliot actively Americanizes Tulita through the habits of Euro-American domesticity. Where domesticity in *Monica* is more of a frame, or a common experience, through which the white girl can influence the Indian/Hispanic girl, it functions here as the mark of a civilized Indian who is willing to cooperate with white Americans, thus earning the respect of those Americans. As Baym points out, Raymond tells readers in the preface that Patience, who is "simple and modest, yet courageous and, if need be, daring," is the new model for the American girl to emulate (203). Indeed, Raymond explicitly encourages readers to make friends with Patience so that "each daughter of America, east or west, who reads this story, realizes that she is also a Princess in her own right, a being to whom all nobility is possible, and so realizing, walk uprightly, with that graciousness that sets her apart as one in whom the eyes of all the world delight" (6). Reflecting popular beliefs about the effects of reading, Raymond offers a story of American girlhood that she expects will alter the material lives of the actual American girls who read it. To this end, the novel delineates roles for various types of girls.

From the opening scenes, Raymond creates a world of binary oppositions, where Patience's role is to bring goodness and light to the degenerate and dark world of Tulita, whose role, in turn, is to follow Patience's lead to become a civilized American. As in *Monica, Daughter of the West* opens with the white heroine touring the Hispanic part of a Southern California town. In this case, on a trip through Los Angeles with her father, Patience wants to ride through the "Mexican quarter" because it is "ever so much more picturesque" than the Anglo part of the city (12). Also like Monica, Patience romanticizes the architecture of the area, noting that "the long, low rambling old adobe structures looked almost squalid, at first sight, in contrast with the palatial buildings of the streets they had just left; but the locality had a charm of its own for the Eliots" (14). Patience soon meets Tulita, the "lion tamer," who puts on streetshows with live pumas for the entertainment of tourists. When the domesticated pumas get loose and play-attack Patience, Tulita is almost arrested for the attack (and because a shop owner accuses her of theft) until Patience stands between her and the police officer, and the crowd gazes with wonder on this unlikely pair: "A wider contrast could scarcely have been afforded between the haughty, ill-clad, but strangely beautiful Indian 'princess' and the fair-haired wealthy daughter of a higher civilization, and people paused to watch them as they stood thus for a moment side by side—protector and protected—but American both, from the crowns of their shapely heads to the tips of their restless feet" (28). The girls have seen each other in the streets, but from this encounter springs a "full-fledged friendship, impetuous and unreasoning as [Patience's] nature was generous and trusting" (28). Friendship, then, also becomes a civilizing force in the novel. Even though the relationship between Patience and Tulita is always colonial—Patience is of the "higher civilization"—their friendship and the premise that Tulita is already American in some way paves the way for Patience to complete Tulita's process of Americanization.

Tulita's Americanization began at a mission school; while listening to

Tulita defend herself with dignified speech during the puma incident, an onlooker says, "That ain't no common Injun. She's been taught in some mission, that's plain; and she's purty, too, for a redskin" (32). Another crowd member replies, "Greaser, more like. A greaser is good for nothing but to kill!" (33). On the way home, Patience and her father also talk about Tulita's speech and bearing that seem so unusual for an "Injun," and Patience worries that Tulita's feelings might be hurt by the accusation of theft. She also worries about what kind of living conditions Tulita must endure because "she must be very, very poor, I should think, to be willing to train wild-cats for a living" (49). Patience decides she's going to help Tulita prove the townsfolk wrong who misjudge her as a thief or a "greaser," even though her father warns her against taking on this kind of "*protégé*" (51). Patience soon realizes that Tulita's dress and domesticity keep people from recognizing her as a civilized American, for she dresses in native garb and lives in a "rude" mud hut (40). After the girls solidify their friendship when Tulita reciprocates the rescue and rescues Patience (who has been kidnapped by the dastardly Indian, Ouleon), Patience begins the work of completing Tulita's Americanization in earnest.

Patience's and Tulita's roles in this Americanization process through the rest of the novel are so contrived as to be, without a doubt, didactic models for young female readers. Patience decides on the immersion method for Tulita's transformation, inviting her to "come with me. Live with me for a time and learn all that is to be learned" (268). By coming to live in Patience's house on her family's ranch, Santa Paula, Tulita sees firsthand the workings of Euro-American domesticity. To clear any confusion regarding her role in the household, Tulita asks if she is to live in the house as a "waitress, or—" and Patience interrupts, "I have called you *sister*. I mean it. You are to be my equal in all things which I can control for you. A waitress is a servant, and I am too good an American ever to be served by a princess of the line! Save in the service of love, which we shall render toward one another" (271). Assured of Patience's goodwill, Tulita then volunteers to wear clothes like Patience's so that she can "appear as thou dost," even though she admits she will be "miserable in them. But what is a little discomfort of the body to the discomfort of a soul? No; if thou wilt give them to me—whatever is fitting—I will wear them, and learn to do so quickly" (272). Of course, Patience is delighted and finds clothing that "would completely change Tulita's appearance," and the narrator tells us that "indeed, it was quite wonderful how swiftly Tulita adapted herself to all the Santa Paula ways. Her native intelligence, her early training at the mission school . . . , but most of all her intense desire to please Patience in all things, made her efforts wonderfully successful in a wonderfully brief time" (273).

Tulita's transformation is complete, as can be seen in the novel's illustrations (figures 3.8–10). Depicting Patience and Tulita's yearlong trip to New York City and back with Patience's aunt, Mrs. Rutger, the illustrations echo the before/after photographs of Indian girls at boarding schools. In figure 3.8, Tulita is most Indian in her native dress, in her adobe community, talking to an Indian man. In figure 3.9, Tulita is talking to Mr. Eliot in his study. She is still in her native clothing but is surrounded by Euro-American home decor; she has moved into a space where she can be civilized. In figure 3.10, Tulita is wearing Euro-American clothing on the streets of New York City. Patience has domesticated her, and their position in front of a shop—another space where American women increasingly belong as the twentieth century gets rolling—suggests Tulita is also learning to be a consumer. The watching children learn lessons too: if white ladies befriend Indians, then maybe Indians can be ladies too. Maybe they too could befriend Indians. Patience's role is to facilitate the Americanization of Indians through experiences with Euro-American habits of dress and domesticity, and Tulita's role is to cooperate with and learn from these experiences.

This cooperation has national implications in the novel, as we see when Tulita has a vision that foreshadows her experiences with Patience: "We two girls, speaking that one word [*friend*], have solved the problems of two nations. Thou wilt see. It has been revealed to me. . . . Our hands, clasped above the hatred of two peoples, shall hide it forever. . . . I see it—I see it! The comfort—the beauty—the peace shall be over all this, through us, two princesses of one land, two handmaidens of one Great Spirit!" (215). Before commenting on Tulita's vision, I include two more extended passages from the novel's final pages that show her prophecy fulfilled. Taken together, these three passages distill Raymond's lesson to young female readers, making the moral of the story hard to miss:

> When they all were safely home at Santa Paula they set immediately about putting into practical shape the plans they had formed during

Figures 3.8–3.10 Charles Copeland illustrations from Evelyn Hunt Raymond's *Daughter of the West* (1899). Author's collection.

> their long tour and today, where was once the humble Indian village by the arroyo, stands a beautiful town. The houses are no longer built of adobe mud, but tastefully and conveniently arranged "model homes," such as one sees everywhere in thrifty New England towns, sheltering busy and happy households. The people who dwell in these homes are still Indian, but Indians who command the respect of their white brothers the world over. (344)

Tulita ends up as the head of an agricultural college, Patience "spends a goodly portion of her time among her cherished protégées," and together they are part of a "powerful object lesson on the famous 'Indian question'" (346). One of the local ranchers has the last didactic lines of the novel: "we've never seen a more touching or prettier sight anywhere than those two princesses of ours joining hands like sisters across all the—the great mistakes of the past century or so. Little white hand and little red one, God bless them both! Tender of touch and true as steel, long may they hold close to the bond that's between them—*Love!*" (346–47).

That Raymond herself calls the story of Patience and Tulita a "powerful object lesson" leaves little doubt that young female readers were meant to emulate these characters and plotlines. By reading Raymond's novels within the history of children's literature and American colonialism, we can see how, as Richards writes, popular fiction is one of many ways a culture transmits and controls its values and customs. Though Richards writes about imperialism in English adventure fiction for boys, his premise—that imperialism dominated the English national consciousness from the mid-nineteenth to the mid-twentieth centuries (*Imperialism* 2)—transports across the Atlantic and across the gender divide to describe American fiction for girls. Similarly, Claudia Marquis argues that late nineteenth-century evangelical European culture pitted girls against "the savage" (63) and notes that Victorian female characters often have a spirit of independence and practicality that extends rather than resists colonial endeavors (62). Karen Sánchez-Eppler reads Victorian American Sunday school tracts for children, arguing that "manifestations of imperial domesticity were already anticipated in the relations Sunday school stories construct between the American child, home, nation, and the world beyond. Such complex narratives precede and produce the complexly gendered contours of American international imperialism and coincide with America's continental expansion." In short, Sánchez-Eppler argues that such stories teach children "how to incorporate the nation's own racial and religious others" (188, 187).

Daughter of the West, then, along with the other Raymond novels I discuss here, tries to teach young, female white American readers how to participate in the colonial project of Americanizing the Indians and Hispanics they might encounter in their continental travels. It is a given in these novels that white American girls will travel and that they will travel west. Specifically, as we see performed so well by Patience, the white girl must bring the tenets of Euro-American domesticity with her on her travels so she can domesticate Indian girls. If children's literature offers role models for child readers to emulate, Patience herself would have had plenty of women to emulate in her own historical period. White women were highly active in Indian and Mexican communities all across the continent during this time period. As we have seen, Jane E. Simonsen, Peggy Pascoe, and other historians have shown how white female missionaries, teachers, nurses, and members of such organizations as the Women's National Indian Association took it upon themselves to lift their nonwhite neighbors out of their supposed squalor by inculcating Euro-American habits of housework and hygiene.[8] In 1891, for instance, Amelia Stone Quinton wrote, in an essay titled "Care of the

Indian," that "the work of women for the Indians within our national limits has been important and of many kinds. It would require much more than the space of a single volume fitly to describe the labor, self-sacrifice, and heroism of women in connection with the various missionary organizations on behalf of the red man" (373). Quinton names several women, such as Helen Hunt Jackson and Alice C. Fletcher, to argue that, whether as secretaries, field agents, teachers, writers, ethnographers or archaeologists, "gifted women of high culture have devoted some of their best years to the elevation of the red race" (373). With *Daughter of the West*, Raymond draws Patience Eliot as an exemplar of such reforming women that young white readers should aspire to become.

Indian girls were also readers. To the colonialist mind, Indian girl readers would have the ideal model in Tulita, who also plays her role perfectly in this novel. She not only builds and occupies her own model home but turns her whole village into a replica of a New England town. Like the ex-students of Carlisle who returned to their communities and built Euro-American homes and like Stiya, who returns home and teaches her parents how to build and keep a proper household, Tulita assimilates the civilizing ideals of domesticity and gains the respect of the white world. Moreover, she takes part in community planning and teaches at an Indian school, actions that mirror the actual history of boarding schools and federal bureaus that recruited Indian teachers and agents who became (self-consciously or not) what reformers would see as the ultimate examples of and tools for assimilation (but what Tulita would likely experience as the syncretism of mimcry).

If Patience is a model reformer, she represents the new generation of such reformers. Raymond contrasts her attitude toward Tulita with Mrs. Rutger's when Patience first brings the Indian girl home to live with them. Mrs. Rutger, Patience's aunt, "had fancied she was most cordially interested in the 'Indian question,' with a leaning toward affection for the much-discussed red man, yet when her young relative put a similar predilection into practice it was . . . '[a] black horse of quite another color'" (270). Similarly, "Tulita in her buckskin attire, riding over the plains, seemed to the Easterner quite the 'correct thing,' but the same Tulita, in the same garments, seated opposite herself at table, gave her a very uncomfortable feeling—almost as if she herself were a part of some great 'Wild West Show'" (270–71). Mrs. Rutger, then, represents an older generation of "friends of the Indian" who spoke about helping

Indians—even admiring them from a distance—but were uncomfortable in the presence of actual Indians or stood silently by while the federal government stole Indian lands and lives. By stressing that Tulita is her sister, Patience represents a kinder, gentler colonizer who believes that philanthropy and friendship are enough to heal the wounds caused by "the great mistakes of the past century or so" (347). By stressing the girls' friendship and drawing the image of red and white hands joined in love, Raymond argues that the new American girl-reformer befriends Indians with the belief that friendship goes farther than intimidation in influencing Indians to dress in American clothes and live in American houses. For despite all this sentimental talk of love and friendship, we cannot forget that Tulita is acceptable to Mrs. Rutger and Patience only after she dons Patience's clothes and builds model homes for her community, and only then can she receive the respect of the surrounding white world. By acknowledging past wrongs and attempting to right these wrongs with friendship, Raymond evinces a degree of sympathy toward Indians and even remorse for the treacherous dealings with Indians by the US government. But racist comments and descriptions still permeate this novel and the others I discuss here, and Indians still stand in need of intervention and help from white girls—in particular, help in the form of white domesticity. In this way, these novels exude a more insidious racism: the kind that masquerades as philanthropy but is still motivated by discomfort with difference. Even more insidious is the fact that this racism is part and parcel of the object lessons Raymond's books deliver to young, presumably impressionable, female readers.

Because they share so many similarities in plot, theme, and character development, *A Yankee Girl in Old California* and *Polly, the Gringo* can be discussed together. Both novels begin with scenes of the teenaged heroines traveling alone from towns in New England to San Diego, California. In *Yankee Girl*, the orphaned Edith Hale travels by train to live with her mother's people, the Garcelons. In *Polly*, the motherless Polly Pancoast secures passage on a stranger's ship and sails to San Diego in pursuit of her sea-going father. When she cannot find him right away, she fortunately happens upon the ranch of her father's longtime friend, Doña Delores Ysidro. In *Monica* and *Daughter of the West* the young white heroines live with their parent(s) in Southern California, either as long-term tourists or as permanent ranchers, and they make friends with Hispanic/Indian girls. In *Yankee Girl* and *Polly*, the white heroines reunite with Spanish families that their European American parents already know. This difference might indicate a progression of westward expansion and the colonial project or at least an assumption of progress, in Raymond's perspective. Our first two heroines—Christine and Patience—might represent the first or an earlier wave of white people exploring the West. They both encounter Hispanic/Indian girls for what seems like the first time, and—especially in Patience's story—they take an active role in domesticating these native girls in order to Americanize them.

Our second pair of heroines—Edith and Polly—represents a return to the West. In both cases, their parents have already explored the region and, to some extent, Americanized the people they've encountered there. Edith's father married a Spanish woman from California, Americanizing her through that marriage and by bringing her east to live in New England. As the product of that marriage, Edith, it would seem, was born to bridge the cultural gap between white Americans and Hispanic Americans. Edith says that her parents left instructions in their will that she was to live with the Garcelons when she turned eighteen because "they hoped by giving me this two-sided sort of raising, I might develop a 'noble, well-rounded character, free from prejudices and bigotry'" (135). Especially in children's literature, Edith may be one of the first characters of mixed-blood an author presents unapologetically or without a complicated explanation as fully white or fully American. On the other hand, Polly's father has forged a friendship with the Ysidros through trade. In this way, Captain Pancoast Americanizes the Ysidro family by inviting them to participate in American consumer culture. In a conversation between Polly and Doña Delores's son, José, he tells her that her father "is our friend. We of Santa Rosa are proud to have friendship with honorable Americanos, los gringos, si. It is from them we get our clothes, our shoes, and dresses for the women, our blankets, our sugars—ah! Of many things we are the debtors to the ships and the sailors" (104). Moreover, both Edith and Polly return to Spanish landowning families, which is a key distinction between the Hispanics in *Yankee Girl* and *Polly* and the Hispanics/Indians in *Monica* and *Daughter of the West*, who are supposedly living in complete squalor and poverty when their rescuing white heroines find them. Even though the Garcelon and Ysidro families have lost much of their fortunes and are living in reduced circumstances when Edith and Polly find them, their history of economic success marks these two families as more white and thus more American than their Mexican or Indian acquaintances. In this way, Raymond engages a western racial discourse much as María Amparo Ruiz de Burton does when she writes about the history of Spanish landowners and Spanish American whiteness in *The Squatter and the Don.*

As in the first two novels, domesticity frames the heroines' actions in at least three key ways. It helps them sort out the ranches' racial hierarchies. The ranches' ramshackle domesticity moves the girls to pity the proud yet dilapidated Doñas and motivates them to find new financial resources to restore the homes to their former grandeur. And through domesticity, along with book learning the girls transport modernity to the ranches, allowing the ranches not only to persist but to prosper. Parsing race and class seems a central task of both novels, as we see through Edith's and Polly's observations of domestic roles at the ranches. At least three categories of race separate the people who live on and around the ranches: Spanish (white), Mexican, and Indian (the latter two nonwhite). In *Yankee Girl,* Edith learns from a neighbor who drives her from the train station to the ranch that the Garcelons are so "pesky proud of their old Castilian strain" (136) that they won't take help or learn new methods of ranching from anyone in San Diego. Because Edith is convinced "of their own blue-bloodedness" (137), the neighbor believes that Edith is the one who can help save the Garcelon ranch from going under. When Edith arrives at the ranch, Santa Rosa, she is met by her grandmother, Señora Dora Rosa Garcelon, who extends her "fair white hands" in greeting (143).

Señora Rosa's hands are white because she is pure Castilian; they are fair because she does not perform the domestic labor of her household. Her Indian daughter-in-law keeps house. Upon her arrival at the ranch Edith notices a prickly pear fence, which the neighbor tells her is "about six to ten foot thick, and a hundred years old if it's a day. Look's if 'twould keep the Indians out, don't it? That was what it was planted for, I 'low" (138). But the fence evidently did not work as a barrier between the Spaniards and the Indians because Señora Rosa's son married Ysidra, an apparently Indian woman who is "as strongly in contrast to the elder lady as possible. She was swarthy and rotund and her features so ill-matched that each might have been selected from some different face" (145). Ysidra is figured as the squaw drudge of the household, perhaps because her apparent dim wit (314) makes her most fit for mindless domestic tasks, or perhaps because learning the values of domesticity (albeit antiquated Spanish domesticity, in this case) might make her seem white enough to have a place in the Garcelon household. At the breakfast table on Edith's first morning, she observes Ysidra's position in the household as Ysidra

> poured the coffee and passed the cakes. Edith looked up and greeted the silent woman with a bright: "Good morning!" which received no other attention than if she had been a hired servant. Although she was Alarico's mother and the daughter-in-law of Doña Rosa, her position in the household seemed a much lower one than Maria's at the parsonage [Edith's New England housemaid]. It was all very puzzling and unsatisfactory. (167–68)

Edith seems to internalize Ysidra's raced separation from the family. At first, her repeated attempts to befriend Ysidra are continually "repulsed" by the "unfriendly creature" (237), and when she attends an ostrich race at the fully modernized and highly lucrative San Pedro ostrich ranch, she compares Ysidra to the housemaid there: "she was a clean, wholesome looking middle-aged body, in a neat gingham gown and spotless apron, while a dainty, be-ribboned cap set off her waving hair. She was so trim and brisk and sociable that Edith could not help contrasting her with the dowdy and melancholy Ysidra, who ruled over the domestic affairs of Santa Rosa" (197).

Noticeably absent from this description is any mention of this housemaid's complexion. Because the description is absent, we can assume this woman is white and that she is part of a newly organized, paid female workforce that Edith herself joins later in the novel in her attempt to save the ranch. Though following this line of thinking would take me too far from the focus of this chapter, it is worth noting that, at least in Raymond's Southern California, domestic work is financially rewarded when performed by neat, attractive white female bodies; but that same work is expected, without pay, from unkempt, supposedly unattractive brown (or red) female bodies as a means of securing one's basic needs in a racist white household. Despite Edith's seeming participation in racializing Ysidra, and though Ysidra's position in the family never changes, Edith comes to respect Ysidra's work for the family, nearly granting true womanhood status to her domesticity:

> I honor my aunt Ysidra Garcelon more than any other woman I ever knew. It is almost nine months since I came to Santa Rosa, and in all that time I have never seen one single act of selfishness on her part. She has toiled for all of us early and late. She has hidden her sorrows in her own heart. She has gone without the food she needed more than any of us lest we should suffer hunger. She has gone without sleeping that she might weave her bits of lace and sell them to buy us bread. (339)

It could be that Edith comes to recognize Ysidra's domestic servitude as selfless domesticity because she has internalized her own position as a white family member and romanticizes Ysidra's work instead of recognizing it as involuntary labor. Or it could be that Edith now understands Ysidra's position as the undesirable in-law (a Cinderella, the unwanted and overworked step-daughter) and respects her work with sympathy and compassion. Or perhaps Edith's new perspective on Ysidra comes from a combination of factors, including the possibility that Edith now looks at Ysidra's work as a proud teacher would look at her student's progress because Edith teaches the Garcelon household the tenets of her New England domesticity.

This preoccupation with race and household roles also runs through *Polly, the Gringo.* As soon as Polly arrives at Don Santiago Ysidro's ranch—also called Santa Rosa—her observations about space and race echo Edith's observations in *Yankee Girl.* As neighbor Luther Dow drives her into the ranch, "Polly's amazement at the mighty cactus hedge aroused many questions and exclamations," to which Luther's only answer is "Indians" (92). While Polly has just arrived at the exterior of the ranch, the narrator tells us that the ranch is composed of "many Indian servants and Mexican vaqueros" (93). One of them welcomes Polly by calling, "Hola! the Gringo!" (93). Noticing that Polly seems uncomfortable with this unfamiliar term, Doña Delores explains that "'Gringo' is no word of reproach but only that name by which all are known who come from the land of the Americanos" (95). The narrator explains that Polly was "soon to learn, as her hostess informed her, that this was the common term used to distinguish the easterners, or 'Americanos' from the native Californians, and in no sense insulting" (96). The Ysidro family describes itself as both native Californian and purely Spanish, adding more layers to the already precariously stacked racial hierarchy of nineteenth-century Spanish-Californian landowning culture, a racializing phenomenon that historians and novelists such as Ruiz de Burton have described.

This racial hierarchy plays out in the ranch's interior as well. Indian servants perform domestic tasks. Polly is assigned her own servant, and she struggles to understand the "custom of this new land" when "Juana the Indian woman" helps her dress and undress, bathe, and even sits watch over her while she sleeps (98, 99). When she dines with the family on her first night at Santa Rosa, Polly observes that "there seemed almost as many servants as guests, and these were mostly Indians, Mission trained and lifetime members of the household, though here and there a Mexican moved among them, deft, solicitous, and as talkative as his fellows were silent" (107–8). So delineated are the roles of each raced house servant and ranch hand that Inez Peralta, a girl from a neighboring ranch whom Polly befriends (like the Christine/Monica and Patience/Tulita friendships), scolds her for making her own bed: "'Caramba! Why do you do that? Is it not a task for her?' pointing to the Indian maid" (125). In *Yankee Girl*, and perhaps even more in *Polly*, the eastern white girls arrive in the unfamiliar world of California race relations to find that making these distinctions between Spanish landowners, Indian servants, and Mexican vaqueros is central to maintaining the class hierarchies that keep the Spanish householders in positions of power.

In much the same way that, in *Monica*, Christine evaluates the status of the Riveras' domesticity when she first sees their home, both Edith and Polly assess the status of the Garcelons' and Ysidros' civility and economic vitality by surveying their architectural and habitual domesticity. The heroines often contrast the decor of their ascetic New England households with the decaying decadence of the Spanish-style ranch homes. In *Yankee Girl*, this contrast provokes Edith's pity when she views the Garcelons' performances of wealth against such crumbling architectural and spatial backdrops. Early on, Edith notices how large and sprawling their mansion is and notes that, "despite the air of decay everywhere visible, a mansion it still remained" (147). Later, while she takes a light supper in the garden with Señora Rosa and a neighbor, Edith worries about the "rickety" chairs as she gazes with "astonishment" (152) at the poor quality of the food and table set before her:

> A fine, but well-darned napkin covered the center of the warped table, and upon this were placed a few dishes of rare china, with a

> silver goblet and pitcher. The silver was dingy and the water had lost its sparkle, while the only eatables in sight were some pieces of hard dried meat with a small, equally uninviting, pile of biscuits. . . . However, the Señora found nothing wanting or out of common; and while her guests tried their utmost to do justice to her hospitality—and nearly choked themselves in the attempt—she entertained them with discourse about her garden. (152–53)

This contrast between what Edith sees and what the Señora sees when they look at the dining table serves as an example of the history of encounters between white women reformers and Hispanic women in the Southwest. These white women reformers came to the Southwest from various American institutions to civilize, Christianize, and Americanize the Hispanic and Indian women, mistaking differences in domestic habits as a complete lack of domestic rituals and routines. For example, Presbyterian missionaries Robert McLean and Grace Petrie Williams, in 1916, wrote from their experiences in the Southwest that "home has seldom been a sacred place, and family relations have not been held sacred. . . . It is a most important work that [Spanish American] women be taught to make the home attractive to the men and children of the family. . . . A real home would tend to make husbands more faithful and woman's lot brighter" (138–39). Just as McLean and Williams believed that the women they encountered needed "more Bible women, more district nurses, and more settlement women" (138) to teach them how to keep a proper home, so Señora Rosa needs Edith to show her how "warped" (152), "dingy" (152), and "uninviting" (152) is the domesticity where she herself "found nothing wanting or out of common" (153).

In this way, the teenaged Edith not only becomes another woman in a long line of white woman reformers, she also teaches a lesson to Raymond's young girl readers: white women need to help civilize the nonwhite women of the West. Even though Raymond figures the Señora as white, Edith sees the Señora's whiteness as compromised by her terrible housekeeping. Edith directly contrasts the domesticity at her New England and California homes:

> A frayed and coarse towel had been added to the preparations for the bath and a piece of soap such as Maria [the New Hampshire housemaid] would have disdained for even laundry purposes; and

> though these were but trifles they were enough to make the girl realize that the new life upon which she had entered was to be indeed, entirely different from what she had known or anticipated. Her heart sank with a fresh access of homesickness, and . . . she made preparations and went to bed. "Such a bed! It's like the soap and the towel!" (156)

Just as Señora Rosa does not see the shabbiness of her table setting, the maid who lays out Edith's linens also does not see (or is not concerned) that the towel, soap, and bed are not in pristine condition. Edith acknowledges that these matters are "but trifles," but her upbringing in Euro-American domesticity makes Edith equate cleanliness and neatness with home and security. And Edith cannot help thinking this way, for she is one of a long line of domestic heroines who, as Avery argues, have a "passionate feeling for home and domesticity. For Americans, the household community was a microcosm of the ideal republic they saw themselves to have created; all its members were independent and working towards the same purpose, for the good of the whole" ("Home and Family" 44). The California climate, landscape, architecture, and people do not make Edith realize how different her life will be here, but the apparent lack of domesticity makes her feel the difference and motivates her, as it did the woman reformers of her time, to find the resources to make Santa Rosa "a microcosm of the ideal republic" by teaching Anglo domesticity to the Garcelon women.

Edith seems to recognize her role in bringing domesticity to Santa Rosa when she attends the San Pedro ostrich races, "for San Pedro was a typical Southern Californian ranch at its best" (190). In a conversation with Mrs. Eastman, a white woman who owns the land that borders Santa Rosa, Edith also realizes that the Garcelon ranch needs domesticity combined with modernity to achieve a modern version of its former grandeur. Mrs. Eastman says that, at the San Pedro ranch, "all the prosperity so evident was due to simple common sense and a 'determination to get away from tradition'" (209). Mrs. Eastman wants to partner with the Garcelons to bring an irrigation system to both ranches, a notion that Señora Rosa has refused: "she belongs to the old 'Californians,' a race in itself almost extinct. She lives up to her traditions. . . . They believe, these Garcelons, that they are a little better than their neighbors in the world and that it is for them to dictate, not the others. They cling to everything that is old and hate everything which is new and progressive. . . . You old Garcelons are land poor" (212). Echoing the sentiments of white women reformers, Mrs. Eastman sets up herself (and, ultimately, Edith) as the bringer of modernity, and thus, the savior of these proud old Californians whose insistence on tradition is causing them to wither away. Edith promises Mrs. Eastman that she can persuade her grandmother to speak with her, and so begins Edith's work of modernizing the Garcelon's antiquated domesticity.

She goes about this task in several ways. First, she seeks out her Aunt Ysidra (the Indian in-law) to "beg to be allowed a share in the household tasks" (248–49) because "the idleness which was so irksome to her [was] so natural to her new friends. The ordinary avocations of an eastern housewife were unknown here. Very little sweeping or dusting was done, and this in only the most primitive way, by Ysidra, who still resented what she considered interference, whenever Edith attempted to help her" (250). Of course, as Newman points out, the fact that the "Indian problem" had become an aspect of the "woman question" was fraught with contradictions, as Edith's own contradictory feelings and attitude toward Ysidra perfectly exemplify: sometimes she praises Ysidra's domesticity in terms of true womanhood, sometimes she sees her work as primitive and counterproductive. Newman explains that "on the one hand, white women posited that all women, civilized and primitive, could serve as the agents and promoters of civilization," which is why the Indian schools trained Indian girls in the rigors of Euro-American domesticity. But "on the other hand," Newman continues, "white women considered Indian women, especially ones who 'return to the blanket,' the main impediment, not just to the racial progress of the tribe, but to the future of the United States" (117). Young female readers would see a good example in Edith of one who pitches in and helps with the household chores, by extension, training Ysidra, the Indian, to be an "agent of civilization." But these readers might not recognize the judgment that motivates Edith's desire to help: Ysidra's methods are primitive and inadequate. Whether or not they realize the judgment, though, young female readers might also pick up on the other lesson of Edith's example: young white women need to teach Hispanic and Indian women the proper way to keep a house.

In a bit of a rabbit-trail plotline, Raymond experiments with the debate about woman's work outside the home, but the goal of this plot is still to perpetuate ideal domesticity at Santa Rosa. Edith also goes to work in an olive factory for a short time to help keep money coming into the Garcelon household, and, ultimately, she accomplishes this task by finding resources to restore the Garcelons' wealth. Susana, a stereotypically drawn Indian prophetess, comes to Edith in the night and tells her that she is the key to restoring Santa Rosa and gives her a treasure map, presumably to a gold mine. Edith tells her grandmother not to worry about the family finances because, "Don't you remember what old Susana says? I have come to make you rich!" (256). The gold mine turns out to be water, a "natural-made reservoir of immeasurable capacity" (380) that runs under Santa Rosa and will be used to irrigate the ranch. So the novel ends with a flash-forward five years into the future when just "one glimpse of the old adobe" (382) will show how much has changed: the old adobe "is quite restored wherever it had fallen into the decay of our first acquaintance with it" (382), complete with a "wide table on the beautiful veranda" (383) that replaces the warped table at which Edith sat during her first dinner at Santa Rosa. Edith's New England family moves west to live on the Garcelon ranch too, and the still-learning Ysidra finds the perfect mentor and helper in Maria, the New England housemaid.

Polly also sizes up the domesticity of her host family when she arrives at their San Diego ranch. But where Edith compares Spanish American domesticity to her New England domesticity in *Yankee Girl* and finds it sorely lacking, Polly sees elegance in the Spanish style of housekeeping and dress that makes her own New England habits seem dull and austere in comparison. In marked contrast to Edith's first dinner with the Garcelons, Polly feels she has been transported to a "picture of 'fairyland'" when she joins the Ysidros and their many guests for dinner:

> Candles innumerable, augmented by the picturesque hanging lamps, cast a radiance almost dazzling over the beautifully-spread table, with its plate and glass—of priceless value, since it had been brought long before from far-away Spain and could never be replaced. Charming women in evening dress, such as Polly had never before seen; and men in short knee-breeches and deerskin leggings, enriched by gold or silver lace, a sash knotted about the waist and surmounted by a jacket and vest gaily decorated with buttons of the same glittering gold. As for the young folks, they were but smaller

> editions of their elders, though the girls were, invariably, in white. But alas! white with such a difference from the stranger's own attire, with its long sleeves, its high neck, its ungraceful big skirt—made "to grow in"—and suggesting now, even to its once proud owner, nothing so much as a nightgown. (106–7)

Like Edith, Polly comes to Santa Rosa and sees the ranch and its people through her own lens of New England domesticity with the presupposition that they will need to be taught the values of domesticity and that she is the one who can teach them. But somewhat differently from Edith's experiences, Polly realizes right away that the Ysidro household runs according to its own strict and functional domestic rules. Inez Peralta, Polly's newfound friend, teaches her that the Indian women do the housework and the Spanish women (read: white women) wear fine clothes and preside over beautifully arrayed dining tables.

Where Edith brings change to the Garcelon family, Polly is also changed *by* the Ysidro family, for it is not long before "the little gringo found herself whirled out of her own gown and petticoats and into the things Inez had procured" (125). As "both white-faced girls" rushed to the mirror to admire the transformation, Polly "scarcely recognized herself, her appearance was so altered by the clothes she wore" (126). This scene of assimilation is a complete role reversal from the similarly structured scene in *Daughter of the West.* In that novel, Tulita, the Indian girl, is transformed by donning the Euro-American clothes of her white friend, Patience. Here this is less a scene of reverse assimilation, or of a white girl "going native," but more a recognition of the whiteness of both girls, as the description above implies. What at first might seem like a move by Raymond to encourage white girls to learn from Hispanic (read: nonwhite) girls and appreciate Hispanic culture is actually a reaffirmation of the racial hierarchy that stratifies Santa Rosa. In this dress-up scene, where the "white girls were shrieking with laughter" over the fun they are having, Juana, "the phlegmatic Indian maid" who always watches from the shadows, even "smiled now and then" (125). At Santa Rosa, a gringo is white, a Spaniard is white, and an Indian is a squaw drudge at best and a raiding savage at worst.

The idea of the raiding savage brings us back to Polly's recognition of domesticity at Santa Rosa. In *Yankee Girl,* Edith does not recognize Spanish domesticity and feels compelled to teach Euro-American domesticity and find financial resources to restore the ranch because the Garcelon family has lived in poverty long before her arrival. In *Polly*, on the other hand, Polly finds the Ysidro family living a wealthy, even luxurious, life. The Ysidros do not need Polly's domesticity because "such knowledge and accomplishments as they themselves possessed mothers passed to their daughters. Also, they trained their children to be notable housewives, so that no matter how large the establishment, its mistress might have an eye and hand ready for any part of it or any duty that arose" (147). As I have noted, Polly recognizes this domesticity because she recognizes the Ysidros' whiteness. The Ysidros do need Polly for book learning, though, and she helps preserve their way of life when she makes sure the ranch is evacuated one night before raiding Indians destroy it. Where poverty destroyed the Garcelon ranch, greedy Indians destroy the Ysidro ranch, and this major plot device is metonymic for the racial hierarchy that organizes both Santa Rosa and the entire novel.

What seems, then, like an improvement over Christine's romanticization of the Rivera adobe in *Monica, the Mesa Maiden* and Patience's Americanization of Tulita's body, home, and community in *Daughter of the West* is, in *Polly*, actually a reification of whiteness by contrasting Hispanic and Anglo characters with Indian characters. It is another example of the US belief that Indians need white people to patiently and methodically civilize the Indianness right out of them. What might seem to modern readers like an acceptance of Hispanic (read: nonwhite) Americans is a typically nineteenth-century-Californian recognition of Spanish culture as white culture (along the lines of Ruiz de Burton or Helen Hunt Jackson); figuratively, Indians still stand outside this white civilization but literally support it from the inside as house servants and, in this novel, superintendents at the mission school for Indian neophytes. Polly and the Ysidro family have to live at the mission until Santa Rosa can be rebuilt after the raid, and Polly is amazed that the "white wall-church . . . was well filled, and most of the kneeling worshipers were neophytes, or Christianized Indians. Men and women, with little children, all of them so devout, that she rubbed her eyes to stare at them again. Could it be possible that these were of the same race which had come out of the wilds to ravage and destroy such homes as Santa Rosa?" (197). While *Daughter of the West* ends with a utopian scene where Tulita leads her entire Indian community to live in Anglo houses and wear European clothes, in *Polly*, published six years later, there is no such vision of assimilation for California Indians. Here the most civilized Indians are still being trained at the mission or are working in Spanish households, and the wild Indians (presumably the natural Indians) raid ranches and are mowed down by whites with guns: "A half-dozen white men can conquer a hundred redskins—dastards that they are" (189).

These distinctions between dastardly and domesticated Indians are disturbing enough in and of themselves and still more insidious in children's novels. If young white female readers can learn from Christine, Patience, and Edith to befriend Hispanics and Indians and teach them American domesticity, then they can also learn—especially from Polly—that all Indians desperately need white help and, moreover, that some Indians are beyond help and are just wild, savage, greedy, and dastardly. But child readers are surely not reliably aware that the Indian character they are reading about is not only fictional but is also a fiction constructed from the bias of a white mind. And what are Indian and Hispanic girls supposed to learn from these stories? Educators at the Indian schools believed that if the students read *Stiya*, *Little Women*, and maybe even Raymond's novels or others like them, then they would have that much more exposure to domesticity's civilizing tenets and would be ready and willing to circulate this domesticity throughout their home communities.

But how else might Indian children respond to Raymond's depictions of Indians? Would they cooperate like Tulita? Feel angry and hurt at Raymond's stereotypical descriptions or betrayed by Tulita's cooperation? Not only do white children see racism reinforced in novels like Raymond's, giving them "horrible ideas about what other people were like" (11), as Doris Seale argues in her highly influential *Through Indian Eyes: The Native Experience in Books for Children*. But during the civil rights movement of the 1960s, Seale continues, teachers and librarians began to wonder if it would also be harmful for "the children of the *other* people to be wounded in their sense of self by the things they read in books" (11). Debbie Reese maintains a website dedicated to critiquing the portrayal of Indians in children's books, and Seale and Beverly Slapin have presented a collection of stories told by contemporary Indian children and parents who encountered stereotypical Indian characters in children's books and cartoons (*A Broken Flute: The Native Experience in Books for Children*).[9] The stories help answer my questions about how Indian and Hispanic girls might respond to reading about Tulita or Monica or

Ysidra or Inez. To be sure, Victorian Indian readers of Raymond's books might have responded to these didactic tales of assimilation in the ways that white colonizers hoped; like other people surrounded by a larger culture, many American Indians did and do assimilate European American ways of life. Indeed, every North American assimilates or does not assimilate certain mores and habits of mainstream American culture. But Indian girls reading Raymond's books at the turn into the twentieth century might also have felt like the respondents to Seale and Slapin's questions about seeing themselves in children's books by white writers: sad, confused, shamed, scared, angry, and inspired to resist such stereotypes, even when assimilating dominant ways of life. The ways that Indian women negotiate such seemingly contradictory responses to imperial domesticity—both assimilation and resistance—are the focus of my next chapter about Indian women writers.

CHAPTER FOUR

Practicing Domesticity

From Domestic Outing Programs to Sovereign Domesticity

Annie Goyitney, a Laguna Pueblo and a graduating student at the Carlisle Indian Industrial School in Pennsylvania, asks in her 1901 commencement address, "What Should Be the Aim of a Carlisle Indian Girl?" As part of the answer to her question Goyitney writes,

> The Indian girl, perhaps, does not realize the value of her education, for she does not know what it is to struggle for a living as other girls do who have had no Government aid to depend upon. Yet many of us are afraid to start in life for ourselves, but we should be womanly and face whatever comes. If a girl finds that she must go home to her parents, she can be a great help to them, as she can teach them the right ways of living and make the home comfortable and cheerful for them. She may at first find hardships in their way of living but her aim should be to show them that the ways of the white people bring more comfort and happiness. (2)

That Goyitney's address smacks of the rhetoric of colonialism and the dogma of domesticity is no accident. She would not have been allowed to speak otherwise. To be sure, these lines from her speech bear striking resemblance to portions of Marianna Burgess's now-familiar novella, *Stiya, A Carlisle Indian Girl at Home: Founded on the Author's Actual Observations*, published by Riverside Press in 1891 after first circulating in 1889 in *Indian Helper*, an earlier version of the school's newsletter where Goyitney published her essay. The novella, of course, served the boarding schools as a central piece of propaganda: Stiya, the protagonist, performs "the right ways of living" for readers who were intended to be—we must remember—Carlisle Indian girls returning home. Writing *Stiya,* Burgess—a white administrator of the Carlisle school—constructed the "ideal" Indian girl who unquestioningly internalized her domestic education at Carlisle, returned home to her family, and in turn lifted her Native parents out of their Indian savagery and into American civilization. Jane E. Simonsen writes that the visit from Stiya's Carlisle teachers at novel's end sanctifies her homemaking achievements (93). Without a doubt, Stiya's clean white sheets and her clean tablecloth signal her accomplishment: she has whitewashed her family and is now a shining example of the assimilation desired by her teachers, by the Carlisle school, and by the federal government.

In this chapter, I attend to the writings of American Indian women who encountered the colonial, domestic education propagated by federal Indian schools and white women reformers who lived and worked in Indian communities throughout North America. I use the term *propagate* and its association with breeding and reproduction intentionally; as I show, federal officials used domestic education to reproduce American Indian women as copies of Euro-American women. By virtue of their newly acquired domestic skills and sentimental values, newly domesticated Indian women would, in turn, propagate American values among their families and communities. I also choose *propagate* for its etymological relation to the word *propaganda,* both words that find their origins in the Catholic Church and eighteenth-century treatises for disseminating the faith; some critics describe the curriculum for the federal boarding schools as thinly disguised colonial propaganda. The Indian women writers I discuss altered the course laid out for them by these reformers and teachers, for in learning to practice the rituals of domesticity they also learned to *write* about those domestic rituals and sentimental values.

I am aware of a decades-long critical debate about how the texts by these Indian women writers should be approached. Some literary scholars see these texts as too contaminated by whiteness to be read as Indian literature (for example, Craig Womack), some assert that the texts are not literary at all (for example, Gretchen M. Bataille and Kathleen Mullen Sands), some barely even see them as texts and call them "preliterate" (for example, David H. Brumble III); and many read these texts as autobiographical, historical, or ethnographic representations of a "real" life or culture rather than as artistic creations (for example, Alanna Kathleen Brown, Linda K. Karell, Dexter Fisher, and others). I approach these texts as literary, artistic creations, defining literature, as Jace Weaver does, "as the total written output of a people. Even biographies, autobiographies, and tribal histories would come under such a definition, because to impress form on the relative formlessness of a life or a culture, to exercise authority over what is to be included and what excluded, is an act of literary creation" ("Assimilation" ix). And despite the controversy surrounding his book, I also agree with David Treuer on this basic point: "if Native American literature is worth thinking about at all, it is worth thinking about as literature" (195).

I begin by contextualizing my readings of boarding school literature at a historical intersection where Indian reform movements and the rise of public domesticity collide. From there, I interpret articles and poems written by young girls at various Indian schools around the country; several of these pieces—as far as I know—no critics have discussed. I argue that the schoolgirls' practice of writing about domesticity laid the groundwork for American Indian women writers to engage the rhetorics of sentimentalism and domesticity that characterize much of the writing about Indians by Euro-American women in the decades surrounding the turn into the twentieth century. Through their curriculum of domestic education, female reformers and school officials did their best to control how Indian girls learned, practiced, and propagated the rituals of Euro-American domesticity. But once taught to write, these Indian girls matured into writers who could influence their own responses to their domestic education and would manipulate the sentimental discourse in ways reformers and officials could have never predicted and would have never desired. The Indian women writers I discuss later in this chapter—Estelle Armstrong (Nez Perce), Sophia Alice Callahan (Creek), Mourning Dove (Okanogan), Ella Cara Deloria (Dakota Sioux), Sarah Winnemucca Hopkins (Paiute), and Zitkála-Šá (Yankton Sioux)—all engage the sentimental and domestic rhetoric to narrate and negotiate complicated responses to their domestic educations, positing a syncretic, sovereign domesticity.

Indoctrinating Domesticity

Writings such as Burgess's and Goyitney's engage the overlapping histories of white women reformers, the boarding schools, and the colonizing manipulations of Euro-American domesticity that both the reformers and the schools performed in efforts to Americanize American Indians. It was no coincidence that Indian education efforts—especially the education of Indian girls—centered on the home and domestic life. As Simonsen points out, several historians argue that "domesticity was an imperial construct used by the white middle class to uphold its power in a diversifying and expansionist nation" (3). Among others, Amy Kaplan, Anne McClintock, Margaret D. Jacobs, and Peggy Pascoe show how domesticity and women's work were indispensable tools for Americanizing the indigenous peoples of the North American landmass now known as the United States. Religious groups such as Council of Women for Home Missions, nondenominational reform clubs such as the Women's National Indian Association, and groups associated with the Works Progress Administration and the Indian New Deal gave white women, from the mid-nineteenth century to the mid-twentieth century, the opportunity to take up the cause of the Indian "less fortunate" and extend their own influence beyond the confines of their home and immediate and familial social circles and out into the public sphere.

Ironically, the very confines they sought to transcend—the private sphere of home and family—provided the tools and values they used to colonize Indian women. Pascoe and Siohban Senier argue that these white women reformers were likely more motivated by their own desire for moral authority and self-authorization than by philanthropic or compassionate impulses to better the lives of those around them. Alison Bernstein questions the appropriateness of the methods of such programs as the Women's National Indian Association or the Indian New Deal, arguing that replacing Indian gender roles with white gender norms was indeed a "cultural imposition," even though its participants saw it as "progressive." Bernstein notes that "the Indian New Deal made a conscious effort to include Indian women as part of its programs and activities"—particularly those that "provided training in cooking, sewing, childcare, and handcrafts"—but she argues that "this attempt to give Indian women the status white women enjoyed also seriously ignored the traditional" roles Indian women filled in their tribes (16).

Working to replace tribal gender roles with Euro-American ideals, white women lived and worked in and near Indian communities all over the United States, and this work spilled over—not surprisingly—into the curriculum of the federal Indian schools, especially at the boarding schools. To lesser or greater extents, nearly every historian and critic of the boarding schools points out the intentional efforts among school officials to instill domestic values in female students.[1] These scholars have established, comprehensively and inarguably, the centrality of the ideology of domesticity to the schools' express purpose: "Kill the Indian, and save the man." Indeed, Richard Pratt and other boarding school officials imagined that the most direct course to "saving" Indian men was "chiefly through their women" (Mason 238). The Indian schools received standardized curricula from Washington, DC. *Course of Study for the Indian Schools of the United States. Industrial and Literary* (1901), written by Estelle Reel, shows that this training in domesticity was organized at the federal level and was equally prioritized alongside reading, writing, and arithmetic. Perhaps domesticity even held higher priority, for in the "Housekeeping" lesson, Reel instructs teachers thus: "if there is time for nothing else, housekeeping must be taught" (152).

The domestic curriculum Reel and others wrote and implemented was founded on white racist assumptions that Indian parents—and particularly Indian mothers—were sorely lacking in their ability to raise children who could in any way adapt to life under the new regime of settler colonialism. Mollie V. Gaither, a school official from Oregon, captures this assumption in an article for the Superintendent of Indian Schools' report in 1897:

> The Indian girl comes to us from a home where the mother is the drudge and beast of burden, and if the daughter thinks at all on the subject she knows that this is the part expected of her in the life which lies before her; hence the most readily accepted training in our schools is that which in their province of nursery for true womanhood teaches the young girl not only to knit and sew, to bake and to mend, to wash and to scrub, to care for the young, the old, and the sick, but also gives her the strength of character to become an independent, self-reliant woman, capable of assuming any burden that life in its manifold chances and changes may lay upon her. (Child 78)

Once an Indian girl was removed from her own mother's supposedly inept influence, the boarding schools provided replacement mothers—school matrons, usually but not always white women—whose job was to "serve as a more wholesome replacement for the girls' darker and immoral natural mothers. . . . If the superintendent was the stern patriarch of the institution, the matron was its instinctive mother" (Child 79). We can read two conflicting goals of this domestic education in Gaither's statement. First, in calling the schools the "nursery for true womanhood," Gaither implies that Indian girls were taught the domestic arts and sentimental values she lists so that they too could be true women who would marry, have children, and tend to their homes and families.

Devon A. Mihesuah also writes about the educational goal of creating Indian true women at the Cherokee Female Seminary. The Cherokee Female Seminary differed markedly from the other boarding schools and is an exceptional case, primarily because it was not federally sponsored but also because of different assumptions about its clientele and different designs for its curriculum. Mihesuah notes that the school, established in 1851, was unique in that it was tribally maintained and required tribal enrollment for admission and offered a course of study modeled on the curriculum at Mount Holyoke Seminary rather than designed by federal reformers (1). The seminary shared the goals of federal institutions in that "one of the Cherokee National Council's rationales for establishing the school was to train the young women of the tribe in order to make them educated, dutiful, and 'useful' wives for prominent Cherokee husbands" (3). Whereas the federal schools assumed, as Gaither did, a cultural ineptness (at best) in Indian women, the seminary assumed the opposite. Mihesuah asserts that "'women's values' and the ideal of the 'true woman' are often assumed to be a part of the white woman's world exclusively. But a number of Cherokee females were economically, socially, and physiologically nearly identical to Victorian society's white women, and many seminary students subscribed to the same value system as whites even before they enrolled" (3). So despite these important differences, the goals at the seminary resembled those at federal schools, in that the girls' "education would serve to reform or mold Cherokee society into a copy of white society, a goal that many Cherokees shared. Educated females would become pious homemakers and companions to their prominent husbands, whose self-esteem was undoubtedly elevated by placing women in a position that seemed exalted yet was subservient" (21). And even though at its opening, the seminary, like Mount Holyoke, did not include domestic science courses because of the belief that Cherokee mothers were capable of training their daughters themselves, it eventually implemented a domestic science curriculum. Mihesuah notes that by the end of the nineteenth century, the school felt pressure from the national push for the "'professionalization' of housework" and from parents who "had been pushing administrators to teach their daughters the 'most essential qualities that are so important to housewivery'" (60, 61). By 1905 the school implemented the new curriculum with courses in cleaning, cooking, sewing, and gardening (60–61).

Despite the stated intentions of the federal institutions and the obvious exception of the Cherokee Female Seminary's goals of creating true women out of their female Indian students, other historians question this intention and its results by arguing that the schools trained the girls to join the domestic workforce as servants and laborers in white women's houses. Indeed, the work of the boarding schools exemplify Homi Bhaba's assertion that "colonial mimicry is the desire for a reformed, recognizable Other, *as a subject of difference that is almost the same, but not quite*" (122). The goal of the boarding schools' domestic education programs, some argue, was to create Indian women who were near approximations of white women; they could perform Victorian domesticity, but the performances would be enacted as servants in whites' homes under the watchful eye of the lady of the house. K. Tsianina Lomawaima writes that Chilocco's domestic education program "was in step with the unreality of the times, as patriarchal American society envisioned women's place in the home. Indian women's place reflected the double burden of gender and race. Their domesticity training prepared them not to labor in their homes but as employees of white women or the boarding schools that trained them" (81). Lomawaima, Child, and Myriam Vuckovic all write about the outing programs at various Indian schools that placed Indian girls with white, middle-class families where they did the families' housework. Vuckovic writes about the domestic science cottages at Haskell that were models of the ideal, modern American home, where eight Indian girls would stay for a ten-week practicum in the routines of domesticity. Vuckovic argues that although the girls surely enjoyed this diversion from their regular academic routines and dormitory life, "the cottage was the closest they would ever come to a white middle-class lifestyle. . . . The cottage was a modern home with electric lights, running water, and a furnace—conditions that only few girls would actually find upon their return home" (119).

Lomawaima, Child, and Vuckovic argue that the outing program never maintained a steady placement rate, suggesting that "the development of subservience among Indian women rather than realistic training for employment" (Lomawaima 87) was the objective of the schools' domestic curriculum. The internal contradiction of Gaither's article, then—and the ultimate contradiction of the federal domestic education curriculum for Indian girls—is that, even though the schools trained Indian girls in the values of true womanhood, their teachers never really expected them to embody what that ideal entailed. Instead of becoming wives, mothers, and keepers of their own homes, Indian girls were actually being trained as domestic workers. Gaither writes that Indian girls were taught to be "independent, self-reliant wom[e]n," something that true women never had to be, nor were supposed to be. In Gaither's article, then, "independent" and "self-reliant" connote "worker," not "wife."

It is in this context of domestic education that Carlisle circulated Burgess's *Stiya* and Goyitney's address as part of the curriculum. Several scholars have discussed the roles that literary domesticity, or the sentimental form, played for female Indian students who navigated the ideological quagmires that were the boarding schools. Amelia V. Katanski and Ernest Stromberg, for instance, address the work of Francis La Flesche, Charles Eastman, and Zitkála-Šá, focusing primarily on what they wrote *after* they were students. Janet Dean discusses *Stiya* and S. Alice Callahan's sentimental novel, *Wynema*, focusing on *reading* as a site of colonial indoctrination and Native resistance. But in taking the pseudonym Embe and writing *Stiya* as a first-person narration of a Carlisle girl's return home, Burgess also imagined an Indian girl *writing*. *Stiya* functioned as federal propaganda, but it also stood as both a model for student writing and a plot against which students could react and write. Indeed, a vast archive of newspapers and magazines from boarding schools across the country yields this indisputable fact: Indian girls were writing—many more than we can realize if we focus only on writers who would become famous, such as La Flesche, Zitkála-Šá, and Callahan. School publications contain numerous articles, essays, stories, and poems about domesticity written by anonymous or relatively unknown Native girls at these federal institutions. Much like a military draft, the schools drafted Indian girls into Euro-American-style domestic service—at school, in white women's homes, and in their own homes as daughters and, allegedly and eventually, as wives.

But while at school, Indian girls also drafted sentimental literature. As Dean astutely argues, Indian students were taught to "read right" in order to "feel right" about their colonial educations. The next lesson was learning to *write right.* Structuring this chapter is the argument that, unwittingly, the boarding schools trained a generation of Native women writers who repurposed the dominant, feminized discourses in the United States in the decades surrounding the turn into the twentieth century.[2] Through their curriculum of domestic education, female reformers and school officials did their best to control how Indian girls learned, practiced, and propagated the rituals of Euro-American domesticity. But once taught to write, these Indian girls became women writers who shaped their own responses to their domestic education and would manipulate the sentimental discourse in ways reformers and officials did not anticipate. Reading boarding school writing in this way, as Beth H. Piatote writes, helps "make visible the resilience of the tribal-national domestic by centering the intimate domestic (the Indian home and family) as the primary site of struggle against the foreign force of U.S. national domestication" (4). The sentimental texts I discuss show how writing into such dominant discourses is central to the Indian students' survivance and subverts the before-and-after aims of the boarding schools, thus disrupting not only the plot of domestic ideology but the conventions of sentimental form.[3] If we look at this archive of boarding school texts as a product of a writing circle that spans decades, student writing like Goyitney's becomes foundational to the more widely circulated work of Estelle Armstrong, Zitkála-Šá, and others. Students write, other students read that writing, more students write, students graduate and some continue writing, and more students read what graduates wrote. In this way, boarding school writing perpetuated a discursive circle in which American Indians narrated and read about their own lives as lived out in a colonial context.

Perhaps because of *Stiya*'s success as propaganda—Leslie Marmon Silko says it was meant to "inoculate" Carlisle graduates "against their 'uncivilized' families"—scholars have been hesitant to discuss boarding school student writing as literary constructs. That *Stiya* was originally published serially in *Indian Helper* is but one telling example of how administrators used school newspapers to disseminate Euro-American values to Indian students. Daniel Littlefield and James Parins write that the school publications served an "essentially propagandistic purpose" (1) by spreading these values among the students and, as Katanski indicates, to show the general population that the institutions inculcated Americanness and assure them that the "Indian problem" was under control. Katanski also points out that Burgess and Pratt regularly wrote and published articles in the school's papers that looked as if Indian students wrote them—"paper Indians"—in addition to publishing articles that were actually written by Indian students but were carefully edited to appear in print as a total assimilation to the school's mission. Burgess's and Pratt's paper Indians exemplify the typical late nineteenth- and early twentieth-century belief in the ideological power of reading to sway readers to think, believe, or do one thing or the other.[4]

It is no wonder, given this belief in the power of reading,[5] that educators like Burgess and Pratt appropriated student writing for its indoctrinating purposes. The logic makes sense: reading what your peers write seems an effective form of peer pressure. As Dean points out, this belief and logic certainly permeated boarding school curriculum. But while many scholars have discussed Indian student readers and writers, a hesitant approach to student-authored texts still characterizes the scholarship. Vuckovic includes excerpts and interpretations of several Haskell student texts, but she does not include any on the subject of domesticity. Katanski also acknowledges Indian student writing. But she does not provide examples of it or contextualize it, instead dismissing it as written under coercion and thus not worth studying. And while Jessica Enoch discusses the performative roles of the Carlisle school newspapers and the ways Zitkála-Šá "erases Carlisle's script" (124) with her publications in *Atlantic Monthly*, she also does not present or interpret any student writing. Alicia Cox too, in her insightful essay on Polingaysi Qoyawayma's memoir of her education at the Sherman Institute (*No Turning Back: A Hopi Indian Woman's Struggle to Live in Two Worlds*), reads issues of the school's newspaper without discussing student writers. Amy Goodburn is one of the few scholars to engage student writings, arguing that the girls' essay form changed from personal narrative to step-by-step instructions to performing domestic tasks; as such, they "echoed the national project of manifest destiny" (93). In a chapter that traces a trajectory of Native education through Native educational narratives, Robert Warrior discusses Native student workers at school printing presses, a Carlisle student's essay (Dennis Wheelock, Oneida, 1887) about the US government's policy not to teach with Indian languages, and more recent literature about boarding school life and Indian education. Lori Ostergaard, Amy Mecklenburg-Faegner, and Henrietta Rix Wood include a brief discussion of Haskell's the *Indian Leader* as part of their comparison of three high schools (1897–1930) that encouraged girls to engage public discourses via writing. Though they cite a couple of essays by Indian girls, they seemingly do so in order to craft their portrait of *Indian Leader*'s early editor, the white Helen W. Ball, as resisting "the villain-victim binary" of boarding school history (43).

Without a doubt, officials at the boarding schools used their newspapers and magazines to circulate and reinforce the fiction that the process of assimilating Native students was going exactly as planned. Just as the school papers used before-and-after images of domesticated Indian students to assure the reading public that the "Indian problem" was under control (as Piatote and Laura Wexler have discussed), so they used student writing to show that domesticated Indians are not a novelty or a contradiction. But as Scott Richard Lyons writes, "All Indian texts are x-marks, all texts contend with discursive contexts, and Indian space is where this all gets played out. . . . writing Indians are no longer seen as an inherent contradiction" (26). To continue disregarding student writing as literary production because we judge it as assimilative or coerced is to continue disregarding the agency of Indian students. I agree with Child, who cautions that "newspapers reflected the culture of boarding schools; even articles authored by American Indians were destined for a public audience that must therefore be approached with a measure of skepticism" (xii). But I would argue that most literary critics approach most texts with some measure of skepticism, and coercion does not necessarily keep student writing from being literary documents worthy of serious scrutiny. Student writings from boarding schools can be read as what Lyons calls "x-marks":

> The x-mark is a contaminated and coerced sign of consent made under conditions that are not of one's making. It signifies power and a lack of power, agency and a lack of agency. It is a decision one makes when something has already been decided for you, but it is still a decision. Damned if you do, damned if you don't. And yet

> there is always the prospect of slippage, indeterminacy, unforeseen consequences, or unintended results; it is always possible, that is, that an x-mark could result in something good. (*X-Marks* 3)

Goyitney's commencement address suggests that a decade after *Stiya*, Carlisle's teachers continued to administer the "Stiya inoculation" to help students build a resistance to the supposedly uncivilized Indian ways that awaited Carlisle students on their return home. But whether Carlisle trained Indian schoolgirls to be housewives or housekeepers, the federal institutions also taught them to be readers and writers; and these skills allowed Indian women writers to transcend the destinies designed for them by the schools and to speak back using the very rhetorical and ideological tools colonizers taught them.

Figuring out ways of thinking about this archive of writing, an archive that is usually only referred to as exemplary of indoctrination, requires abandoning the polarized ways of thinking about Indian responses to colonization—as either assimilation or resistance. Thinking about these texts requires dwelling in the often uncomfortable, interstitial spaces where the terms of engagement are not clearly defined, spaces such as the contact zone (Mary Louise Pratt), the middle ground (Richard White), or "the detonation zone of culture bombs" (Warrior referencing Ngugi wa Thiong'o, *People* 121). Perhaps we can approach such ideologically complex texts remembering that "discourses can always be appropriated and challenged . . . but they cannot be ignored. When the Indian speaks, it always speaks as an Indian, and it must do so in a discursive context that, thanks to colonization, is never of pure Native origin. This is why all Indian texts are x-marks" (Lyons, *X-Marks* 25). Indeed, Lyons builds on Simon J. Ortiz's foundational assertion that "the indigenous peoples of the Americas have taken the languages of the colonialists and used them for their own purposes. Some would argue that this means that Indian people have succumbed or become educated into a different linguistic system and have forgotten or have been forced to forsake their native selves. This is simply not true. . . . they have used these languages on their own terms" (10). Perhaps Gerald Vizenor's concept of survivance can also help us see the ways these student writers demonstrate their "active presence over absence, deracination, and oblivion" and renounce "dominance, detractions, obtrusions, the unbearable sentiments of tragedy, and the legacy of victimry" (*Survivance* 1). What follows here, then, are close readings that show how literary texts produced by boarding school students "appropriate and challenge" the ideology of domesticity and the genre of sentimentalism. Cox describes decolonization as "the ongoing processes of removing or transforming the pernicious cultural effects of colonization—for example, the myth of the assimilated Indian" or, in the context of this essay, the myth of the domesticated Indian (55). As Warrior asserts, boarding school narratives "persist as gifts of intelligence and artistry. To assume otherwise is to hamstring written Native literature as an innocent outgrowth of Native literacy and to view Native writers as writing simply because they could" (*People* 117). While at school and after they left, Native women writers decolonized these homogenizing discourses and used them for their own strategic purposes: to recast the rhetorics of domesticity and sentimentalism on their own terms, a syncretic yet sovereign domesticity.

Drafting Domesticity

Finding themselves in a physical and discursive space that sought to annihilate them—at least culturally and linguistically, when not corporeally—boarding school students wrote for self-determination. The sovereign domesticity they drafted with their pens and paper was the result of and the motivation for the syncretism that shaped their writings. Many of the essays, poems, and stories seem merely to ventriloquize Euro-American domestic rhetoric. But if we read them not as ventriloquism but as mimicry, we see that Bhaba's concept of "ambivalence" characterizes the students' writings, for while they are grounded in the rhetoric of domesticity, their mimicry "continually produces its slippage, its excess, its difference" (122). In particular, the student writers disrupt the before/after transformation plot of domestic ideology and replace the discrete space-time settings of conventional sentimental writing with a sense of longing for elsewhere and elsetime. With these methods, whether in combination or separately, they subvert the ironically depersonalizing model/copy logic of both domestic ideology and sentimental writing and blur that line of supposed distinction between the model and the copy (of American womanhood) that Gilles Deleuze theorizes in his concept of the simulacrum.

Domesticity, by definition, centers on the household and a particular devotion to home life. It could go without saying, then, that domestic or sentimental writing features the home as the nuclear setting around which the heroine acts. So how do girls writing at school, away from their homes and families, use domesticity as a literary motif? One way is to describe a before/after process of domestication. Several of the student writers use this method, tellingly varying the setting they define as before or after. In the following examples, the boarding school figures as a pivotal yet paradoxical setting for the before/after plotline: school is both before and after for these writers.

Edith (Cherokee) writes a before/after vignette in her "View from Our Seminary" for an 1854 issue of *Cherokee Rose Buds*. She describes the prairies and woodlands she sees from the school grounds, noting that "peeping from among the trees of the [groves], instead of the rudely constructed *wigwams* of our forefathers which stood there not more than half a century ago, elegant white dwellings are seen. Everything around denotes taste, refinement and the progress of civilization among our people: long may they vie with the long enlightened inhabitants of the *east*" (403). We can read these "white dwellings" as a double entendre: the siding might actually be painted white, but Edith implies that they are also styled like Euro-Americans' homes and so signify how civilized her people are. And while her tale of transformation does not so neatly describe school or home as the setting for the before or after, we can infer that the school—from where the view inspires her reverie—stands as both product and perpetuator of Cherokee "taste," "refinement," "progress," "civilization," and "enlighten[ment]."

Writing for Haskell's the *Indian Leader*, two girls pen third-person autobiographies that read like boarding school bildungsromans. In "Autobiography of an Indian Girl" (1897), Bright Eyes[6] describes her journey from "a family who were not civilized," whose "home was a small teepee with no furniture to make it comfortable and with no bed to sleep on," to Haskell Institute, where "the first English word she had learned was 'pincushion'" (415).

Domestic and linguistic habits mark Bright Eyes's narrative of transformation. While at school, she "learned to love her new home" and "learned the English Language" (415). After being at school for three years, she goes home to visit her father and stepmother but is shocked to find her father "with Indian clothes on"; "she had not thought of seeing him in that condition" (415). Bright Eyes chafes when her family "jabbered away in Indian" since she could now only "understand a few words" (416). And even though she marvels to see that her father has built "a small, white, frame house," she fumes when she realizes they all still sleep in their teepee, and she finds "herself lying on the hard ground. She said: 'How I wish I was back to my dear old school home and could lie between two clean white sheets instead of on the ground'" (416). Bright Eyes sticks it out with her family for four months, then successfully "coaxed her father" to send her back to her "dear old school home" (416). Much like Stiya's story in Burgess's novella, Bright Eyes sees the school as the "after" to the life she lived with her family before going to school. She describes her life before school in terms of domestic lack and measures her family's degree of civilization by its dwelling structure and furnishings. At school, she adds language as a measure of civilization. But then the setting shifts and school becomes the "before" to the life she might live after she returns home. The setting shifts one more time before Bright Eyes concludes her story, and once again her home is the "before" to the "after" that is the school.

Published anonymously, "An Indian Girl's History, Written by Herself" (1899) also traces the life of a girl born "in an Indian teepee" (417) who ends up "very glad to think she has the privilege of going to school" at Haskell (417, 418). Before going to school, the girl "lived in a house made out of bark," and "whenever the white folks came to their house she would go out in the woods to hide" (417). But after ten years at Haskell, the girl "was very proud to think she went. She did not dress like an Indian girl now," and she soon learned English (418). In both autobiographies, the school replaces the girls' homes. Bright Eyes chooses to go back to her "dear old school home" after returning to her family, and both girls stay at Haskell for more than ten years. Karen L. Kilcup suggests that the anonymous narrative, "with its odd third-person perspective, suggests a high degree of teacher intervention" (*Native American* 400). The same could be said for Bright Eyes's piece, also written in third person. As Katanski points out, teachers commonly edited heavily or even wrote entirely some articles attributed to students in the schools' publications. It is also possible that, much as in modern high schools, teachers instructed the girls not to write school essays in the first or second person. Many of us who teach writing have had to contend with the similarly awkward third-person phrasings of our students, who try to make their writing sound academic by going far out of their way to avoid using *I* or *you*.

Whatever the degree of teacher intervention, the schools published student writings on domesticity as evidence that assimilation programs worked. Bright Eyes's piece is prefaced by an introduction, presumably written by one of her teachers:

> Having been asked to write an oration to be delivered before her fellow students in the assembly hall, she said she did not know what theme to write upon, unless it was her own life experience. The idea having been approved, she wrote the story which is here reproduced from her manuscript as she wrote it herself. The plain school-girl style in which it is written greatly enhances the interest awakened by the pleasing recital. The story is valuable as a proof taken from the actual life experience of a full-blooded Indian, demonstrating the effective manner in which the rising generation of the American Indian can be, and actually is, being introduced into civilized life by the training they receive at the US government schools for Indians. (415)

Of course, we should not take the teacher's word for it that she is reproducing Bright Eyes's essay exactly as she wrote it. The teacher might be protesting too much here. On the other hand, we should not dismiss Bright Eyes's piece as too mediated or assume that she did not write it because her teachers might have edited it or because it is too assimilative. History shows that many Indians did and do assimilate and that many had happy experiences at boarding schools. Lomawaima has recorded interviews with Indian women who attended Chilocco's domestic education program. Though one Cherokee, Winona, says she was a "little bit resentful because we felt that the home economics course was the only course that was open to us," she also laughs and says, "I found that it was something I've always been able to use in my own home" (88). Irene (Potawatomi) says she thought the practice cottage was a "*wonderful* way to teach you," and Juanita (Cherokee) recalls that the cottage "was a play house, it was fun, we liked it" (89).

The essays written by Bright Eyes and the anonymous student at Haskell differ from Lomawaima's socio/anthropological data, though, in that they end at the boarding school—the "after" setting. Unlike Irene, who told Lomawaima that she found her domestic education useful in her own home, these two Haskell writers do not—perhaps cannot—imagine an "after" in their own Indian homes. In this way, the girls not only suggest the cognitive and cultural dissonance boarding school students experienced, but they also disrupt the before/after plot of transformation so heralded by school officials. As the following examples corroborate, Indian women's writings about domesticity are a site of ideological struggle. School officials imagined some sort of standardized transition from Indian home life to boarding school domestic education to a civilized version of Indian home life once the girls finished school; but as these writings indicate, the students struggle to articulate an "after" setting that contains their newly acquired habits of Euro-American domesticity.

Where early students at Haskell solved this problem by using school as their "after" and avoiding talk of their futures after finishing school, a later Haskell student, Alice Bellanger (Ojibwe), complicates the before/after setting while speculating about her post-school future. In "Home-Making" (1915), she details building and decorating a home, as do many of the boarding school writers. But Bellanger's statements about the power of home disrupt the before/after transformation plot in that—here again—defining a setting as before or after remains elusive:

> the influence of a home follows us wherever we go, helping mold our sentiments and shape our lives. . . . If children are brought up as good Christians they will be happier and the better for it. It will make the home a happy one and that home will be an influence and an example to the whole community. . . . Good citizenship depends upon home training. Good men and women are wanted and where shall we get them if the home training is neglected? (10)

How does Bellanger define "home" in the opening sentence of this passage? Read one way, we might think she is ventriloquizing boarding school discourse, highlighting the importance of how she will raise her own potential children. Likely learned at school, Christianity is what will make Bellanger's home and children happy. Christianity would mold and shape their sentiments and lives, making them better citizens and good examples (of Christian citizens?) to their communities. Read this way, Bellanger's "before" is both her Ojibwe home and her school training and her "after" is a Christian home of her own; the essay coheres with the official plot of transformation of Native girls into approximations of white women.

Read another way, Bellanger's definition of home is not so stable. If "the influence of a home follows us wherever we go, helping mold our sentiments and shape our lives," she might also refer to her Ojibwe home. She is at school, but Ojibwe lifeways still guide her. What follows in the passage, then, seems characterized by an anxiety about how to synthesize her Ojibwe upbringing with her domestic education at school. Certainly, Bellanger could have experienced Christianity in her home community. But the rhetoric of "good Christians" and "[g]ood citizenship," combined with the emphasis on "home training" and being an example to others, is just as certainly something she would have learned at school. Her closing question highlights her anxiety but also suggests that home training can be and is "neglected." Domestic indoctrination, when struggled through in writing, seems easier accomplished in theory than in practice.

The anxieties Bellanger and Goyitney imply about their domestic futures underscore the tentativeness, or perhaps belie the narrative, of the boarding schools' before/after plot. As Mark Rifkin and Alicia Cox discuss, the writings of Zitkála-Šá, Qoyawayma, and these unknown female students offer "a counternarrative to administrative efforts to impose a detribalizing teleology justified as the achievement of real and stable love, home, and family, instead connecting romance to the maintenance of indigenous collective identity and forms of self-determination" (Rifkin, "Romancing" 29). School officials carefully packaged this detribalizing teleology as the uplifting rituals of domesticity, but as the boarding school writers show, the school's version of domesticity was really the practice of creating an *illusion* of transformation. Much like sentimental fiction creates an illusion that nuclear families living in clean, sparkling homes equals happiness, healthiness, morality, Christianity, and Americanness, so the schools' domestic ideology sought to clean up and make presentable the messy work of killing Indians and saving men. At the same time, the schools used their publications to persuade the reading public that domesticating Indians was a neat, tidy, before/after process. At stake here is Indian futurity: How does a Native girl, educated at federal boarding schools, enter the world upon graduation?

In much of boarding school writing, home is merely an idea projected onto some other place and time. Goyitney's commencement address reflects as much on the ideology of domesticity as it does on her years at Carlisle and disrupts conventional notions of setting, echoing a sense that home is somewhere else at some other time. Saying that many Indian girls are afraid to start their own lives suggests that life at school was a suspension of living their lives. Using the conditional if-then sentence structure to describe her potential domestic life after graduation indicates that this home so promoted by the schools may not be her own home with her own husband and children after all; it may likely be a life trying to convince her backward parents that the ways of the white people bring more comfort and happiness. Bellanger's essay too, even though it might be read as an affirmation of the before/after transformation with a more clearly defined setting for the "after," uses the same sentence structure and future tense to describe the children she "will" raise. In addition, then, to describing school life as their "afters," many of the student writers disrupt the transformative process of domesticity by describing vague settings for home—settings that are neither now nor then, here nor there.

Several more student-writing examples dislocate domesticity from its typical grounding in space-time. As with the earlier examples, these pieces can read like mere playback from their classroom recordings of domestic ideology. But the space-time disruptions that ripple through student writings highlight the incomplete transfer of Euro-American domestic values from white teachers to Indian students. Alma Mollie, a Pima student at the Phoenix Indian School in Arizona, wrote "Housekeeping" for the 1906 commencement issue of the school's newspaper, the *Native American*. Mollie opens with the assertion that three things a housekeeper needs "that she may properly manage the home in which she lives are intelligence, common sense, and industry" (189). The rest of her brief article reads like a job application for a housekeeping position: "I would like to tell you how I would manage the affairs of this household in a cleanly and orderly way" (189). Then she lists the ways she would perform the duties of preparing breakfast, making beds ("in the way I was taught at the Phoenix school"), sweeping and dusting, arranging furniture "so that my home be as pleasing and attractive as possible" (190), cooking and serving dinner and supper promptly, and sitting down to a quiet evening of needlework. Surely used by the Phoenix school as evidence of her assimilation of American domestic ideology,

Mollie's use of the conditional verb tense distances herself from it by displacing it onto some other time and space.

Similar articles came out in the 1911, 1914, and 1915 commencement issues of *Indian Leader*. In 1911 Wyandot student Grace Crotzer published "The Value of Thorough Domestic Training" to assert that "all girls should be taught to cook and sew and to keep every part of a home. This is quite as essential to a girl as reading, writing and arithmetic and should be equally as compulsory in all schools" (2). Oneida student Margaret Doxtator shows a more acute awareness of the national stakes of students' domestic training in her 1914 "The Importance of Making the Home Attractive." Doxtator argues that the home is "the center of love, order, faith, unselfishness, and reverence" and that as such, "it is quite important to open our eyes to the possibilities of development of character-building in an attractive, orderly living place, and as young people are the assets of the nation our best thought should be directed toward having the right influences at work here" at home (9). She reminds her fellow female students that "the household affairs are as important as any other occupation in the world" and that, "as the homemaker comes in contact with almost every variety of retail merchant, the home certainly has a close and intimate relation to the business world in general" (9, 9–10). More explicitly than the writings of the other girls, Doxtator's essay resonates with the rhetoric of republican motherhood—that an American woman best serves her nation by raising patriotic, capitalist, and Christian citizens in her home—so thoroughly researched and theorized in the pivotal work of scholars such as Mary Kelley and Gillian Brown. But even as Mollie, Crotzer, and Doxtator seem like poster girls for the thoroughness of domestic indoctrination, they seemingly keep the ideology at arm's length. They (or perhaps, more accurately, their narrative personas) do not seem intimately connected to the domestic spaces and rituals they discuss, as do many white women writing in sentimental mode such as Louisa May Alcott or Catherine Beecher or Harriet Beecher Stowe. Perhaps this is simply due to the physical fact that they are at school while writing about home. As Bhaba points out, though, writing emerges between mimesis and mimicry. Where mimicry, by definition, describes an action (i.e., the girls practicing housekeeping methods), mimesis describes a literary or artistic rendering of the real world (i.e., the girls writing about housekeeping methods). And here, in writing, is where the slippages of ideological colonization can be seen.

Margaret Beauregard, an Ojibwe at the Chilocco Indian School in Oklahoma, writes "The Indian Girl as a Home-maker" as a commencement address in 1910 that was then published in the school's newspaper, *Indian School Journal.* Beauregard's article echoes another line of rhetoric that dominates women's writings at the turn into the twentieth century, that of true womanhood. Her account of true womanhood has a racialized twist, however. She writes that Indian girls have to work harder to be true women than do white girls because they have to catch up on centuries of "civilization" and English-language speaking to be a true woman, who she defines as "one who knows her place in life and who attends strictly to her own business [in the home] and not to that of anyone else." Although she asserts that it is no wonder white girls are naturally better homemakers than Indian girls, Beauregard values her time at Chilocco, for it was there that "I have been especially fortunate in being brought into contact with good Christian women who have taught me both by precept and example, that, in order that we may live the life up to the standard that has been set for us, we must live the life of a Christian." In addition, she vows to emulate the "true woman who is always trying to make her home just the very best and most comfortable place for her husband and children." Beauregard's remarks signal at least a nascent awareness of the duplicity of the schools' domesticating project. Defining true womanhood and civilization by practicing domesticity and speaking English, she seems to know she is being made into a copy of white womanhood. She also seems to know that she and her Indian classmates will never be a complete copy of the model; white girls, she says, have been practicing European (and Euro-American) domestic habits for centuries. While she says it's the Indian girls' job to "work our way up," she also says, "it is not an easy matter to begin all over as we have had to do" (51).

About halfway through her address, Beauregard slips some constructive criticism of Chilocco's curriculum into her speech:

> Perhaps, if we could have been taught in our own native tongue, we might not have been so slow in learning the ways of civilization and could have taken our places side by side with the white people long ago. Taking all these things into consideration you can plainly see why the white girl ought to be a far better home-maker than the Indian girl. But I know many Indian girls who are good home-makers in every respect. (51)

The disruptions in Beauregard's before/after transformation narrative ("we will never be as good at this as white girls") and her displacement of domestic space-time ("we must at some point appropriate these habits even if we won't be as good at them as white girls") belie the boarding schools' assimilative goals. She jabs at the language policy of the schools (English only) and in so doing exposes the fact that the goal for Indian students was never to have them take their places "side by side with the white people." The slippages in Beauregard's address highlight an inherent contradiction in colonial ideology: the colonizer desires the colonized to be "almost the same, but not quite." The slippages (here and in other students' writings) might also confirm that, despite some scholars' insistence on questioning all Native writing mediated by white editors, Beauregard and other student writers did, in fact, write these pieces.

If we read the students' essays through the propagandistic intentions of boarding school officials, then the authorship of these writings might not matter all that much. If the schools were creating illusions of transformations anyway, then whether students actually penned the pieces or instructors ghosted them becomes a moot point when considered as but another trick in the hat of a master illusionist. Federal officials used domestic education programs to remake American Indian girls into copies of Euro-American women who, by virtue of their newly acquired domestic skills and sentimental vocabulary, would, in turn, propagate American values among their families and communities. This model/copy logic gets reinforced at the boarding school not only by the forced change in dress, habits, and hairstyles but also in the curriculum, the school newspapers and magazines, and the (hypothetical) potential that Indian girls could perform the ideals of Euro-American gender roles.[7] Writing about abolitionist texts, Karen Sánchez-Eppler shows how sentimental fiction is a prime genre for tracing "the implications of a bodily definition of identity" (2). Similarly, writing about the role of seduction and democracy in American sentimental novels, Elizabeth Barnes asserts, "sentimental literature contributes to broader cultural discourse that obscures the differences between real and fictional bodies and attempts to dramatize anxieties about the material body through fictions that replicate the sympathetic process" (7–8).

In my readings of these boarding school stories, essays, and poems, I'm thinking with and against Barnes's idea of "sympathetic identification," the notion that sentimental literature offers a model for "imagining oneself in another's positions" (ix). School officials used sentimental literature for that reason, creating space in school publications for Indian girls to imagine themselves as white in their writings about domesticity. Conversely, the schools purported to imagine the Other in one's own position: to imagine that Indian girls, via domestic education and practices, could become white citizens. But in actual fact, the girls were trained for domestic service in white households and taught housekeeping habits to take back to the reservation. Indian girls were supposed to imagine themselves in the white woman's position when they were writing about domesticity, but, as the boarding school writings show, they do not. Instead, they imagine an Indian home elsewhere. In this way, illustrating Bhaba's theory of colonial mimicry, it would not matter which girl wrote what because of the "metonymy of presence": "the desire of colonial mimicry—an interdictory desire—may not have an object, but it has strategic objectives" (128). There is no ex-Indian girl or ex-Indian home on the other side of federal domestic education for Indians. The Indian girl-turned-woman would still be Other because she would still be Indian (despite Pratt's injunction to "kill the Indian, and save the man").

But on the other hand, the authorship of boarding school writings matters greatly, particularly because white writers often masqueraded as Indian in the school newspapers. If, as Barnes suggests, "sentimental literature teaches a particular way of reading both texts and people that relies on likeness and thereby reinforces homogeneity" (4), then the way Native domestic writers subvert the tropes and forms of the sentimental genre also defies this depersonalizing and homogenizing model/copy logic. Whether constructing fictional characters or narrating personal experiences, each of these writers maintains her subjectivity and those of her characters by drafting pieces that are almost-the-same-but-not-quite replicas of sentimental convention. Students Maude Cooke (Mohawk, New York) and Agnes Hatch (Chippewa, Michigan), cowrote "Our Cottage" for Carlisle's publications, a poem that disrupts the replication process of the model cottage program.[8] For most of the poem, the speakers hum along with dactyls, singing the joys of

> This Model Home banner which teaches so true,
> The ways of plain home life and happiness, too,—

> The planning and serving of different foods,
> That would set grouchy people in pleasurable moods. (238)

Cooke and Hatch echo a central tenet of sentimentalist rhetoric: that a simple home life and home-cooked meals can have restorative effects on even the most resistant and unhappy person. Even though most of the poem is in dactyls, the rhythmic needle skips here and there, possibly reflective of Indian students' thinking and writing from two lexicons. But the rhythmic disruptions could also be metonymic for the ways the ideologic recording machines that were the boarding schools never quite made clean copies of domesticated Indians. The needle skipped, and the girls' writings and lives are "*original bicultural composite composition*[s]" (Krupat, *For Those* 31).

After continuing to present other facets of domesticity, such as decorating with plain, economical furnishings and keeping a warm, happy hearth, Cooke and Hatch's cheery dactyl duet shifts to a more subdued, perhaps ironic, tone:

> The days come and go like swift aeroplanes,
> But this is no reason why we should complain;
> For with each fleeting moment we all hope to gain,
> A knowledge which may be both useful and sane. (238)

They might feel like complaining because their joyful stint in the model cottage will soon be over. But if, as they say, this is no reason to complain, we might wonder: What *is* their reason to complain, then? Would they complain if they could? The last two lines suggest an answer. The speakers might truly believe they are gaining useful knowledge with every quickly passing moment. But here again, the usage of the word "sane" raises questions. Of course, it rhymes with "complain," which may be the reason Cooke and Hatch use it. But following the same line of questioning, might the word "sane" conjure the opposite—"insane"? If so, the lilting meter of the poem takes on a more maniacal tone, and the girls don't complain about how quickly their time in the cottage is going because, despite their hopes, they either feel they have not had enough time in the cottage to master the new skills or they cannot imagine a practical application of these new skills when they return home. Even if school officials edited this poem before publication, a scuffling with domestic ideology and the sentimental form creeps through the lines and suggests a disruption of the copying process.

As we are seeing, these same ideological and generic disruptions ripple just below, if not right on top of, the surface of the archive of student writing about their domestic educations. Like the previous writers discussed, Sara Hoxie (Nomlacki, California) sets domesticity in some other time and place even as she employs the before/after plot. Her piece in the *Red Man* describes how Indians lived "contentedly in the forests" (29) before contact with whites. But after their educations at Carlisle—where the boys learned in "various shops, viz., carpenter, blacksmith, tin, wood, and the printing department" and the girls learned in the "laundry, sewing room, housekeeping, the normal for teachers and the office for stenographers"—the Indian has "adopted the white man's method of living. Instead of finding the Indians residing in wigwams we now see the most of them living in frame houses comparing favorably with those of the white man" (30). Hoxie's essay indicates her understanding that as a young, federally educated Indian woman, it is her responsibility to work for "our advancement and promotion to a happier, nobler, and more civilized life" (30). Hoxie's use of "contentedly" could signal a sense of regret for a way of life she sees as lost, indicating a disturbance in the process of copying domestic ideology.

In a pair of vignettes about Cherokee home life, "Two Scenes in Cherokee Land," two girls draw markedly different pictures of Indian domesticity. Na-Li describes a primitive Cherokee family:

> In rudeness and uncivilization, we find the inmates bearing a striking resemblance to their little hut. In one corner is a roll of buffalo skins, which doubtless serve for beds. The floor is the earth upon which the hut stands. A woman is seated by the fire-side, smoking a pipe. . . . No little stand of books, no vase of flowers, filling the room with fragrance, no neat papers are to be seen. . . . In the mean time the girls have finished beating the Conihany.[9] A large kettle, filled with the Conihany, is placed on the fire; the little ones of the family sit watching it with great eagerness. . . . Thus pass the days of their wild life, without any intellectual pleasures or enjoyments, only varied from the same, monotonous round by some great gathering or public festival. The most noted of these were the "*green corn dances*." (408)

In marked contrast, Fanny describes a progressive Cherokee family:

> By the fenced fields of wheat and corn, we see that civilization and nature are here united in Cherokee land. White cottages peep forth from the same spot, perhaps, where some warrior's rude wigwam once stood. What a contrast to the scenes of olden times! The Missionaries came and brought with them the BIBLE. They taught our ancestors the precepts of religion and the arts of civilization; to cultivate farms and erect neat little cottages. . . . Let us enter one of these white cottages. . . . Within the cottages we find ourselves in a room most tastefully arranged. . . . Books, flowers, music, and what is far better, the *Holy Word* of GOD is here to study. . . . But where are the occupants of the dwelling? Have they gone to celebrate the festival of some *Unknown Power*? Have they gone to *ball-play*, or to have a gossip at a *green-corn-dance*, as in days gone by? No; for the general observance of these customs have ceased. (408–9)

Instead of watching the Conihany cook or participating at tribal festivals, Fanny's Cherokees engage in school activities "where the *mind* is exercised instead of the *body*" and where she can "hope we may advance, never faltering, until all the dark clouds of ignorance and superstition and wickedness flee from before the rays of the Suns of *Knowledge* and *Righteousness*" (409). We can imagine that teachers instructed Na-Li to write the "before contact" essay and Fanny to write the "after contact" essay; even the girls' names suggest that while Na-Li still holds to tribal customs, Fanny has assimilated Euro-American ones. But even Na-Li's "before" vignette is not without evidence of contact, for she presents traditional Cherokee customs and describes the family's domesticity in terms of lack. Na-Li's yard is not manicured, the hut is not decorated, and books and papers are nowhere to be found. Mihesuah asserts that the girls "took pleasure in comparing the old Cherokee ways with the new-and-improved lifestyles of the tribe to show that many tribe members had progressed past savagery and were on their way to equality with whites" (41). Again, it is also highly probable that the girls wrote the vignettes in such contrasting terms because that's what they were told to do. But we could infer too, that Na-Li's fictional family knows about Euro-American domesticity and has chosen to reject it and maintain traditional domestic habits. Whatever the circumstances of their writing,

Na-Li and Fanny show that boarding school officials saw domesticity and domestic spaces as primary stages for performing the dramas of assimilation and resistance. The fact that Na-Li's and Fanny's vignettes were also published in the June 1858 edition of *Godey's Lady's Book* further suggests the performative, persuasive power of student essays about domesticity. Illustrating this point, the editors—Louis Antoine Godey and Sarah Josepha Hale—preface the vignettes: "The descriptions convey a clearer notion of the great change wrought by the missionaries among these wild children of the forest more than anything we could say" (563).

Printed in one of the most famous women's magazines of the period alongside other domestic texts such as Alice B. Haven's "Margaret's Home: A Household Tale," Na-Li's and Fanny's essays circulated in a discussion of domesticity's homogenizing cultural work that was surely wider than they could have anticipated when they wrote them at their student desks.

In figure 4.1, we see the beginnings of Della Mae John's (Oneida) report on the dinner and reception celebrating the opening of Carlisle's domestic science program (see also figure 4.2). Her prose details the menu, table settings, guests of honor, toasts, and musicians' offerings. More interesting, though, is the poem and illustration printed above John's article. The drawings are initialed "J. G.," but the author is otherwise anonymous. The poem's last line reiterates the progressive theme of the two sketches—"But civilized man cannot live without cooks"—and argues that the domestic education the girls' receive at Carlisle civilizes Indians more effectively than any other discipline or program. The drawings tell a before-and-after story centered on domesticity. On the left, the Indian woman cooks over an open flame with a spoon in her left hand and some other rude utensil in her right. She is outside, and a dog sits near her cooking area. She wears a plain dress, flat boots, and long braids, and her sunken cheeks, dark and deep-set eyes, and angular neck, chin, and nose suggest a hard life of toil, hunger, and exposure to the elements. On the right, the "new" Indian woman stands at a modern counter complete with drawers and shelf space, has several Euro-American utensils at her disposal, and kneads dough in a large mixing bowl. Some kind of modern appliance sits at the ready in the corner of the counter. She works inside in a presumably clean environment—there is no dog in this kitchen. She wears a dress with a long coverall apron

Figure 4.1 "Inauguration of Domestic Science Course." An illustration by "J. G." printed with Della Mae John's report about the celebration of the new domestic science curriculum. *Carlisle Arrow*, 14 June 1915: 26. Courtesy American Indian and Indigenous Studies Collection, Newberry Library, Chicago, Illinois.

Figure 4.2 Carlisle's publications often featured photographic "evidence" that female students were learning their domestic lessons. This photo depicts girls in cooking class, a routine experience that surely served as the inspiration for J. G.'s illustration (shown in figure 4.1). Courtesy Special Collections Division, J. Willard Marriott Library, University of Utah.

and heeled boots, and her hair is tucked up under a lacy cap. Her plump arms, cheeks, and neck suggest an easier workload with plenty of food and protection from the elements. The woman also stands on a floor and has a window with a shade that shields her from direct sunlight. This, the drawing suggests, is the potential of Indian civilization and the goal of every federal boarding school.

But at the same time, as with the other writings, disruptions in the ideological copying creep through the official redactions. While at first glance the poem affirms the transformation plot—the Indian woman can now be a "real" cook in a kitchen—the illustration shows us that *both* Indian women are cooks. Whether inside or outside, the same life-sustaining task is being performed, after *and* before domestication. Additionally, reading the drawing from left to right—as we read words in English—suggests a narrative of progress from savagery to civilization. But if we look to the left and up to the poem, we see that because the artist draws both women as cooks, the speaker's phrasing of "civilized man" applies to whites *and* Indians. Further, even if J. G. consciously drew this cartoon as a story of progress, she (or he) also makes the scenario on the left seem far more appealing. In scale, the woman on the left appears larger, thus taking more visual space on the page and signifying greater importance. The woman on the right is small in comparison, and the straight lines on the walls and window (which is opaque) signify confinement, as if the kitchen imprisons her. That sense of restriction is heightened when one looks back at the image on the left. This woman is outside, the sun is shining, her dog (another life form) is nearby, and the round lines of her body, the kettle, the sun, and mountains exude an expansiveness and freedom that is missing from the image on the right. What at first glance seems nothing other than one more example of boarding school indoctrination is, in fact, a subtle subversion of the transformative and improving power of domestic ideology and sentimental convention.

As we will see, adult Indian women also wrote to wrestle with the ideological colonization of domesticity. We cannot dismiss sentimental or domestic writings by Indians as too assimilative or because they may have been assigned by a teacher or written under coercion. The binary that I have been using for most of this chapter—Euro-American domesticity versus Native lifeways—is already false by the time these girls are writing. By the late nineteenth century, as writers such as Sarah

Figure 4.3 Marie L. Baldwin (Chippewa) was one of the speakers and moderators who gathered at the first conference of the Society of American Indians in 1911. Courtesy Main Library, University of Illinois at Urbana–Champaign.

Winnemucca and S. Alice Callahan show, domesticity and sentimentality were also *Native* literary modes. Schoolgirls might also have read domestic texts by Indian women, and we know that Native women influenced boarding school curriculum as well as white women by the early twentieth century.

At the first annual conference for the Society of American Indians held at Ohio State University in 1911, Marie L. Baldwin (Chippewa) gave an address titled "Modern Home-Making and the Indian Woman" (figure 4.3). Baldwin graduated from Washington School of Law in 1914 and worked in the Education Division of the Bureau of Indian Affairs after graduation. (Littlefield and Parins 169). She describes the history of the North American Indian woman as a history of domestic duties to argue that the Indian woman is already equipped, by her own traditions and nature, to perform the tasks of domesticity taught by white women. Baldwin sees domesticity as a means of assimilation, acculturation, and survival for Indian women:

> To secure welfare and happiness she must adapt and wisely adjust her inherent and acquired talents to these modern surroundings. Many of the things that were useful and necessary, yea, sacred, to her own mother, must now be laid aside. Methods of producing, securing, and preserving shelter and the necessaries of life must be adopted

> or changed or discarded altogether to meet the new conditions of life on this continent. And the American Indian woman who fails to realize this duty and obligation to her race in her home-making fails completely to read aright the signs of the time. (66–67)

Baldwin stresses change and adaptation for Indian survival, arguing that the tenets of domesticity are not all that different—though the methods are—from the duties Indian women have performed for millennia. In figures 4.4 and 4.5, cover illustrations from the December 1911 and November 1913 issues of the *Red Man* tell another before/after story and imply an evolving Indian femininity pushed along by Carlisle and echoed at the other boarding schools.

Figure 4.4 depicts a Hopi girl watching a Hopi woman—perhaps her mother—making piki bread. Though this woman performs a decidedly

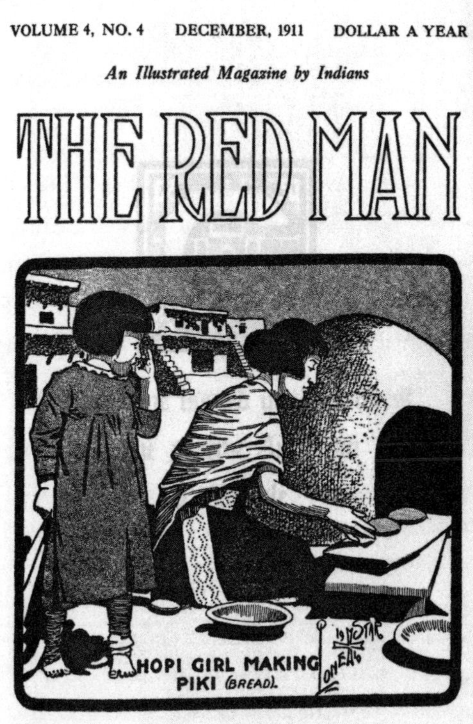

Figure 4.4 *Hopi Girl Making Piki (Bread)*. Illustration by William H. Dietz, *Red Man* 4 [1911]: cover. Courtesy American Indian and Indigenous Studies Collection, Newberry Library, Chicago, Illinois.

domestic task that falls within the realm of a true woman's motherly duties, this acknowledgement of Hopi cooking did not translate into awareness among whites that Indian women do, in fact, perform domesticity. Perhaps this contradiction flowed through the pen of the illustrator, William H. "Lone Star" Dietz, whose (part-Sioux) Indian identity was challenged in courts. Dietz surely knew firsthand the challenges of performing authentic Indianness and mimicking whiteness. But considered alongside Baldwin's assertions about adaptive domesticity, perhaps this image affirms Native domesticity even as it relegates traditional piki making to the past.

If the piki-making image illustrates a "before" method of domestic labor, figure 4.5 suggests an alternative "after" for Indian femininity. Also drawn by Dietz, this cover of the *Red Man*, from November 1913, illustrates a female "Indian Stenographer" who, presumably, learned the trade while a student at Carlisle. Though Lomawaima, Child, and Vuckovic assert that the schools never intended to give female students marketable skills, this illustration suggests that Carlisle also trained Indian girls to enter the workforce as something other than a domestic laborer. At school, the Indian girl could leave her primitive ways of life and take up that most modern of American identities: the working girl. During the same year (1913), Edna Ferber published the third book in a series about Emma McChesney, an upwardly mobile, divorced white mother for whom stenography is but a menial stop along her path to partnership in a clothing company. Carlisle trained Indian women, apparently, to perform the jobs white women were tired of doing: housework and secretary work. Again, considered alongside Baldwin's admonishment for adaptation, these cover images might betray an anxiety that is as much about shifting roles for Indian femininity as it is about modifying methods of Indian domesticity. Perhaps questions of identity surfaced for Baldwin and the boarding school writers who found themselves at this cultural crux during the Progressive Era: If I don't make piki the traditional way, am I still Indian? If I'm a stenographer and not at home, who will make the piki at all? Am I less a woman if I'm not at home all day? These last two questions were certainly ones white women wrestled with too. But the first question highlights the difference: whatever the white woman does with her time, she will always be white. And, most threatening to the colonial project, is the opposite reality that whatever the Indian woman does with her time, she will always be Indian. No

Figure 4.5 *The Indian Stenographer*. Illustration by William H. Dietz, *Red Man* 6 [1913]: cover. Courtesy American Indian and Indigenous Studies Collection, Newberry Library, Chicago, Illinois.

matter how much Indian girls write about their future lives characterized by Euro-American domesticity, what their teachers and administrators failed to understand was that they would only ever be "almost the same, but not white." Indeed, this is the *menace* of mimicry and why Indian girls writing domesticity is crucial to their survivance. For as Bhaba describes, "what emerges between mimesis and mimicry is a *writing*, a mode of representation, that marginalizes the monumentality of history, quite simply mocks its power to be a model, that power which supposedly makes it imitable" (125, italics mine). In writing before/after, elsewhere-and-elsetime disruptions of the model/copy curriculum of their domestic educations, Indian girls subverted the expectations of school officials and highlighted contradictions in the logic of the schools' use of domestic ideology as a colonial tool.

Deploying Domesticity

A writing process began at the boarding schools that turned the discourses of domesticity and sentimentality on their heads. By redirecting the before/after plot and the discourse of transformation, by imagining home as elsewhere and elsetime, and by causing hiccups in the model/copy process, Indian women writers highlight the inherent contradictions and incompleteness of using domestic ideology as a colonial tool. But where student writers could only use irony, subtlety, and displacement to question the lessons of their colonialist teachers, adult Indian writers could overtly criticize boarding schools and the federal government and claim rhetorical and ideological power for themselves. Native sentimental writing repurposes domesticity in ways that white reformers and educators could not have seen coming: claiming Indian women's power to educate white women in the superior methods of Native domesticity and crafting a sovereign domesticity.

Having experienced the rhetorical power of sentimental and domestic rhetoric as both readers and writers at federal boarding schools, several Indian women went on to publish writings that deployed these discourses for purposes that claim and reframe domesticity and sentimentalism as a tool and marker of self-determination. Whether publishing autobiographies, novels, stories, essays, ethnographies, or some hybrid of these genres, Armstrong, Callahan, Mourning Dove, Deloria, Winnemucca, and Zitkála-Šá write texts that exemplify complicated responses—both assimilative and resistant—to their education in general and their domestic education specifically.[10] I use these binary terms—assimilation and resistance—to label the continuum along which these women moved in responding to colonialism, but in my readings of their work I see their *movement* between these poles as the most realistic response a colonized people makes toward their colonizers. That is, I do not expect complete assimilation or utter resistance in their work or lives, nor do I see their negotiations between assimilation and resistance as pathological or self-sacrificial or their collaboration with white editors and their manipulation of white genres as antithetical to their tribal and Indian identities.[11] So while I will point out moments of assimilation or resistance in their texts, I ultimately read the work of these women as syncretic, though not quite hybrid (as Bhaba defines it), responses to colonialism that manipulate the discourses available to them in the literary culture they share with Euro-Americans.[12] Some critics apologize for Indian women writers' use of sentimentalism and domesticity for various reasons, dismissing it as a Euro-American cultural imposition, as mere imitation, or as somehow less-than-Indian.[13] Some critics admire the ways these writers put sentimentalism and domesticity to work as subversion, resistance, and protest rhetoric, on the one hand, or, on the other hand, as "meeting grounds" (Bernardin, "Meeting Grounds" 209) for cross-cultural conversations about the shared sentiments of home, family, and community. Armstrong, Callahan, Mourning Dove, Deloria, Winnemucca, and Zitkála-Šá appropriate the tandem discourses of sentimentalism and domesticity in both the form and the content of their writings in order to shape a response to their colonial educations that challenges stereotypes and assumptions about Indian women, questions the moral authority and ideals of white women, and asserts a model of Indian domesticity and motherhood that rivals Euro-American feminine ideals such as republican motherhood, true womanhood, and new womanhood.[14]

Each of these writers manipulates the forms and narrative conventions of nineteenth-century sentimental women's writing. Some Indian students—especially female students—had opportunities to read domestic fiction like *Little Women* or dime novels like *The Brand* (1909). And even if Winnemucca, Callahan, and the others never read a word of domestic fiction, we know that they were exposed to the structures and themes of sentimental literature through the schools' curricula and student newspapers. Therefore, I approach these women as writers as well as readers of the texts and rhetorics of Euro-American culture. We also know that these women writers were familiar with white women and white discourses in their own lives, coming into contact with them not only at school but in their own tribal communities; and eventually most of these women joined the lecture circuit themselves, listening to and giving speeches in the sentimental mode.[15] How they learned it, though, is less important than how they used sentimental narrative structures for their own purposes. Like student writers at boarding schools, these Indian women writers disrupt the before/after plots of domestic (and/or) marital transformation by positing post-school, self-determined futures for Indian women. Unlike the student writers, though, these writers ground their domestic settings in particular times and spaces, claiming a present that will shape their futures via articulations of sovereign domesticity, futures that self-consciously "almost the same, but not quite" copy the models for femininity they learned to emulate at school.

Estelle Armstrong, a Carlisle alumnus and a Nez Perce writer best known to scholars of early Indian literature for her short story "The Return" (and for her nonfiction book, *The Indian Special*), not only bends sentimental conventions in that her protagonists are male but also in that their sense of home differs greatly from the orderly, pleasant, and nurturing spaces typically found in domestic fiction.[16] Instead, Armstrong portrays Indian domesticity *and* a transition to boarding school domesticity as a bewildering, painful and displacing process. Though "The Debut of Aloyasius" (1910) is about a young boy's first experiences at school, his troubles are narrated in decidedly domestic terms. The story opens on Aloyasius at his home that has a distant view of the "glaring, red roofs" (17) of the government Indian school. He "hated most the sight" (14) of it, but he knew he would have to go there soon. He also knew his "feeble grandparents might not get their monthly rations unless the children were sent in; so the Indian Agent had said, and the Indian Agent was to be feared above all else" (14). His family could barely feed him, and even though he knew that boarding school children got more food than they could ever eat, he still did not want to go. Armstrong depicts Aloyasius's home as lacking—lacking the food, safety, and security typically associated with Euro-American homes in the sentimental genre.

Aloyasius's tale follows a narrative trajectory that is now hauntingly familiar among stories of boarding school life. Although he did not want to go, the inevitable occurs, and he soon finds himself welcomed into the school by a woman with confusingly red hair: "strange as the woman looked, she did things still more strange" (15). Aloyasius is utterly befuddled when the woman fills a huge tub with clear water—which to him "was something infinitely precious and not to be wasted" (15)—and then made him get into it. The bath is frightening and painful; the woman "had taken a cloth and something smooth and slippery that made a white foam when she rubbed it, and had washed him. She got the white foam in his eyes and mouth and they smarted" (15). After the bath comes a parade of perplexing rituals: putting on close-fitting clothes, getting the "neeil" combed out of his hair and his hair washed with kerosene—"he had supposed they belonged there and had accepted them without questioning" (16)—tucking a white cloth under his chin and using a spoon and fork at dinner, changing his clothes several times a day, wearing a nightgown, and praying before bed (16–17). At the end of that harrowing first day, Aloyasius "crept between the white sheets and lay very still. His heart ached for his corner in the sand at home where he curled up at night with his mother's gay shawl, or his father's coat, thrown over him. He drew the despised government blanket over his throbbing head and cried his little heart out beneath the shelter of the glaring, red roofs" (17). Aloyasius yearns for his old bed, but home, in the sentimental sense, is not with his grandparents, and he does not find it at school either despite the fact that the matron subjects him to every trapping of Euro-American home life that is so central to domesticity and the domestication of Indians.

"The Debut of Aloyasius" paints a pessimistic portrait of children's initiation into boarding school life, surprisingly so since it was published in Carlisle's the *Red Man*. It may have served school administrators' purposes of letting new students know they were not alone in the difficult transition they were undertaking. But whatever the publisher's intentions, Armstrong draws on sentimentalist rhetoric to invite the reader to empathize with Aloyasius. And whatever Armstrong's own stance on the assimilative practices at the boarding schools, her story suggests two things. First, the story signals Armstrong's awareness that domesticity was a primary tool for forcing Indian students to assimilate. Second, it suggests her belief in the inevitability of the domesticating, civilizing process.

But if this process of domestication was inevitable, one can still ask about the *product* of domestication. How did girls actually implement domesticity when they returned home? It is one thing to regurgitate information on an essay exam (as some might describe the student-written pieces), but another thing entirely for these students to go home and implement these domestic practices. In what reads like a sequel to "The Debut of Aloyasius," but with a different protagonist, Armstrong follows the young Jose home from Carlisle in "The Return." The narrator tells us that "the innate hatred for the white man's dominating activity, with its resulting absorption of their own purposeless lives, eggs them on to use in retaliation the only weapon left them, often undoing by their witless ridicule of returned students what years of study and careful training has inculcated" (115). The narrator continues, "I select the home-coming of Jose as typical of many such that I have witnessed, and having witnessed have marveled, not at the half failure sometimes resulting, but at the optimism that dared to expect success" (115). Jose looks forward to seeing his home and parents with fondness, for the "remembrance of the squalor and meanness of his early years had faded from his mind" (116). The "open, grass-thatched hovels" he passes on his way home give him pause, and he hesitates to say the word "mother" when he sees her condition in their "poor hut": "old and bent with many years, her hair matted above her sunken eyes, her only garment a shred of filth that stopped above her knees, her unhuman hands ending in talons" (117). His father he found lying in the sand wrapped in nothing but a loincloth, in marked contrast to Jose's own "altered features and alien clothes" (117). Jose seems shocked by his parents' appearances and domesticity; "as in a dream Jose sat down on a nearby log and gazed about him. He saw the mean hut in its squalor and poverty; the heaps of rags in the sand on which his parents slept; the open fire over which hung the kettle of soup containing the coming meal . . . [and] the form of his mother as she bent again over the pot of soup" (118).

The narrator interjects to conclude the story, leaving readers with an opposite perspective on the experience of boarding school than "The Debut" offers. Four years after his return, Jose still wears his "overalls and work shirt neat and whole, his hair closely cut and his face showing no signs of dissipation beneath its grime and sweat. He looked as I believe he is, an honest youth engaged in honest work, and my heart rejoiced for him. . . . I challenge you to declare his education vain or to proclaim his life a failure" (118). Where "The Debut of Aloyasius" describes the boy's domestic assimilation to boarding school life in terms of culture shock, in "The Return," going home is a culture shock for Jose. As with Aloyasius, Jose's sense of home is always elsewhere and elsetime. While at school he longs for the home of his parents—clearly not feeling at home at school—but when he returns to his parents' home, he judges it by the foreign standards of domesticity that he learned at school. And Jose finds that his parents don't meet his new standards. The odd interjection by the narrator suggests that, while Aloyasius's life at boarding school will be bleak and depressing, Jose's time at school was productive. Despite the serious flaws in colonialist philosophies, Armstrong ironically implies, Indians can derive some good from learning modern domestic habits—that is, they can recognize and be disgusted by their slovenly families. In this way, Aloyasius and Jose disrupt the before-and-after plot of the boarding schools. Neither boy feels a sense of home in the rituals of domesticity at the boarding schools. And while Jose expects to bring these rituals to his parents' house, he is unsuccessful in changing their habits. He stands, instead, as an outsider to both worlds; he is "almost the same, but not quite [white]" and is still Indian. Armstrong dramatizes the more likely events that would unfold when students returned home—more likely than *Stiya's* return home, than the schoolgirls' projections of their domestic futures, than the *Red Man's* illustrative suggestion that Indian girls would become office girls, than Marie L. Baldwin herself, who was still a small minority among ex-students of the boarding schools. She was the first Indian woman to earn a law degree, and she had a public platform at the first meeting of the Society of the American Indians, pronouncing the benefits of incorporating Euro-American domesticity into the habits of native domesticity.

S. Alice Callahan's novel, *Wynema: A Child of the Forest*, published in 1891, is arguably the first known novel written by an American Indian woman. Of all the sentimental narrative structures I discuss here, *Wynema* is also perhaps the most obviously sentimental in both form and content. Susan K. Bernardin argues that sentimentality is "one of the few meeting grounds" for American women of various cultures ("Meeting Grounds" 209). Sentimental conventions bolster Native writing rather than threaten it by inviting a dialogue with mainstream cultural discourses. Indeed, Dean suggests that Callahan actually read *Stiya* and wrote *Wynema* "in response to Burgess's racist denigration of Native life" and to critique the reeducation programs celebrated in Burgess's propagandistic fiction" (216, 217). At the structural level, the double-romance plot of *Wynema* mirrors many other romance novels from the period, as Jacqueline Shea Murphy points out. In the opening chapter, we meet one character from each would-be romance: Wynema, the "Tepee" Indian child in her forest whose thirst for knowledge brings her into the path of Gerald Keithly, the young, handsome white Methodist missionary teacher who lives among the Tepees. Aware of Wynema's intelligence and curiosity, Keithly puts out a call among "the great Methodist assembly" (4) for a female teacher to instruct her. Genevieve Weir answers his call, "one from the sunny Southland—a young lady, intelligent and pretty, endowed with the graces of heart and head, and surrounded by the luxuries of a Southern home" (22). Genevieve is beautiful, but like so many sentimental heroines, she is also frail (23) and, as it turns out, racist, so the double-romance plot is enhanced by a female bildungsroman plot in which Genevieve must grow stronger both physically and morally.

Genevieve's southern home is central to the sentimental structure of this novel; her knowledge of southern womanhood makes her the perfect teacher for Wynema, whose education will consist of not only learning English and mathematics and so on but also learning the mores of white womanhood. Turn-into-the-twentieth-century sentimental fiction endowed white women with a tripartite structure of influence that included domesticity, religion, and education. Callahan's novel focuses on the educational branch of sentimental domesticity. *Wynema* describes Genevieve's role as a missionary teacher among Indians as an extension of her domestic influence, and Wynema's presumed role is to mimic Genevieve's performances. At the level of the romance plot, this multifaceted education—in academics, in domesticity, in femininity—puts Wynema in the position of meeting and being seen as a potential romance interest for Genevieve's brother, Robin. Of course, Keithly is attracted to Genevieve and proposes marriage but, in a conventional romantic twist, finds that she is already engaged to another man. Maurice Mauran, it turns out, is the romantic villain. But instead of preying on Genevieve's purity and piety, attempting to ruin her and leave her sullied, as do most romance-novel villains, Maurice's misogyny takes the opposite approach. He wants to keep her under his thumb as the virtuous angel-in-the-house wife and mother who has no interest in public concerns. Leaving Maurice is also part of Genevieve's bildungsroman. Her interests in suffrage, education, and Indian concerns make her a better match for Keithly, and, in the end, Genevieve and Keithly, as well as Wynema and Robin, are happily married with children. What seems like Wynema's assimilation of her rightful domestic duties, then, actually illustrates Callahan's manipulation of domestic rhetoric. Wynema ends up teaching her teacher how, when it comes to Indian affairs and race relations, domesticity without empathy rings hollow.

At least two structural aberrations keep *Wynema* from being just another sentimental romance novel, in addition to the simple facts that it was written by an Indian woman and includes an Indian woman as part of the major romance plotline. As A. LaVonne Brown Ruoff notes, the novel shows how an Indian author can draw on nineteenth-century literary sentimentalism to her own advantage ("Two Ideas" 128). The first aberration is that the narrative takes an abrupt break from the romance plots—and from its implied setting in Indian Territory—in chapter 8, when the narrative switches to discussions concerning the West, including the Dawes Act, the Wounded Knee Massacre, the Ghost Dance controversy, and the ethics of Buffalo Bill. Contrary to critics who read this disruption as one more—and perhaps the worst—problem in Callahan's novel, Lisa Tatonetti contends that "*Wynema*'s depiction of the 1890 Ghost Dance and the Wounded Knee Massacre has the potential to expand our understanding of both the tensions and possibilities that underlie Native visions of American Indian identities in the late nineteenth century" (128). I read this shift in narrative style and function as a signal of Callahan's awareness of the broader cultural work that sentimental literature can perform. As Jane Tompkins argues, white women reformers used sentimental fiction in the nineteenth century to support all sorts of causes—temperance, suffrage, abolition, and here, the "Indian problem"—the most notable of these are Harriet Beecher Stowe's *Uncle Tom's Cabin* and Helen Hunt Jackson's *Ramona*. Despite Callahan's uneven and unsophisticated execution of narrative modifications, her novel stands as one of the first examples of Indian women's writing that engages women's concerns from a decidedly Indian-centered platform and the first in a novel.

The second departure Callahan takes from the traditional sentimental romance plot is not only that she includes interracial marriage between the main characters but, more importantly, that the couple can live with a presumed level of acceptance in white society. While some critics criticize this as another example of its assimilationist stance, this plot device is perhaps one of the earliest literary examples of an interracial married couple that does not flee polite or mainstream white American society. For example, Catharine Maria Sedgwick's *Hope Leslie* (1827) includes a white-Indian marriage where the title character's sister, Faith, grows up to marry one of the family's Indian servants, Oneco. Oneco and Faith leave her Puritan community to live with his family in the woods of western Massachusetts, and, after many years go by, Hope reunites with her sister to find that Faith has thoroughly "gone native," wearing Indian dress and forgetting how to speak English. Similarly, in Jackson's *Ramona*, the orphaned Ramona, born of a Scottish father and a California Indian mother who is raised by her aunt, Señora Moreno, elopes with Moreno's Indian sheepherder, Alessandro. The racial coding is complex and convoluted in Jackson's novel, but the idea remains: there is no place in white society for such racial mixing (keeping in mind that Señora Moreno considered herself Mexican aristocracy and as such was able to claim the privileges of whiteness as it was defined in mid-nineteenth-century California). Ramona and Alessandro live on the run for their entire married life.

In yet another example, Pauline Hopkins's *Winona: A Tale of Negro Life in the South and Southwest* (1902), the escaped slave Winona marries her white rescuer, Maxwell, who coincidentally (as it seems) is a lawyer from England who came to America to find Winona, who, in a strange twist of fate, is the heiress to a large fortune in England. They find American society inhospitable to such an interracial union, so the two live out their married life in England. *Winona* differs from *Hope Leslie* and *Ramona* in that it does not obviously treat Indian-white marriages. But it is similar in surprising and strange ways, as Winona was actually raised in a Seneca community in upstate New York, and Hopkins often attributes Winona's physical and moral strength to the Indian traits she acquired while living among the Seneca. In this context of other sentimental fiction, Callahan's ending to her novel is remarkably progressive; Wynema and Robin live together in harmony with Keithly and Genevieve on the grounds of Keithly College in the American South.

Rather than evidence of Callahan's belief in assimilation, as some scholars see it, this harmonious conclusion exemplifies Callahan's use of Malea Powell's "rhetorics of Survivance." As Kelly Sassi suggests, Callahan reclaims and refigures white stereotypes about Indian practices and Indian spaces, claiming syncretic, domestic spaces for Indian women: inside the home, inside the nation, and inside the discourse of domestic sentimentalism.

Mourning Dove, like Callahan, appropriates generic conventions from sentimental and romantic fiction in her 1927 novel, *Cogewea, The Half-Blood: A Depiction of the Great Montana Cattle Range.*[17] But where Callahan primarily follows the narrative structures and purposes of sentimental literature, Mourning Dove also draws from several other forms, including the dime novel, the new woman novel, political pamphlets, and, most innovatively, Okanogan tales. *Cogewea* actually begins as if it were a new woman novel, where the heroine longs for a life outside the confines of home, marriage, and family; is freed from these confines by a job opportunity; and does or does not return home after this work experience but in the end has a broader scope of influence and a heightened awareness of her place in the world outside traditional gender roles. Charlotte J. Rich and Maureen Honey read *Cogewea* as both appropriating and challenging the new woman ideal, arguing that Mourning Dove points out the ways that this ideal does not serve the needs of nonwhite women and often perpetuates stereotypes about racialized Others. The narrator tells us that Cogewea's "longings were vague and shadowy; as something not to be attained within the narrow limits of her prescribed sphere" (22). After Cogewea's return from Carlisle, "her everyday companions had been the cowboys of the range," and she much prefers riding and reading to housework (17). Even after the romance plot begins, Mourning Dove does not entirely abandon the new woman plot, as we rarely see Cogewea inside domestic spaces but rather in the outside spaces of the ranch, the woods, and the town.

Her primary sphere of influence is not her husband and children, like her sister's, but is instead the ranch hands she manages, and her regular speeches championing suffrage and "preacher women or school-marm[s]" (33) who make their own living, align her with new woman heroines. At least initially, Cogewea resists joining a romance plot, holding onto the freedom and independence she sees in single women around her. The narrator describes her as having "the feminine longing to be loved and cared for" (32), but that description comes in relation to Cogewea's musings about her grandmother, not about a man. When Jim first proposes to Cogewea, she declines at first on the grounds that she sees him as a brother. She falls back on sentimental notions about romantic love but then supports her refusal with another reference to "an industrious class of women and mostly school-marms all making their own living" (113), suggesting that she values independence over the supposed stability of a marriage.

Despite the narrative potential that *Cogewea* could be a new woman novel, it is ultimately a romance novel based on the sentimental tradition and one of its literary ancestors, the dime novel. More specifically, *Cogewea* is structured much like the cautionary tale of the late eighteenth- and early nineteenth-century seduction novel. Justine Dymond argues that *Cogewea* can also be seen as a modernist novel that "enters sentimental subjectivity in order to undo its racial and geographic enclosures" (301). The love triangle with Jim, Cogewea, and Densmore is a stock plot for a sentimental novel, and the dastardly Densmore is as predacious and villainous a suitor as John Montraville in Susanna Rowson's *Charlotte*

Temple: A Tale of Truth (1791). But where Rowson's book is a tragedy meant to shock young female readers into chastity and piety—the unwed Charlotte dies giving birth to Montraville's child—Mourning Dove narrates a romantic comedy that ends happily with Jim and Cogewea's marriage. Even Densmore's seduction attempts resemble comic antics more than aggressive advances. Scenes where he dictates a letter to his mother *through* Cogewea and *about* Cogewea or where he steals Cogewea's money and ties her to a tree are more in line with cartoon Western scenes of the villain tying the fair maiden to the railroad tracks and then running off while rubbing his hands together and giggling in depraved delight than they are with Montraville's rape and abandonment of Charlotte. On the other hand, Densmore's depravity might run a bit deeper than Montraville's, given the racist overtones that characterize most of his comments and all of his narrated thoughts.

As Rich points out, Mourning Dove's privileging of racial concerns over gender concerns makes her appropriation of sentimental conventions challenge stereotypically racist tropes in sentimental fiction, but it also challenges assumptions common among critics that Mourning Dove's appropriation of such forms is necessarily an assimilative gesture. *Cogewea*'s narrative collage has led scholars to criticize the novel as "schizophrenic" (Dearborn 20) and "maimed" (Allen, *Sacred Hoop* 83), seeing in this generic multiplicity the contaminating manipulations of Mourning Dove's white male editor, Lucullus V. McWhorter. But critics who insist on formal unity in the text often insist as well on unity of identity in the writer. As several other critics have aptly shown, Mourning Dove's own syncretic identity—as one who had both white and Indian parentage and participated in both white and Indian cultures—makes her syncretic text more legible and, ironically, more reliable.[18] Alicia A. Kent argues that Mourning Dove's manipulation of several genres signals her "refusal to play the role of the native informant and instead claimed [her] position as [an] author of artistic fiction" ("Native Americans" 85). Not only does Mourning Dove disrupt the conventional seduction plot by giving the villainous suitor his comeuppance—the novel ends on a scene of Densmore sitting alone in a shabby hotel, reading about Cogewea's large inheritance in the newspaper—or even by creating a new kind of space, as Bernardin, Harry J. Brown, Susan M. Cannata, and Louis Owens suggest, where the mixed-blood couple can live peacefully with all the syncretic elements of their identity without having to choose white culture or Indian culture. More critically, Mourning Dove incorporates Okanogan tales—including a cautionary tale about seduction within the larger seduction plot—that further the plot and help structure the narrative, a move that, as Kent suggests, shows Mourning Dove's refusal to separate narratives that are supposedly white from narratives that are supposedly Indian. In this way, *Cogewea* argues against notions that unity of narrative and identity is a question of essential singularity.

Ella Deloria's novel *Waterlily*, presumably completed in 1944 but not published until 1988, is perhaps the most "Indian" of the novels I discuss here, with its focus on Sioux *tiyospaye* (group of tepee) culture and its passing references to the distant presence of whites. Most critics read this novel primarily as part of Deloria's ethnographic work, though Beatrice Medicine contends that approach would have "displeased" Deloria and argues that *Waterlily* is a novel—a narrative creation—and not a work of ethnography or a mirror of Sioux culture (281).[19] Ruth J. Heflin argues that examining the conventional literary elements in *Dakota Texts* can show us how Deloria combined Sioux and western literary traditions to construct a "modernist, interstitial" novel with *Waterlily* (139). She continues to assert, to "many of the high modernists, the resurrection and synthesis of older literary traditions with innovations created by the modern writers is the natural response to modern life, and the primary outcome of modernism. From that point of view, most of Deloria's works are modernist" (141). I also read this novel as a literary construction (though I do not see it as primarily modernist), and like Callahan's and Mourning Dove's novels, as a manipulation of Euro-American sentimental narrative conventions.

Told from a decidedly Siouan, tiyospaye cultural perspective, Deloria structures her tale within the frames of the seduction plot and the more happily ending domestic novel. The novel opens with Blue Bird giving birth to Waterlily during her camp circle's move from one space to another; in this way, the novel seems to use the disruption strategy of displacing home elsewhere and elsetime that the boarding school writers use. For Blue Bird, home is literally neither here nor there. Further, she is alone during the birth, just as she is alone in her parenting. Deloria uses the narrative techniques of flashback and memory to show readers why Blue Bird is alone; she has been seduced and abandoned by an opportunistic suitor. But unlike Mourning Dove's novel, where Cogewea's evil suitor is a white stranger, in *Waterlily* the villainous suitor is a Sioux man, Star Elk, who is known in their camp circle as "headstrong and unfriendly" (12) and "lazy, petulant and given to jealous fits" (14). Deloria describes Blue Bird as the ideal prey for a man like Star Elk, for, like Charlotte Temple, Blue Bird is an orphan, and the women gossip about her marriage to him: "Well, what could you expect since the girl is very young and pretty and lacks a mother to guide her? What could a tottering grandmother do, anyway? It is good that the girl did not get into real trouble and bear a fatherless child" (14).

In these ways, Deloria sets up her story much as Euro-American sentimental novelists do: take an orphaned, vulnerable girl; introduce her to a treacherous sexual predator; then watch her fall into disgrace as the man takes advantage of her and abandons her. Through the dialogue of the women of the camp circle, Deloria also signals her awareness of the Euro-American sacralization of motherhood and its protective, guiding function. Like Mourning Dove, Deloria even includes a cautionary tale of seduction within the larger seduction plot. In this instance, though, Blue Bird uses her own seduction tale to caution her maturing daughter, Waterlily, against men who "may only be playing at courtship. Many do, to try a woman out. If she is too easy, they do not want her for life, knowing they cannot trust her" (135). This differs from the Stemteema's cautionary tale, told to Cogewea about another woman's life. It also differs from fallen heroines in other cautionary tales, like *Charlotte Temple*, because Blue Bird herself can reflect on and narrate her own life and has the narrative opportunity to find redemption and love for herself and through Waterlily. Waterlily's romance plot dovetails with her mother's plot and carries out the conventions of sentimental fiction: she is attracted to one man, is bought in marriage by another, is widowed, and, in a typically sentimental turn of events, meets and marries her dead husband's cousin, who also happens to be the first man she was attracted to as a young woman.

In addition to manipulating sentimental conventions at the narrative, structural level, Deloria also puts the language and themes of sentimentalism to work in *Waterlily*, challenging assumptions by white women reformers and educators—such as Molly V. Gaither and Estelle Reel—that Indian mothers are negligent and ignorant and that, consequently, Indian children are without guides toward a moral center. As I suggest above, the fact that Blue Bird uses her life experience to teach Waterlily about morality directly contradicts these assumptions. Throughout *Waterlily*, Deloria uses the phrases and themes of the stock rhetoric of domesticity that would have been familiar to readers of sentimental fiction. As Blue Bird's grandmother recalls the days when Star Elk was courting Blue Bird, she thinks that Blue Bird "must be warned at once that many a girl had come to ruin by taking [reckless young men's] wooing seriously" and hopes she will be "honorably married before any trouble can befall her" (12). The phrases "come to ruin" and "honorably married" would ring familiar to readers well-versed in sentimental conventions and would invite them to sympathize with Blue Bird and detest Star Elk, who "lured the girl away" on "shabby terms," triggering the grandmother's worry that "too often an elopement ended disastrously for the girl, while the man always went free" (13).

Star Elk and Blue Bird married in "the least honorable way" (13), according to Dakota customs, but readers would already be suspicious of Star Elk and they would nod their heads in sad agreement with the gossipy camp-circle women who cluck their tongues and say, "what could you expect since the girl . . . lacks a mother to guide her?" (14). Unfortunately, we do not know to what extent Deloria used sentimental rhetoric in the novel, for the publisher's preface to *Waterlily* notes that "a few dated slang expressions and turns of phrase out of keeping with the tone of the story . . . have been revised editorially: for example, 'the eternal question in a man's heart' (referring to courtship), 'sweet young thing' (a young girl), 'sinful' (evil), 'thank heaven' (thankfully)" (xi). These omissions exemplify the anthropological and ethnographic approaches critics and historians have taken to Deloria's novel; reading these omissions alongside the sentimental rhetoric that survived the editors' cuts indicates Deloria's engagement with the domestic rhetoric of the period.[20]

Deploying these stock phrases and themes allows Deloria to connect with her readers in a commonly understood rhetoric. But more importantly, Deloria's textual sentimentalism argues for a version of domesticity within both the familial and social kinship networks of tiyospaye culture that offers more avenues of support and redemption than does the Euro-American version of domesticity centered on the model nuclear-family home and the nurturing qualities of one individual mother. For instance, Deloria couches a discussion of the Dakota custom of men having plural wives—a custom that would be foreign and, no doubt, deplorably immoral to Victorian sensibilities—within the familiar terms of domesticity. After Waterlily's marriage to Sacred Horse, she follows custom and moves to his family's tiyospaye to find that his father, Good Hunter, has several wives and thus that she has several mothers-in-law that she must learn to cooperate with. In typical domestic-fiction style, the narrator launches into a description of their tepee's construction and interior, of their living spaces, and of their arrangements for cooking and childcare. Good Hunter's tepee

> required thirty-four poles . . . the interior was very spacious, for a tipi [*sic*]. . . . Each wife had her own compartment, which she shared with her small children, while the senior wife occupied the hostess's space on the righthand [*sic*] side nearest the entrance. . . . There were spaces for them all. Often, too, some traveler or outsider sought shelter for a night, having no other place to stop. It was Good Hunter's boast that no wayfarer was ever turned away and no visitor, even a casual caller, was allowed to leave without first eating his meal. . . . All the wives—two being sisters and one their cousin—were equally responsible for cooking. . . . Likewise, all the women were equally responsible for all the children, being mothers to them all. Indeed, until an outsider was well acquainted, he could not tell which woman was the real mother of any child, except the nursing baby. (166)

This passage could read as another example of Deloria's ethnographic writing. But this one passage contains so many references to customs valued by the Euro-American cult of domesticity that another conclusion can be drawn as well. Deloria draws on this rhetoric to argue that Indian women—Dakota Sioux women in particular—already have a system of domesticity in place. Contrary to white reformers such as Gaither and Reel, who assume that Indian women are without proper methods of housekeeping, Deloria drafts a domestic scenario that works more efficiently than the Euro-American system. Her references in this passage to spacious yet privatized interiors, generous hospitality, food preparation, and childcare echo domestic values of the Republican and Victorian eras, amidst whatever differences they also sustain. Moreover, the fact that the wives enjoy an effective and harmonious system of cooperative housekeeping and childcare evokes Progressive Era attempts at professionalizing and sharing domestic duties, recalling utopian experiments that writers such as Charlotte Perkins Gilman and Edith Summers Kelley wrote about and participated in.[21] Margaret Beauregard, the student writer from Chilocco, lamented that white girls' domesticity was so much more advanced than Indian girls' that she and her classmates could never catch up. But Deloria argues in this passage that Dakota Sioux women are far ahead of white women reformers who believe their own versions of domesticity will be the salvation of the poor, Indian squaws who are their students.

Winnemucca, Zitkála-Šá, Callahan, and Mourning Dove also use domestic rhetoric and themes to challenge white reformers and educators and, ultimately, to assert versions of tribal domesticity that rival Euro-American ideals of femininity, be it republican motherhood, true womanhood, or new womanhood. Critics have already and exhaustively discussed Winnemucca's book as an autobiography and, as such, an appropriation of this non-Indian generic form.[22] But fewer critics have noted the ways that Winnemucca uses domestic and sentimentalist rhetorical conventions to engage her white audience. At the level of language, Winnemucca sprinkles her text with direct addresses to her readers, perhaps one of the most common of the sentimentalist writers' moves. Her "dear readers" sections direct readers' attention to moral atrocities, just like white sentimentalists' "dear readers." Stowe's addresses to her readers, for example, interpellate the sympathetic white women and men she sought to recruit to the abolitionist cause. Winnemucca directs readers' attention to corrupt Office of Indian Affairs agents—"Now, dear readers, this is the way all the Indian agents get rich" (86)—or to the hypocrisy of white Christians among the Paiutes (as Margo Lukens discusses) or to the sexual violence of white men against Paiute women (as Gregory Wright discusses), and, most relevant to this discussion, to the dubious benevolence of white women reformers. Brigitte Georgi-Findlay points out various caricatures of white women that Winnemucca draws in *Life Among the Piutes: Their Wrongs and Claims*. Her address—"Dear reader, this is the kind of white women that are in the West. They are always ready to condemn me"—comes after she describes an altercation she had with a white woman who says, "I would see the horses pull her to pieces with good grace" and "[r]ope is too good to hang her with" (168). This is in marked contrast to an earlier characterization of Mrs. Parrish, the white woman who helped Winnemucca open a school for Paiute children. Winnemucca writes that "Mrs. Parrish, the dear, lovely lady, was very kind to the children. We all called her our white lily mother" (117).[23] These descriptions of two different white women could be merely that: simple recognition of different qualities in different people. But taken together with all Winnemucca's "dear readers" and her outspoken challenges to white institutions such as the federal government and the Christian Church, these seemingly contradictory comparisons might also signal her awareness of the duplicitous tendencies of some white women reformers and educators. On the surface, these women, like Mrs. Parrish, seem full of benevolent intentions for bettering the living conditions of Indian people. But underneath the placid surface of the group of white women reformers at large lurks the monstrous assumptions held by women like the one who would see Sarah drawn and quartered, assumptions that "these Indian people" need help to find salvation from their own savage selves.

Chapter 1 of Winnemucca's book, "Domestic and Social Moralities," can then be read as her response to the assumptions of white women who suppose, like Gaither, that Indian women are without domestic rituals or values. Like Deloria, Winnemucca presents a picture of Indian life that not only challenges those assumptions but also asserts a superior Indian domesticity. Winnemucca's white editor, Mary Mann, highlights this assertion, noting that Paiute child-rearing is "worthy the imitation of whites" (51n1). The opening line of this chapter—"Our children are very carefully taught to be good" (45)—argues that Paiute parents deliberately and methodically instruct their children. Parents tell instructional stories, grandmothers help girls through the transition of puberty, and fathers must grant permission before their daughters can begin courtship. A father even "assumes all his wife's household work" during her pregnancy (50), yet another example Winnemucca gives of the ways Paiutes cooperate in child-rearing rather than placing the bulk of the burden of child-rearing on an individual mother's shoulders. Paiute women, according to Winnemucca, are also better off than white women in that they have full participation privileges in their tribal council, where "anybody can speak who has anything to say, women and all" (53). And the result of "the way my people teach their children" is that Paiute children grow up to be better members of society than do white children: she writes, "I never in my life saw our children as rude as I have seen white children and grown people in the streets" (51).

Katharine Rodier connects Winnemucca's use of domestic rhetoric to her collaboration with the Peabody sisters (one of whom became Mary Mann when she married Horace Mann), seemingly granting more narrative control to the Peabody sisters than to Winnemucca. Siobhan Senier also notes that "Mann echoes . . . other white women reformers, who moved, often uncomfortably, between claiming power for themselves at the expense of Indian peoples and seeking a genuine recognition of those peoples' humanity. 'Domestic and Social Moralities' thus suggests compromises as well as mutual dialogues and possibilities" (*Voices* 111). I certainly agree that *Life Among the Piutes*, along with the other texts I interpret in this chapter, bears the undeniable marks of collaboration with or influence by white writers. But Winnemucca's "dear readers," her treatise on Paiute domesticity in chapter 1, and Mann's editorial comments work together to deploy the twinned rhetorics of sentimentality and domesticity for a purpose that white reformers and educators could not have seen coming: claiming her own power to educate white women in the superior methods of Indian domestic rituals and values.

Zitkála-Šá's writings can perform the same function, particularly her autobiographical essays originally published in the *Atlantic Monthly* in 1900: "Impressions of an Indian Childhood," "The School Days of an Indian Girl," and "An Indian Teacher Among Indians." Ruoff discusses these essays within the context of the sentimental tradition ("Early Native American Women Authors"), and Stromberg notes that Zitkála-Šá's use of the "sentimental literary trope familiar to readers in the late nineteenth century" shows a "remarkable understanding of the values" of those readers (108). As going to and returning from federal boarding school is a major theme and plot element in these essays, several critics have written about Zitkála-Šá's lived experiences with and textual representations of the schools. Wexler argues that Zitkála-Šá's experience at boarding schools so indoctrinated her with sentimentality that her autobiographical writings "had no Indian in them that was left untouched by western codes" ("Tender Violence" 33). I disagree with Wexler's assertion that Zitkála-Šá's education taught the Indian out of her and her writings. My reading of her work echoes Bernardin's argument that, as "the first literary response to the era's Indian education system, Zitkála-Šá's stories effectively use the language of domesticity to scrutinize sentimental ideology's foundational role in compulsory Indian education as well as its related participation in national efforts to 'Americanize' the Indian" ("Lessons" 213).[24]

Where Goyitney, Beauregard, and the other student writers structure their essays around the Euro-American rituals of domesticity that they learned at school and will supposedly perform after they return home or in job placements, Zitkála-Šá structures her first essay around the domestic rituals that her mother *already* performs. Penelope Myrtle Kelsey argues that Zitkála-Šá's subversion of sentimentality "has roots in Dakota familial and gender norms" and that "by centering her narrative around domestic issues of home and family, [Zitkála-Šá] intentionally places her autobiography within a larger discussion about Dakota nationhood and sovereignty" (66, 66–67). Catherine Kunce's reading goes beyond characterizing Zitkála-Šá's mother as a sovereign figure and nearly sacralizes her as a deity: "by likening her mother to the Judaic-Christian God, Zitkála-Šá simultaneously unsettles the foundation of racism, patriarchy, and theological hierarchy" (76). In this way, Zitkála-Šá uses literary sentimentalism in much the same ways as white women writers from the same period; as Tompkins and others argue, by both sanctifying and politicizing motherhood, writers claim a space for national influence in the public sphere for women who lived their lives primarily in the private sphere.

In what reads like an apologetic for Native American domesticity, Zitkála-Šá recalls in "Impressions of an Indian Childhood" that every "morning, noon, and evening" her mother retrieved water from the Missouri River for their "household use" (37); every day, her mother built a fire to cook a "simple breakfast" of "dried meat with unleavened bread and . . . strong black coffee." At their noon meal, passersby regularly "stopped to rest, and to share our luncheon with us, for they were sure of our hospitality" (38). The young narrator "loved best the evening meal," though, because then the family and neighbors gathered to share food and the "old legends" (38). She recalls long evenings where she curled up in the warmth of her mother's lap, listening to her grandmother and uncle tell stories (39), and then another, similar day would dawn, and her mother would begin beadwork or making moccasins for her (40). The arrival of white missionaries ultimately interrupts the comfort and consistency of this domestic scene, when they take the young girl away to boarding school where a "paleface woman," who turns out to be a "cruel woman," replaces the mother's rituals with the school's "iron routine" that was "next to impossible to leave" once "the civilizing machine had begun its day's buzzing" ("School Days" 190).

The student writers likely had no choice but to write about the "civilizing machine" of their domestic education as the welcome introduction of routine and order to their previously unkempt lives and likely felt pressure to commit, in writing, to educating their own, supposedly uncivilized, mothers in the virtuous values of Euro-American domesticity. But Zitkála-Šá, having left school and secured sustaining work and a sympathetic publisher, was freer to write something that surely more closely resembles the truth of the matter. The *Atlantic*'s motives for publishing Zitkála-Šá's work may have matched those of Pratt and Burgess, who used Carlisle's newspapers to showcase how well the school carried out the federal assimilation program, as Enoch and Katanski suggest. Perhaps the *Atlantic*'s editors viewed Zitkála-Šá—an Indian woman writer—as a novelty to be collected, as if the magazine were a cabinet of curiosities. Patricia Okker argues that her canonization "ironically began with the popular fascination with the 'exotic Indian' at the beginning of the twentieth century" (89).[25] Regardless of the *Atlantic*'s motives, reading Zitkála-Šá's autobiographical essays within their original context strengthens an argument that she was indeed seeking to educate a reading public that, like federal education officials, assumed that Indian women were either squaws and drudges or tribal princesses. These three essays were published in the January, February, and March 1900 issues of *Atlantic* alongside essays about world and American politics, as well as sentimental serialized stories such as "Mother" by Margaret L. Knapp and "To Have and to Hold" by Mary Johnston.[26] Johnston's story is a captivity narrative, set in Jamestown, where two Englishmen are captured and held prisoner by Powhatan's clan. Its departure from the typically gendered captivity narrative—where white women are captured and then released by Indians—is interesting in and of itself, but the theme of the story highlights white American nativism and exceptionalism when compared to Zitkála-Šá's essays. In the January installment, with "Impressions of an Indian Childhood," Johnston offers a chapter titled "In Which an Indian Forgives and Forgets" (54) that marks the turning point in the story when the Indians decide to release the Englishmen. One of them, Captain Percy, has a conversation with Nantauquas, the spokesman for the "dark Emperor" Opechancanough, who says that

> Opechancanough is very wise indeed. . . . He says that now the English will believe in his love indeed when they see that he holds dear even one who might be called his enemy, who hath spoken against him at the Englishmen's council fire. He says that for five suns Captain Percy shall feast with Opechancanough, and that then he shall be sent back free to Jamestown. He thinks that then Captain Percy will not speak against him anymore, calling his love to the white men only words with no good deeds behind. (58)

With this speech, full of stereotypical, white-writerly versions of Indian-inflected English, Johnston characterizes Opechancanough as an adherent to the New Testament teachings of Jesus Christ: love your enemies, turn the other cheek, forgive those who mistreat you, and follow words of love with actions of love. We might see this as Johnston's attempts at a complimentary characterization of the very Indians that most whites of the period saw as essentially depraved and too animallike to be capable of morality. We might see it this way, except for the naïveté of Opechancanough's thought process; only a non-Indian writer could imagine an Indian who thinks that capturing and then safely returning a white man is really going to prove his love and goodwill toward white people. Moreover, the charity of the "dark Emperor" still serves whites' purposes, for with him Johnston imagines an Indian who is willing simply to forgive and forget the atrocities and thievery committed by whites against Indians.

The forgive-and-forget kind of Indian must have been what school officials like Pratt were hoping for when they sent students like Zitkála-Šá out into the world bearing the unmistakable marks of a federal boarding school education. Enoch and Katanski discuss Pratt's responses to Zitkála-Šá's published essays and his express disappointment that she would be anything but grateful for her education. Zitkála-Šá and Johnston surely had little, if any, control over exactly when or which portions of their writings were published by the *Atlantic.* But it is probably more than coincidence that the last three installments of "To Have and to Hold" were published simultaneously with the first three essays of "American Indian Stories." As if in deliberate response to Johnston's "In Which an Indian Forgives and Forgets" chapter, Zitkála-Šá's "The School Days of an Indian Girl" came out in February. Unlike Opechancanough, who seems willing to turn a blind eye to colonial erasure of Indian ways of life, the young narrator in "School Days" unabashedly calls her teacher on the carpet:

> I grew bitter, and censured the [paleface] woman for cruel neglect of our physical ills. I despised the pencils that moved automatically, and the one teaspoon which dealt out, from a large bottle, healing to a row of variously ailing Indian children. I blamed the hard-working, well-meaning, ignorant woman who was inculcating in our hearts her superstitious ideas. (190)

Zitkála-Šá reverses reformist assumptions that the Indian woman is benighted by her superstition and mired in ineffective rituals by calling Christianity a superstition and modern medicine a ridiculous cure-all notion. P. Jane Hafen notes that Zitkála-Šá's essays show the "complexity of popular sentimentality mixed with oral tradition and political indignation" ("Zitkála-Šá" 32), and Heflin argues that her "stories are meant to influence and *change* Euro-American opinions about Indians, opening their eyes to abuses" (111). Ruth Spack points out that "Zitkala-Ša's case" aptly exemplifies federal failures at making over Indian girls into "paragons of domestic virtue" ("Dis/engagement" 181). Gaither and other white reformers who dehumanized Indian women as drudges and beasts of burden met their rhetorical match in Zitkála-Šá who, in return, dehumanizes boarding schools and their officials, characterizing them as an unthinking, unfeeling "civilizing machine" that worked to churn out equally unthinking, unfeeling, robotic Indian replicas of itself that would go back to the reservations and steer Indian families to its superior "iron routine."

Callahan also challenges reformist ideologies with *Wynema.* She fashions an Indian girl who is already ready to soak up knowledge and who doesn't need an iron routine to mechanize the Indian out of her. Keithly, the missionary teacher, recognizes and awakens in Wynema "the slumbering ambition for knowledge and for a higher life" (20), and her father, recognizing the same, agrees to let Keithly build a school in their community for Wynema to attend. In Callahan's novel, then, Indians do not need to be convinced of their children's need for education and for tools to adapt to white society. Several critics have taken Callahan to task for her assimilative bent in this novel (and for her use of stereotypically racist turns of phrase and characterizations). But fewer critics address the fact that drawing Wynema—who needs less intervention then reformers would assume—allows Callahan to construct Genevieve Weir—a prototypical southern true woman—as the one who needs reprogramming. Bernardin points out that Genevieve can read like the "missionizing" white woman reformer ("Meeting Grounds" 213), and Melissa Ryan asserts that while *Wynema* appears to be a novel about educating Indians, it is actually about educating white women reformers (31). Anne Ruggles Gere sees Wynema as an "alternative to stereotypical Indian identity, one that mirrored white middle-class domesticity and sexuality as well as professionalism" (41). Arguably, all of these Indian women writers work in one way or another to reeducate Americans about Indian life. But as these critics suggest, if there is a bildungsroman plot in this novel, Genevieve seemingly grows and changes more than Wynema.

In several telling scenes, Genevieve betrays her cultural biases and prejudices. While having a blue corn dumpling dinner with Wynema's family, she "took a small morsel of the dumpling in her mouth, for she was not prepossessed with its looks, and ate it with difficulty for it was tough and tasteless" (31). The narrator, both thinking through Genevieve's perspective and poking fun at it, notes,

> it is strange that, though always accustomed to such fare, the Indians are not a dyspeptic people. We of this age are constantly talking and thinking of ways and means by which to the idea of placing blue dumplings on our table! And yet, we are a much more dyspeptic people than the "blue dumpling" eaters, struggle though we do to ward off the troublesome disease. (32–33)

This moment exemplifies narrative slippages common in the novel, where one moment the narrative "we" is white people and the next moment the "we" is Indian people. But more importantly, this bit of narrative fun that comes at Genevieve's expense also takes shots at the domestic science models of housekeeping that rose up out of the Republican era, grew throughout the Progressive Era, and flourished into the modern period and informed the domestic educational curriculum at federal Indian schools. Genevieve's progress is recursive as she moves forward in enlightened moments and backward in racist moments when she wonders when "the Indians would quit these barbaric customs!" (46). She seems to recognize her uneven progress—"It seems I can never see things as they are, in the true light" (56)—which, perhaps, might be a kind of progress in itself. But in the last pages of the novel, when listening to her brother, Robin, read a sympathetic newspaper article about the Wounded Knee Massacre, Genevieve says, "I think the editor is rather bitter" (163), and she has to be corrected by Robin: "Yes, dear, . . . but if you had seen the Indians slain on the battle-field as we did, and could have heard the groans of the wounded you would not think so" (163).

The (re)education of Genevieve Weir, though incomplete, is Callahan's reversal of the domestic education script. Senier cautions against "overstating the case" or seeing Genevieve's transformation as complete, arguing that "Genevieve is certainly affected by her experiences, but while she learns to be sympathetic to Indians, it is not quite true that she ever learns to be more like them in anything resembling Wynema's Indian-to-white Bildungsroman" ("Allotment Protest" 429, 429–30). Like Senier, I am not sure that white-to-Indian is the goal of Callahan's (re)education of Genevieve. Rather, just as federal agents believed that Indian lifeways could be replaced by Euro-American habits through education, Genevieve's reprogramming, which also attempts to override a lifetime of cultural input, is a fragile, nascent worldview that needs protection and guidance. As Kara Mollis suggests, perhaps the goal of cross-cultural education, as we see it in *Wynema,* is simply Callahan's "proposal that an appreciation of cultural difference fosters socially desirable affectional bonds, the central philosophical ethos of sentimentalism, [and] invites us to reconsider more radically that relationship" (124). Rather than a contaminating element, then, sentimentalism in Indian women's fiction might be an early stepping-stone on the journey of cross-cultural understanding.

Mourning Dove also bucks the system's script for federally educated Indian girls, not only by becoming a writer who challenges the ethics of that system but by creating a character—Cogewea—who self-consciously resists Carlisle's expectations of her. Unlike Annie Goyitney, the Carlisle student who answers the question "What Should Be the Aim of a Carlisle Indian Girl?" with rhetorical allegiance to the cult of domesticity, Cogewea is not fulfilling her teachers' hopes for her. Cogewea's preference to work outside at the ranch underscores her unhappiness in the "prescribed sphere" (22) of home and family. Like so many writers of domestic fiction, Mourning Dove takes time to describe the interior of the ranch house. But unlike other writers, who then narrate the heroine as an integral part of that interior space, Mourning Dove describes Cogewea's discomfort in and detachment from that space. Cogewea lives with her sister, who married a white man, and the house is decorated in the stereotypically western style of white imagination, complete with buffalo-, bear-, and mountain lion-skin rugs scattered on the floor and deer and elk antlers and a buffalo head mounted on the wall. The narrator says that "the fixed glassy eyes [of the buffalo head] haunted her, as a ghost of the past. With her people had vanished this monarch of the plains" (31). Instead of assimilating the Euro-American values and habits of domesticity she was taught at Carlisle, Cogewea is uncomfortable in "white" interiors and associates them with the desecration of the natural landscape and the diminishing of her people's ways of life.

Goyitney and the other student essayists realized they were expected to narrate their plans to put their domestic education to its intended use, and because they were writing at school, they knew they had to follow the federal script for this narration. But once away from school, students such as Deloria, Winnemucca, and Zitkála-Šá turned this script on its head and used sentimentalist rhetorical devices practiced during their educational experiences to carve out different courses for themselves that resisted the federal demand that Indians must assimilate. Callahan and Mourning Dove likewise negotiated narratives of survivance that pushed back against these prescriptions written out by white women reformers and federal educational officials. As Cari M. Carpenter argues in the introduction to her study on anger and sentimentality in Indian women's literature, "early Native American women writers use sentimentality as one means of buttressing their own nationhood. Sentimentality as a means of nation-making is not, in other words, the sole prerogative of white women" (*Seeing Red* 17). Indeed, Indian women writers construct a syncretic literary domesticity that asserts a sovereign practical domesticity and melds Native traditions with Euro-American rituals. Whether disrupting the before/after transformation plot, displacing the idea of home elsewhere and elsetime, or disturbing the model/copy process, American Indian women writers carve a space for a feminine domestic ideal that highlights and reinforces systems of power where Native women exercise tribal influence. Similar to the way nineteenth-century white writers propagated the Euro-American ideal of republican motherhood—and utterly dissimilar to US assumptions about Indians—Indian writers build on the conventions of sentimental domestic fiction to craft a feminine ideal that predates, coincides with, and menaces white domesticity—and to assert a sovereign domesticity.

EPILOGUE

Fashioning Femininity

"Types of American Girls," "Types of Indian Girls," and the "Wrong Kind of [Mexican] Woman"

Mexican American and Native American women writers belie the many fictions of American domesticity. This book corroborates the work of other scholars who show that literary domesticity did not end with the nineteenth century; domesticity's influence travels far beyond the four walls of a woman's home; and all sentimental novelists did not laud domesticity, nor all modernist novelists scorn it. This study pushes on the work of historians to show how the literature of American domesticity participates in the colonial project of making over indigenous women of North America into properly feminized and domesticated Americans. Ironically, perhaps the most insidious instances of colonial domesticity hide in plain sight—in the glossy pages of popular magazines and the apparently innocent chapters of children's books. But this project also shows how colonized women manipulate domestic colonialism's imposition of cultural values and rituals for their own literary, artistic, and political purposes. Mexican and Indian writers contradict some of American domesticity's largest, most lasting, and possibly surreptitious assumptions: that indigenous women have no values or rituals of domesticity and thus *need* the intervention of white women; that nonwhite women will assimilate Euro-American domesticity indiscriminately; and, paradoxically, that Mexican and Indian women writers threaten their indigenous authenticity when adopting practical and literary modes, motifs, and images that might look *too* white. On the contrary, the nonwhite women writers discussed in this project prove that domesticity's cultures and literary conventions permeate the imaginary borders colonialists construct to separate themselves from the colonized.

In chapter 2, I discuss the ways Mexican American women writers fictionalize the tripartite spheres of domestic influence—home, school, and church—to engage and correct Euro-American ideas that Mexican Americans do not value or even have domestic mores. Jovita González and María Amparo Ruiz de Burton, among others, draft characters and scenes that promote Tejana and Californiana domesticity and expose Euro-American domesticity as predatory and hypocritical. Sarah Winnemucca (Paiute) and Zitkála-Šá (Yankton Sioux) construct similar scenarios. Ora V. Eddleman Reed (Cherokee) also uses the sentimental conventions of domestic rhetoric to fictionalize—and image—another sphere of supposedly feminized Euro-American influence: fashion. In her fiction and photographs, Eddleman Reed pushes against Euro-American stereotypes of Indian garb and derelict domesticity even as she incorporates Euro-American fashion and domestic ideals.

At just eighteen years old, Eddleman Reed began her editorial career at one of the first popular magazines in Indian and Oklahoma Territories: *Twin Territories: The Indian Magazine* (figure 5.1). Published for just six years, from 1898 to 1904, the magazine ran articles about Indian events and territorial news, as well as essays, poetry, and short stories by local writers (D. Morrison 136). Eddleman Reed contributed many mostly sentimental stories that feature Indian girls who, as Daryl Morrison points out, represent "the education, abilities, and cultures of the Indians" (145). In "The Honor of Wynoma: A Thanksgiving Story by a Cherokee Girl" (1902), Eddleman Reed spins a tale of romance and deceit and of racial passing and cultural blending that echoes Ruiz de Burton's novels and anticipates the romance plot in Edna Ferber's *Cimarron*.

Set in "the West"—presumably Indian Territory—"The Honor of Wynoma" opens on a domestic scene, where Mr. and Mrs. Boynton sit at their kitchen table drinking coffee. Mrs. Boynton laments news she has just received in a letter from her son, Horton: he is engaged to marry an Indian girl. While Mr. Boynton quietly tells his wife they can't tell their son who to love and tries to end his wife's tirade by asking for another cup of coffee, she rants about the "preposterous" notions that her daughter-in-law would be "a rough, uncouth Indian" and her "grandchildren [would] have the blood of savages in their veins" (372, 373, 373). Another letter in the mailbag momentarily distracts Mrs. Boynton from her

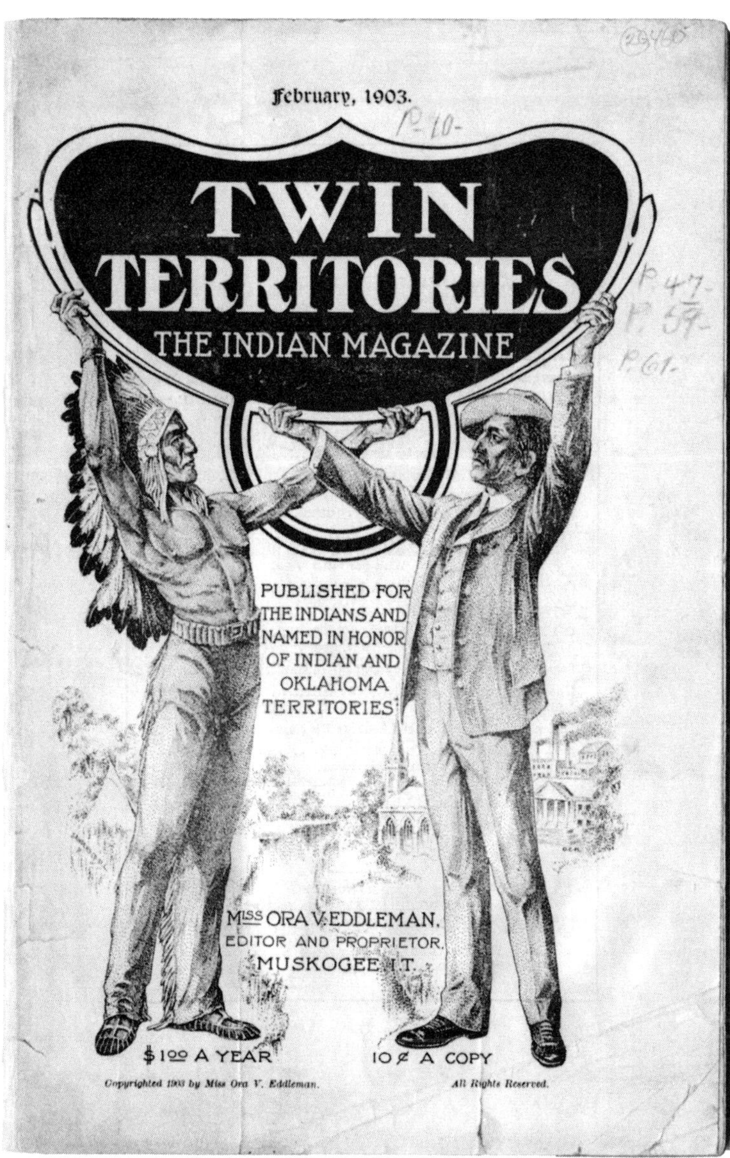

Figure 5.1 This cover image for the February 1903 issue of *Twin Territories: The Indian Magazine*—a magazine "published for the Indians and Named in Honor of Indian and Oklahoma Territories"—illustrates the face-off between Indians and settlers. The attire of each man in the foreground, as well as the architectural depictions of each man's culture in the background, suggest that Ora V. Eddleman Reed was well aware of what was at stake in this clash of cultures. Courtesy Manuscripts, Archives, and Special Collections, Washington State University Libraries, Pullman.

tirade—her daughter, Madge, wants to bring a friend home from school for Thanksgiving dinner—but only ends up fueling her fury. Horton can't bring his Indian fiancée home because she might corrupt his sister: "dainty Madge," says Mrs. Boynton, "wouldn't touch an Indian" (373). In a twist of literary fate, Horton does not bring his fiancée home, but Madge brings her friend, who is, of course, Horton's fiancée, Miss Wynoma Littleheart. The three young people know of this coincidence ahead of time and agree to deceive the Boyntons, hoping that the parents will fall in love with Wynoma before they reveal the truth. Wynoma easily passes as white. Her father, John Littleheart, is a "prominent half-breed Indian" who "belonged to a progressive tribe" and had money enough to buy her "any advantage that money could buy," including fine clothes, a beautiful home, and an eastern education (373). The narrator tells us that Wynoma's "home, instead of the tepee which Mrs. Boynton had pictured, was a spacious white house surrounded by grounds as lovely as Mrs. Boynton's own. The interior furnishings, too, were equal in taste, beauty and value to those found in other homes" (373). Mr. Boynton recognizes his daughter and her friend from afar at the train station because they "were two well dressed young ladies among those who alighted when the train stopped" (374). In her performances of domesticity and dress, Wynoma presents as white, so much so that Mrs. Boynton pronounces "she's our kind" and contrives to play matchmaker for Wynoma and Horton, hoping Horton will forget all about his "wild Indian girl" (375).

Wynoma keeps up the ruse through a painful conversation with Mrs. Boynton about making Horton forget his Indian fiancée, and even though she wonders how Horton's mother could be so "cold-hearted" and "calculating" (375). Mrs. Boynton has defined Wynoma's racial identity by assessing her upbringing, her manners, and her attire as white. Like Wynoma's classmates at school who do not believe she is Indian because "they couldn't see what I had done with my paint and feathers" (374), Mrs. Boynton does not see Wynoma as Indian because of her own presuppositions about Indian authenticity. At this point in the story, readers might be frustrated with Wynoma, perhaps even disgusted by her willingness to deny her Indianness to obtain the love of a white man and his family. But soon after this conversation, Horton proposes again when he and Wynoma go out for a drive. Wynoma refuses:

> we've deceived your mother into willingness! She knows you are going to marry, and she had rather it be I than, to quote her, "a low-born Indian girl!" I can't bear it. Only this morning she told me that she was so glad to see the change in you—so glad she was "rid of that Indian girl." I tell you, Horton, I'm sick of it! I am an Indian girl, but I am not the kind that deceives! It was weakness in this plan of ours. I should have owned my Indian blood, and accepted the consequences. As it is, my honor has asserted itself in time. I shall go no further. If you could not take me in the face of your mother's prejudice and opposition, you are not deserving of me, and it is best that we part. (376)

Wynoma and Horton do part ways. She goes home to take care of her father, who has fallen ill, and for the next year she and Horton do not speak. But when Thanksgiving arrives again, it brings Mrs. Boynton and Wynoma back together, this time at Wynoma's home. Mrs. Boynton apologizes for being "ignorant and prejudiced" (376), asks for Wynoma's forgiveness, and implores her to take Horton back. "Let's give thanks that the past is gone," Mrs. Boynton says. "I acknowledge it, Wynoma—the Indian girl is my daughter's equal, yes, in some respects, my daughter's mother's superior!" (376). The story ends happily: Wynoma forgives Mrs. Boynton and goes home with her to marry Horton.

In "The Honor of Wynoma," Eddleman Reed reverses Euro-American stereotypes about Indians. Wynoma is no squaw, but she is no princess either. She is not savage. Indeed, her honorable behavior foils the savagery of Mrs. Boynton's ignorance and prejudice. Playing on the tropes of the first Thanksgiving, Eddleman Reed suggests that whites need only recognize syncretic Indian identities to eradicate stereotypes and achieve racial harmony. Wynoma knows that she does not have to wear "paint and feathers" or live in a tepee to perform Indianness; she also knows that wearing Victorian gowns and living in a "spacious white house" do not compromise her Indianness or indicate attempts to pass as white. The only thing that compromises Indian identity, Eddleman Reed seems to suggest, is *denying* it.

Twin Territories also ran a photographic series that represents syncretic performances of Indian identity called "Types of Indian Girls," featuring Indian women in Victorian American fashions (figure 5.2).

Eddleman Reed apparently felt compelled to defend the series, contending "there is nothing improper or bold in a young lady allowing her picture to appear in these columns. This is not a police Gazette or a show or a revised edition of Sam Jones' sermons, but a well-meant effort to show the world that the Territory people are up-to-date" (72). Daryl Morrison notes that Eddleman Reed's depiction of Indian women was vastly different from the popular Euro-American stereotype of the squaw (145), and Alexia Kosmider asserts that she "wanted more than anything to eradicate negative Indian images" that Euro-Americans held about Indian women (112). In her fiction and her photography, Eddleman Reed works to replace Euro-American imaginary images of American Indians with actual images that imply the range of identity performances that can signify Indianness.

As we see in these pages from various issues of *Twin Territories*, Eddleman Reed features pictures of girls in white Victorian dress with captions that state their parentage, their accomplishments, or their blood quantum (figures 5.2 and 5.3). Unfortunately, the quality of these images is poor; hard copies of the magazines are rare, and microfilm leaves much to be desired. But we can see enough to understand that the images of Victorian-dressed girls, combined with the statements that identify the girls as Cherokee, Creek, Sauk and Fox, and Cheyenne, would disrupt Euro-American perceptions that relegated Indian women to the categories of erotic princess or squaw drudge. Indeed, these images speak a challenge to white women viewers: see, we can dress like you. Not coincidently, Eddleman Reed likely addressed this challenge to Indian viewers, as well. As Kosmider suggests, these images "mirror [Euro-Americans'] own models of proper womanhood," but more importantly, they "collapse the binary of white and red" (117).

Perhaps Eddleman Reed's photo project was necessary given the stereotypical, usually demeaning images of Native women proliferating through popular media, whether as part of the emerging field of anthropology or on consumer product labels ranging from shampoo bottles to tobacco boxes (figures 5.4 and 5.5). But the *Twin Territories* photos call to mind similar photos published in federal Indian boarding school publications, like those from Carlisle's *Red Man* (see chapter 3) that show how thoroughly Indian girls have learned the domestic arts of laundry, childcare, sewing, and milk processing. Boarding school publications circulated to thousands of American homes, and these photos, in which

Types of Indian Girls.

TYPES OF INDIAN GIRLS.

Figure 5.2 (*left*) The "Types of Indian Girls" series ran through most of *Twin Territories'* volumes. Courtesy Missouri Valley Special Collections, Kansas City Public Library, Kansas City, Missouri.

Figure 5.3 (*right*) Portrait of Miss Leota Crabtree in Victorian dress, "one of the most popular young ladies of Indian Territory." Photograph by Ora V. Eddleman Reed, *Twin Territories* [1903]: 52. Courtesy Manuscripts, Archives, and Special Collections, Washington State University Libraries, Pullman.

students certainly had no choice about what to wear, served one of the main goals of the schools and the magazines: to civilize Indian students and prove to the white reading public their assimilation of Euro-American mores. Among others, Laura Wexler, Susan K. Bernardin, and Melody Graulich write about photographing Indians as a violent erasure of individual and tribal identity. But what about when Indians turn cameras on themselves? In *Twin Territories* we see adult Indian women who presumably choose to dress in this fashion and an Indian editor who uses these images, as Kosmider asserts, to prove the civility, modernity, and desirability of Indian women and of living in Indian and Oklahoma Territories (figure 5.6).

Perhaps Eddleman Reed's project was also necessary because she

Figures 5.4 and 5.5 Also reproduced in Rayna Green's essay, "The Pocahontas Perplex," these advertisements circulated far and wide for decades and illustrate the stereotypical, sexualized appropriation of Native women's bodies for commercial purposes. The ad for James Moran & Co.'s Indian Girl Fine Cut Chewing Tobacco (ca. 1874), featuring a larger-than-life, bare-breasted Indian woman beckoning travelers with tobacco leaves, is available even today on posters and various other items. Courtesy Library of Congress, Prints and Photographs Division. The ad for Wildroot Dandruff Remedy was a point-of-purchase ad (ca. 1910), made of cardboard, printed in full color, and likely wrapped around the bottle. The label features the head of an American Indian woman on the bottle with a white family peeking around from behind. Courtesy Warshaw Collection of Business Americana—Hair, Archives Center, National Museum of American History, Smithsonian Institution, Washington, DC.

realized that popular magazines presented Indian women *only* in these stereotypically objectifying ways. Eddleman Reed's "Types of Indian Girls," and "Types of Indian Women" echo a series of images that ran in other popular magazines during the same years. Thomas Mitchell Pierce's "Types of American Women," as they appeared in the December 1902 issue of *Everybody's Magazine*, became so popular that they were recirculated as postcards and calendars (figures 5.7–5.12). As we move through the images, visiting fashionably dressed, implicitly white women in their home cities of New York, Chicago, New Orleans, San Francisco, and Boston, we notice that a short poem accompanies each woman's picture describing the personality .of the women that live in each city. We should also notice that there is no woman from Muskogee included here. Earlier in 1902, a similar series of images ran in the April issue of

TYPES OF INDIAN WOMEN.

MRS. CZARINA COLBERT CONLAN.

Prominent in Indian Territory Club Circles. First Vice President of the Indian Territory and Oklahoma Territory Federation of Clubs. Mrs. Conlan will edit new Club Department in TWIN TERRITORIES.

Figure 5.6 Portrait of Mrs. Czarina Colbert Conlan. Photograph by Ora V. Eddleman Reed, *Twin Territories* [1903]: 13. Courtesy General Research Division, New York Public Library, Astor, Lenox, and Tilden Foundations.

Everybody's Magazine titled "Girls of Many Nations." Drawn by Penrhyn Stanlaws, these images represent white girls from England, Ireland, Scotland, France, and Germany (figures 5.13–19). In other publications, Stanlaws also illustrated American girls, and his drawings were so popular that the *New York Times* included "his girl" when celebrating artists who "won prominence through his delineation of American girls" ("Girl of Today" 5). As with Pierce's "Types of American Women," though, we should notice that in Stanlaws's list of "Girls of Many Nations" there is no girl from the Cherokee Nation or any other Native nation.

Instead, the very next feature in the same issue of *Everybody's Magazine* is Zitkála-Šá's short story "The Warrior's Daughter." The illustrations, drawn by E. S. Blumenschein, depict the warrior's daughter, Tusee, in stereotypically Indian garb (figures 5.20 and 21). One image shows her

Figures 5.7–5.12 Illustrator Thomas Mitchell Pierce did not include Indians among his "Types of American Women." *Everybody's Magazine* 7 [1902]. Courtesy Boise Public Library, Boise, Idaho.

in an off-the-shoulder (and nearly off-the-chest) buckskin dress adorned with fringes and beads. Reflecting another Euro-American idea of Indian women's appearance, Tusee's long black hair covers her shoulders and large shell-like earrings peek out from beneath her hair. In the next illustration, Tusee sits "Indian style" on the floor of her tepee, stringing beads and coyly fielding the obvious advances of the suitor who leans in close to her. This time her buckskin dress covers more of her shoulders and her hair is in braids, suggesting, from the perspective of white fashion, a childlike innocence that contradicts the previous illustration. Of course, the illustrator worked off Zitkála-Šá's story for the content of his drawings, and it seems that Zitkála-Šá can't win with modern critics who study her work. Either she is criticized by Bernardin and others for allowing herself to be photographed in Indian buckskin and for writing sappy stories like "The Warrior's Daughter" that seemingly pander to whites' stereotypes of Indians or she is criticized for being photographed in Victorian whites, like Eddleman Reed's girls, and for using the conventions of domestic sentimentalism to write about her childhood. Either way, Eddleman Reed's "Types of Indian Girls" and "Types of Indian Women" navigate this same minefield of identity politics and posturing in a popular discourse that, at least in *Everybody's Magazine*, excludes Indian women from its list of "Types of American Women" and ignores

Figure 5.13 "Girls of Many Nations" by Penrhyn Stanlaws. *Everybody's Magazine* 6 [1902]. Author's collection.

Figures 5.14–5.19 Indian girls are noticeably absent from Penrhyn Stanlaws's "Girls of Many Nations." Author's collection.

the nationhood of individual Indian tribes in its list of "Girls of Many Nations." Instead, *Everybody's Magazine*—and others like it, even though they publish stories by Indian writers—insist on imaging Indians as museum relics or curiosities in some cultural sideshow.

Speaking of sideshow curiosities, Indian girls were, in fact, included in circuit Chautauqua and lyceum programs that traveled the country during the early twentieth century to offer patriotic information, education, and inspiration to small-town Americans. Theodore Roosevelt called these programs "the most American thing in America." Woodrow Wilson said they were "an integral part of national defense." But Sinclair Lewis sneered that they were "nothing but wind and chaff . . . the laughter of yokels," and William James lamented they were "depressing from [their] mediocrity" (Canning 2000). One such program was titled "The American Girls," a musical sponsored by the Redpath Lyceum Bureau. James Redpath—I have found no indication that his name signifies anything Indian—started this company in 1868, and it became one of the most popular and prolific of the lyceum companies. As we see in these images from the program's brochure, Indian girls are included only as characters presumably played by white girls and as relics, not as modern women with agency. According to the brochure, *The American Girls*, first performed in 1916, presented

> the many charming things about a truly typical American girl as we have known her in history since the time of the discovery of the American continent and as we have known her in our own day. . . . As we consider these types of American girls we find that the modern girl is, in a measure, a sort of summing up of all the others. She represents the freedom of the Indian maiden, the Puritanical instincts of the Quaker, the romance of the Colonial girl, the dignity of the girl who wore hoop skirts and the queer conceit of the girl with the basque [Figure 5.22] . . . The idea is to show, not a cheap comedy, but a fine example of American girlhood. . . . It will be

Figures 5.20 and 5.21 Even though it was published on the very next page after Penrhyn Stanlaws's "Girls of Many Nations," illustrations from Zitkala-Ša's "The Warrior's Daughter" suggest that the editors and illustrators of *Everybody's Magazine* saw Indian women and Indian nations as Other: not fully female, not fully sovereign. Author's collection.

> a historical number showing glimpses of American girl life and bringing out in prominent view the part she has played in American historical events and the social life of the nation. (6)

The brochure explains that the story line is built around creating the American flag and "other events in history in which the American girl has played a conspicuous part." If the spinning wheel illustrated here refers to Betsy Ross sewing the flag, one can only guess who and what event the Pilgrim-style blunderbuss references (figures 5.22 and 23). Other photographs in the brochure show American girls holding their instruments poised and ready to play, with one photo bordered by an illustration of the American bald eagle and the other bordered by a ship at sea—perhaps representing the *Niña*, the *Pinta*, or the *Santa María*, or maybe the *Mayflower* (figures 5.24 and 5.25). But no girl holds a blunderbuss or poses against a backdrop that would clearly explain it. Two other pages from the program, however, suggest potential contexts for the weapon.

In figure 5.26, six girls crouch in the entrance of a tepee. The girls wear stereotypical headbands with feathers and appear to wear faux buckskin dresses with fringed sleeves. The tepee is marked with what its designers presumably considered Indian art, and the vase in the foreground matches in design. Both the tepee (used by Indians on the western Great Plains, not on the East coast) and the stage backdrop (with its distant view of snowcapped mountains that look more like the Rockies than the Appalachians) signify the Redpath Lyceum Bureau's reproduction of Native stereotyping. Though the Bureau had offices in cities across the country, it originated in Boston, and if *The American Girls* program celebrated the Indian maiden who helped shape the social history of the United States, then the stories the show told were likely about Indian girls from the eastern woodlands, not the West. For all its rhetoric about how the "freedom of the Indian maiden" shaped American history, *The American Girls* seems to use the stereotyped image of the Indian girl as the baseline for an evolution of American girls that progresses from primitive to modern, from savage to civilized.

We see in another page of images that the girls are arranged so as to suggest such an evolution, starting with the Indian girl and moving through the Puritan girl, the Colonial girl, the hoop-skirt girl, the Basque girl, and finally, the modern girl in her simple, unadorned, and

Figures 5.22–5.27 *The American Girls* program of the Redpath Lyceum Bureau, a popular company that traveled the circuit Chautauqua in the late nineteenth and early twentieth centuries. Courtesy of *Traveling Culture: Circuit Chautauqua in the Twentieth Century*, Records of the Redpath Chautauqua Collection, University of Iowa Libraries, Iowa City.

unrestrictive white gown (figure 5.27). In this progression, the writers of *The American Girls* can include the Indian girl as one of its types because she is relegated to the past. And going by the images on this page, one could infer that it is the modern girl who forces the Indian girl out of civilized modernity. Perhaps only by the happenstance of an editor's layout, the girl in the upper-right-hand corner of the page, in her simple modern dress and her early-1900s-era shoe boots, almost points a fencing foil at the Indian girl. With the foil laid out against a shield decorated like an American flag, the subtle but undeniable message is that the Indian girl of the past must either die or assimilate to this fashionable march of progress. The foil (or, in the earlier image, the blunderbuss) joins the spinning wheel as weapons American girls can wield to shape American Indian modernity, either by deadly violence or by homespun fashion.

The American Girls program traveled the circuit twelve years after the last issue of Eddleman Reed's *Twin Territories*. Maybe the way Redpath relegates Indian girls to a distant past is evidence that her work was in vain. But Eddleman Reed's venture still seems a necessary and urgent enterprise: to image and reimage Native women to show that Indian women are alive and adaptable and have sophisticated understandings of the performative and political attributes of personal dress. For even though Eddleman Reed presents Indian women in white Victorian garb, she also presents them in traditional Native garb, images that complicate the idea that only an Indian in Victorian dress is a civilized Indian or that movement away from one's tribal clothing is a primary marker of progress. Eddleman Reed included as part of her types girls who wore tribal dress, and she had no qualms about laying out images of girls in tribal dress on the same page as girls in Victorian dress. On one particular page, Eddleman Reed published photos of "Full-Blood Creek Indian Girls—Showing the famous Creek pottery" alongside "Misses Pauline McCoy (full-blood Sauk and Fox Indian), and Mattie Block, (half-blood Cheyenne), graduates from Haskell Institute." Perhaps Eddleman Reed presents these Creek girls as authentic Indians; by not naming them and instead focusing on their tribal affiliations, she nods to the importance of community over the individual. In this way, she denies the Creek girls individuated subjectivity and shows a preference for the Victorian American definition of a civilized woman. But in every other photo in her "Types of Indian Girls," Eddleman Reed provides an individual and a tribal name. On this same page, Pauline McCoy is also presented as "full-blood," suggesting that an Indian girl in Victorian dress could be just as authentic as one in tribal dress.[1] Kosmider notes that Eddleman Reed "implies that one image does not supersede or suppress the other" (122). This is especially the case when Eddleman Reed presents two images of Mrs. Florence Stephens-Lennon—one in stereotypically Indian huntress attire and one in a Victorian gown (figures 5.28 and 29). In the huntress image, which Eddleman Reed titled *A Graceful 'Diana' of the Cherokees*, she plays to Euro-American expectations of an Indian's appearance; white viewers would recognize the bow and

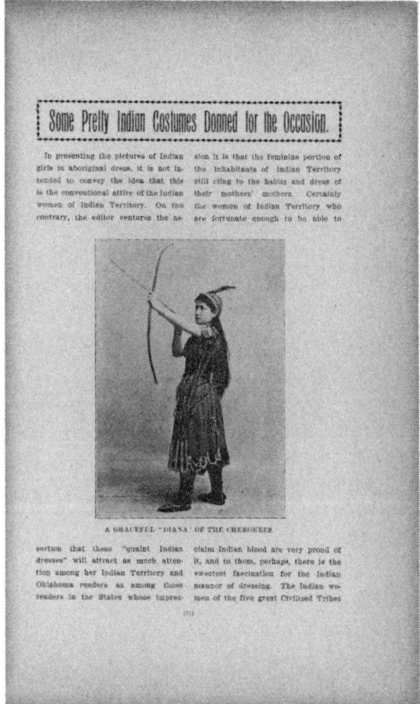

Some Pretty Indian Costumes Donned for the Occasion.

In presenting the pictures of Indian girls in aboriginal dress, it is not intended to convey the idea that this is the conventional attire of the Indian women of Indian Territory. On the contrary, the editor ventures the assertion that these "quaint Indian dresses" will attract as much attention among her Indian Territory and Oklahoma readers as among those readers in the States whose impression it is that the feminine portion of the inhabitants of Indian Territory still cling to the habits and dress of their mothers' mothers. Certainly the women of Indian Territory who are fortunate enough to be able to claim Indian blood are very proud of it, and to them, perhaps, there is the sweetest fascination for the Indian manner of dressing. The Indian women of the five great Civilized Tribes

A GRACEFUL "DIANA" OF THE CHEROKEES.

14 TWIN TERRITORIES

MRS. FLORENCE STEPHENS-LENNON.

A Beautiful Cherokee Woman. One of the Most Accomplished Musicians of Indian Territory.

Figure 5.28 (*left*) Mrs. Florence Stephens-Lennon shows the adaptability of gender performance. In a photograph under the headline "Some Pretty Indian Costumes Donned for the Occasion," she dresses as *A Graceful "Diana" of the Cherokees.* Photograph by Ora V. Eddleman Reed, *Twin Territories*, Nov. 1902. Courtesy General Research Division, New York Public Library, Astor, Lenox and Tilden Foundations.

Figure 5.29 (*right*) In this image, Mrs. Florence Stephens-Lennon's outfit contrasts with the one in figure 5.28. She is a Cherokee and a musician and a Victorian lady. Courtesy General Research Division, New York Public Library, Astor, Lenox and Tilden Foundations.

arrow as a signifier of Indianness and perhaps think: "there is an Indian woman." But those same white viewers might note the evening gown and the book in the second image and see themselves—white genteel ladies. Eddleman Reed's hope, surely, was that viewers would also see the caption of the second picture, "Mrs. Florence Stephens-Lennon, A Beautiful Cherokee Woman. One of the Most Accomplished Musicians of Indian Territory," and think: "there is an Indian woman."

And even though she never included a photograph of herself in the "Types of Indian Women" series, Eddleman Reed published a picture of herself dressed in skins and pelts in a 1903 issue of *Twin Territories*, which she captioned, "an Indian Huntress costume, Cherokee." Years later, in 1920, she sat for a portrait with her sons, dressed and posed as the all-American mother (see D. Morrison's article for these portraits). Karen L. Kilcup notes that Eddleman Reed, along with other well-known Native women such as Zitkála-Šá, Sarah Winnemucca, and Pauline Johnson, was adept at performing both the "Indian princess" and the "Victorian lady," that these women were experts at "playing Indian" (*Writing* 194).

While this is surely true, it is only true because Eddleman Reed and others understood that Indian women perform gender and tribal identity through fashion in multiple ways. And instead of assimilating her and her models' performances of identity into *Everybody's Magazine*'s "Types of American Women," Eddleman Reed rejected that homogenizing and vague label—"American"—choosing instead the term "Indian" to describe her subjects. Of course "Indian" is itself a vague and homogenizing label. But while the precious poems that accompany Pierce's "Types of American Women" erase each woman's personal identity in favor of a local type, Eddleman Reed's photo captions maintain each subject's personal and tribal identity. And while Redpath Lyceum Bureau's *The American Girls* implies that the Indian girl must be made over into the American girl through fashion, Eddleman Reed's subjects argue for an Indian modernity that includes both tribal fashions and Euro-American apparel as markers of identity and as sites of cultural negotiation.

In closing, I offer a brief discussion of Felicia Luna Lemus's 2003 novel, *Trace Elements of Random Tea Parties*, to suggest that nonwhite women in the western United States—in fiction and in life—still find themselves subject to varying definitions of what it means to be an American woman. A story about a Chicana lesbian's coming of age, the novel pressures mainstream American definitions of femininity via sexuality, domesticity, and fashion as the main character, Leti, negotiates the haunting discourses—past and present, dead and alive, folklore and fact—that would circumscribe her identity. In writing about Leti's negotiations of identity, Lemus joins a growing collective of writers and scholars such as Gloria Anzaldúa, Cherríe L. Moraga, Martha P. Cotera, and others who espouse a Xicanisma, or Chicana feminism, that "confronts and undermines patriarchy as it cross-cuts forms of disempowerment and silence such as racism, homophobia, class inequality, and nationalism" (Arredondo 2). Whereas Reed portrays individual Indian women in various fashions and settings to define a collective femininity, Lemus invokes a collective of Mexican and Mexican American women through which Leti defines her individual femininity. Legendary women who provide master narratives that traditionally define a woman's life haunt Leti throughout the novel. Many of these women loom large as mother figures: La Llorona (whom Leti calls "my gal Weeping"), La Malinche, La Virgen de Guadalupe, her own mother, her grandmother (Nana), and her great-grandmother (Mama Estrella). Others are pop culture icons such as Dolores del Río and Maria Callas. As I have shown throughout this book, American femininity is prescribed in print culture as much as in other cultural traditions such as religion, education, fiction, and folklore. The images included in this section illustrate the ways print culture also influences Leti.

In her characteristic pithy syntax, Leti summarizes the legends of La Llorona, La Malinche, and La Virgen for readers—both Chicana/o and not—who are unfamiliar with them:

> Weeping Woman traveled by wind in the night, stopping at windows and howling deep and mournful wails because she was bad and wanted to take bad children to be her own. She was the Weeping because she birthed a little girl whose father was a Spaniard. She cried because she had a mixed baby, one her Indian family and neighborhood despised. That is why she threw her little girl into the river that storming night, the night when the lightning's gleam on her baby's hazel eyes finally drove her mad. The Weeping Woman, she cried because she was La Malinche reborn.
>
> You don't know that story, either? Didn't you ever spend *any* time with your nana?
>
> La Malinche. Everyone was taught to despise la Malinche because she loved a conquistador. Or so he said. As did his buddies. And the entire empire they set up. La Malinche. Yes, that woman, the archetype of the Wrong Kind of Woman. Not surrounded by cherubs and pink roses like the Virgen de Guadalupe, our blessed patron mother saint. Not pasted on candles in textured tall glasses that we lit for thanks. No, the Weeping Woman, and her cousin Malinche, they were bad, bad, bad girls, those two were.
>
> Those two girls, their fierce rebel lasting power made people

Figure 5.30 Leti's "my gal Weeping" enjoys a vibrant popularity well into the twenty-first century as artists and filmmakers, producers of goods, and tellers of urban legends reimagine, renarrate, and recirculate her image and her story. A Google Image search of "La Llorona" yields hundreds of images that show La Llorona is still haunting modern imaginations. This painting captures several key elements: La Llorona is often figured as tragically beautiful and dangerously alluring, in or near water, and accompanied in some way by her three children. Here, in keeping with the artist's depiction of Llorona with a Mexican sugar-skull face, the children appear as three skulls on the Weeping Woman's necklace. Painting by Cathy Ashworth, *La Llorona*, 2015, acrylic on canvas. Courtesy of the artist, image use courtesy of CATbox Art Studio, www.CATboxartstudio.com.

Figure 5.31 (*top left*) This woodblock print of La Llorona captures a few other elements of the legend: she is depicted as a frightening vision searching the water, in the darkness, for the children she drowned. Some makeup artists create a version of the Weeping Woman that is grotesque and horrifying, making her look like a decaying zombie instead of an ethereal ghost. Print by Maria Cristina Tavera, *La Llorona (The Crying Woman)*, 2014, woodblock print. Courtesy of Maria Cristina Tavera. © All rights reserved.

Figure 5.32 (*bottom left*) La Malinche also figures largely in Mexican and Mexican American popular culture, as she clearly has since the early 1500s, when Tlaxcala artists rendered this codex that narrates Malinche's interactions with Cortez. Courtesy http://blogs.histoireglobale.com/wp-content/uploads/2014/06/La-Maninche.jpg.

Figure 5.33 (*right*) The image of La Virgen de Guadalupe is as ubiquitous in popular culture as is La Llorona's and La Malinche's. Found everywhere from children's coloring pages to cartoons, tattoos to candles, Mexican and Mexican American women are ever reminded of the patriarchal requirement of chastity until motherhood. Author's collection.

> remember them long after they died. They were everything I wanted to be. (18–19) (See figures 5.30–33.)

Leti invokes all three legendary women, but it is "my gal Weeping" that haunts her throughout the novel, particularly in quiet moments when change is on the horizon.

Leti's character challenges a definition of femininity that is inextricably tied to heterosexuality and motherhood. The legendary women who haunt her—including the women in her family—depict versions of heterosexuality that Leti rejects, even though she says Llorona and Malinche "were everything I wanted to be" (19). By invoking La Llorona, heterosexual femininity and motherhood is figured as dangerous, victimized, insane—even sadistic or sadomasochistic. By invoking La Malinche, heterosexual femininity and motherhood is figured as natural yet treacherous, familial yet epic. By invoking La Virgen, heterosexual femininity and motherhood is figured as passive, chaste, sacred, and sacrificial. Leti's biological mothers are no less legendary. Her mother gave birth to her after she was clinically dead. Her grandmother and great-grandmother—Nana and Mama Estrella—raise her, trying to replicate their own roles in patriarchal Mexican culture by insisting Leti perform a highly stylized heterosexual femininity that will eventually end in marriage and motherhood.

With Leti's lesbian sexuality, Lemus dramatizes the tension of the individual and the collective. Leti says she wants to be "everything" these legendary women are, but perhaps she would be more accurate in saying that she wants to be included in their legends, that she does not want to distance herself from the collectivity of Mexican women that have shaped her life and culture. Instead of distancing herself from the collective, Leti claims the individual strengths that the collective represents: the power to define one's own identity and future even in the face of overwhelming, and sometimes opposing, cultural pressures. For we could say that La Malinche insists on her own desires despite the perceived betrayal of her own people; that La Llorona insists on her indigenous identity despite horrifically murdering her own (half-Spanish) children; that even La Virgen braves certain ridicule or shaming by insisting on her virgin motherhood. Domino Renee Perez argues that "the prominence Lemus gives La Llorona and the way she is put to use in a novel about young, queer, primarily working-class youths indicate the capacity of the lore to accommodate contemporary concerns about multiple cultural and sexual realities" and that "by recasting the sexual dynamics of the legend, Chicana lesbians write themselves into Chican@ oral and literary traditions to, at times, radically alter the tale" (29). Leti claims these powers of self-definition and self-narration even as she speaks into the discursive history of Mexican femininity.

Leti's definition of her sexuality gets worked out in the novel, then, in the stereotypically feminine realms of domesticity, family, and fashion. Just as she narrates her sexuality as a modern retelling of legendary feminine narratives, she claims these additional realms as her birthright and reshapes and reframes collective traditions as individual expressions of self. In the very first pages of the novel, Lemus sets the main characters—"chicana dykes"—and the scenes—domestic spaces. In the novel, Edith is Leti's first girlfriend, and by their third date in Leti's small apartment, she is wrapping herself up in purple plastic wrap for "bouts of all-night hygienic sex" (5). Leti recognizes the stereotypical heterosexuality of this particular activity, saying,

> I felt like a desperate and misguided mamasita, all gussied up in kitchen paraphernalia to greet her hunka-hunka at the door and try to cook up some loving. I've read about stuff like that in *Good Housekeeping* at the dentist's. You know, the path to sexual happiness is through his digestive tract, that sort of thing. It's strange for two chicana dykes to live *Good Housekeeping* lust, but the way Edith's eyes shimmered when she'd airtight me with the Saran, I was willing to do anything to see that wild glow. (5)

Leti invokes heterosexual fantasies as she narrates sex with a woman, queering the fantasy even as she reveals her anxiety about the queering. Further, she names a popular ladies' magazine—*Good Housekeeping*—that has circulated white middle-class heteronormativity since 1885. As I have discussed throughout this book, popular magazines and other ephemera of print culture reinforce ideologies of gender, race, sex, and class. But by invoking print culture, Lemus dramatizes the adaptability of ideologies that seem cemented by more than a century of tradition and discourse. Sex is sex, Lemus seems to say; but Leti's anxiety about her sexuality (she feels desperate and misguided and calls her plastic-wrapped sex "strange") highlights the seemingly inevitable tension that arises when an individual performs a group-defined role in a way the collective would see as Other.

Readers see scenes rife with similar tensions throughout the novel—scenes set in domestic spaces that, in other novels or stories, would reiterate centuries of patriarchal, heteronormative narratives. But in *Trace Elements*, domesticity does not connote the repression of women. Instead, the domesticity in *Trace Elements* is usually playful and experimental, allowing the lesbian characters to reshape collective narratives about what it means to be a woman, what it means to make a home, and what it means to be a family. For the most part, Leti's domesticity is characterized by experiments in happiness. When she starts dating K (short for Berenike), they make homes of their separate apartments, working out routines that bring them together yet allow for individual space. After they had been dating a few months and reshaping yet another collective narrative—the joke among lesbians that the second date involves a U-Haul—Leti and K move into apartments that share a wall, but they still don't move in together. They continue their previous routines and make new ones. They laugh when they can hear each other through the wall while they talk on the phone, when they can hear the other one showering through the rattling of the shared pipes, when they work out tapping codes on the shared wall in the closets. When that gets old—they "almost busted a hole through the teasing common wall"—but after beginning what was clearly going to be a tedious process of tearing down that wall, Leti and K rediscover the charm in alternating sleepovers (148). They throw themselves into "homemaking efforts" that their apartment manager thought was "amusing or cute" but that signify the girls' continued blending of heteronormative, white, domestic traditions with their Chicana ethnicity and lesbian sexuality (149). The "silver lining" of trying to knock down the common wall, for example, "added tool-belt sex to the variety pack" (148). After K paints the bathroom cabinets bright orange, she warns Leti that she'd "have to bake chocolate-chip cookies Vargas Girl style if I got toothpaste globs on the cabinet. Done" (149).

Both sexual fantasies, the tool belt and the Vargas Girl indicate heterosexual, even male-dominated, play appropriated as same-sex play. Lemus notes that the colors the girls choose to paint their bathrooms and bedrooms—cobalt blue, apple red, bright orange, silver—echo the graffiti that K paints of "fierce Aztec women [who] stood at the top of

Figure 5.34 Alberto Vargas was a Peruvian immigrant who would become one of the most famous pinup-girl artists. He began his career of sketching and painting female nudes for Hollywood studios and, in New York, for the Ziegfeld Follies in the 1920s. His "Vargas girls" were favorite pinups in *Esquire* magazine in the 1940s and were eventually featured as centerfolds in *Playboy* magazine from the 1950s through the 1970s. The girl in this image is dressed up in a sheer purple nightie and matching heeled slippers, recalling Leti's and Edith's purple plastic-wrap sex and Leti's and K's jokes about baking cookies "Vargas Girl style." In Leti's sexual play that invokes popular heterosexual fantasies, she complicates the idea of the male gaze, showing that females enjoy viewing and dressing up the female form too. Illustration by Alberto Vargas, *March, 1962*. Reproduced by permission of the Estate of Max Vargas.

Aztlán pyramids with their lightning-bolt-licked long blue-black hair whipping" (149) in the wind. Lemus, it seems, anticipates Judith Halberstam's call for "a much more rigorous understanding of the gendering of domestic space" (8) and an articulation of what she dubs "queer space," which she defines as "the place-making practices within postmodernism in which queer people engage and it also describes the new understandings of space enabled by the production of queer counterpublics" (6). Michael Warner defines *counterpublics* as groups that are "formed by their conflict with the norms and contexts of their cultural environment, and this context of domination inevitably leads to distortion. Mass publics and counterpublics, in other words, are both damaged forms of publicness, just as gender and sexuality, are, in this culture, damaged forms of privacy" (63). While Leti and K redefine their domestic spaces as queer spaces, and while we could consider those home spaces—and the more public spaces such as Crystal's dyke bar that they also share with Edith and Nolan—inhabited by counterpublics, Lemus does not suggest that these spaces are distorted. "Distortion" is usually used in a negative or wrong sense (as in, "the media distorts the issue" or "the virus distorts the cell"). On the contrary, except for the inevitable tensions of inhabiting a counterpublic, Leti's and K's cultural disruptions are creative and productive. They queer and Chican-ize their domesticity, resisting an American narrative that says proper domesticity is the realm of white middle-class women even while claiming the feminized narrative of domesticity for themselves.

As the novel progresses, Leti shows that her reappropriation of heteronormative narratives of sexuality and domesticity also intersects with generational and class differences. She and K eventually move into a single-family house together, where they continue to hone their "touch of punk Martha Stewart-goes-dyke Home Depot" style (163). And in an amusing yet dead-serious debate with Nana over where to place the huge green velvet second-hand sofa, Lemus suggests that different generations of Mexican American women negotiate hegemonic feminine ideals in different ways. Class difference adds to generational difference when Leti and K and Edith and Nolan go on a road trip to visit Edith's parents. In her dress, demeanor, and descriptions of her past, Edith has led the other three girls to believe that she is just like them—that is, a Chicana dyke from a working-class family. So when they pull into Edith's family neighborhood—the ultra-affluent Nob Hill in San Francisco, no less—Leti "wasn't the only one confused" (106). Edith's family is rich, and Leti refers to another ladies' magazine dedicated to perfect domesticity as they walk into the "*House Beautiful* foyer where nothing was to be touched and everything was insured" (109). Mrs. Contreras wears Chanel and keeps up a rigorous cosmetic enhancement routine. Mr. Contreras is a corporate lawyer who is on his fifth gin sour by the time their French Swiss maid serves them all a gourmet dinner.

The dinner conversation recalls the class positioning of the nineteenth-century New Mexico and California writers who claimed whiteness as class status. Not about to let Edith get away with her lies, Nolan says, "This sure is a nice place you have here, Mr. Contreras. And here we always thought Edie came from the Mission district, isn't that funny?" Mr. Contreras's reply shows the reader why the girls are so upset at Edith's lies. "The Mission?" he asks, incredulous. "What a damned insult. Edith's grandparents still live there, but I can't fathom how they bear it. The whole area smells of tortillas and menudo, and that damned ranchero music with its ludicrous polka insanity, too many damned lazy beaners without any ambition" (110). While the rest of the girls sit in stunned, angry silence and Mrs. Contreras tries desperately to change the subject, Nolan "gunned her engines all over again, 'Mr. Contreras, I'm shocked to hear you call anyone a "beaner." It seems so self-deprecating. You and Mrs. Contreras are Mexican by heritage, aren't you?" With barely contained fury, he corrects her, "I am Hispanic, thank you very kindly, and, young missy, I have had just about enough of this interrogation" (111). Just as nineteenth-century ranchero-owning nuevomexicanas and Californianas distanced themselves from their indigenous Mexican heritage and called themselves Spanish American, so do the Contreras parents distance themselves from their Mexican heritage by using the US census term to label themselves "Hispanic." Further, the Contreras parents are examples of members of marginalized groups in the United States who internalize negative stereotypes circulated about their group by members of the dominant group (as described in Frantz Fanon's foundational discussions of internalized racism). Mr. Contreras—and surely his wife too—has internalized the idea that all Mexicans are lazy and smelly and out of touch with modernity. Using the racial epithet "beaner," he also indicates his belief that Mexicans are poor, only and always eating beans, presumably because they can't afford anything else.

In turn, the fact that Edith lies to her friends about her family's class status indicates that she operates on the internalization of stereotypes too. Clearly embarrassed by her parents' internalized racism as much as by their conspicuous consumption, Edith performs a role she believes is more authentically Mexican in the opening years of the twenty-first century: that of working-class Chicana dyke. To be sure, as is well documented, the Chicano movement started among the working class. Edith's friends would have been offended at her parents' comments and behavior no matter how Edith performs her identity. But their anger at Edith is a response to her class positioning, which is a slumming of sorts. Edith's behavior unconsciously says, in effect, the exact same thing her parents' does: Mexicans (Chicana/os) are poor and perhaps lazy and smelly and backward (which gets reinterpreted by Edith and the girls as retro); in order to distance myself from my overtly racists parents and be accepted by these girls I see as more authentically Chicana, I need to dress, talk, and act in the exact ways my parents describe Mexicans even though I know my parents' descriptions are racist. To put it another way, then, the girls are as angry at Edith's racism and capitalist subterfuge as her lies and pretenses.

Edith's racist pretenses, though, illustrate what underlies Leti's quest to perform her most authentic identity: her dissatisfaction with being forced to define herself at all. Experiments with fashion accompany her forays into domesticity and adventures in sexuality as she struggles, throughout the novel, to perform her selfhood in ways that are both expressive of and independent from her Mexican American heritage. Whereas Eddleman Reed's "Types of Indian Girls" defy racial stereotypes with their Victorian fashions, Leti defies both racial and gender stereotypes with her sartorial choices. She uses fashion to play into gendered expectations of those around her, such as when she dons a "classy blouse," irons her pants, spit shines a pair of high heels, and "played Emily Post Perfect" for an interview with a realtor and when she perpetually carries a cardigan to cover her tattoos in Nana's presence (152, 153). But she also uses fashion to resist Nana's expectations of her femininity.

Even as the legendary La Llorona, La Malinche, and La Virgen haunt Leti's self-perception, Nana is a living legend whose memory of Leti's girlhood haunts her perceptions and expectations of Leti in the present. Nana does not approve of Leti's fashion choices, whether they are ratty, retro housedresses or boy-sized t-shirts and baggy jeans purchased from "The Willy's" (the Goodwill). Leti expresses gratitude to her Nana and Mama Estrella for teaching her to sort through the clothes racks to "snag never-been-worn name brands," but she wants the

> undersized tee-shirts she said even little boys wouldn't make mud pies in. The shirts worn to display my Weeping Woman tattoo, my beautiful lady perfectly bronze-skinned, warm on the upper half of my right arm permanently muscled from years of stocking the store's shelves. Around Nana, I slipped on a cardigan out of respect to hide the ink job a girlfriend needled into my skin during college. (29)

Leti understands the fluidity and performativity of gender even if she is never quite comfortable with the realization. Indeed, the realization is likely what makes Leti uncomfortable. She knows what Nana expects of her—which is why she uses a cardigan—but she still gets the tattoos, still wears boys clothes, even though

> Nana made it perfectly clear, she did not appreciate my carefully honed boyness. Raw deal. I mean, Nana couldn't care less that K was so boy. But with me, ay no. No go. See, as far as Nana could tell, K had always been able to pass as dude if she wanted to. Not me. Nana remembered my girl as well as she remembered the endless days she spent crafting its precise style. Nana hadn't ever braided K's hair. She hadn't ever taught K how to humble girl into the Virgen's flowing gowns. Basically Nana didn't look at K's boy and see years of upbringing being actively denied. (168–69)

The trouble with gender, as I have discussed throughout this book, is its prescription. Nana sees in Leti's "boyness" not an expression of Leti's selfhood, but a rejection of Nana's own performance of her gender and her "years of upbringing being actively denied" (169). When one woman presumes to know how another woman should perform her femininity, problems arise for both women.

Leti's gender trouble cuts both ways. In a particularly poignant moment in the novel, she thinks about the "Diagonal Crossing Allowed" street signs and compares pedestrian traffic to gender performance. She wonders why, even when signs allow for diagonal crossing, people still

Figure 5.35 The girl featured on the cover of Felicia Luna Lemus's *Trace Elements of Random Tea Parties* illustrates Leti's tattooed girl-boy gender performance. Cover design by Gia Giasullo, Studio eg. Cover photo by Marion Ettlinger. Author's collection.

tend "to walk lines perpendicular to the well-traveled roads. Why? Fuck if I know. What I did know was that my life depended on me crossing the street diagonally, sometimes in a winding circular pattern for that matter." Leti thinks, "I wasn't a boy, not entirely at least, but at times I wasn't a girl either." She also knows that the pressure to choose a gender and perform it regularly does not come solely from cisgender women like Nana. Such pressures have existed among lesbian and transgender women from the earliest "1950s bar days," when Leti knows she would have been labeled a "ki-ki, a neither-nor" (169). She thinks about how even Rob, her first college girlfriend, would have "accused me of being a traitor for claiming part boy" (while noting the irony of this girlfriend going by the name "Rob"):

> Rob would have accused me of bringing the communal growl down for saying I'm part boy. And pre-Stonewall dykes would have wanted me to call my game. What kind of dyke was I anyway? Good question. Simple and complicated all at once, I wasn't a pigeon to be tucked away neatly into a hole. I didn't wear a fixed category without feeling pain. I was more, or less, or something different entirely. (170)

Leti and her friends might be a productive illustration of Lisa Duggan's observations about performances of gender and sexuality under late capitalism. She writes, "new neo-liberal sexual politics . . . might be termed the new homonormativity—it is a politics that does not contest heteronormative assumptions and institutions, but upholds them and sustains them, while promising the possibility of a semobilized gay constituency and a privatized, depoliticized gay culture anchored in domesticity and consumption" (50). As readers watch Leti struggle and grow throughout the novel, we realize that she's haunted as much by her peers' homonormative definitions and categories as by the traditions of her Nana and the impositions of heteronormative culture. We understand that Leti invokes these legendary women—La Llorona, La Malinche, La Virgen—not as prescriptions of femininity but as examples of women who crossed diagonally, who insisted on performing their ethnic, sexual, and class identities in ways that engaged the collective while expressing their individuality, even when that performance garnered ridicule and certain death.

The US history of westward expansion is narrated, in part, by white women who say to the Indian and Mexican women they met, "This is how to be an American woman." The Indian women writers I've discussed say in response, "This is how I am a Paiute woman, or a Laguna woman, or a Cherokee woman, *and* an American woman." The New Mexican and California women writers say, "This is how I am a Spanish, Mexican, *and* American woman. And as we see in *Trace Elements*, Nana tells Leti, "This is what it means to be a Mexican American woman." Even the Chicana dykes say to her, "This is how to be a Chicana lesbian." In response, calling on the strength of the legendary women who forged their own identities in the face of overwhelming pressure to perform one role or another, Leti says, "Bullshit."

APPENDIX

Advertisements for and Reviews of Evelyn Hunt Raymond Novels

The following is a list of contemporary advertisements for and reviews of the four novels by Evelyn Hunt Raymond discussed in chapter 3, in chronological order.

Monica, the Mesa Maiden

Annual American Catalogue. 1892
Current Literature: A Magazine of Record and Review. Sept.–Dec. 1892 (vol. 11)
Dial. Sept. 1 and Dec. 1, 1892
Publishers Weekly. Sept. 21, 1892
Book News. Sept. (vol. 1) and Dec. (vol. 2) 1892
New York Herald Tribune. Oct. 22, 1892
Book Buyer: A Summary of American & Foreign Literature. Dec. 1892 (vol. 9)
Catholic World. Dec. 1892 (vol. 56)
Review of Reviews (American edition). Dec. 1892 (vol. 6)
Literary World. Dec. 3, 1892
Christian Union. Dec. 3, 1892
New York Herald. Dec. 5, 1892
Congregationalist. Dec. 15, 1892
Public Opinion. Jan. 14, 1893
Saturday Morning Citizen/Beverly (MA) Citizen. Jan. 20, 1893

A Daughter of the West: The Story of an American Princess

Annual American Catalogue. 1899
Plain Dealer (Cleveland, Ohio). Apr. 29, 1899
Literary World. Nov. 25, 1899
Dial. Dec. 1, 1899
Anaconda (MT) Standard. Dec. 3, 1899

A Yankee Girl in Old California: A Story for Girls

Annual American Catalogue. 1901–1905
Literary World. Oct. 1, 1901
Publishers Weekly. Oct. 26, 1901 and Nov. 30, 1901 ("Christmas Bookshelf")
Salt Lake Telegram. June 4, 1904 and May 15, 1911
Boise Idaho Statesman. Nov. 16, 1913

Polly, the Gringo: A Story for Girls

Publishers Weekly. Oct. 28, 1905 and Nov. 25, 1905 ("Christmas Bookshelf")
Baltimore (MD) American. Nov. 18, 1905
Springfield (MA) Daily Republican. Nov. 30, 1905
Bookseller, Newsdealer, and Stationer. Dec. 1, 1905

NOTES

Introduction

1. With this plotline, Ferber engages the fraught history of black Indians in Oklahoma, which I discuss more fully in my article "Peyote in the Kitchen: Gendered Identities and Imperial Domesticity in Edna Ferber's *Cimarron*."

2. Coining the term *new woman* in 1894, Sarah Grand asserts that the defining feature of the new woman is that she would take the nurturing, virtuous morality that made her a true woman out into the world and mother men. As the twentieth century began, the ideal of the new woman grew and changed, as several historians and literary critics have discussed, to describe a woman who was liberated from the expectations of motherhood and domesticity; artistic or a reformer or a suffragist; sexually free or asexual; and white and middle class. The turn into the twenty-first century brought scholarship on the new woman ideal that, as Charlotte J. Rich's does, highlights the racist and classist aspects of this model for American femininity. As this book shows, the white women reformers were often new women or aspired to the freedoms of new womanhood but often at the expense of the nonwhite and/or poor women who were the targets of their reform efforts.

3. Although Eve Raleigh (the pseudonym of Margaret Eimer) is listed as coauthor of this book, most literary historians agree that González was the primary creative force and refer to her as the sole author. I will follow that pattern in this book.

4. Many scholars have intervened with critical historical and biographical readings, and they often read the autobiographical writings of these Mexican American women writers as resistance literature. These scholars include, among others, Leticia M. Garza-Falcón, Becky Jo Gesteland McShane, Amelia María de la Luz Montes, Charles Montgomery, and Elizabeth Salas.

5. Ramón A. Gutiérrez provides a detailed history of racial intermarriage in New Mexico; John M. Nieto-Phillips writes about blood discourse in constructing New Mexican Spanish American identity; and these scholars, among others, have critiqued intermarriage and claims to whiteness in Ruiz de Burton's and González's novels: Jesse Alemán, John Morán González, Margaret D. Jacobs, José E. Limón, David Luis-Brown, Joséf Raab, Pablo Ramirez, Andrea Tinnemeyer, and Elisa Warford. Other scholars have produced influential readings of these writers that do not fit easily in the critical

categories I discuss in chapter 2, including Sarah E. Chinn, Melanie V. Dawson, Timothy Deines, James Diego Frazier, Susan Gillman, Melody Graulich, Kirsten Silva Gruesz, Bernadine M. Hernández, Lene M. Johannessen, María Irene Moyna, Gretchen Murphy, Raymond A. Paredes, John-Michael Rivera, Forrest Robinson, J. Javier Rodríguez, Ralph E. Rodriguez, Jennifer S. Tuttle, and Priscilla Solis Ybarra.

6. Throughout the United States, even after the Civil War, white women took as servants the black, Native, and/or Mexican women living near them, delegating their domestic tasks to women of color. This book focuses on how literary domesticity also delegates domestic labor to women of color, particularly (for this study) to Native and Mexican women in the West. Other scholars have written about Southern domesticity and black women, such as Louise Michele Newman, Claudia Tate, Elizabeth Ammons, Charlotte J. Rich, and Toni Morrison. Black women domestics are stereotyped and commodified in American literature and culture just as much as the Indian and Mexican women I discuss in this book; the perennial appeal of the mammy figure, as caricatured by Aunt Jemima's pancake syrup or as revived by Kathryn Stockett's novel-turned-film, *The Help* (2009, 2011; both hugely popular), are but two cases in point. In this study, I show how Native and Mexican women join black women in their critique of first-wave feminism that was primarily concerned with "white women's rights" (as Newman so brilliantly puts it), and not *all* women's rights.

7. Throughout the book I evoke historically derogatory terms such as *Indian problem, Indian question, blanket Indian,* and even the insulting term *squaw.* Sometimes I am quoting white people who used the term in their speeches or writings and sometimes I use these terms in my prose as a reference to the colonial history of framing Indians and Indian cultures as a problem that needs to be fixed or a way of life that needs to be altered. Part of the work of this book is to show how Indian women writers reframed the Indian problem for themselves. They engaged sentimental and domestic discourses to argue that the Indian problem is actually a white problem: a racist misrecognition of Native lifeways, survivance, and sovereignty.

Chapter One

1. Portions of this chapter appear in my similarly titled article in *Western American Literature,* "Peyote in the Kitchen: Gendered Identities and Imperial Domesticity in Edna Ferber's *Cimarron.*" Where this chapter focuses mainly on constructions and performances of femininity, in that article, I also discuss racialized performances of masculinity in *Cimarron* and in John Joseph Mathew's *Sundown.*

2. See introduction, note 1.

3. Susan J. Rosowski discusses masculinity and the western hero's use of or resistance to language, using Owen Wister's *The Virginian* and N. Scott

Momaday's *The Man Made of Words* (among other texts) as case studies. Language is central to *Cimarron*; Yancey is supposed to be a "man made of words" as a newspaper man, and this scene of linguistic exchange between him and Big Elk exemplifies Rosowski's assertions that "the dichotomy informing the history of Indian-white relations is realized by this difference in language" and that the "Western is about language far more than it is about land" ("Western Hero" 174, 175).

4. Because so many critics have written about Cather for so many years, this list is representative, not comprehensive. Though I list these methods separately, they overlap in most cases, so that one critic might write about domesticity and empire in the same essay.

5. Naming the baby "Jack Demps" could refer to famous 1920s boxer Jack Dempsey's mixed (Cherokee and Irish) heritage. Though Stone never uses this name again, it seems probable given the Third Grade, Mexican students' self-consciousness about their own mixed heritages.

6. Shawn Michelle Smith argues that *Ladies' Home Journal*'s publications of family photographs—particularly pictures of white babies—bears a "startling correlation" to "the reproduction of white supremacy" (9). Further, when interpreting photographs included in the American Negro display at the Paris Exposition in 1900, Smith asserts that photographs figured centrally "in envisioning racially codified identities at the turn of the century" (10).

Chapter Two

1. Here I add to my comments about identity labels in the introductory chapter. We cannot refer to Ruiz de Burton, Jaramillo, González, Cabeza de Baca, and Otero-Warren as Chicana because they predate the Chicano movement and because their writings do not align with Chicano politics. The New Mexican writers—Jaramillo, Cabeza de Baca, and Otero-Warren—called themselves Spanish American. González was a Tejana and Ruiz de Burton a Californiana.

Chapter Three

1. Readers might wonder why I discuss Raymond's novels in the context of the history of children's literature and not Stone's novel about Mexican children, *The Laughingest Lady*. While Mexican children are some of the main characters in Stone's novel, the teacher—Katherine Nevin—is the protagonist, not the students. The "lessons" Katherine teaches readers are how to Americanize the nonwhite Others living in the United States. Further, *The Laughingest Lady* was published serially in *Woman's Home Companion*, a magazine whose primary audience was adult women. Raymond's novels were marketed to girls, as the covers of the novels proclaim: "A Story for Girls from 9–16."

Raymond's lessons were directed at girl readers, teaching them how to befriend and uplift American Indian and Mexican American girls.

2. Laura Wexler reads similar photographs from the Hampton Institute in Virginia to argue that "'before and after' institutional images show very clearly the exact dimension of change that the students are to demonstrate" (*Tender Violence* 109).

3. Oskison was a Stanford- and Harvard-educated Cherokee who had a successful career as a magazine writer and editor and was a member of the Society of American Indians; he worked for a time as an associate editor and a special writer for *Collier's Weekly*. The *Red Man* misspells his name as "Oskinson"; he is widely known as John Milton Oskison.

4. Elena Byanuaba, a New Mexican Pueblo student at Haskell, writes, "I have read these books: 'Self Help,' 'To Have and to Hold,' 'Ramona,' 'Ben Hur,' 'When Knighthood Was in Flower,' 'Uncle Tom's Cabin' and a few others" (Kilcup, *Native American* 419).

5. Today the insistence that books transmit cultural mores likely comes more from buyers than from writers of children's books. That is to say, parents want to see—or don't want to see—certain cultural phenomena in their children's books, and writers, editors, and publishers likely feel pressured to cater to these desires in order to sell books.

6. Raymond might have paid money for this privilege, but she was also included in the 1910–1911 edition of *Who's Who in America: A Biographical Dictionary of Notable Living Men and Women of the United States* and the 1914–1915 edition of *Woman's Who's Who in America: A Biographical Dictionary of Contemporary Women of the United States and Canada.* Born in Watertown, New York, and educated at private schools, including Mt. Holyoke College in South Hadley, Massachusetts, Raymond wrote most of her novels while living in Baltimore, Maryland.

7. I am very grateful to Nina Baym for calling my attention to Raymond before her own book went to print. Honey does not mention the Raymond novels I discuss here. She concerns herself with the *Dorothy* series that children's serial books publishing giant Edward Stratemeyer commissioned her to write and focuses only on the letters written between Stratemeyer and Raymond.

8. See the epigraph to this chapter, taken from Leupp's field report about female missionaries working among Native women.

9. See also Nora Murphy's article on American Indians in children's literature.

Chapter Four

1. In the large and growing body of scholarship on federal Indian schools, some scholars—primarily historians such as David Wallace Adams, Frederick E. Hoxie, Jorge Noriega, and Elizabeth Cook-Lynn—focus on Indian education

and assimilation more generally. Other historians—such as Nicholas Beck, Brenda J. Child, Jean A. Keller, Matthew Sakiestewa Gilbert, K. Tsianina Lomawaima, Devon A. Mihesuah, Dorothy R. Parker, and Robert Trennert, who each write histories of the Phoenix school, and Myriam Vuckovic, who writes on the Haskell school—focus on specific regions or specific schools. Other historians and critics— including Margaret D. Jacobs, Michael C. Coleman, Amanda J. Cobb, Ruth Spack, Jessica Enoch, and Amelia V. Katanski—chronicle the boarding schools from more specific angles.

2. Several historians and literary scholars put this discussion of women and US culture on the academic map. See Ann Douglas, Mary Kelley, Jane Tompkins, Nina Baym, Linda Kerber, and Lora Romero.

3. Survivance: Gerald Vizenor's seminal concept for reading American Indian texts.

4. Federal educators directed what Indian students read to indoctrinate and attempt ideological control. Vuckovic notes that teachers at Haskell (and, logically, we can suppose the same at other schools), encouraged reading as a means to civilize students, and school officials stocked the library with books and magazines that promoted the values and culture of mainstream America (102). In terms of indoctrinating domesticity, "even though Indian girls would never belong to the white middle class, the values taught in these stories [such as Alcott's *Little Women*]—modesty, compassion, chastity and piety—were regarded as essential to the process of assimilation." (103). These lessons were apparently effective. Elena Byanuaba, a New Mexican Pueblo student at Haskell, writes, "I have read these books: 'Self Help,' 'To Have and to Hold,' 'Ramona,' 'Ben Hur,' 'When Knighthood Was in Flower,' 'Uncle Tom's Cabin' and a few others." And apparently these books helped Byanuaba learn her domestic lessons, for she also writes, "I like the sewing work very much" and "I admire these virtues: The best of character, a good Christian girl, honesty, cleanliness, promptness and politeness, and I do the best I can" (Kilcup, *Native American* 419, 419–20). Indian women writers were indeed readers and were well aware of the cultural work that literature—particularly domestic, sentimental fiction—was supposed to do. Indian novelists Mourning Dove and S. Alice Callahan also highlight the importance of reading novels to their English education. Joanna Brooks and other historians note Mourning Dove's voracious reading, and Jay Miller has written a short biography from the perspective of what fueled her desires to be an author. Mourning Dove constructs Cogewea, a Carlisle-educated character who not only reads American Western novels but also performs an extended critical reading of Therese Broderick's *The Brand* (as Peter G. Beidler discusses). Callahan's Indian heroine, Wynema, is also a reader. In keeping with Callahan's agenda to construct a "naturally" intelligent Indian student who needs but little guidance from white teachers, Wynema reads British classics by Shakespeare, Scott, Dickens, and Defoe instead of tawdry dime novels. Other critics, including H. David Brumble III and Cheryl Walker, have argued that we

cannot know what Indian women writers at large read; but records of student reading survive.

5. See chapter 3 for an extended discussion on theories regarding reading's influence on children.

6. This Bright Eyes is apparently not the same person as the well-known writer Susette La Flesche, who often went by the same name. Karen L. Kilcup includes this piece by Bright Eyes in her *Native American Women's Writing: An Anthology, c. 1800–1924* in the "Various Authors" section and includes La Flesche in a section of her own. Bright Eyes may also have been a pseudonym; the Haskell teacher who wrote an introduction to her essay writes that Bright Eyes is "the name which the author of this story gives to herself" (415). I have so far been unable to match this student author to another name or tribal affiliation.

7. I use *model/copy* in the Deleuzian sense, particularly as Thomas J. Catlaw discusses it:

> Consider the example of the term *human*. The term is the general category within which a particular set of entities is collected. The criterion for inclusion is the possession of some property or characteristic that is common to a set of entities—call it "humanity." Humanity is the universal possession of entities designated as human. The challenges of category-making immediately become evident. First, the term itself needs content or to be specified beyond the emptiness of humanity or being human. In representation, as will be argued below, the temptation is to see these descriptors in naturalistic, organic, and purely descriptive terms. However, categorization rests on a *decision*. This is evident in the racist, sexist, and highly discriminatory practices that have excluded by definition certain beings from the human by determining the human in specific terms (e.g., whiteness, male, heterosexual, able-bodied) or by defining certain humans in nonhuman terms (e.g., as property or "animals"). The word *model* is used here because these categories are not used only to organize, catalog, and describe. Rather, they are used for judgment among the various copies, or representations, out in the world; they define criteria for judgment and, further, permit or discourage certain lines of action. For example, when African slaves or white women are categorized as nonhuman or property a determination is made, in the case of slaves, that they are categorically distinctive; white women (in restricted instances) may be included as human but make "poorer copies of a model of humanity defined in terms of maleness. Certain actions, such as the legitimate infliction of violence, may also be permitted in a political community by virtue of the categorical decision to *exclude* entities from a given grouping." (62–63)

8. In addition to outing programs, where the schools farmed out Indian girls as domestic apprentices (read: servants) in white homes, the schools also

built model cottages on school grounds that served as domestic laboratories. See page 238 of Vuckovic for more information about the domestic science cottages at Haskell.

9. According to a specialist at the Cherokee Language Program, "Conihany" is a phonetic spelling for the Cherokee word ᏍᏃᎮᏂ (kanoheni), meaning hominy (Zachary Barnes, pers. comm.).

10. Many biographers and critics of these women note their federal educations. See, for example, Gae Whitney Canfield and Sally Zanjani (Winnemucca); Cathy Davidson and Ada Norris, David L. Johnson and Raymond Wilson (Zitkála-Šá); María Eugenia Cotéra and Janet L. Finn (Deloria); Dexter Fisher and Jay Miller (Mourning Dove); and Gary Sligh and A. Lavonne Brown Ruoff (Callahan).

11. For example, Mary Dearborn describes *Cogewea* as a "slightly schizophrenic book" that is a "text gone crazy" (20) and Paula Gunn Allen writes that the novel is "maimed—I should say martyred" by Mourning Dove's collaboration with Lucullus McWhorter (*Sacred Hoop* 83). Many critics have written many pages criticizing these Indian women writers for collaborating with whites, for not writing texts that are "Indian enough," or for being trapped by their own liminality. These include Gretchen M. Bataille and Kathleen Mullen Sands, Alanna Kathleen Brown, Kathleen M. Donovan, Linda K. Karell, Charles R. Larson, Margo Lukens, and Jeanne Smith.

12. Harry J. Brown, Ron Carpenter, Alicia A. Kent, Noreen Groover Lape, Andrew S. McClure, Malea Powell, Gerald Vizenor, and others offer nuanced and sophisticated discussions of hybridity theory and indigenous identity.

13. Some critics all but apologize for these authors' use of domesticity and sentimentalism, such as Dexter Fisher and Louis Owens (*Other Destinies*).

14. Though they do not engage Indian women's writing, a number of literary critics and historians have written about these ideals for American femininity as they operate in women's fiction, including Jane Tompkins, Gillian Brown, Lora Romero, Mary Kelley, and others.

15. Siobhan Senier, Katharine Rodier, and Pat Creech Scholten, for example, discuss Winnemucca's acquaintance, work, and travel with white women, particularly the Peabody sisters.

16. Paula Gunn Allen introduces and includes Armstrong's "The Return" in her 1994 collection, *Voice of the Turtle: American Indian Literature, 1900–1970.*

17. Mourning Dove finished writing *Cogewea* in 1917, but it took her ten years to see it to publication.

18. See note 9.

19. For example, even in literary readings of *Waterlily*, María Eugenia Cotéra, Janet L. Finn, Susan Gardner, and John Prater privilege Deloria's work as an anthropologist and ethnographer under the tutelage of Franz Boas.

20. Gardner, "Though It Broke," traces the editorial history of and "textual tampering" (676) with *Waterlily* as a process over which Deloria had little control.

21. See my discussion of class and geographic discrepancies in utopian experiments for cooperative mothering in "Maternal Economies: The Estranged Sisterhood of Edith Summers Kelley and Charlotte Perkins Gilman."

22. See, for example, Brumble, Ruoff, and Deborah Gilbert.

23. *Sarah Winnemucca's Practical Solution of the Indian Problem*, a pamphlet published by Elizabeth Palmer Peabody in 1886, describes Winnemucca's establishment of the school for Paiute children and appropriates it as an achievement of white women reformers.

24. Winnemucca and Callahan had already responded in print to the educational system, albeit from a different, slightly less confrontational stance. Callahan's novel had not yet been recovered when Bernardin published this article.

25. Charles Hannon discusses the magazine writings of Zitkála-Šá—particularly those in *Harper's*, the *Atlantic*, and *Everybody's Magazine* in 1900–1901—as they are situated in print along with writings rife with Anglo-Saxon nativism. He argues that the magazines function as a state apparatus in the Althusserian sense and that Native Americans were not "American" by contemporary definition because they were not Anglo-Saxon—particularly English—in heritage.

26. Johnston's *To Have and To Hold* was published as a novel by Houghton Mifflin later in 1900. Elena Byanuaba lists this book among the titles she read while a student at Haskell.

Epilogue

1. Only ten libraries in the world hold physical copies of *Twin Territories: The Indian Magazine*. I first found the image I describe here on microfilm, the resolution of which is not suitable to be reproduced in a book. Unfortunately, I could not locate a physical copy of the issue with this image to secure a high-resolution reproduction in time to go to press.

BIBLIOGRAPHY

Acocella, Joan. *Willa Cather and the Politics of Criticism.* Vintage, 2000.

Adams, David Wallace. *Education for Extinction: American Indians and the Boarding School Experience, 1875–1928.* UP of Kansas, 1995.

Alemán, Jesse. "Citizenship Rights and Colonial Whites: The Cultural Work of María Amparo Ruiz de Burton's Novels." *Complicating Constructions: Race, Ethnicity, and Hybridity in American Texts,* edited by David S. Goldstein and Audrey B. Thacker, U of Washington P, 2007, pp. 3–30.

———. "Historical Amnesia and the Vanishing Mestiza: The Problem of Race in *The Squatter and the Don* and *Ramona.*" *Aztlán: A Journal of Chicano Studies,* vol. 27, no. 1, 2002, pp. 59–93.

———. "Novelizing National Discourses: History, Romance, and Law in *The Squatter and the Don.*" Gutiérrez and Padilla, pp. 38–49.

———. "'Thank God, Lolita Is Away from Those Horrid Savages': The Politics of Whiteness in *Who Would Have Thought It?*" Montes and Goldman, pp. 95–111.

Allen, Paula Gunn. Introduction. *Spider Woman's Granddaughters: Traditional Tales and Contemporary Writing by Native American Women,* by Allen, Beacon, 1989, pp. 1–21.

———. *The Sacred Hoop: Recovering the Feminine in American Indian Traditions,* 1986, Beacon, 1992.

———. *Voice of the Turtle: American Indian Literature: 1900–1970.* Toronto: One World/Ballantine, 1995.

The American Girls. 1916. *Traveling Culture: Circuit Chautauqua in the Twentieth Century.* Records of the Redpath Chautauqua Collection, University of Iowa Libraries, Iowa City. digital.lib.uiowa.edu/cdm/ref/collection/tc/id/39939. Accessed 8 July 2016.

Ammons, Elizabeth. "Cather and the New Canon: 'The Old Beauty' and the Issue of Empire." *Cather Studies,* edited by Susan J. Rosowski, vol. 3, U of Nebraska P, 1996, pp. 256–66.

———. *Conflicting Stories: American Women Writers at the Turn into the Twentieth Century,* Oxford UP, 1992.

"Another Redskin." Minute Tapioca Cereal. Advertisement. *Woman's Home Companion,* vol. 51, no. 11, Nov. 1924, p. 69.

Anzaldúa, Gloria. *Borderlands/La Frontera.* 2nd ed., Aunt Lute, 1999.

Aranda, José F., Jr. "Breaking All the Rules: María Amparo Ruiz de Burton Writes a Civil War Novel." *Recovering the U.S. Hispanic Literary Heritage,* edited by María Herrera-Sobek and Virginia Sánchez Korrol, vol. 3, Arte Público, 2000, pp. 61–73.

———. "Contradictory Impulses: María Amparo Ruiz de Burton, Resistance Theory, and the Politics of Chicano/a Studies." *American Literature*, vol. 70, no. 3, 1998, pp. 551–79.

———. "Returning California to the People: Vigilantism in *The Squatter and the Don*." Montes and Goldman, pp. 11–26.

———. *When We Arrive: A New Literary History of Mexican America.* U of Arizona P, 2003.

Armstrong, Estelle. "The Debut of Aloyasius." *Red Man*, vol. 3, no. 1, Sept. 1910, pp. 10, 15–17.

———. "The Return." *Red Man*, vol. 5, no. 3, Nov. 1912, pp. 115–18.

Arredondo, Gabriela F., editor. *Chicana Feminisms: A Critical Reader.* Duke UP, 2003.

Ashworth, Cathy. *La Llorona.* 2015, acrylic on canvas, private collection.

Atwater, Helen W. *Home Economics: The Art and Science of Homemaking.* American Library Association, 1929. Reading With a Purpose No. 50.

Austin, Mary. "The Basket Maker." *The Land of Little Rain.* Houghton Mifflin, 1903, pp. 161–80.

———. *Earth Horizon.* Literary Guild, 1932.

———. *Santa Lucia: A Common Story.* Harper and Row, 1908.

Avery, Gillian. *Behold the Child: American Children and Their Books, 1621–1922.* Johns Hopkins UP, 1994.

———. "Home and Family: English and American Ideals in the Nineteenth Century." *Stories and Society: Children's Literature in Its Social Context*, edited by Dennis Butts, St. Martin's, 1992, pp. 37–49.

Baldwin, Marie L. "Modern Home-Making and the Indian Woman." *Report of the Executive Council on the Proceedings of the First Annual Conference of the Society of American Indians.* Washington, DC, 1912, pp. 58–67.

Barker, Joanne. *Sovereignty Matters: Locations of Contestation and Possibility in Indigenous Struggles for Self-Determination.* U of Nebraska P, 2005.

Barnes, Elizabeth. *States of Sympathy: Seduction and Democracy in the American Novel.* Columbia UP, 1997.

Bastille, Gretchen M., and Laurie Lisa, editors. *Native American Women: A Biographical Dictionary.* 2nd ed., Routledge, 2001.

Bataille, Gretchen M., and Kathleen Mullen Sands. *American Indian Women: Telling Their Lives.* U of Nebraska P, 1984.

Baym, Nina. *Women Writers of the American West, 1833–1927.* U of Illinois P, 2011.

Beauregard, Margaret. "The Indian Girl as a Home-maker." *Indian School Journal*, vol. 10, June 1910, pp. 51–52.

Beck, Nicholas. "The Vanishing Californians: The Education of Indians in the Nineteenth Century." *Southern California Quarterly*, vol. 69, no. 1, Mar. 1987, pp. 33–50.

Beecher, Catherine E. *Treatise on Domestic Economy for Use of Young Ladies at Home and School.* 1841. Boston, 1843.

Beecher, Catherine E., and Harriet Beecher Stowe. *The American Woman's Home, or Principles of Domestic Science; Being a Guide to the Formation and Maintenance of Economical, Healthful, Beautiful and Christian Homes.* New York, 1869.

Beidler, Peter G. "Literary Criticism in *Cogewea*: Mourning Dove's Protagonist Reads *The Brand.*" *American Indian Culture and Research Journal*, vol. 19, no. 2, 1995, pp. 45–65.

Bellanger, Alice. "Home-making." *Indian Leader*, vol. 18, no. 41, June 11, 1915, pp. 9–10.

Bennett, Kay. *Kaibah: Recollection of a Navajo Girlhood.* Los Angeles: Westernlore, 1964.

Bennett, Paula Bernat. *Poets in the Public Sphere: The Emancipatory Project of American Women's Poetry, 1800–1900.* Princeton UP, 2003.

Berch, Victor. "More on Elinore Cowan Stone." 22 Jan. 2007, *Mystery File.* mysteryfile.com/blog/?m=200701&paged=2. Accessed 2 Mar. 2012.

Berlant, Lauren. *The Female Complaint: The Unfinished Business of Sentimentality in American Culture.* Duke UP, 2008.

Bernardin, Susan K. "The Lessons of a Sentimental Education: Zitkala-Ša's Autobiographical Narratives." *Western American Literature*, vol. 32, no. 3, Fall 1997, pp. 212–38.

———. "Mixed Messages: Authority and Authorship in Mourning Dove's *Cogewea, The Half-Blood: A Depiction of the Great Montana Cattle Range.*" *American Literature*, vol. 67, no. 3, Sept. 1995, pp. 487–509.

———. "On the Meeting Grounds of Sentiment: S. Alice Callahan's *Wynema: A Child of the Forest.*" *American Transcendental Quarterly*, vol. 14, no. 3, Sept. 2001, pp. 209–24.

Bernardin, Susan K., et al. *Trading Gazes: Euro-American Women Photographers and Native North Americans, 1880–1940.* Rutgers UP, 2003.

Bernstein, Alison. "A Mixed Record: The Political Enfranchisement of American Indian Women during the Indian New Deal." *Journal of the West*, vol. 23, no. 3, 1984, pp. 13–20.

"Best Books for Boys and Girls." Advertisement. *A Yankee Girl in Old California: A Story for Girls*, by Evelyn Hunt Raymond. Penn, 1901, p. 181.

Better Babies Score Card. Pamphlet. Author's collection. *Woman's Home Companion.* Crowell, 1913.

"Better Babies: The Bureau Celebrates Its Tenth Birthday." *Woman's Home Companion*, vol. 51, no. 10, Oct. 1924, p. 128.

Bhaba, Homi. *The Location of Culture.* Routledge, 1994.

"Blackfeet Indians Visiting the Carlisle Indian School." *Red Man*, vol. 5, no. 9, May 1913, p. 429.

Bloom, Edward A., and Lillian D. Bloom. "On the Composition of a Novel."

Willa Cather's Gift of Sympathy. Southern Illinois UP, 1962. Rpt. in *Willa Cather and Her Critics,* edited by James Schroeter, Cornell UP, 1967, pp. 323–55.

Blumenschein, E. S. Illustrations. "The Warrior's Daughter," by Zitkála-Šá. *Everybody's Magazine,* vol. 6, no. 4, Apr. 1902, pp. 346–65.

"Books You Want to Read and Own." *Chicago Daily Tribune,* 9 July 1927, p. 6.

Bost, Suzanne. "West Meets East: Nineteenth-Century Southern Dialogues on Mixture, Race, Gender, and Nation." *Mississippi Quarterly,* vol. 56, no. 4, 2003, pp. 647–56.

Bradley, Jennifer L. "To Entertain, To Educate, To Elevate: Cather and the Commodification of Manners at the *Home Monthly.*" Stout, *Willa Cather,* pp. 37–65.

Bright Eyes. "Autobiography of an Indian Girl." *Indian Leader,* June 1897. Rpt. in Kilcup, *Native American,* pp. 415–16.

Broderick, Therese. *The Brand: A Tale of the Flathead Reservation.* Alice Harriman, 1909.

Brooks, Joanna. "Sacajawea, Meet *Cogewea*: A Red Progressive Revision of Frontier Romance." *Lewis and Clark: Legacies, Memories, and New Perspectives,* edited by Kris Fresonke and Mark Spence, U of California P, 2004, pp. 184–97.

Brown, Alanna Kathleen. "The Choice to Write: Mourning Dove's Search for Survival." *Old West—New West: Centennial Essays,* edited by Barbara Howard Meldrum, U of Idaho P, 1993, pp. 261–71.

———. "Collaboration and the Complex World of Literary Rights." *American Indian Quarterly,* vol. 21, no. 4, 1997, p. 595,

———. "Looking through the Glass Darkly: The Editorialized Mourning Dove." *New Voices in Native American Literary Criticism,* edited by Arnold Krupat, Smithsonian Institution Press, 1993, pp. 274–90.

———. "Mourning Dove." *Handbook of Native American Literature,* edited by Andrew Wiget, Garland, 1996, pp. 259–64.

———. "Mourning Dove" (Humishuma, 1888–1936). *Legacy,* vol. 6, no. 1, 1989, pp. 51–56.

———. "Mourning Dove's Voice in *Cogewea.*" *Wicazo Sa Review,* vol. 3, no. 2, Autumn 1988, pp. 2–15.

Brown, Gillian. *Domestic Individualism: Imagining Self in Nineteenth-Century America.* U of California P, 1990.

Brown, Harry J. "From Biological to Cultural Hybridity in *Cogewea, Sundown,* and Twentieth-Century Magazine Fiction." *Injun Joe's Ghost: The Indian Mixed-Blood in American Writing,* edited by Brown, U of Missouri P, 2004, pp. 150–218.

Brumberg, Joan Jacobs. "Defining the Profession and the Good Life: Home Economics on Film." *Rethinking Home Economics: Women and the History of a Profession,* edited by Sarah Stage and Virginia B. Vincenti, Cornell UP, 1997, pp. 189–202.

Brumble, H. David, III. "The Preliterate Traditions at Work: White Bull, Two Leggings, and Sarah Winnemucca." *American Indian Autobiography*, U of California P, 1988, pp. 21–71.

Bucker, Park. "'That Kitchen with the Shining Windows': Willa Cather's 'Neighbour Rosicky' and the *Woman's Home Companion*." Stout, *Willa Cather*, pp. 66–112.

Burgess, Marianna (Embe). *Stiya, A Carlisle Indian Girl at Home: Founded on the Author's Actual Observations*. 1891. General Books, 2010.

Byanuaba, Elena. "An Autobiography." *Indian Leader*, 31 Jan. 1902. Rpt. in Kilcup, *Native American*, pp. 419–20.

Bynum, Ruth. "Bibliography of Occupational Fiction for Junior High School Readers." *English Journal*, vol. 27, no. 8, Oct. 1938, pp. 678–81.

Cabeza de Baca Gilbert, Fabiola. "Foods for Easter in the Old Tradition." *New Mexico Magazine*, vol. 35, Apr. 1957, pp. 23, 47.

———. *The Good Life: New Mexico Traditions and Food*. 1949. Museum of New Mexico Press, 1982.

———. *Historic Cookery*. 1931. La Galeria de los Artesanos, 1970.

———. "New Mexican Diets." *Journal of Home Economics*, vol. 34, Nov. 1942, pp. 668–69.

———. *We Fed Them Cactus*. 1954. U of New Mexico P, 1979.

Cahill, Cathleen D. *Federal Fathers and Mothers: A Social History of the United States Indian Service, 1869–1933*. U of North Carolina P, 2011.

Callahan, S. Alice. *Wynema: A Child of the Forest*. Philadelphia, 1891.

Camino Bueno Alastuey, María. "À qui appartient l'Histoire? évision par la littérature/Does History Only Belong to You? Revision through Literature." *Revue LISA/LISA e-journal*, vol. 1, no. 4, 2004, pp. 195–210, lisa.revues.org/2944. Accessed 5 Apr. 2017.

Campbell, Donna. "Domestic or Sentimental Fiction, 1820–1865." *English Dept.*, Washington State University, 9 Feb. 2017, public.wsu.edu/~campbelld/amlit/domestic.htm. Accessed 27 Mar. 2017.

———. "'Written With a Hard and Ruthless Purpose': Rose Wilder Lane, Edna Ferber, and Middlebrow Regional Fiction." *Middlebrow Moderns: Popular American Women Writers of the 1920s*, edited by Lisa Botshon and Meredith Goldsmith, Northeastern UP, 2003, pp. 25–44.

Cane, Aleta Feinsod, and Susan Alves. "American Women Writers and the Periodical: Creating a Constituency, Opening a Dialogue." *"The Only Efficient Instrument": American Women Writers and the Periodical, 1837–1916*, edited by Cane and Alves, U of Iowa P, 2001, pp. 1–19.

Canfield, Gae Whitney. *Sarah Winnemucca of the Northern Paiutes*. U of Oklahoma P, 1983.

Cannata, Susan M. "Generic Power Plays in Mourning Dove's *Co-go-we-a*." *American Indian Quarterly*, vol. 21, no. 4, 1997, p. 703.

Canning, Charlotte. "What Was Chautauqua?" *Traveling Culture: Circuit Chautauqua in the Twentieth Century*. Dec. 2000. Records of the Redpath

Chautauqua Collection, University of Iowa Libraries, Iowa City, lib.uiowa.edu/spec-coll/tc/. Accessed 13 Nov. 2012.

"Carlisle Indian Girls Under the Outing System—In Pennsylvania Homes." *Indian Craftsman*, vol. 1, no. 9, May 1910, p. 14.

Carpenter, Cari M. "Detecting Indianness: Gertrude Bonnin's Investigation of Native American Identity." *Wicazo Sa Review*, vol. 20, no. 1, Spring 2005, pp. 139–59.

———. *Seeing Red: Anger, Sentimentality, and American Indians*. Ohio State UP, 2008.

———."Tiresias Speaks: Sarah Winnemucca's Hybrid Selves and Genres." *Legacy*, vol. 19, no. 1, 2002, pp. 71–80.

Carpenter, Ron. "Zitkala-Ša and Bicultural Subjectivity." *Studies in American Indian Literature*, vol. 16, no. 3, Fall 2004, pp. 1–28.

Carr, Jean Ferguson. "Nineteenth-Century Girls and Literacy." *Girls and Literacy in America: Historical Perspectives to the Present*, edited by Jane Greer, ABC-CLIO, 2003, pp. 51–77.

Carson, Gerald Hewes. "Good—Better—Best Short Stories." *Bookman: A Review of Books and Life*, vol. 61, no. 3, May 1925, pp. 348–51.

Cassidy, Ina Sizer. Introduction. *The Good Life: New Mexico Traditions and Food*, by Cabeza de Baca Gilbert, 1949, Museum of New Mexico Press, 1982, pp. 1–4.

Cather, Willa. *Death Comes for the Archbishop*. 1927. Vintage, 1990.

———. *The World and the Parish: Willa Cather's Articles and Reviews, 1893–1902*, edited by William M. Curtin, vol. 1, U of Nebraska P, 1970.

Catlaw, Thomas J. *Fabricating the People: Politics and Administration in the Biopolitical State*. U of Alabama P, 2007.

Child, Brenda J. *Boarding School Seasons: American Indian Families, 1900–1940*. U of Nebraska P, 1998.

Chinn, Sarah E. "'No Heart for Human Pity': The U.S.-Mexican War, Depersonalization, and Power in E.D.E.N. Southworth and María Amparo Ruiz de Burton." *Prospects*, vol. 30, 2005, pp. 339–62.

Chvany, Peter A. "'Those Indians Are Great Thieves, I Suppose?': Historicizing the White Woman in *The Squatter and the Don*." *White Women in Racialized Spaces: Imaginative Transformation and Ethical Action in Literature*, edited by Samina Najmi and Rajini Srikanth, State U of New York P, 2002, pp. 105–18.

Clark, Suzanne. *Sentimental Modernism: Women Writers and the Revolution of the Word*. Indiana UP, 1991.

Cobb, Amanda J. *Listening to Our Grandmothers' Stories: The Bloomfield Academy for Chickasaw Females, 1852–1949*. Bison, 2007.

———. "Understanding Tribal Sovereignty: Definitions, Conceptualizations, and Interpretations." *American Studies*, vol. 46, nos. 3–4, Fall/Winter 2005, pp. 115–32.

Coleman, Michael C. *American Indian Children at School, 1850–1930.* UP of Mississippi, 1993.

Cooke, Maude, and Agnes Hatch. "Our Cottage." *Carlisle* 1917. Parker, *Changing Is Not Vanishing*, p. 237.

Cook-Lynn, Elizabeth. *Why I Can't Read Wallace Stegner and Other Essays: A Tribal Voice.* U of Wisconsin P, 1996.

Cotéra, María Eugenia. "Engendering a 'Dialectics of Our America': Jovita González's Pluralist Dialogue as Feminist Testimonio." *Las obreras: Chicana Politics of Work and Family*, edited by Vicki L. Ruiz, Chicano Studies Research Center, 2000, pp. 237–56.

———. "Jovita González Mireles: A Sense of History and Homeland." *Latina Legacies: Identity, Biography, and Community*, edited by Vicki L. Ruiz and Virginia Sánchez Korrol, Oxford UP, 2005, pp. 158–74.

———. *Native Speakers: Ella Deloria, Zora Neale Hurston, Jovita González, and the Poetics of Culture.* U of Texas P, 2008.

———. "Recovering "Our" History: *Caballero* and the Gendered Politics of Form." *Aztlán: A Journal of Chicano Studies*, vol. 32, no. 2, 2007, pp. 157–71.

———. "Refiguring 'The American Congo': Jovita González, John Gregory Bourke, and the Battle over Ethno-Historical Representations of the Texas Mexican Border." *Western American Literature*, vol. 35, no. 1, Spring 2000, pp. 75–94.

———. "A Woman of the Borderlands: 'Social Life in Cameron, Starr and Zapata Counties' and the Origins of Borderlands Discourse." Introduction. *Life along the Border: A Landmark Tejana Thesis*, by González and Raleigh, Texas A&M UP, 2006, pp. 3–34.

Cotera, Martha P. *The Chicana Feminist.* Info Systems Development, 1977.

Cox, Alicia. "Remembering Polingaysi: A Queer Recovery of *No Turning Back* as a Decolonial Text." *Studies in American Indian Literatures*, vol. 26, no. 1, Spring 2014, pp. 54–80.

Crotzer, Grace. "The Value of Thorough Domestic Training." *Indian Leader*, vol. 15, nos. 7–8, 9 June 1911, p. 2.

Davidson, Cathy. "Preface: No More Separate Spheres!" *American Literature*, vol. 70, no. 3, Sept. 1998, pp. 443–63.

Davidson, Cathy, and Ada Norris. Introduction. *American Indian Stories*, by Zitkála-Šá, Penguin, 2003, pp. xi–xliii.

Davidson, Margaret Garcia. "Borders, Frontiers, and Mountains: Mapping the History of 'U.S. Hispanic Literature.'" *Reading the West: New Essays on the Literature of the American West*, edited by Michael Kowalewski, Cambridge UP, 1996, pp. 177–96.

Dawson, Melanie V. "Ruiz de Burton's Emotional Landscape: Property and Feeling in *The Squatter and the Don.*" *Nineteenth-Century Literature*, vol. 64, no. 1, June 2008, pp. 41–72.

Dean, Janet. "Reading Lessons: Sentimental Literacy and Assimilation in *Stiya: A Carlisle Indian Girl* and *Wynema: A Child of the Forest*." *ESQ: A Journal of the American Renaissance*, vol. 57, no. 3, 2011, pp. 200–40.

Dearborn, Mary V. *Pocahontas's Daughters: Gender and Ethnicity in American Culture.* Oxford UP, 1986.

DeHuff, Elizabeth. "Intriguing Mexican Dishes." *Holland's, the Magazine of the South*, vol. 54, Mar. 1935, pp. 34–47.

Deines, Timothy. "Interrogating the Moral Contract in Ruiz de Burton's *The Squatter and the Don*." *REAL: The Yearbook of Research in English and American Literature*, vol. 22, 2006, pp. 269–89.

Deleuze, Gilles. "Plato and the Simulacrum." Translated by Rosalind Krauss. *October*, vol. 27, Winter 1983, pp. 45–56.

Deloria, Ella Cara. *Dakota Texts.* U of Nebraska P, 1932.

———. *Waterlily.* U of Nebraska P, 1988.

Deloria, Philip J. *Playing Indian.* Yale UP, 1998.

Deloria, Vine, Jr. "Intellectual Self-Determination and Sovereignty: Looking at the Windmills in Our Minds." *Wicazo Sa Review*, vol. 14, no. 1, Spring 1998, pp. 25–31.

Deutsch, Sarah. *No Separate Refuge: Culture, Class, and Gender on an Anglo-Hispanic Frontier in the American Southwest, 1880–1940.* Oxford UP, 1987.

Dietz, William H. "Lone Star." *Hopi Girl Making Piki (Bread).* Illustration. *Red Man*, vol. 4, no. 4, Dec. 1911, cover.

———. *The Indian Stenographer.* Illustration. *Red Man*, vol. 4, no. 4, Nov. 1913, cover.

Dippie, Brian. *The Vanishing American: White Attitudes and U.S. Indian Policy.* Wesleyan UP, 1982.

Dodd, Lee Wilson. "A Hymn to Spiritual Beauty." *Saturday Review of Literature*, vol. 4, 10 Sept. 1927, p. 101. Rpt. in O'Connor, p. 316.

Dole, Nathan Haskell. "Notes from Boston." *Book News*, vol. 1, no. 121, Sept. 1892, pp. 1–3.

Dollar, J. Gerard. "Misogyny in the American Eden: Abbey, Cather, and Maclean." *Reading the Earth: New Directions in the Study of Literature and the Environment*, edited by Michael P. Branch, Rochelle Johnson, Daniel Patterson, and Scott Slovic, U of Idaho P, 1998, pp. 97–105.

Donovan, Kathleen M. "Owning Mourning Dove: The Dynamics of Authenticity." *Feminist Readings of Native American Literature: Coming to Voice*, by Donovan, U of Arizona P, 1998, pp. 99–120.

Dooley, Patrick K. "Biocentric, Homocentric, and Theocentric Environmentalism in *O Pioneers!*, *My Antonia*, and *Death Comes for the Archbishop*." *Willa Cather's Ecological Imagination*, edited by Susan K. Rosowski, vol. 5., U of Nebraska P, 2003, pp. 64–76.

Dorey, Annette K. Vance. *Better Babies Contests: The Scientific Quest for Perfect Childhood Health in the Early Twentieth Century.* McFarland, 1999.

Douglas, Ann. *The Feminization of American Culture.* Knopf, 1977.

Douglas, Mary. *Purity and Danger: An Analysis of Concepts of Pollution and Taboo.* Routledge, 1966.

Downs, M. Catherine. *Becoming Modern: Willa Cather's Journalism.* Associated University Presses, 1999.

Doxtator, Margaret. "The Importance of Making the Home Attractive." *Indian Leader,* vol. 17, [?] June 1914, pp. 9–10.

Duggan, Lisa. *The Twilight of Equality: Neoliberalism, Cultural Politics, and the Attack on Democracy.* Beacon, 2003.

Dymond, Justine. "Modernism(s) Inside Out: History, Space, and Modern American Indian Subjectivity in *Cogewea, the Half-Blood.*" *Geomodernisms: Race, Modernism, and Modernity,* edited by Laura Doyle and Laura Winkiel, Indiana UP, 2005, pp. 297–312.

East, C. W. *Better Baby Conference: What It Is—Why It Is—How to Organize and Conduct It.* Illinois Department of Public Health, Division of Child Hygiene and Public Health Nursing. Illinois Printing, 1922.

Eddleman Reed, Ora V. "Full-Blood Creek Indian Girls"; "Misses Pauline McCoy and Mattie Block." *Twin Territories: The Indian Magazine,* Mar. 1903.

———. *A Graceful 'Diana' of the Cherokees.* Photograph. *Twin Territories: The Indian Magazine,* Mar. 1903.

———. "The Honor of Wynoma: A Thanksgiving Story by a Cherokee Girl." *Twin Territories: The Indian Magazine,* Nov. 1902. Rpt. in Kilcup, *Native American,* pp. 372–76.

———. Mrs. Florence Stephens-Lennon. Photograph. *Twin Territories: The Indian Magazine,* Jan. 1903.

———. "Types of Indian Girls." *Twin Territories: The Indian Magazine,* Feb. 1903, p. 51.

———. "Types of Indian Girls, Miss Leota Crabtree." *Twin Territories: The Indian Magazine,* Feb. 1903, p. 52.

———. "Types of Indian Women, Mrs. Czarina Colbert Conlan." *Twin Territories: The Indian Magazine,* Jan. 1903, p. 13.

———. *Untitled. Twin Territories: The Indian Magazine,* Feb. 1903, cover.

Edgett, Edwin Francis. Review of Cather. *Boston Evening Transcript,* 17 Sept. 1927, p. 6. Rpt. in O'Connor, p. 324.

Edith. "View from Our Seminary." *Cherokee Rose Buds,* 1854. Rpt. in Kilcup, *Native American,* p. 403.

Educating the Indians—A Female Pupil of the Government School at Carlisle Visits Her Home at Pine Ridge Agency. Illustration. *Frank Leslie's Illustrated Newspaper,* 15 Mar. 1884, cover. Library of Congress, Prints and Photographs Online, LC-USZ62-100543, loc.gov/pictures/item/90712911/. Accessed 17 July 2016.

Embe [Marianna Burgess]. *Stiya, A Carlisle Indian Girl at Home: Founded on the Author's Actual Observations.* 1891. General Books, 2010.

Emmerich, Lisa E. "'Save the Babies!': American Indian Women, Assimilation

Policy, and Scientific Motherhood, 1912–1918." *Writing the Range: Race, Class, and Culture in the Women's West*, edited by Elizabeth Jameson and Susan Armitage, U of Oklahoma P, 1997, pp. 393–409.

Endres, Kathleen L., and Therese L. Lueck, editors. *Women's Periodicals in the United States: Consumer Magazines.* Greenwood, 1995. Historical Guides to the World's Periodicals and Newspapers.

Engs, Ruth Clifford. "Better Babies Movement." *The Eugenics Movement: An Encyclopedia*, edited by Engs, Greenwood, 2005.

Enoch, Jessica. "Resisting the Script of Indian Education: Zitkala-Ša and the Carlisle Indian School." *College English*, vol. 64, no. 2, Nov. 2002, pp. 117–41.

"Eradicating Tribal Distinctions." *Red Man*, vol. 3, no. 4, Dec. 1910, pp. 156–57.

Fanon, Frantz. *The Wretched of the Earth.* 1963. Grove, 2005.

Ferber, Edna. *Cimarron.* Grosset and Dunlap, 1929.

———. *A Kind of Magic.* Doubleday, 1963.

———. *A Peculiar Treasure.* 1939. Doubleday, 1960.

Finn, Janet L. "Ella Cara Deloria and Mourning Dove: Writing for Cultures, Writing Against the Grain." *Women Writing Culture*, edited by Ruth Behar and Deborah A. Gordon, U of California P, 1995, pp. 131–47.

———. "Walls and Bridges: Cultural Mediation and the Legacy of Ella Cara Deloria." *Frontiers*, vol. 21, no. 3, 2000, pp. 158–82.

Fisher, Beth. "The Captive Mexicana and the Desiring Bourgeois Woman: Domesticity and Expansionism in Ruiz de Burton's *Who Would Have Thought It?*" *Legacy*, vol. 16, no. 1, 1999, pp. 59–69.

———. "Precarious Performances: Ruiz de Burton's Theatrical Vision of the Gilded Age Female Consumer." Montes and Goldman, pp. 187–205.

Fisher, Dexter. Introduction. *Cogewea, The Half-Blood: A Depiction of the Great Montana Cattle Range*, by Mourning Dove, U of Nebraska P, 1981, pp. v–xxix.

———. "The Transformation of Tradition: A Study of Zitkala-Ša and Mourning Dove, Two Transitional American Indian Writers." *Critical Essays on Native American Literature*, edited by Andrew Wiget, G. K. Hall, 1985, pp. 202–11.

———. "Zitkala Sa: The Evolution of a Writer." *American Indian Quarterly*, vol. 4, no. 3, Aug. 1979, pp. 229–338.

Ford, Lillian C. Review of *Death Comes for the Archbishop. Santa Fe New Mexican*, 23 Sept. 1927, p. 4. Rpt. in O'Connor, p. 327.

Forrest, Suzanne. *The Preservation of the Village: New Mexico's Hispanics and the New Deal.* U of New Mexico P, 1989. New Mexico Land Grant Series.

Foucault, Michel. *Discipline and Punish: The Birth of the Prison*, translated by Alan Sheridan, 1975. 2nd ed., Vintage, 1995.

Fowler, Catherine S. "Sarah Winnemucca, Northern Paiute, 1844–1891." *American Indian Intellectuals: 1976 Proceedings of the American Ethnological Society*, edited by Margot Liberty, West, 1978, pp. 32–42.

Frazier, James Diego. "*The Squatter and the Don*": The Title Page as Paratextual Borderland." *ANQ: A Journal of Short Articles, Notes, and Reviews*, vol. 22, no. 2, Spring 2009, pp. 30–36.

Frederick, Christine. *Efficient Housekeeping, or Household Engineering: Scientific Management in the Home*. Home Economics Association, 1925. Correspondence Course of the American School of Home Economics.

Friedman, Moses. "Able Indian Girls." *Red Man*, vol. 6, no. 3, Nov. 1913, p. 126.

———. "Encouraging Home Building Among Indians." *Red Man*, vol. 5, no. 4, Dec. 1912, pp. 171–72.

———. "The Improvements at the Carlisle Indian School: By the Superintendent." *Indian Craftsman*, vol. 1, no. 1, Feb. 1909, pp. 3–16.

Gardner, Susan. "'Though It Broke My Heart to Cut Some Bits I Fancied': Ella Deloria's Original Design for *Waterlily*." *American Indian Quarterly*, vol. 27, nos. 3–4, Summer/Fall 2003, pp. 667–96.

———. "'Weaving an Epic Story': Ella Cara Deloria's Pageant for the Indians of Robeson County, North Carolina, 1940–1941." *Mississippi Quarterly*, vol. 60, no. 1, Winter/Spring 2007, pp. 33–57.

Garvey, Ellen Gruber. *The Adman in the Parlor: Magazines and the Gendering of Consumer Culture, 1880s to 1910s*. Oxford UP, 1996.

Garza-Falcón, Leticia M. "The Historical Fiction of Jovita González: Complex and Competing Class Identities." *Gente Decente: A Borderlands Response to the Rhetoric of Dominance*, by Garzon-Falcón, U of Texas P, 1998, pp. 74–132.

Georgi-Findlay, Brigitte. *The Frontiers of Women's Writing: Women's Narratives and the Rhetoric of Western Expansion*. U of Arizona P, 1996.

Gere, Anne Ruggles. "Indian Heart/White Man's Head: Native-American Teachers in Indian Schools, 1880–1930." *History of Education Quarterly*, vol. 45, no. 1, Spring 2005, pp. 38–65.

Gilbert, Deborah. "Sarah Winnemucca Hopkins: Performer, Activist, and Educator Teaching History in the First Person." *Journal of the West*, vol. 43, no. 4, 2004, pp. 24–31.

Gilbert, Julie. *Ferber: Edna Ferber and Her Circle*. Applause, 1999.

Gillman, Susan. "The Squatter, the Don, and the Grandissimes in Our America." *Mixing Race, Mixing Culture: Inter-American Literary Dialogues*, edited by Monika Kaup and Debra Rosenthal, U of Texas P, 2002, pp. 140–59.

"'Girl of Today' Jury Famous for American Types." *New York Times*, 7 Dec. 1913, p. 5.

"Girl Students of Carlisle in Pennsylvania Households under the School's Outing System." *Red Man*, vol. 4, no. 1, Sept. 1911, p. 11.

Godey, Louis Antoine, and Sarah Josepha Hale. *Godey's Lady's Book and Magazine*, vol. 56, June 1858, pp. 563–64.

Godfrey, Eveline C. "A Century of Children's Books." 1906. *A Peculiar Gift: Writings on Books for Children*, edited by Lance Salway, Kestrel, 1976, pp. 92–105.

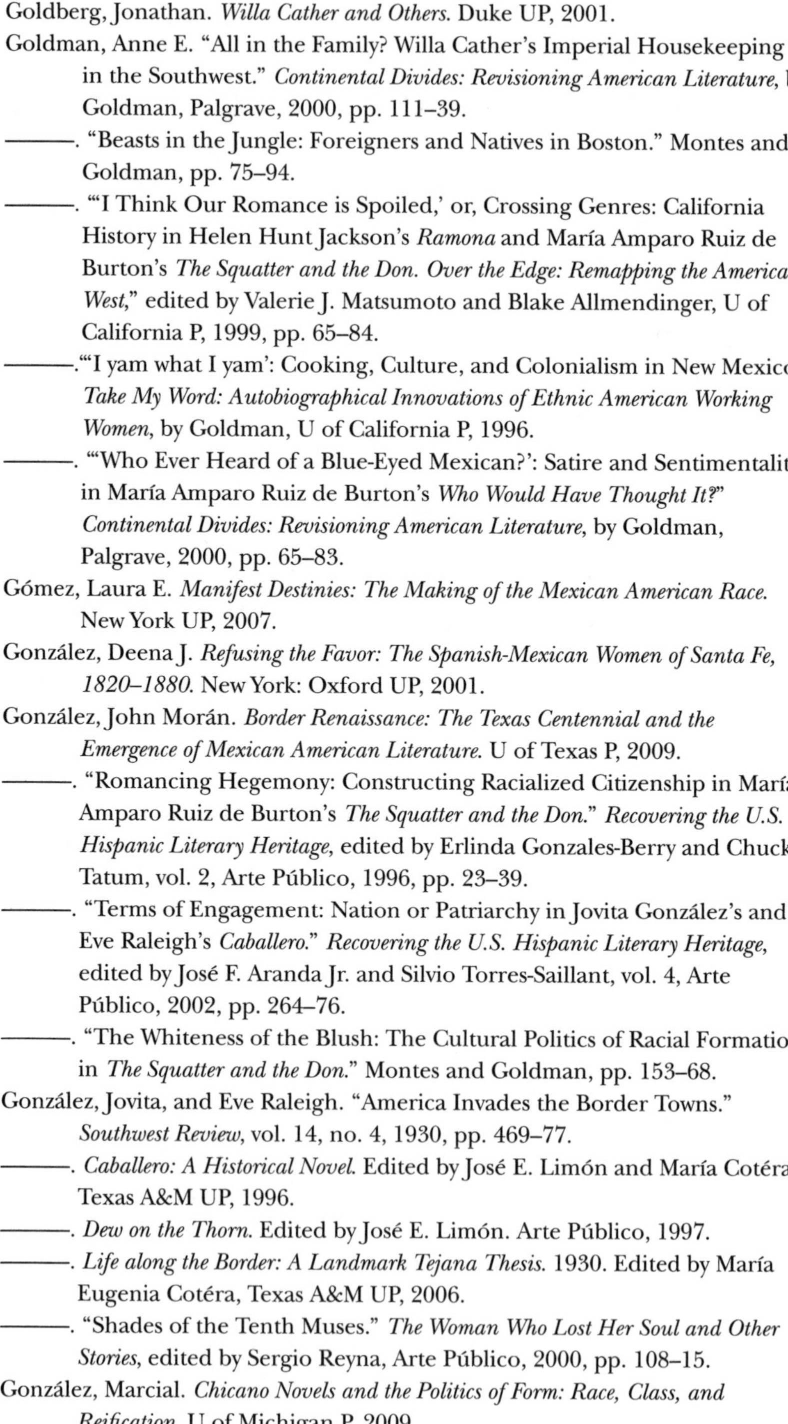

Goldberg, Jonathan. *Willa Cather and Others.* Duke UP, 2001.

Goldman, Anne E. "All in the Family? Willa Cather's Imperial Housekeeping in the Southwest." *Continental Divides: Revisioning American Literature,* by Goldman, Palgrave, 2000, pp. 111–39.

———. "Beasts in the Jungle: Foreigners and Natives in Boston." Montes and Goldman, pp. 75–94.

———. "'I Think Our Romance is Spoiled,' or, Crossing Genres: California History in Helen Hunt Jackson's *Ramona* and María Amparo Ruiz de Burton's *The Squatter and the Don. Over the Edge: Remapping the American West,*" edited by Valerie J. Matsumoto and Blake Allmendinger, U of California P, 1999, pp. 65–84.

———."'I yam what I yam': Cooking, Culture, and Colonialism in New Mexico." *Take My Word: Autobiographical Innovations of Ethnic American Working Women,* by Goldman, U of California P, 1996.

———. "'Who Ever Heard of a Blue-Eyed Mexican?': Satire and Sentimentality in María Amparo Ruiz de Burton's *Who Would Have Thought It?*" *Continental Divides: Revisioning American Literature,* by Goldman, Palgrave, 2000, pp. 65–83.

Gómez, Laura E. *Manifest Destinies: The Making of the Mexican American Race.* New York UP, 2007.

González, Deena J. *Refusing the Favor: The Spanish-Mexican Women of Santa Fe, 1820–1880.* New York: Oxford UP, 2001.

González, John Morán. *Border Renaissance: The Texas Centennial and the Emergence of Mexican American Literature.* U of Texas P, 2009.

———. "Romancing Hegemony: Constructing Racialized Citizenship in María Amparo Ruiz de Burton's *The Squatter and the Don.*" *Recovering the U.S. Hispanic Literary Heritage,* edited by Erlinda Gonzales-Berry and Chuck Tatum, vol. 2, Arte Público, 1996, pp. 23–39.

———. "Terms of Engagement: Nation or Patriarchy in Jovita González's and Eve Raleigh's *Caballero.*" *Recovering the U.S. Hispanic Literary Heritage,* edited by José F. Aranda Jr. and Silvio Torres-Saillant, vol. 4, Arte Público, 2002, pp. 264–76.

———. "The Whiteness of the Blush: The Cultural Politics of Racial Formation in *The Squatter and the Don.*" Montes and Goldman, pp. 153–68.

González, Jovita, and Eve Raleigh. "America Invades the Border Towns." *Southwest Review,* vol. 14, no. 4, 1930, pp. 469–77.

———. *Caballero: A Historical Novel.* Edited by José E. Limón and María Cotéra, Texas A&M UP, 1996.

———. *Dew on the Thorn.* Edited by José E. Limón. Arte Público, 1997.

———. *Life along the Border: A Landmark Tejana Thesis.* 1930. Edited by María Eugenia Cotéra, Texas A&M UP, 2006.

———. "Shades of the Tenth Muses." *The Woman Who Lost Her Soul and Other Stories,* edited by Sergio Reyna, Arte Público, 2000, pp. 108–15.

González, Marcial. *Chicano Novels and the Politics of Form: Race, Class, and Reification.* U of Michigan P, 2009.

Goodburn, Amy. "Girls' Literacy in the Progressive Era." *Girls and Literacy in America: Historical Perspectives to the Present,* edited by Jane Greer, ABC-CLIO, 2003, pp. 79–101.

Goodman, Audrey. *Translating Southwestern Landscapes: The Making of an Anglo Literary Region.* U of Arizona P, 2002.

Goyitney, Annie. "What Should Be the Aim of a Carlisle Indian Girl?" *Red Man and Helper,* vol. 16, no. 38, Mar. 22, 1901, p. 2.

Grand, Sarah. "The New Aspect of the Woman Question." 1894. *A New Woman Reader: Fiction, Articles, Drama of the 1890s,* edited by Carolyn Christensen Nelson, Broadview, 2002, pp. 141–46.

Graulich, Melody. "Western Biodiversity: Rereading Nineteenth-Century American Women's Writing." Kilcup, *Nineteenth-Century,* pp. 47–61.

"Great White Fleet." Advertisement. *Forum,* vol. 77, no. 1, Jan. 1927.

Green, Rayna. "The Pocahontas Perplex: The Image of Indian Women in American Culture." *Massachusetts Review,* vol. 16, no. 4, 1975, pp. 698–714.

Gruesz, Kirsten Silva. *Ambassadors of Culture: The Transamerican Origins of Latino Writing.* Princeton UP, 2002.

Gutiérrez, Ramón A. *When Jesus Came, the Corn Mothers Went Away: Marriage, Sexuality, and Power in New Mexico, 1500–1846.* Stanford UP, 1991.

Gutiérrez, Ramón A., and Genaro M. Padilla, editors. Introduction. *Recovering the U.S. Hispanic Literary Heritage,* by Gutiérrez and Padilla, vol. 1, Arte Público, 1993, pp. vii–xii.

Hafen, P. Jane. "A Cultural Duet: Zitkala-Ša and The Sun Dance Opera." *Great Plains Quarterly,* vol. 18, no. 2, Mar. 1998, pp. 102–11.

———. "Zitkala-Ša: Sentimentality and Sovereignty." *Wicazo Sa Review,* vol. 12, no. 2, Fall 1997, pp. 31–41.

Halberstam, Judith. *In a Queer Time and Place: Transgender Bodies, Subcultural Lives.* NYU P, 2005.

Halverson, Cathryn. *Playing House in the American West: Western Women's Life Narratives, 1839–1987.* U of Alabama P, 2013.

Handley, William R. "Willa Cather: 'The West Authentic,' the West Divided." *True West: Authenticity and the American West,* edited by William R. Handley and Nathaniel Lewis, U of Nebraska P, 2004, pp. 72–94.

Hannon, Charles. "Zitkala-Ša and the Commercial Magazine Apparatus." *"The Only Efficient Instrument": American Women Writers and the Periodical, 1837–1916,* edited by Aleta Feinsod Cane and Susan Alves, U of Iowa P, 2001, pp. 179–201.

Heflin, Ruth J. *"I Remain Alive": The Sioux Literary Renaissance.* Syracuse UP, 2000.

Henkin, David M. *City Reading: Written Words and Public Spaces in Antebellum New York.* Columbia UP, 1998.

Hernández, Bernadine M. "Rewriting Space in Ruiz de Burton's *Who Would Have Thought It?*" *CLCWeb: Comparative Literature and Culture,* vol. 11, no. 2, June 2009, pp. 1–9, connection.ebscohost.com/c/

literary-criticism/43930872/rewriting-space-ruiz-de-burtons-who-would-have-thought-it. Accessed 26 Apr. 2010.

Herring, Scott. "Catherian Friendship: Or, How Not To Do the History of Homosexuality." *Modern Fiction Studies*, vol. 54, no. 1, 2006, pp. 66–91.

Higham, John. *Strangers in the Land: Patterns of American Nativism, 1860–1925.* 1955. Rutgers UP, 2002.

Holt, Marilyn Irvin. *Linoleum, Better Babies, and the Modern Farm Woman, 1890–1930.* U of New Mexico P, 1995.

"Home and Family of Mr. Benjamin Caswell and Leila Cornelius. . . ." *Red Man*, vol. 3, no. 9, May 1911, p. 381.

"Homes of Carlisle Ex-Students. . . ." *Red Man*, vol. 3, no. 7, Mar. 1911, p. 284.

"Homes of Indians Educated at Carlisle. . . ." *Red Man*, vol. 5, no. 9, May 1913, p. 430.

Honey, Emily. *From Spiritual Guides to Eager Consumers: American Girls' Series Fiction, 1865–1930.* Dissertation, University of Massachusetts Amherst, 2010. ProQuest, 2010

Honey, Maureen. "'So Far Away From Home': Minority Women Writers and the New Woman." *Women's Studies International Forum*, vol. 14, no. 4, 1992, pp. 473–85.

Hopkins, Pauline. *Winona: A Tale of Negro Life in the South and Southwest.* 1902. *The Magazine Novels of Pauline Hopkins*, by Hopkins, Oxford UP, 1988.

"How Healthy Are the Babies in Your Town?" Advertisement. *Woman's Home Companion*, vol. 40, no. 7, July 1913, p. 50.

Hoxie, Frederick E. *A Final Promise: The Campaign to Assimilate the Indians: 1880–1920.* U of Nebraska P, 1984.

Hoxie, Sara. "The American Indian." *Indian Craftsman*, vol. 1, no. 4, Dec. 1909, pp. 29–30.

Huhndorf, Shari M. *Going Native: Indians in the American Cultural Imagination.* Cornell UP, 2001.

Hunt, Peter. *An Introduction to Children's Literature.* Oxford UP, 1994.

"Indian-detour." Santa Fe Railway. Advertisement. *Forum*, vol. 77, Jan.–June 1927.

"The Indian Girl." *Red Man*, vol. 3, no. 3, Nov. 1910, p. 136.

"An Indian Girl's History, Written by Herself." *Indian Leader*, Oct. 1899. Rpt. in Kilcup, *Native American*, pp. 417–18.

Indian Homes (Best of the New Type). Photograph. Leupp, p. 64.

"Industrial Talks—Benefits of the Outing System." *Indian Craftsman*, vol. 1, no. 4, May 1909, p. 23.

"Industrial Training—Lesson in Domestic Science, Carlisle School." *Red Man*, vol. 3, no. 3, Nov. 1911, p. 20.

Inness, Sherrie A., editor. *Nancy Drew and Company: Culture, Gender, and Girls' Series.* Bowling Green State UP, 1997.

Jackson, Helen Hunt. *A Century of Dishonor: A Sketch of the United States Government's Dealings with Some of the Indian Tribes.* New York, 1881.

———. *Ramona.* 1884. Modern Library, 2005.

Jacobs, Elizabeth. "New Mexican Narratives and the Politics of Home." *Journal of American Studies of Turkey*, vol. 12, 2000, pp. 39–49, researchgate.net/publication/49310737_New_Mexican_Narratives_and_the_Politics_of_Home. Accessed 5 Apr. 2017.

Jacobs, Margaret D. *Engendered Encounters: Feminism and Pueblo Cultures, 1879–1934*. U of Nebraska P, 1999.

———. "Maternal Colonialism: White Women and Indigenous Child Removal in the American West and Australia, 1880–1940." *Western Historical Quarterly*, vol. 36, no. 4, 2005, pp. 453–76.

———. "Mixed-Bloods, Mestizas, and Pintos: Race, Gender, and Claims to Whiteness in Helen Hunt Jackson's *Ramona* and María Amparo Ruiz de Burton's *Who Would Have Thought It?*" *Western American Literature*, vol. 36, no. 3, 2001, pp. 212–31.

———. *White Mother to a Dark Race: Settler Colonialism, Maternalism, and the Removal of Indigenous Children in the American West and Australia, 1880–1940*, by Jacobs, U of Nebraska P, 2009.

James Moran & Co.'s Indian Girl Fine Cut Chewing Tobacco. Label. 1874.

Jameson, Elizabeth, and Susan Armitage, editors. *Writing the Range: Race, Class, and Culture in the Women's West*. U of Oklahoma P, 1997.

Jaramillo, Cleofas M. *The Genuine New Mexico Tasty Recipes*. 1939. Ancient City, 1981.

———. *Romance of a Little Village Girl*. 1955. U of New Mexico P, 2000.

———. *Shadows of the Past (Sombras del Pasado)*. 1941. Ancient City, 1980.

Jensen, Carol. "Cleofas M. Jaramillo on Marriage in Territorial Northern New Mexico." *New Mexico Historical Review*, vol. 58, no. 2, Apr. 1983, pp. 153–71.

Jensen, Joan M., and Darlis A. Miller. *New Mexico Women: Intercultural Perspectives*. U of New Mexico P, 1986.

J. G. Cartoon. *Carlisle Arrow*, vol. 11, no. 38, 4 June 1915, p. 26.

Johannessen, Lene M. "Disillusion and Defiance in María Amparo Ruiz de Burton's *The Squatter and the Don*." *Threshold Time: Passage of Crisis in Chicano Literature*, by Johannessen, Rodopi, 2008, pp. 61–80.

John, Della Mae. "Inauguration of Domestic Science Course." *Carlisle Arrow*, vol. 11, no. 38, 4 June 1915, pp. 26–27.

"Johnny Soap." Ivory Soap. Advertisement. *Woman's Home Companion*, vol. 52, no. 3, Mar. 1925, pp. 58–59.

Johnson, David L., and Raymond Wilson. "Gertrude Simmons Bonnin, 1876–1938: 'Americanize the First American.'" *American Indian Quarterly*, vol. 14, no. 1, Winter 1988, 27–40.

Johnston, Mary. "To Have and To Hold." *Atlantic Monthly*, vol. 85, nos. 507–509, Jan./Mar. 1900, pp. 54–65, 205–18, 335–54.

Kaestle, Carl F., and Janice A. Radway. *Print in Motion: The Expansion of Publishing and Reading in the United States, 1880–1940*. U of North Carolina P, 2009.

Kaplan, Amy. *The Anarchy of Empire in the Making of U.S. Culture*. Harvard UP, 2002.

———. "Manifest Domesticity." *American Literature*, vol. 70, no. 3, Sept. 1998, pp. 581–606.

Kaplan, Barry B. "Forever Diamonds: A Powerful Company, a Catchy Slogan, and How They Forever Changed the Way We Value Diamonds." *Gemnation*, gemnation.com/forever_diamonds_1.jsp. Accessed 8 July 2015.

Karell, Linda K. "A Question of Perspectives: Collaboration and Literary Authority in Mourning Dove's *Cogewea*." *Writing Together/Writing Apart: Collaboration in Western American Literature*, by Karell, U of Nebraska P, 2002, pp. 64–91.

Karo Syrup. Advertisement. *Woman's Home Companion*, vol. 57, no. 4, Apr. 1930, p. 198.

Karush, Deborah. "Bringing Outland Inland in *The Professor's House*: Willa Cather's Domestication of Empire." *Willa Cather's Canadian and Old World Connections*, edited by Robert Thacker and Michael A. Peterman, vol. 4, U of Nebraska P, 1999, pp. 144–71. Cather Studies.

Katanski, Amelia V. *Learning to Write "Indian": The Boarding School Experience and American Indian Literature*. U of Oklahoma P, 2005.

Kaup, Monika. "The Unsustainable Hacienda: The Rhetoric of Progress in Jovita González and Eve Raleigh's Caballero." *Modern Fiction Studies*, vol. 51, no. 3, 2005, pp. 561–91.

Keller, Jean A. *Empty Beds: Indian Student Health at Sherman Institute, 1902–1922*. Michigan State UP, 2002.

Kelley, Mary. *Private Woman, Public Stage: Literary Domesticity in Nineteenth-Century America*. Oxford UP, 1984.

Kelly, R. Gordon. *Mother Was a Lady: Self and Society in Selected American Children's Periodicals, 1865–1890*. Greenwood, 1974.

Kelsey, Penelope Myrtle. "Narratives of the Boarding School Era from Victimry to Resistance." *Atenea*, vol. 23, no. 2, Winter 2003, pp. 123–38.

———. *Tribal Theory in Native American Literature: Dakota and Haudenosaunee Writing and Indigenous Worldviews*. Lincoln: U of Nebraska P, 2008.

Kent, Alicia A. "Mourning Dove's *Cogewea*: Writing Her Way into Modernity." *MELUS*, vol. 23, no. 3, Fall 1999, pp. 39–66.

———. "Native Americans: Moving from Primitive to Postmodern, Mourning Dove and D'Arcy McNickel." *African, Native, and Jewish American Literature and the Reshaping of Modernism*, by Kent, Palgrave Macmillan, 2007, pp. 71–112.

Kerber, Linda. "The Republican Mother: Women and the Enlightenment—An American Perspective." *American Quarterly*, vol. 28, no. 2, Summer 1976, pp. 187–205.

Kilcup, Karen L., editor. *Native American Women's Writing: An Anthology, c. 1800–1924*. Blackwell, 2000.

———, editor. *Nineteenth-Century American Women Writers: A Critical Reader*. Blackwell, 1998.

———. "Writing in the Real World." *Legacy*, vol. 24, no. 2, June 2008, pp. 193–210.

King, Rosemary A. "Claiming Space: Domestic Places, National Divides." *Border Confluences: Borderland Narratives from the Mexican War to the Present*, by King, U of Arizona P, 2004, pp. 3–29.

Kinyon, Henry H. "South America, Land of Contrasts." *Forum*, vol. 77, no. 1, Jan. 1927, 38–45.

Kline, Wendy. *Building a Better Race: Gender, Sexuality, and Eugenics from the Turn of the Century to the Baby Boom.* U of California P, 2001.

Kosmider, Alexia. "Strike a EuroAmerican Pose: Ora Eddleman Reed's 'Types of Indian Girls.'" *American Transcendental Quarterly*, vol. 12, no. 2, June 1998, pp. 109–31.

Krupat, Arnold. *Ethnocriticism: Ethnography, History, Literature.* U of California P, 1992.

———. *For Those Who Came After: A Study of Native American Autobiography.* 1985. U of California P, 1989.

———. "From 'Half-Blood' to 'Mixedblood': *Cogewea* and the Discourse of Indian Blood." *Red Matters: Native American Studies*, by Krupat, U of Pennsylvania P, 2002, pp. 76–97.

Kunce, Catherine. "Fire of Eden: Zitkala-Ša's Bitter Apple." *Studies in American Indian Literatures*, vol. 18, no. 1, Spring 2006, pp. 73–82.

La Malinche and Cortez, Lienzo de Tlaxcala. Illustration c. 1560. Reproduction c. 1890.

Lape, Noreen Groover. "Double Consciousness in the Borderlands: The Frontier Autobiographies of James P. Beckworth and Sarah Winnemucca Hopkins." *West of the Border: The Multicultural Literature of the Western American Frontiers*, by Lape, Ohio UP, 2000, pp. 19–56.

———. "'I would rather be with my people, but not to live with them as they live': Cultural Liminality and Double Consciousness in Sarah Winnemucca Hopkins's *Life Among the Piutes: Their Wrongs and Claims.*" *American Indian Quarterly*, vol. 22, no. 3, Summer 1998, pp. 259–79.

Larson, Charles R. *American Indian Fiction.* University of New Mexico P, 1978.

Lears, Jackson. *Fables of Abundance: A Cultural History of Advertising in America.* Basic, 1994.

Lemus, Felicia Luna. *Trace Elements of Random Tea Parties.* Seal, 2003.

Leonard, John W. "Raymond, Evelyn Hunt." *Women's Who's Who in America: A Biographical Dictionary of Contemporary Women of the United States and Canada, 1914–1915*, by Leonard, American Commonwealth, 1914, p. 674.

Leupp, Francis E. *In Red Man's Land: A Study of the American Indian.* Fleming H. Revell, 1914.

Lima, Lázaro. "Negotiating Cultural Memory in the Aftermath of the Mexican-American War: Nineteenth Century Mexican American Testimonials and *The Squatter and the Don.*" *The Latino Body: Crisis*

Identities in American Literary and Cultural Memory, by Lima, New York UP, 2007, pp. 22–55.

Limón, José E. "Folklore, Gendered Repression, and Cultural Critique: The Case of Jovita González." *Texas Studies in Literature and Language*, vol. 34, no. 4, 1993, pp. 453–73.

———. "Mexicans, Foundational Fictions, and the United States: *Caballero*, a Late Border Romance." *The Places of History: Regionalism Revisited in Latin America*, edited by Doris Sommer, Duke UP, 1999, pp. 236–48.

———. "Nations, Regions, and Mid-Nineteenth-Century Texas: History in *On the Long Tide* and *Caballero*." *Amerikastudien/American Studies*, vol. 54, no. 1, 2008, pp. 97–111.

Lindemann, Marilee. *Willa Cather: Queering America*. Columbia UP, 1999.

Littlefield, Daniel. "Short Fiction Writers of Indian Territory." *American Studies*, vol. 24, no. 1, 1982, pp. 23–38.

Littlefield, Daniel, and James Parins. *American Indian and Alaska Native Newspapers and Periodicals*. Greenwood, 1984.

———. *A Biobibliography of Native American Writers, 1772–1924: A Supplement*. Scarecrow, 1985.

Lomawaima, K. Tsianina. *They Called It Prairie Light: The Story of Chilocco Indian School*. U of Nebraska P, 1994.

Lorde, Audre. "The Master's Tools Will Never Dismantle the Master's House." 1984. *Sister Outsider: Essays and Speeches*, by Lorde, Crossing, 2007, pp. 110–14.

Loughran, Trish. *The Republic in Print: Print Culture in the Age of U.S. Nation Building, 1770–1870*. Columbia UP, 2007.

Love, Heather. "Willa Cather's Sad Kindred." *Feeling Backward: Loss and the Politics of Queer History*, by Love, Harvard UP, 2007, pp. 72–99.

Lovett, Laura L. *Conceiving the Future: Pronatalism, Reproduction, and the Family in the United States, 1890–1938*. U of North Carolina P, 2007.

"Lucerne-in-Maine." Advertisement. *Forum*, vol. 77, no. 1, Jan. 1927.

Luis-Brown, David. "'White Slaves' and 'Arrogant Mestiza': Reconfiguring Whiteness in *The Squatter and the Don* and *Ramona*." *American Literature*, vol. 69, no. 4, 1997, pp. 813–39.

———. "'White Slaves' and 'Arrogant Mestiza': Reconfiguring Whiteness in *The Squatter and the Don* and *Ramona*." *Waves of Decolonization: Discourses of Race and Hemispheric Citizenship in Cuba, Mexico, and the United States*, by Luis-Brown, Duke UP, 2008, pp. 35–66.

Lukens, Margo. "The American Indian Story of Zitkala-Ša." *In Her Own Voice: Nineteenth-Century American Women Essayists*, edited by Sherry Lee Linkon, Garland, 1997, pp. 141–55.

———. "Her 'Wrongs and Claims': Sarah Winnemucca's Strategic Narratives of Abuse." *Wicazo Sa Review*, vol. 14, no. 1, Spring 1998, pp. 93–108.

———. "Mourning Dove and Mixed Blood: Cultural and Historical Pressures on Aesthetic Choice and Authorial Identity." *American Indian Quarterly*, vol. 21, no. 3, 1997, p. 409.

Lyons, Scott Richard. "Rhetorical Sovereignty: What Do American Indians Want from Writing?" *College Composition and Communication*, vol. 51, no. 3, 2000, pp. 447–68.

———. *X-Marks: Native Signatures of Assent.* U of Minnesota P, 2010.

Lystad, Mary. *At Home in America: As Seen through Its Books for Children.* Schenkman, 1984.

MacLeod, Anne Scott. *American Childhood: Essays on Children's Literature of the Nineteenth and Twentieth Centuries.* U of Georgia P, 1994.

———. *A Moral Tale: Children's Fiction and American Culture, 1820–1860.* Archon, 1975.

Madigan, Mark J. "Willa Cather and the Book-of-the-Month Club." *Willa Cather as Cultural Icon*, edited by Guy Reynolds, vol. 7, U of Nebraska P, 2007, pp. 68–85. Cather Studies.

Manriquez, B. J. "Argument in Narrative: Tropology in Jovita González's Caballero." *Bilingual Review/La Revista Bilingue*, vol. 24, no. 2, 2000, pp. 172–78.

Marcus, Leonard S. *Minders of Make-Believe: Idealists, Entrepreneurs, and the Shaping of American Children's Literature.* Houghton Mifflin, 2008.

Marquis, Claudia. "Romancing the Home: Gender, Empire, and the South Pacific." *Girls, Boys, Books, Toys: Gender in Children's Literature and Culture*, edited by Beverly Lyon Clark and Margaret R. Higonnet, Johns Hopkins UP, 1999, pp. 53–67.

Mason, Otis T. *Woman's Share in Primitive Culture.* New York, 1894.

Massmann, Ann M. "Adelina 'Nina' Otero-Warren: A Spanish-American Cultural Broker." *Journal of the Southwest*, vol. 41, no. 4, 2000, pp. 877–96.

McClintock, Anne. *Imperial Leather: Race, Gender, and Sexuality in the Colonial Contest.* Routledge, 1995.

McClure, Andrew S. "Sarah Winnemucca: [Post]Indian Princess and Voice of the Paiutes." *MELUS*, vol. 23, no. 2, Summer 1999, pp. 29–51.

McCombs, Vernon Monroe. *From over the Border: A Study of the Mexicans in the United States.* Council of Women for Home Missions and Missionary Education Movement of the United States and Canada, 1925.

McCullough, Kate. "María Amparo Ruiz de Burton's Geographies of Race, Regions of Religion." *Regions of Identity: The Construction of America in Women's Fiction, 1885–1914*, by McCullough, Stanford UP, 1999, pp. 131–84.

McGraw, Eliza. *Edna Ferber's America.* U of Louisiana P, 2013.

McLean, Robert, and Grace Petrie Williams. *Old Spain in New America.* Association Press, 1916.

McMahon, Marci. "Politicizing Spanish-Mexican Domesticity, Redefining *Fronteras*: Jovita González's *Cabellero* and Cleofas Jaramillo's *Romance of a Little Village Girl*." *Frontiers*, vol. 28, nos. 1–2, 2007, pp. 232–59.

McShane, Becky Jo Gesteland. "In Pursuit of Regional and Cultural Identity: The Autobiographies of Agnes Morley Cleaveland and Fabiola Cabeza de Baca." *Breaking Boundaries: New Perspectives on Women's Regional Writing*, edited by Sherrie A. Inness and Diana Royer, U of Iowa P, 1997, pp. 180–96.

Medicine, Beatrice. "Ella C. Deloria: The Emic Voice." *Learning to Be an Anthropologist and Remaining "Native": Selected Writings*, edited by Sue Ellen Jacobs, U of Illinois P, 2001, pp. 269–88.

Melzer, Richard and Francisco Sisneros. "Proud Residents Refer to La Joya as 'The Jewel.'" *El Defensor Chieftain* [Socorro, NM], 5 Apr. 2008, dchieftain.com/proud-residents-refer-to-la-joya-as-the-jewel/article_bf404c5d-762b-5a04-be99-3e8211532d80.html. Accessed 29 Mar. 2017.

Mexicans? No! They Are Americans in the Making! Photograph. *From over the Border: A Study of the Mexicans in the United States*, edited by Vernon Monroe McCombs, Council of Women for Home Missions and Missionary Education Movement of the United States and Canada, 1925, p. 64.

Michaels, Walter Benn. *Our America: Nativism, Modernism, and Pluralism.* Duke UP, 1995.

Mignon, Charles W. "Textual Essay." *Death Comes for the Archbishop*, edited by John J. Murphy and Charles W. Mignon, U of Nebraska P, 1999, 515–63. Willa Cather Scholarly Edition Series.

Mihesuah, Devon A. *Cultivating the Rosebuds: The Education of Women at the Cherokee Female Seminary, 1851–1909.* U of Illinois P, 1993.

Miller, Jay. "Mourning Dove: The Author as Cultural Mediator." *Being and Becoming Indian: Biographical Studies of North American Frontiers*, edited by James A. Clifton, Dorsey, 1989, pp. 160–82.

———, editor. *Mourning Dove: A Salishan Autobiography.* Lincoln: U of Nebraska P, 1990.

"The Modern Indian Girl." *Sunday Magazine, Red Man*, vol. 2, no. 3, Nov. 1909, pp. 23–25.

Mollie, Alma. "Housekeeping." *Native American*, 16 June 1906, pp. 189–90.

Mollis, Kara. "Teaching 'dear Mihia': Sentimentalism and Cross-Cultural Education in S. Alice Callahan's *Wynema: A Child of the Forest.*" *MELUS*, vol. 33, no. 3, Fall 2008, pp. 111–29.

Montes, Amelia María de la Luz. "*Es Necesario Mirar Bien*: Nineteenth-Century Letter Making and Novel Writing in the Life of María Amparo Ruiz de Burton." *Recovering the U.S. Hispanic Literary Heritage*, edited by María Herrera-Sobek and Virginia Sánchez Korrol, vol. 3, Arte Público, 2000, pp. 16–37.

———. "María Amparo Ruiz de Burton Negotiates American Literary Politics and Culture." *Challenging Boundaries: Gender and Periodization*, edited by Joyce W. Warren and Margaret Dickie, U of Georgia P, 2000, pp. 202–25.

———. "See How I Am Received: Nationalism, Race, and Gender in *Who Would Have Thought It?*" *Decolonial Voices: Chicana and Chicano Cultural Studies in the Twenty-First Century*, edited by Arturo J. Aldama and Naomi H. Quinonez, Indiana UP, 2002, pp. 177–94.

———. "'We Were Born to Do Something More Than Simply Live': María Amparo Ruiz de Burton and the Nineteenth Century." *Symbolism*, vol. 4, 2004, pp. 293–309.

Montes, Amelia María de la Luz, and Anne Elizabeth Goldman, editors. *María Amparo Ruiz de Burton: Critical and Pedagogical Perspectives.* U of Nebraska P, 2004.

Montgomery, Charles. *The Spanish Redemption: Heritage, Power, and Loss on New Mexico's Upper Rio Grande.* U of California P, 2002.

———. "The Trap of Race and Memory: The Language of Spanish Civility on the Upper Rio Grande." *American Quarterly*, vol. 52, no. 3, Sept. 2000, pp. 478–513.

Moraga, Cherríe L. *Loving in the War Years: Lo Que Nunca Pasí por Sus Labios.* 1983. South End, 2000.

Morgenstern, John. *Playing with Books: A Study of the Reader as Child.* McFarland, 2009.

Morrison, Daryl. "*Twin Territories: The Indian Magazine* and Its Editor, Ora Eddleman Reed." *Chronicles of Oklahoma*, vol. 60, no. 2, Summer 1982, pp. 136–66.

Morrison, Toni. *Playing in the Dark: Whiteness and the Literary Imagination.* Vintage, 1992.

Mourning Dove. *Cogewea, The Half-Blood: A Depiction of the Great Montana Cattle Range.* 1927. U of Nebraska P, 1991.

Moyna, María Irene. "Portrayals of Spanish in 19th-century American prose: María Amparo Ruiz de Burton's *The Squatter and the Don.*" *Language and Literature*, vol. 17, no. 3, 2008, pp. 235–52.

Mullen Sands, Kathleen. "Indian Women's Personal Narrative: Voices Past and Present." *American Women's Autobiography: Fea(s)ts of Memory*, edited by Margo Culley, U of Wisconsin P, 1992, pp. 268–94.

Mulsified Cocoanut Oil Shampoo. Advertisement. *Woman's Home Companion*, vol. 51, no. 5, May 1925, p. 48.

Murphy, Gretchen. "A Europeanized New World: Colonialism and Cosmopolitanism in *Who Would Have Thought It?*" Montes and Goldman, pp. 135–52.

———. *Hemispheric Imaginings: The Monroe Doctrine and Narratives of U.S. Empire.* Duke UP, 2005.

Murphy, Jacqueline Shea. "Picking Up the Master's Tools." *Women's Review of Books*, vol. 15, no. 1, 1997, p. 10.

Murphy, John J. "Historical Essay." *Death Comes for the Archbishop*, edited by John J. Murphy and Charles W. Mignon, U of Nebraska P, 1999, pp. 325–72, 515–63. Willa Cather Scholarly Edition Series.

Murphy, Nora. "Starting Children on the Path to the Past: American Indians in Children's Historical Fiction." *Minnesota History*, vol. 57, no. 6, Summer 2001, pp. 284–95.

Na-Li and Fanny. "Two Scenes in Cherokee Land. *A Wreath of Cherokee Rose Buds.* 1855. Rpt. in Kilcup, *Native American*, pp. 408–9.

NEA Book Survey. "Willa Cather in Somber Mood as She Writes Story of Taos and Santa Fe of Early Days." *New Mexico State Tribune*, 10 Sept. 1927, p. 6. Rpt. in O'Connor, pp. 315–16.

Nealon, Christopher. "Feeling and Affiliation in Willa Cather." *Foundlings: Lesbian and Gay Historical Emotion before Stonewall*, by Nealon, Duke UP, 2001, pp. 61–97.

New Citizens from Over the Border. Photograph. *From over the Border: A Study of the Mexicans in the United States*, edited by Vernon Monroe McCombs, Council of Women for Home Missions and Missionary Education Movement of the United States and Canada, 1925.

Newman, Frances. "The American Short Story in the First Twenty Five Years of the Twentieth Century." *Bookman: A Review of Books and Life*, vol. 62, no. 2, Apr. 1926, pp. 186–93.

Newman, Louise Michele. *White Women's Rights: The Racial Origins of Feminism in the United States.* Oxford UP, 1999.

Nieto-Phillips, John M. *The Language of Blood: The Making of Spanish-American Identity in New Mexico, 1880s–1930s.* U of New Mexico P, 2004.

Noriega, Jorge. "American Indian Education in the United States: Indoctrination for Subordination to Colonialism." *The State of Native America: Genocide, Colonization, and Resistance*, edited by M. Annette Jaimes, South End, 1992, pp. 371–402.

O'Connor, Margaret Anne, editor. *Willa Cather: The Contemporary Reviews.* Cambridge UP, 2001.

Ojibway Tepees (Typical of the Passing Old Life). Photograph. Leupp, p. 64.

Okker, Patricia. "Native American Literature and the Canon: The Case of Zitkala-Ša." *American Realism and the Canon*, edited by Tom Quirk and Gary Scharnhorst, U of Delaware P, 1994, pp. 87–101.

Ordover, Nancy. *American Eugenics: Race, Queer Anatomy, and the Science of Nationalism.* U of Minnesota P, 2003.

Ortiz, Simon J. "Towards a National Indian Literature: Cultural Authenticity in Nationalism." *MELUS*, vol. 8, no. 2, Summer 1981, pp. 7–12.

Oskison, J. M. "Carlisle Commencement as Seen by *Collier's Weekly*." *Red Man*, vol. 4, no. 1, Sept. 1910, p. 18.

Ostergaard, Lori, Amy Mecklenburg-Faenger, and Henrietta Rix Wood. "Making Space for Writing: High School Girls' Newspapers, Writing Clubs, and Literary Magazines, 1897–1930." *Feminist Challenges or Feminist Rhetorics? Locations, Scholarship, Discourse*, edited by Kirsti Cole, Cambridge Scholars, 2014, pp. 39–56.

Otero-Warren, Nina. *Old Spain in Our Southwest.* Harcourt, 1936.

Owens, Louis. *Mixedblood Messages: Literature, Film, Family, Place.* U of Oklahoma P, 1998.

———. *Other Destinies: Understanding the American Indian Novel.* U of Oklahoma P, 1992.

Padilla, Genaro M. "Imprisoned Narrative? Or Lies, Secrets, and Silence in New Mexico Women's Autobiography." *Criticism in the Borderlands: Studies in Chicano Literature, Culture, and Ideology*, edited by Hector Calderón and José David Saldívar, Duke UP, 1991, pp. 43–60.

———. "Lies, Secrets, and Silence: Cultural Autobiography as Resistance in Cleofas Jaramillo's *Romance of a Little Village Girl*." *My History, Not Yours: The Formation of Mexican American Autobiography*, by Padilla, U of Wisconsin P, 1993, pp. 196–227.

Paredes, Raymond A. "Mexican-American Literature: An Overview." *Recovering the U.S. Hispanic Literary Heritage*, edited by Ramón A. Gutiérrez and Genaro M. Padilla, vol. 1, Arte Público, 1993, pp. 31–51.

Parker, Dorothy R. *Phoenix Indian School: The Second Half-Century*. U of Arizona P, 1996.

Parker, Robert Dale, editor. *Changing Is Not Vanishing: A Collection of American Indian Poetry to 1930*. U of Pennsylvania P, 2011.

———. "Nothing to Do: John Joseph Mathews's *Sundown* and Restless Young Indian Men." *The Invention of Native American Literature*, by Parker, Cornell UP, 2003, pp. 19–50.

Pascoe, Peggy. *Relations of Rescue: The Search for Female Moral Authority in the American West, 1874–1939*. Oxford UP, 1990.

Pattison, Mary. *Principles of Domestic Engineering: Or, the What, Why and How of a Home*. Trow, 1915.

Peabody, Elizabeth Palmer. *Sarah Winnemucca's Practical Solution of the Indian Problem*. Cambridge, 1886.

Perez, Domino Renee. *There Was a Woman: La Llorona from Folklore to Popular Culture*. U of Texas P, 2008.

Perez, Vincent. "Remembering the Hacienda: History and Memory in Jovita González and Eve Raleigh's *Caballero: A Historical Novel*." *Look Away! The U.S. South in New World Studies*, edited by Jon Smith and Deborah Cohn, Duke UP, 2004, pp. 471–94.

———. "Remembering the Hacienda: Land and Community in the Californio Narratives." *Remembering the Hacienda: History and Memory in the Mexican American Southwest*, by Perez, Texas A&M UP, 2006, pp. 49–92.

———. "South by Southwest: Land and Community in María Amparo Ruiz de Burton's *The Squatter and the Don* and Maríano Guadalupe Vallejo's Historical and Personal Memoir Relating to Alta California." *Recovering the U.S. Hispanic Literary Heritage*, edited by José F. Aranda Jr. and Silvio Torres-Saillant, vol. 4, Arte Público, 2002, pp. 96–132.

———. "Teaching the Hacienda: Juan Rulfo and Mexican American Cultural Memory." *Western American Literature*, vol. 35, no. 1, Spring 2000, pp. 33–44.

Piatote, Beth H. *Domestic Subjects: Gender, Citizenship, and Law in Native American Literature*. Yale UP, 2013.

Pierce, Georgia Bennett. Letter. *Red Man*, vol. 5, no. 1, Sept. 1912, p. 42.

Pierce, Thomas Mitchell. "Types of American Women." Illustrations. *Everybody's Magazine*, vol. 7, no. 6, Dec. 1902, pp. 509–14.

Powell, Malea. "Princess Sarah, the Civilized Indian: The Rhetoric of Cultural Literacies in Sarah Winnemucca Hopkins's *Life Among the Piutes*." *Rhetorical Women: Roles and Representations*, edited by Hildy Miller and Lillian Bridwell-Bowles, U of Alabama P, 2005, pp. 63–80.

———. "Rhetorics of Survivance: How American Indians *Use* Writing." *College Composition and Communication*, vol. 53, no. 3, Feb. 2002, pp. 396–434.

———. "Sarah Winnemucca: Her Wrongs and Claims." *Rhetorics of Survivance: Word Medicine, Word Magic*, edited by Ernest Stromberg, U of Pittsburgh P, 2006, pp. 69–94.

Prater, John. "Ella Deloria: Varied Discourse." *Wicazo Sa Review*, vol. 11, no. 2, Fall 1995, pp. 40–46.

Pratt, Mary Louise. "Arts of the Contact Zone." *Ways of Reading: An Anthology for Writers*. 11th ed., edited by David Bartholomae, Anthony Petrosky, and Stacey Waite, Bedford/St. Martin's, 2017, pp. 512–32.

Present Day Warriors. Photograph. Leupp, frontispiece.

"Progress of the Indian." *Red Man*, vol. 4, no. 1, Sept. 1911, p. 39.

Qoyawayma, Polingaysi. *No Turning Back: A Hopi Indian Woman's Struggle to Live in Two Worlds*. U of New Mexico P, 1964.

Quinton, Amelia Stone. "Care of the Indian." *Woman's Work in America*, edited by Annie Nathan Meyer, New York, 1891, pp. 373–91.

Raab, Joséf. "Chicanos and Anglos: Mestizaje in Jovita González, Gloria Anzaldúa, and John Sayles." *Zeitschrift Fur Anglistik Und Amerikanistik*, vol. 47, no. 4, 1999, pp. 344–56.

———. "The Imagined Inter-American Community of María Amparo Ruiz de Burton." *Amerikastudien*, vol. 54, no. 1, 2008, pp. 76–95.

Radway, Janice: *A Feeling for Books: The Book-of-the-Month-Club, Literary Taste, and Middle-Class Desire*. U of North Carolina P, 1999.

Ramirez, Pablo. "Resignifying Preservation: A Borderlands Response to American Eugenics in Jovita González and Eve Raleigh's *Caballero*." *Canadian Review of American Studies/Revue Canadienne d'Etudes Américaines*, vol. 39, no. 1, 2009, pp. 21–39.

Raymond, Evelyn Hunt. *A Daughter of the West: The Story of an American Princess*. Boston, 1899.

———. *Monica, the Mesa Maiden*. New York, 1892.

———. *Polly, the Gringo: A Story for Girls*. Penn, 1905.

———. *A Yankee Girl in Old California: A Story for Girls*. Penn, 1901.

"Raymond, Evelyn Hunt." *Who's Who in America: A Biographical Dictionary of Notable Living Men and Women of the United States, 1910–1911*. Vol. 6, A. N. Marquis, 1910, p. 1576.

Rebolledo, Tey Diana. *The Chronicles of Panchita Villa and Other Guerrilleras: Essays on Chicana/Latina and Criticism*. U of Texas P, 2005.

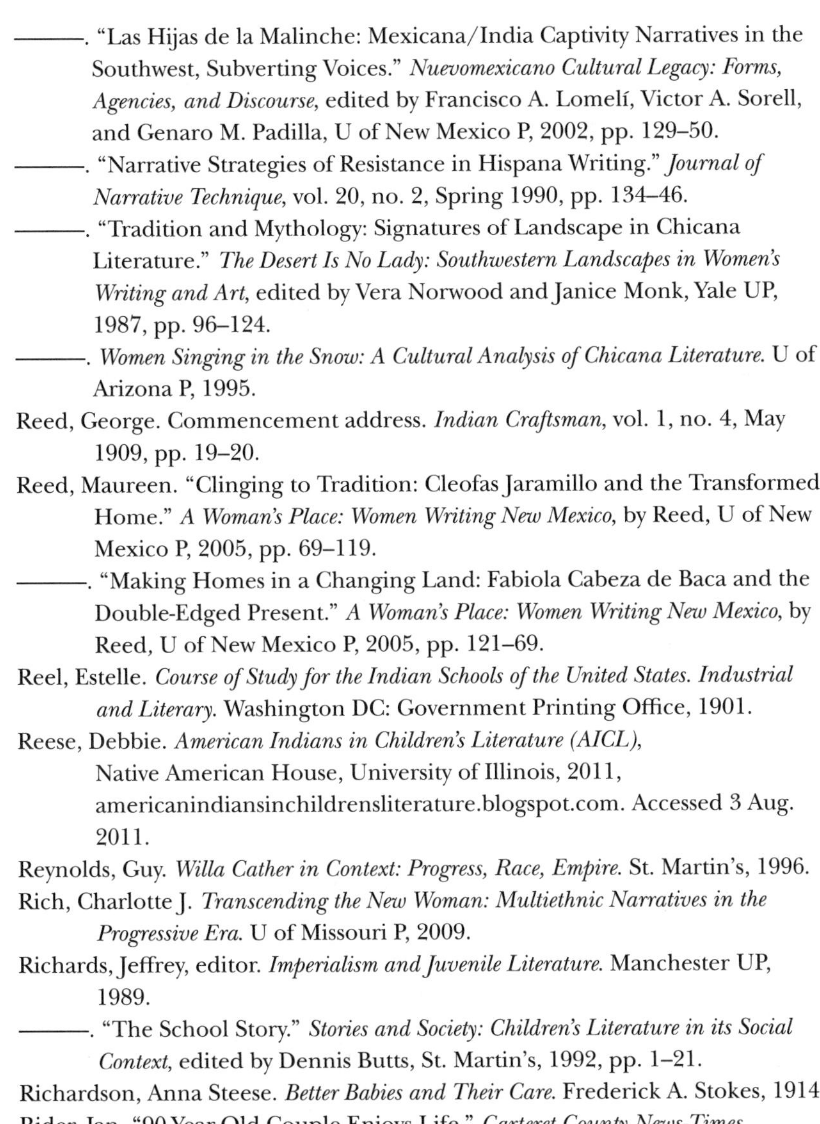

———. "Las Hijas de la Malinche: Mexicana/India Captivity Narratives in the Southwest, Subverting Voices." *Nuevomexicano Cultural Legacy: Forms, Agencies, and Discourse*, edited by Francisco A. Lomelí, Victor A. Sorell, and Genaro M. Padilla, U of New Mexico P, 2002, pp. 129–50.

———. "Narrative Strategies of Resistance in Hispana Writing." *Journal of Narrative Technique*, vol. 20, no. 2, Spring 1990, pp. 134–46.

———. "Tradition and Mythology: Signatures of Landscape in Chicana Literature." *The Desert Is No Lady: Southwestern Landscapes in Women's Writing and Art*, edited by Vera Norwood and Janice Monk, Yale UP, 1987, pp. 96–124.

———. *Women Singing in the Snow: A Cultural Analysis of Chicana Literature*. U of Arizona P, 1995.

Reed, George. Commencement address. *Indian Craftsman*, vol. 1, no. 4, May 1909, pp. 19–20.

Reed, Maureen. "Clinging to Tradition: Cleofas Jaramillo and the Transformed Home." *A Woman's Place: Women Writing New Mexico*, by Reed, U of New Mexico P, 2005, pp. 69–119.

———. "Making Homes in a Changing Land: Fabiola Cabeza de Baca and the Double-Edged Present." *A Woman's Place: Women Writing New Mexico*, by Reed, U of New Mexico P, 2005, pp. 121–69.

Reel, Estelle. *Course of Study for the Indian Schools of the United States. Industrial and Literary*. Washington DC: Government Printing Office, 1901.

Reese, Debbie. *American Indians in Children's Literature (AICL)*, Native American House, University of Illinois, 2011, americanindiansinchildrensliterature.blogspot.com. Accessed 3 Aug. 2011.

Reynolds, Guy. *Willa Cather in Context: Progress, Race, Empire*. St. Martin's, 1996.

Rich, Charlotte J. *Transcending the New Woman: Multiethnic Narratives in the Progressive Era*. U of Missouri P, 2009.

Richards, Jeffrey, editor. *Imperialism and Juvenile Literature*. Manchester UP, 1989.

———. "The School Story." *Stories and Society: Children's Literature in its Social Context*, edited by Dennis Butts, St. Martin's, 1992, pp. 1–21.

Richardson, Anna Steese. *Better Babies and Their Care*. Frederick A. Stokes, 1914.

Rider, Jan. "90-Year-Old Couple Enjoys Life." *Carteret County News-Times* [Morehead City, NC], 22 Mar. 1973.

Rifkin, Mark. "The Erotics of Sovereignty." *Queer Indigenous Studies: Critical Interventions in Theory, Politics, and Literature*, edited by Qwo-Li Driskill, Chris Finley, Brian Joseph Gilley, and Scott Lauria Morgensen, U of Arizona P, 2011, pp. 172–89.

———. "Romancing Kinship: A Queer Reading of Indian Education and Zitkala-Ša's American Indian Stories." *GLQ: A Journal of Lesbian and Gay Studies*, vol. 14, no. 1, 2006, pp. 27–59.

Rivera, John-Michael. "Embodying Greater Mexico: María Amparo Ruiz de

Burton and the Reconstruction of the Mexican Question." *Look Away! The U.S. South in New World Studies,* edited by Jon Smith and Deborah Cohn, Duke UP, 2004, pp. 451–70.

———. "Embodying Manifest Destiny: María Amparo Ruiz de Burton and the Color of Mexican Womanhood." *The Emergence of Mexican America: Recovering Stories of Mexican Peoplehood in U.S. Culture,* by Rivera, New York UP, 2006, pp. 82–109.

Robbins, Frances Lamont. *Outlook,* vol. 147, 26 Oct. 1927, p. 251. Rpt. in O'Connor, pp. 340–41.

Robinson, Forrest. "We Should Talk: Western History and Western Literature in Dialogue." *American Literary History,* vol. 16, no. 1, 2004, pp. 132–43.

Rodier, Katharine. "Authorizing Sarah Winnemucca? Elizabeth Peabody and Mary Peabody Mann." *Reinventing the Peabody Sisters,* edited by Monika M. Ebert, Julie E. Hall, and Katharine Rodier, U of Iowa P, 2006, pp. 108–25.

Rodríguez, J. Javier. "Caballero's Global Continuum: Time and Place in South Texas." *MELUS,* vol. 34, no. 1, Spring 2008, pp. 117–38.

Rodriguez, Ralph E. "Unearthing the Past in 1972: Literary Antecedents and Cultural Capital." *Aztlán: A Journal of Chicano Studies,* vol. 34, no. 1, Spring 2007, pp. 205–18.

Romalov, Nancy Tillman. "Unearthing the Historical Reader, or, Reading Girls' Reading." *Pioneers, Passionate Ladies, and Private Eyes: Dime Novels, Series Books, and Paperbacks,* edited by Larry E. Sullivan and Lydia Cushman Schurman, Haworth, 1996, pp. 87–101.

Romero, Lora. *Home Fronts: Domesticity and Its Critics in the Antebellum United States.* Duke UP, 1997.

Rosowski, Susan J. "The Western Hero as Logos." *Birthing a Nation: Gender, Creativity, and the West in American Literature,* by Rosowski, U of Nebraska P, 1999, pp. 157–76.

———, editor. *Willa Cather's Ecological Imagination.* Vol. 5, U of Nebraska P, 2003. Cather Studies.

Rowson, Susanna. *Charlotte Temple: A Tale of Truth.* 1794. W. W. Norton, 2010.

Ruiz, Julie. "Captive Identities: The Gendered Conquest of Mexico in *Who Would Have Thought It?*" Montes and Goldman, pp. 112–32.

Ruiz de Burton, María Amparo. *The Squatter and the Don.* 1885, edited by Rosaura Sánchez and Beatrice Pita, Arte Público, 1997.

———. *Who Would Have Thought It?* 1872, edited by Rosaura Sánchez and Beatrice Pita, Arte Público, 1995.

Ruoff, A. LaVonne Brown. "American Indian Authors, 1774–1899." *Critical Essays on Native American Literature,* edited by Andrew Wiget, G. K. Hall, 1985, pp. 191–202.

———. "Early Native American Women Authors: Jane Johnston Schoolcraft, Sarah Winnemucca, S. Alice Callahan, E. Pauline Johnson, and Zitkala-Ša." Kilcup, *Nineteenth-Century,* pp. 81–111.

———. "S. Alice Callahan." *Handbook of Native American Literature*, edited by Andrew Wiget, Garland, 1996, pp. 221–23.

———. "Sarah Winnemucca." *Handbook of Native American Literature*, edited by Andrew Wiget, Garland, 1996, pp. 299–302.

———. "Three Nineteenth-Century American Indian Autobiographers." *Redefining American Literary History*, edited by A. LaVonne Brown Ruoff and Jerry W. Ward Jr., MLA, 1990, pp. 251–69.

———. "Two Ideas Above an Oyster: Gender Roles in S. Alice Callahan's *Wynema*." *Native American Women in Literature and Culture*, edited by Susan Castillo and Victor M.P. Da Rosa, Fernando Pessoa UP, 1997, pp. 127–40.

Russell, Danielle. *Between the Angle and the Curve: Mapping Gender, Race, Space, and Identity in Willa Cather and Toni Morrison.* Routledge, 2006.

Ryan, Melissa. "The Indian Problem as a Woman's Question: S. Alice Callahan's *Wynema: A Child of the Forest.*" *ATQ*, vol. 21, no. 1, Mar. 2007, pp. 23–45.

Ryder, Mary R. "Willa Cather as Nature Writer: A Cry in the Wilderness." *Such News of the Land: U.S. Women Nature Writers*, edited by Thomas S. Edwards and Elizabeth A. DeWolfe, UP of New England, 2001, pp. 75–84.

Sakiestewa Gilbert, Matthew. *Education beyond the Mesas: Hopi Students at Sherman Institute, 1902–1929.* U of Nebraska P, 2010.

Salas, Elizabeth. "Adelina Otero Warren: Rural Aristocrat and Modern Feminist." *Latina Legacies: Identity, Biography, and Community*, edited by Vicki L. Ruiz and Virginia Sánchez Korrol, Oxford UP, 2005, pp. 135–47.

Saldívar, José David. *Border Matters: Remapping American Cultural Studies.* Berkeley: U of California P, 1997.

———. "Nuestra America's Borders: Remapping American Cultural Studies." *José Marti's "Our America": From National to Hemispheric Cultural Studies*, edited by Jeffrey Belnap and Raul Fernandez, Duke UP, 1999, pp. 145–78.

Saldívar, Ramón. "Ideologies of Self: Chicano Autobiography." *Chicano Narrative: The Dialectics of Difference.* U of Wisconsin P, 1990, pp. 154–70.

Saldívar-Hull, Sonya. *Feminism on the Border: Chicana Gender Politics and Literature.* U of California P, 2000.

Salmon, Edward G. "What Girls Read." *Nineteenth Century*, vol. 20, no. 116, Oct. 1886, pp. 515–29.

Sánchez, María Carla. "Whiteness Invisible: Early Mexican American Writing and the Color of Literary History." *Passing: Identity and Interpretation in Sexuality, Race, and Religion*, edited by María Carla Sánchez and Linda Schlossberg, New York UP, 2001, pp. 64–91.

Sánchez, Rosaura. "Dismantling the Colossus: Marti and Ruiz de Burton on the Formulation of Anglo America." *José Marti's "Our America": From National to Hemispheric Cultural Studies*, edited by Jeffrey Belnap and Raul Fernandez, Duke UP, 1999, pp. 115–28.

Sánchez, Rosaura, and Beatrice Pita. Introduction. *Who Would Have Thought It?*, by Ruiz de Burton, Arte Público, 1995, pp. vii–lxv.

———. "María Amparo Ruiz de Burton and the Power of Her Pen." *Latina Legacies: Identity, Biography, and Community*, edited by Vicki L. Ruiz and Virginia Sánchez Korrol, Oxford UP, 2005, pp. 72–83.

Sánchez-Eppler, Karen. *Dependent States: The Child's Part in Nineteenth-Century American Culture.* U of Chicago P, 2005.

Sassi, Kelly. "Feminist-Indigenous Rhetorics of Survivance and Discursive Spaces in S. Alice Callahan's *Wynema: A Child of the Forest.*" *Feminist Challenges or Feminist Rhetorics? Locations, Scholarship, Discourse*, edited by Kirsti Cole, Cambridge Scholars, 2014, pp. 264–82.

Scanlon, Jennifer. *Inarticulate Longings: The Ladies' Home Journal, Gender, and the Promise of Consumer Culture.* Routledge, 1995.

Schedler, Christopher. *Border Modernism: Intercultural Readings in American Literary Modernism.* Routledge, 2002.

Scholten, Pat Creech. "Exploitation of Ethos: Sarah Winnemucca and Bright Eyes on the Lecture Tour." *Western Journal of Speech Communication*, vol. 41, no. 4, Fall 1977, pp. 233–44.

Schroeter, James. *Willa Cather and Her Critics.* Cornell UP, 1967.

Seale, Doris. *Through Indian Eyes: The Native Experience in Books for Children.* New Society, 1992.

Seale, Doris, and Beverly Slapin, editors. *A Broken Flute: The Native Experience in Books for Children.* Oyate, 2005.

Sedgwick, Catharine Maria. *Hope Leslie: Or, Early Times in the Massachusetts.* 1827. Rutgers UP, 1993.

Segel, Elizabeth. "'As the Twig is Bent . . . ': Gender and Childhood Reading." *Gender and Reading: Essays on Readers, Texts, and Contexts*, edited by Elizabeth A. Flynn and Patrocinio P. Schweickart, Johns Hopkins UP, 1986, pp. 165–86.

Seguin, Robert. "Willa Cather and the Ambivalence of Hierarchy." *Around Quitting Time: Work and Middle-Class Fantasy in American Fiction*, by Seguin, Duke UP, 2001, pp. 57–81.

Senier, Siobhan. "Allotment Protest and Tribal Discourse: Reading *Wynema's* Successes and Shortcomings." *American Indian Quarterly*, vol. 23, no. 3, Summer 2000, pp. 420–40.

———. *Voices of Assimilation and Resistance: Helen Hunt Jackson, Sarah Winnemucca, and Victoria Howard.* U of Oklahoma P, 2001.

Silko, Leslie Marmon. *Introduction to Native American Literature: A Catalog.* Ken Lopez Bookseller, 1994, lopezbooks.com/articles/silko/. Accessed 8 July 2015.

Simonsen, Jane E. *Making Home Work: Domesticity and Native American Assimilation in the American West, 1860–1919.* U of North Carolina P, 2006.

Sligh, Gary. *A Study of Native American Women Novelists: Sophia Alice Callahan, Mourning Dove, and Ella Deloria.* Edwin Mellen, 2003.

Slote, Bernice. *The Kingdom of Art: Willa Cather's First Principles and Critical Statements, 1893–1896.* U of Nebraska P, 1966.

Slotkin, Richard. *Gunfighter Nation: The Myth of the Frontier in Twentieth-Century America.* U of Oklahoma P, 1992.

Smith, Dorothy Hope. *The Wild Indian. Woman's Home Companion,* vol. 52, no. 8, Aug. 1925, cover.

Smith, Jeanne. "'A Second Tongue': The Trickster's Voice in the Works of Zitkala-Ša." *Tricksterism in Turn-of-the-Century American Literature: A Multicultural Perspective,* edited by Elizabeth Ammons and Annette White-Parks, UP of New England, 1994, pp. 46–60.

Smith, Shawn Michelle. *American Archives: Gender, Race, and Class in Visual Culture.* Princeton UP, 1999.

Smyth, J. E. *Edna Ferber's Hollywood.* U of Texas P, 2010.

Some Homes of Ex-Carlisle Students Who Are Making Good. Photograph. *Red Man,* vol. 3, no. 3, Nov. 1911, p. 121.

Spack, Ruth. *America's Second Tongue: American Indian Education and the Ownership of English, 1860–1900.* U of Nebraska P, 2002.

———. "Dis/engagement: Zitkala-Ša's Letter's to Carlos Montezuma, 1901–1902." *MELUS,* vol. 26, no. 1, Spring 2001, pp. 173–204.

———. "Revisioning Sioux Women: Zitkala-Ša's Revolutionary *American Indian Stories.*" *Legacy,* vol. 14, no. 1, 1997, pp. 25–42.

———. "Translation Moves: Zitkala-Ša's Bilingual Indian Legends." *Studies in American Indian Literatures,* vol. 18, no. 4, Winter 2006, pp. 43–62.

———. "Zitkala-Ša, *The Song of Hiawatha,* and the Carlisle Indian School Band: A Captivity Tale." *Legacy,* vol. 24, no. 2, 2008, pp. 211–24.

Spivak, Gayatri Chakravorty. "Can the Subaltern Speak? Speculations on Widow-Sacrifice." *Wedge,* vol. 7/8, Winter/Spring 1985, pp. 120–30.

———. "Three Women's Texts and a Critique of Imperialism." *Critical Inquiry,* vol. 12, Autumn 1985, pp. 243–61.

Stage, Sarah, and Virginia B. Vincenti, editors. *Rethinking Home Economics: Women and the History of a Profession.* Cornell UP, 1997.

Stanlaws, Penrhyn. "Girls of Many Nations: England, Ireland, Scotland, Italy, France, Germany." Illustrations. *Everybody's Magazine,* vol. 6, no. 4, Apr. 1902, pp. 339–45.

Steele, Frederic Dorr. *Baby Show.* Illustration. "Better Bebbies" by Elinore Cowan Stone. *Woman's Home Companion,* vol. 52, no. 11, Nov. 1925, p. 18.

———. *Health First.* Illustration. "One Uses the Handkerchief" by Elinore Cowan Stone. *Woman's Home Companion,* vol. 51, no. 11, Nov. 1924, p. 20.

———. *Mama Habanera.* Illustration. "Better Bebbies" by Elinore Cowan Stone. *Woman's Home Companion,* vol. 52, no. 11, Nov. 1925, p. 18.

———. *Too Much Water.* Illustration. "José the Onlucky" by Elinore Cowan Stone. *Woman's Home Companion,* vol. 52, no. 5, 5 May 1925, p. 13.

Stern, Alexandra Minna. *Eugenic Nation: Faults and Frontiers of Better Breeding in Modern America.* U of California P, 2005.

Stevens, J. David. *The Word Rides Again: Rereading the Frontier in American Fiction.* Ohio UP, 2002.

Stevenson, Pascha A. "Reader Expectation and Ethnic Rhetorics: The Problem of the Passing Subaltern in *Who Would Have Thought It?*" *Ethnic Studies Review,* vol. 28, no. 2, 2005, pp. 61–75.

Stockett, Kathryn. *The Help.* Putnam, 2009.

Stoler, Ann Laura. "Tense and Tender Ties: The Politics of Comparison in North American History and (Post) Colonial Studies." *Journal of American History,* vol. 88, no. 3, Dec. 2001, pp. 829–65.

Stone, Elinore Cowan. *The Laughingest Lady.* Grosset and Dunlap, 1927.

"A Story for Girls." *Book News,* vol. 1, no. 123, Dec. 1892, p. 167.

Stout, Janis P. *Picturing a Different West: Vision, Illustration, and the Tradition of Austin and Cather.* Texas Tech UP, 2007.

———. *Through the Window, Out the Door: Women's Narratives of Departure, from Austin and Cather to Tyler, Morrison, and Didion.* U of Alabama P, 1998.

———, editor. *Willa Cather and Material Culture: Real-World Writing, Writing the Real World.* U of Alabama P, 2005.

Stowe, Harriet Beecher. *Uncle Tom's Cabin.* 1852. W. W. Norton, 2010.

Stromberg, Ernest. "Resistance and Mediation: The Rhetoric of Irony in Indian Boarding School Narratives by Francis La Flesche and Zitkala-Ša." *American Indian Rhetorics of Survivance: Word Medicine, Word Magic,* edited by Stromberg, U of Pittsburgh P, 2006, pp. 95–109.

Talbot, Francis. "Willa Cather Eulogizes the Archbishop." *America,* vol. 37, 24 Sept. 1927, 572–73. Rpt. in O'Connor, pp. 328–30.

Tarbox, Gwen Athene. *The Clubwomen's Daughters: Collectivist Impulses in Progressive-Era Girls' Fiction.* Garland, 2000.

Tatar, Maria. *Enchanted Hunters: The Power of Stories in Childhood.* Norton, 2009.

Tate, Claudia. *Domestic Allegories of Political Desire: The Black Heroine's Text at the Turn of the Century.* Oxford UP, 1996.

Tatonetti, Lisa. "Behind the Shadows of Wounded Knee: The Slippage of Imagination in *Wynema: A Child of the Forest.*" *Studies in American Indian Literatures,* vol. 16, no. 1, Spring 2004, pp. 1–31.

Tavera, Maria Cristina. *La Llorona (The Crying Woman).* 2014, woodblock print, private collection.

Tinnemeyer, Andrea. "Domestic Captives: Mexicanas in Post-1848 United States." *Identity Politics of the Captivity Narrative after 1848,* by Tinnemeyer, U of Nebraska P, 2006, pp. 19–50.

———. "Enlightenment Ideology and the Crisis of Whiteness in *Francis Berrian* and *Caballero.*" *Western American Literature,* vol. 35, no. 1, Spring 2000, pp. 21–32.

Tompkins, Jane. *Sensational Designs: The Cultural Work of American Fiction, 1790–1860.* Oxford UP, 1985.

———. *West of Everything: The Inner Life of Westerns.* Oxford UP, 1992.

Trennert, Robert. *The Phoenix Indian School: Forced Assimilation in Arizona, 1891–1935.* U of Oklahoma P, 1988.

Treuer, David. *Native American Fiction: A User's Manual.* Graywolf, 2006.

Treviño, Roberto R. *The Church in the Barrio: Mexican-American Ethno-Catholicism in Houston.* U of North Carolina P, 2006.

Tuttle, Jennifer S. "The Symptoms of Conquest: Race, Class, and the Nervous Body in *The Squatter and the Don.*" Montes and Goldman, pp. 56–72.

Urgo, Joseph R. *Willa Cather and the Myth of American Migration.* U of Illinois P, 1995.

———. "Willa Cather's Political Apprenticeship at *McClure's* Magazine." *Willa Cather's New York: New Essays on Cather in the City,* edited by Merrill Maguire Skaggs, Farleigh Dickinson UP, 2000, pp. 60–74.

Van Why, Joseph S. Introduction. *The American Woman's Home, or Principles of Domestic Science; Being a Guide to the Formation and Maintenance of Economical, Healthful, Beautiful and Christian Homes,* by Beecher and Stowe, 1869, Stowe-Day Foundation, 1975.

Veblen, Thornstein. *The Theory of the Leisure Class.* 1899. Dover, 1994.

Velasquez-Treviño, Gloria. "Cultural Ambivalence in Early Chicana Literature." *European Perspectives on Hispanic Literature of the United States,* edited by Genevieve Fabre, Arte Público, 1988, pp. 140–46.

Vigil, Maurilio E. "The Political Development of New Mexico's Hispanas." *Latino Studies Journal,* vol. 7, no. 2, Spring 1996, pp. 3–28.

Vizenor, Gerald. *Manifest Manners: Postindian Warriors of Survivance.* UP of New England, 1994.

———. *Narrative Chance: Postmodern Discourse on Native American Indian Literatures.* U of New Mexico P, 1989.

———. *Wordarrows: Native States of Literary Sovereignty.* U of Nebraska P, 2003.

Vuckovic, Myriam. *Voices from Haskell: Indian Students between Two Worlds, 1884–1928.* U of Kansas P, 2008.

Walker, Cheryl. "Sarah Winnemucca's Mediations: Gender, Race, and Nation." *Indian Nation: Native American Literature and Nineteenth-Century Nationalisms,* by Walker, Duke UP, 1997, pp. 139–63.

Warford, Elisa. "'An Eloquent and Impassioned Plea': The Rhetoric of Ruiz de Burton's *The Squatter and the Don.*" *Western American Literature,* vol. 44, no. 1, Spring 2009, pp. 5–21.

Warner, Michael. *Publics and Counterpublics.* Zone, 2002.

Warrior, Robert. *The People and the Word: Reading Native Nonfiction.* U of Minnesota P, 2005.

———. *Tribal Secrets: Recovering American Indian Intellectual Traditions.* U of Minnesota P, 1994.

Weaver, Jace. "Assimilation, Apocalypticism, and Reform (1900–1967)." *That the People Might Live: Native American Literatures and Native American Community,* by Weaver, Oxford UP, 1997, pp. 86–120.

———. *Other Words: American Indian Literature, Law, and Culture.* U of Oklahoma P, 2001.

Weigle, Marta. *Brothers of Light, Brothers of Blood: The Penitentes of the Southwest.* Sunstone, 2007.

Welter, Barbara. "The Cult of True Womanhood: 1820–1860." 1966. *Dimity Convictions: The American Woman in the Nineteenth Century*, by Welter, Ohio UP, 1976, pp. 21–41.

Wesley, Marilyn C. *Secret Journeys: The Trope of Women's Travel in American Literature.* State U of New York P, 1999.

West Indies, Bermuda, South America. Advertisements. *Forum*, vol. 77, no. 1, Jan. 1927.

Wexler, Laura. *Tender Violence: Domestic Visions in an Age of U.S. Imperialism.* U of North Carolina P, 2000.

———. "Tender Violence: Literary Eavesdropping, Domestic Fiction, and Educational Reform." *The Culture of Sentiment: Race, Gender, and Sentimentality in 19th Century America*, edited by Shirley Samuels, Oxford UP, 1992, pp. 9–38.

Whalen, Terence. *Edgar Allan Poe and the Masses: the Political Economy of Literature in Antebellum America.* Princeton UP, 1999.

White, Richard. *The Middle Ground: Indians, Empires, and Republics in the Great Lakes Region, 1650–1815.* Cambridge UP, 1991.

Wildroot Dandruff Remedy. Label. 1910.

Winnemucca, Sarah. *Life Among the Piutes: Their Wrongs and Claims.* 1883. U of Nevada P, 1994.

Woidat, Caroline M. "The Indian-Detour in Willa Cather's Southwestern Novels." *Twentieth-Century Literature*, vol. 48, no. 1, Spring 2002, pp. 22–49.

Womack, Craig. *Red on Red: Native American Literary Separatism.* U of Minnesota P, 1999.

Wood, James Playsted. *Magazines in the United States.* 2nd ed., Ronald, 1956.

Wright, Gregory. "(Re)Writing the Captivity Narrative: Sarah Winnemucca's *Life Among the Piutes* Records White Male Sexual Violence." *Nevada Historical Society*, vol. 51, no. 3, Fall 2008, pp. 200–18.

Wyeth, N. C., and Charles S. Chapman. *Now Listen, Sabra.* Illustration. "Cimarron: The Return of Yancey and the Trial of Dixie Lee" by Edna Ferber. *Woman's Home Companion*, vol. 57, no. 3, Mar. 1930, p. 32.

———. *She Knew She Must Not Lose Her Dignity.* Illustration. "Cimarron: Prosperity and Decadence; the Coming of Oil in Oklahoma" by Edna Ferber. *Woman's Home Companion*, vol. 57, no. 4, Apr. 1930, p. 29.

Ybarra, Priscilla Solis. "Borderlands as Bioregion: Jovita González, Gloria Anzaldúa, and the Twentieth-Century Ecological Revolution in the Rio Grande Valley." *MELUS*, vol. 33, no. 2, 2009, pp. 175–89.

Zanjani, Sally. *Sarah Winnemucca.* U of Nebraska P, 2001.

Zboray, Ronald, and Mary Saracino Zboray. *Everyday Ideas: Socioliterary Experience among Antebellum New Englanders.* U of Tennessee P, 2006.

Zink, Amanda J. "Carlisle's Writing Circle: Boarding School Texts and the Decolonization of Domesticity." *Studies in American Indian Literatures*, vol. 27, no. 4, Winter 2015, pp. 37–65.

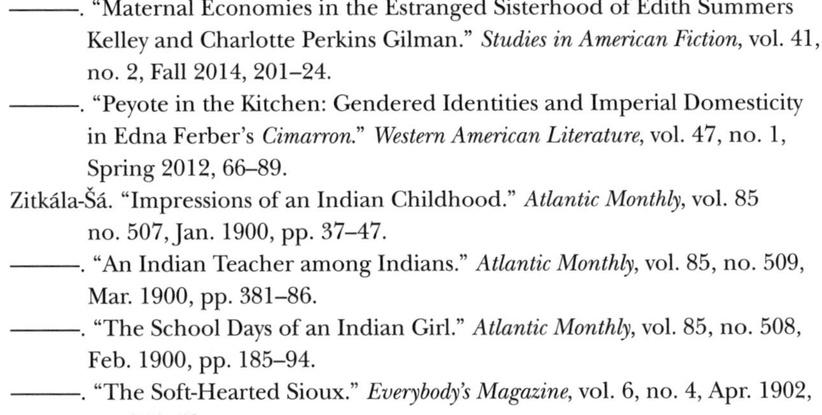

———. "Maternal Economies in the Estranged Sisterhood of Edith Summers Kelley and Charlotte Perkins Gilman." *Studies in American Fiction*, vol. 41, no. 2, Fall 2014, 201–24.

———. "Peyote in the Kitchen: Gendered Identities and Imperial Domesticity in Edna Ferber's *Cimarron*." *Western American Literature*, vol. 47, no. 1, Spring 2012, 66–89.

Zitkála-Šá. "Impressions of an Indian Childhood." *Atlantic Monthly*, vol. 85 no. 507, Jan. 1900, pp. 37–47.

———. "An Indian Teacher among Indians." *Atlantic Monthly*, vol. 85, no. 509, Mar. 1900, pp. 381–86.

———. "The School Days of an Indian Girl." *Atlantic Monthly*, vol. 85, no. 508, Feb. 1900, pp. 185–94.

———. "The Soft-Hearted Sioux." *Everybody's Magazine*, vol. 6, no. 4, Apr. 1902, pp. 346–52.

INDEX